St. George and St. Michael by George MacDonald

IN THREE VOLUMES

George MacDonald was born on December 10th 1824 at Huntly, Aberdeenshire, Scotland where he grew up with the Congregational Church, with its atmosphere of Calvinism to which George never really attached himself.

His mother died when he was only 8 and by 16 George was successful in obtaining a bursary to King's College in Aberdeen and from which he also received his M.A.

In 1846 George had his first poem published anonymously. By 1848 he was attending Highbury Theological College to study for the Congregational ministry and also engaged to Louisa Powell.

By 1850 George was appointed as the pastor of Trinity Congregational Church in Arundel. Later that year he suffered his first severe haemorrhage in what was to become a lifelong battle with declining health. In his ministry his sermons were at odds with the Church and their more segmented views. Three years later he resigned from the pulpit.

His collection of poems 'Within and Without' was published in 1855 and in 1858 so too was 'Phantastes'. His career would now flourish and along with very successful lecture tours were published such classics as 'At the Back of the North Wind', 'Wilfrid Cumbermede', 'The Princess and the Goblin' and 'Exotics'.

From 1880 he and his family moved to Bordighera on the Riviera dei Fiori in Liguria, Italy, where he spent 20 years writing.

But ill health continued to strike at him. By 1898 a stroke had taken his voice.

In 1901 George and Louisa were able to celebrate their Golden Wedding anniversary though sadly Louisa was to pass away on January 13th, 1902 whilst at Bordighera.

On 18th September 1905 George MacDonald died at Sagamore, Ashtead in Surrey. He was cremated and his ashes buried at Bordighera, in the English cemetery, along with his wife Louisa and daughters Lilia and Grace.

Index of Contents

CHAPTER I

DOROTHY AND RICHARD

It was the middle of autumn, and had rained all day. Through the lozenge-panes of the wide oriel window the world appeared in the slowly gathering dusk not a little dismal. The drops that clung trickling to the dim glass added rain and gloom to the landscape beyond, whither the eye passed, as if vaguely seeking that help in the distance, which the dripping hollyhocks and sodden sunflowers bordering the little lawn, or the honeysuckle covering the wide porch, from which the slow rain dropped ceaselessly upon the pebble-paving below, could not give, steepy slopes, hedge-divided into small fields, some green and dotted with red cattle, others crowded with shocks of bedraggled and drooping corn, which looked suffering and patient.

The room to which the window having this prospect belonged was large and low, with a dark floor of uncarpeted oak. It opened immediately upon the porch, and although a good fire of logs blazed on the hearth, was chilly to the sense of the old man, who, with his feet on the skin of a fallow-deer, sat gazing sadly into the flames, which shone rosy through the thin hands spread out before them. At the opposite corner of the great low-arched chimney sat a lady past the prime of life, but still beautiful, though the beauty was all but merged in the loveliness that rises from the heart to the face of such as have taken the greatest step in life, that is, as the old proverb says, the step out of doors. She was plainly yet rather richly dressed, in garments of an old-fashioned and well-preserved look. Her hair was cut short above her forehead, and frizzed out in bunches of little curls on each side. On her head was a covering of dark stuff, like a nun's veil, which fell behind and on her shoulders. Close round her neck was a string of amber beads, that gave a soft harmonious light to her complexion. Her dark eyes looked as if they found repose there, so quietly did they rest on the face of the old man, who was plainly a clergyman. It was a small, pale, thin, delicately and symmetrically formed face, yet not the less a strong one, with endurance on the somewhat sad brow, and force in the closed lips, while a good conscience looked clear out of the grey eyes.

They had been talking about the fast-gathering tide of opinion which, driven on by the wind of words, had already begun to beat so furiously against the moles and ramparts of Church and kingdom. The execution of Lord Strafford was news that had not yet begun to 'hiss the speaker.'

'It is indeed an evil time,' said the old man. 'The world has seldom seen its like.'

'But tell me, master Herbert,' said the lady, 'why comes it in this our day? For our sins or for the sins of our fathers?'

'Be it far from me to presume to set forth the ways of Providence!' returned her guest. 'I meddle not, like some that should be wiser, with the calling of the prophet. It is enough for me to know that ever and again the pride of man will gather to "a mighty and a fearful head," and, like a swollen millpond overfed of rains, burst the banks that confine it, whether they be the laws of the land or the ordinances of the church, usurping on the fruitful meadows, the hope of life for man and beast. Alas!' he went on, with a new suggestion from the image he had been using, 'if the beginning of strife be as the letting out of water, what shall be the end of that strife whose beginning is the letting out of blood?'

'Think you then, good sir, that thus it has always been? that such times of fierce ungodly tempest must ever follow upon seasons of peace and comfort? even as your cousin of holy memory, in his verses concerning the church militant, writes:

"Thus also sin and darkness follow still
The church and sun, with all their power and skill."'

'Truly it seems so. But I thank God the days of my pilgrimage are nearly numbered. To judge by the tokens the wise man gives us, the mourners are already going about my streets. The almond-tree flourisheth at least.'

He smiled as he spoke, laying his hand on his grey head.

'But think of those whom we must leave behind us, master Herbert. How will it fare with them?' said the lady in troubled tone, and glancing in the direction of the window.

In the window sat a girl, gazing from it with the look of a child who had uttered all her incantations, and could imagine no abatement in the steady rain-pour.

'We shall leave behind us strong hearts and sound heads too,' said Mr. Herbert. 'And I bethink me there will be none stronger or sounder than those of your young cousins, my late pupils, of whom I hear brave things from Oxford, and in whose affection my spirit constantly rejoices.'

'You will be glad to hear such good news of your relatives, Dorothy,' said the lady, addressing her daughter.

Even as she said the words, the setting sun broke through the mass of grey cloud, and poured over the earth a level flood of radiance, in which the red wheat glowed, and the drops that hung on every ear flashed like diamonds. The girl's hair caught it as she turned her face to answer her mother, and an aureole of brown-tinted gold gleamed for a moment about her head.

'I am glad that you are pleased, madam, but you know I have never seen them, or heard of them, except from master Herbert, who has, indeed, often spoke rare things of them.'

'Mistress Dorothy will still know the reason why,' said the clergyman, smiling, and the two resumed their conversation. But the girl rose, and, turning again to the window, stood for a moment rapt in the transfiguration passing upon the world. The vault of grey was utterly shattered, but, gathering glory from ruin, was hurrying in rosy masses away from under the loftier vault of blue. The ordered shocks upon twenty fields sent their long purple shadows across the flush; and the evening wind, like the sighing that follows departed tears, was shaking the jewels from their feathery tops. The sunflowers and hollyhocks no longer cowered under the tyranny of the rain, but bowed beneath the weight of the gems that adorned them. A flame burned as upon an altar on the top of every tree, and the very pools that lay on the distant road had their message of light to give to the hopeless earth. As she gazed, another hue than that of the sunset, yet rosy too, gradually flushed the face of the maiden. She turned suddenly from the window, and left the room, shaking a shower of diamonds from the honeysuckle as she passed out through the porch upon the gravel walk.

Possibly her elders found her departure a relief, for although they took no notice of it, their talk became more confidential, and was soon mingled with many names both of rank and note, with a familiarity which to a stranger might have seemed out of keeping with the humbler character of their surroundings.

But when Dorothy Vaughan had passed a corner of the house to another garden more ancient in aspect, and in some things quaint even to grotesqueness, she was in front of a portion of the house which indicated a far statelier past, closed and done with, like the rooms within those shuttered windows. The inhabited wing she had left looked like the dwelling of a yeoman farming his own land; nor did this appearance greatly belie the present position of the family. For generations it had been slowly descending in the scale of worldly account, and the small portion of the house occupied by the widow and daughter of sir Ringwood Vaughan was larger than their means could match with correspondent outlay. Such, however, was the character of Lady Vaughan, that, although she mingled little with the great families in the neighbourhood, she was so much respected, that she would have been a welcome visitor to most of them.

The reverend Mr. Matthew Herbert was a clergyman from the Welsh border, a man of some note and influence, who had been the personal friend both of his late relative George Herbert and of the famous Dr. Donne. Strongly attached to the English church, and recoiling with disgust from the practices of the puritans, as much, perhaps, from refinement of taste as abhorrence of schism, he had never yet fallen into such a passion for episcopacy as to feel any cordiality towards the schemes of the archbishop. To those who knew him his silence concerning it was a louder protest against the policy of Laud than the fiercest denunciations of the puritans. Once only had he been heard to utter himself unguardedly in respect of the primate, and that was amongst friends, and after the second glass permitted of his cousin George. 'Tut! laud me no Laud,' he said. 'A skipping bishop is worse than a skipping king.' Once also he had been overheard murmuring to himself by way of consolement, 'Bishops pass; the church remains.' He had been a great friend of the late sir Ringwood; and although the distance from his parish was too great to be travelled often, he seldom let a year go by without paying a visit to his friend's widow and daughter.

Turning her back on the cenotaph of their former greatness, Dorothy dived into a long pleached alley, careless of the drip from overhead, and hurrying through it came to a circular patch of thin grass, rounded by a lofty hedge of yew-trees, in the midst of which stood what had once been a sun-dial. It mattered little, however, that only the stump of a gnomon was left, seeing the hedge around it had grown to such a height in relation to the diameter of the circle, that it was only for a very brief hour or so in the middle of a summer's day, when, of all periods, the passage of Time seems least to concern humanity, that it could have served to measure his march. The spot had, indeed, a time-forsaken look, as if it lay buried in the bosom of the past, and the present had forgotten it.

Before emerging from the alley, she slackened her pace, half-stopped, and, stooping a little in her tucked-up skirt, threw a bird-like glance around the opener space; then stepping into it, she looked up to the little disc of sky, across which the clouds, their roses already withered, sailed dim and grey once more, while behind them the stars were beginning to recall their half-forgotten message from regions unknown to men. A moment, and she went up to the dial, stood there for another moment, and was on the point of turning to leave the spot, when, as if with one great bound, a youth stood between her and the entrance of the alley.

'Ah ha, mistress Dorothy, you do not escape me so!' he cried, spreading out his arms as if to turn back some runaway creature.

But mistress Dorothy was startled, and mistress Dorothy did not choose to be startled, and therefore mistress Dorothy was dignified, if not angry.

'I do not like such behaviour, Richard,' she said. 'It ill suits with the time. Why did you hide behind the hedge, and then leap forth so rudely?'

'I thought you saw me,' answered the youth. 'Pardon my heedlessness, Dorothy. I hope I have not startled you too much.'

As he spoke he stooped over the hand he had caught, and would have carried it to his lips, but the girl, half-pettishly, snatched it away, and, with a strange mixture of dignity, sadness, and annoyance in her tone, said—

'There has been something too much of this, Richard, and I begin to be ashamed of it.'

'Ashamed!' echoed the youth. 'Of what? There is nothing but me to be ashamed of, and what can I have done since yesterday?'

'No, Richard; I am not ashamed of you, but I am ashamed of—of—this way of meeting—and—and—'

'Surely that is strange, when we can no more remember the day in which we have not met than that in which we met first! No, dear Dorothy—'

'It is not our meeting, Richard; and if you would but think as honestly as you speak, you would not require to lay upon me the burden of explanation. It is this foolish way we have got into of late— kissing hands—and—and—always meeting by the old sun-dial, or in some other over-quiet spot. Why do you not come to the house? My mother would give you the same welcome as any time these last—how many years, Richard?'

'Are you quite sure of that, Dorothy?'

'Well, I did fancy she spoke with something more of ceremony the last time you met. But, consider, she has seen so much less of you of late. Yet I am sure she has all but a mother's love in her heart towards you. For your mother was dear to her as her own soul.'

'I would it were so, Dorothy! For then, perhaps, your mother would not shrink from being my mother too. When we are married, Dorothy—'

'Married!' exclaimed the girl. 'What of marrying, indeed!' And she turned sideways from him with an indignant motion. 'Richard,' she went on, after a marked and yet but momentary pause, for the youth had not had time to say a word, 'it has been very wrong in me to meet you after this fashion. I know it now, for see what such things lead to! If you knew it, you have done me wrong.'

'Dearest Dorothy!' exclaimed the youth, taking her hand again, of which this time she seemed hardly aware, 'did you not know from the very vanished first that I loved you with all my heart, and that to tell you so would have been to tell the sun that he shines warm at noon in midsummer? And I did think you had a little, something for me, Dorothy, your old playmate, that you did not give to every other acquaintance. Think of the houses we have built and the caves we have dug together, of our rabbits, and urchins, and pigeons, and peacocks!'

'We are children no longer,' returned Dorothy. 'To behave as if we were would be to keep our eyes shut after we are awake. I like you, Richard, you know; but why this, where is the use of all this, new sort of thing? Come up with me to the house, where master Herbert is now talking to my mother in the large parlour. The good man will be glad to see you.'

'I doubt it, Dorothy. He and my father, as I am given to understand, think so differently in respect of affairs now pending betwixt the parliament and the king, that—'

'It were more becoming, Richard, if the door of your lips opened to the king first, and let the parliament follow.'

'Well said!' returned the youth with a smile. 'But let it be my excuse that I speak as I am wont to hear.'

The girl's hand had lain quiet in that of the youth, but now it started from it like a scared bird. She stepped two paces back, and drew herself up.

'And you, Richard?' she said, interrogatively.

'What would you ask, Dorothy?' returned the youth, taking a step nearer, to which she responded by another backward ere she replied.

'I would know whom you choose to serve, whether God or Satan; whether you are of those who would set at nought the laws of the land—'

'Insist on their fulfilment, they say, by king as well as people,' interrupted Richard.

'They would tear their mother in pieces—'

'Their mother!' repeated Richard, bewildered.

'Their mother, the church,' explained Dorothy.

'Oh!' said Richard. 'Nay, they would but cast out of her the wolves in sheep's clothing that devour the lambs.'

The girl was silent. Anger glowed on her forehead and flashed from her grey eyes. She stood one moment, then turned to leave him, but half turned again to say scornfully—

'I must go at once to my mother! I knew not I had left her with such a wolf as master Herbert is like to prove!'

'Master Herbert is no bishop, Dorothy!'

'The bishops, then, are the wolves, master Heywood?' said the girl, with growing indignation.

'Dear Dorothy, I am but repeating what I hear. For my own part, I know little of these matters. And what are they to us if we love one another?'

'I tell you I am a child no longer,' flamed Dorothy.

'You were seventeen last St. George's Day, and I shall be nineteen next St. Michael's.'

'St. George for merry England!' cried Dorothy.

'St. Michael for the Truth!' cried Richard.

'So be it. Good-bye, then,' said the girl, going.

'What DO you mean, Dorothy?' said Richard; and she stood to hear, but with her back towards him, and, as it were, hovering midway in a pace. 'Did not St. Michael also slay his dragon? Why should the knights part company? Believe me, Dorothy, I care more for a smile from you than for all the bishops in the church, or all the presbyters out of it.'

'You take needless pains to prove yourself a foolish boy, Richard; and if I go not to my mother at once, I fear I shall learn to despise you, which I would not willingly.'

'Despise me! Do you take me for a coward then, Dorothy?'

'I say not that. I doubt not, for the matter of swords and pistols, you are much like other male creatures; but I protest I could never love a man who preferred my company to the service of his king.'

She glided into the alley and sped along its vaulted twilight, her white dress gleaming and clouding by fits as she went.

The youth stood for a moment petrified, then started to overtake her, but stood stock-still at the entrance of the alley, and followed her only with his eyes as she went.

When Dorothy reached the house, she did not run up to her room that she might weep unseen. She was still too much annoyed with Richard to regret having taken such leave of him. She only swallowed down a little balloonful of sobs, and went straight into the parlour, where her mother and Mr. Herbert still sat, and resumed her seat in the bay window. Her heightened colour, an occasional toss of her head backwards, like that with which a horse seeks ease from the bearing-rein, generally followed by a renewal of the attempt to swallow something of upward tendency, were the only signs of her discomposure, and none of them were observed by her mother or her guest. Could she have known, however, what feelings had already begun to rouse themselves in the mind of him whose boyishness was an offence to her, she would have found it more difficult to keep such composure.

Dorothy's was a face whose forms were already so decided that, should no softening influences from the central regions gain the ascendancy, beyond a doubt age must render it hard and unlovely. In all the roundness and freshness of girlhood, it was handsome rather than beautiful, beautiful rather than lovely. And yet it was strongly attractive, for it bore clear indication of a nature to be trusted. If her grey eyes were a little cold, they were honest eyes, with a rare look of steadfastness; and if her lips were a little too closely pressed, it was clearly from any cause rather than bad temper. Neither head, hands, nor feet were small, but they were fine in form and movement; and for the rest of her person, tall and strong as Richard was, Dorothy looked further advanced in the journey of life than he.

She needed hardly, however, have treated his indifference to the politics of the time with so much severity, seeing her own acquaintance with and interest in them dated from that same afternoon, during which, from lack of other employment, and the weariness of a long morning of slow, dismal rain, she had been listening to Mr. Herbert as he dwelt feelingly on the arrogance of puritan encroachment, and the grossness of presbyterian insolence both to kingly prerogative and episcopal authority, and drew a touching picture of the irritant thwartings and pitiful insults to which the gentle monarch was exposed in his attempts to support the dignity of his divine office, and to cast its protecting skirt over the defenceless church; and if it was with less sympathy that he spoke of the fears which haunted the captive metropolitan, Dorothy at least could detect no hidden sarcasm in the tone in which he expressed his hope that Laud's devotion to the beauty of holiness might not result in the dignity of martyrdom, as might well be feared by those who were assured that the whole guilt of Strafford lay in his return to his duty, and his subsequent devotion to the interests of his royal master: to all this the girl had listened, and her still sufficiently uncertain knowledge of the affairs of the nation had, ere the talk was over, blossomed in a vague sense of partizanship. It was chiefly her desire after the communion of sympathy with Richard that had led her into the mistake of such a hasty disclosure of her new feelings.

But her following words had touched him, whether to fine issues or not remained yet poised on the knife-edge of the balancing will. His first emotion partook of anger. As soon as she was out of sight a spell seemed broken, and words came.

'A boy, indeed, mistress Dorothy!' he said. 'If ever it come to what certain persons prophesy, you may wish me in truth, and that for the sake of your precious bishops, the boy you call me now. Yes, you are right, mistress, though I would it had been another who told me so! Boy indeed I am, or have been, without a thought in my head but of her. The sound of my father's voice has been but as the wind of the winnowing fan. In me it has found but chaff. If you will have me take a side, though, you will find me so far worthy of you that I shall take the side that seems to me the right one, were all the fair Dorothies of the universe on the other. In very truth I should be somewhat sorry to find the king and the bishops in the right, lest my Lady should flatter herself and despise me that I had chosen after her showing, forsooth! This is master Herbert's doing, for never before did I hear her speak after such fashion.'

While he thus spoke with himself, he stood, like the genius of the spot, a still dusky figure on the edge of the night, into which his dress of brown velvet, rich and sombre at once in the sunlight, all but merged. Nearly for the first time in his life he was experiencing the difficulty of making up his mind, not, however, upon any of the important questions, his inattention to which had exposed him to such sudden and unexpected severity, but merely as to whether he should seek her again in the company of her mother and Mr. Herbert, or return home. The result of his deliberation, springing partly, no doubt, from anger, but that of no very virulent type, was, that he turned his back on the alley, passed through a small opening in the yew hedge, crossed a neglected corner of woodland, by ways better known to him than to anyone else, and came out upon the main road leading to the gates of his father's park.

CHAPTER II

RICHARD AND HIS FATHER

Richard Heywood, as to bodily fashion, was a tall and already powerful youth. The clear brown of his complexion spoke of plentiful sunshine and air. A merry sparkle in the depths of his hazel eyes relieved the shadows of rather notably heavy lids, themselves heavily overbrowed, with a suggestion of character which had not yet asserted itself to those who knew him best. Correspondingly, his nose, although of a Greek type, was more notable for substance than clearness of line or modelling; while his lips had a boyish fulness along with a definiteness of bow-like curve, which manly resolve had not yet begun to compress and straighten out. His chin was at least large enough not to contradict the promise of his face; his shoulders were square, and his chest and limbs well developed: altogether it was at present a fair tabernacle, of whatever sort the indwelling divinity might yet turn out, fashioning it further after his own nature.

His father and he were the only male descendants of an old Monmouthshire family, of neither Welsh nor Norman, but as pure Saxon blood as might be had within the clip of the ocean. Roger, the father, had once only or twice in his lifetime been heard boast, in humorous fashion, that although but a simple squire, he could, on this side the fog of tradition, which nearer or further shrouds all origin, count a longer descent than any of the titled families in the county, not excluding the earl of Worcester himself. His character also would have gone far to support any assertion he might have chosen to make as to the purity of his strain. A notable immobility of nature, his friends called it firmness, his enemies obstinacy; a seeming disregard of what others might think of him; a certain sternness of manner, an unreadiness, as it were, to open his door to the people about him; a searching regard with which he was wont to peruse the face of anyone holding talk with him, when he seemed always to give heed to the looks rather than the words of him who spoke; these peculiarities had combined to produce a certain awe of him in his inferiors, and a dislike, not unavowed, in his equals. With his superiors he came seldom in contact, and to them his behaviour was still more distant and unbending. But, although from these causes he was far from being a favourite in the county, he was a man of such known and acknowledged probity that, until of late, when party spirit ran high and drew almost everybody, whether of consequence or not, to one side or the other, there was nobody who would not have trusted Roger Heywood to the uttermost. Even now, foes as well as friends acknowledged that he was to be depended upon; while his own son looked up to him with a reverence that in some measure overshadowed his affection. Such a character as this had necessarily been slow in formation, and the opinions which had been modified by it and had reacted upon it, had been as unalterably as deliberately adopted. But affairs had approached a crisis between king and parliament before one of his friends knew that there were in his mind any opinions upon them in process of formation, so reserved and monosyllabic had been his share in any conversation upon topics which had for a long time been growing every hour of more and more absorbing interest to all men either of consequence, intelligence, property, or adventure. At last, however, it had become clear, to the great annoyance of not a few amongst his neighbours, that Heywood's leanings were to the parliament. But he had never yet sought to influence his son in regard to the great questions at issue.

His house was one of those ancient dwellings which have grown under the hands to fit the wants of successive generations, and look as if they had never been other than old; two-storied at most, and many-gabled, with marvellous accretions and projections, the haunts of yet more wonderful shadows. There, in a room he called his study, shabby and small, containing a library more notable for quality and selection than size, Richard the next morning sought and found him.

'Father!' he said, entering with some haste after the usual request for admission.

'I am here, my son,' answered Roger, without lifting his eyes from the small folio in which he was reading.

'I want to know, father, whether, when men differ, a man is bound to take a side.'

'Nay, Richard, but a man is bound NOT to take a side save upon reasons well considered and found good.'

'It may be, father, if you had seen fit to send me to Oxford, I should have been better able to judge now.'

'I had my reasons, son Richard. Readier, perhaps, you might have been, but fitter, no. Tell me what points you have in question.'

'That I can hardly say, sir. I only know there are points at issue betwixt king and parliament which men appear to consider of mightiest consequence. Will you tell me, father, why you have never instructed me in these affairs of church and state? I trust it is not because you count me unworthy of your confidence.'

'Far from it, my son. My silence hath respect to thy hearing and to the judgment yet unawakened in thee. Who would lay in the arms of a child that which must crush him to the earth? Years did I take to meditate ere I resolved, and I know not yet if thou hast in thee the power of meditation.'

'At least, father, I could try to understand, if you would unfold your mind.'

'When you know what the matters at issue are, my son, that is, when you are able to ask me questions worthy of answer, I shall be ready to answer thee, so far as my judgment will reach.'

'I thank you, father. In the meantime I am as one who knocks, and the door is not opened unto him.'

'Rather art thou as one who loiters on the door-step, and lifts up neither ring nor voice.'

'Surely, sir, I must first know the news.'

'Thou hast ears; keep them open. But at least you know, my son, that on the twelfth day of May last my Lord of Strafford lost his head.'

'Who took it from him, sir? King or parliament?'

'Even that might be made a question; but I answer, the High Court of Parliament, my son.'

'Was the judgment a right one or a wrong, sir? Did he deserve the doom?'

'Ah, there you put a question indeed! Many men say RIGHT, and many men say WRONG. One man, I doubt me much, was wrong in the share HE bore therein.'

'Who was he, sir?'

'Nay, nay, I will not forestall thine own judgment. But, in good sooth, I might be more ready to speak my mind, were it not that I greatly doubt some of those who cry loudest for liberty. I fear that had they once the power, they would be the first to trample her under foot. Liberty with some men means MY liberty to do, and THINE to suffer. But all in good time, my son! The dawn is nigh.'

'You will tell me at least, father, what is the bone of contention?'

'My son, where there is contention, a bone shall not fail. It is but a leg-bone now; it will be a rib to-morrow, and by and by doubtless it will be the skull itself.'

'If you care for none of these things, sir, will not master Flowerdew have a hard name for you? I know not what it means, but it sounds of the gallows,' said Richard, looking rather doubtful as to how his father might take it.

'Possibly, my son, I care more for the contention than the bone, for while thieves quarrel honest men go their own ways. But what ignorance I have kept thee in, and yet left thee to bear the reproach of a puritan!' said the father, smiling grimly. 'Thou meanest master Flowerdew would call me a Gallio, and thou takest the Roman proconsul for a gallows-bird! Verily thou art not destined to prolong the renown of thy race for letters. I marvel what thy cousin Thomas would say to the darkness of thy ignorance.'

'See what comes of not sending me to Oxford, sir: I know not who is my cousin Thomas.'

'A man both of learning and wisdom, my son, though I fear me his diet is too strong for the stomach of this degenerate age, while the dressing of his dishes is, on the other hand, too cunningly devised for their liking. But it is no marvel thou shouldest be ignorant of him, being as yet no reader of books. Neither is he a close kinsman, being of the Lincolnshire branch of the Heywoods.'

'Now I know whom you mean, sir; but I thought he was a writer of stage plays, and such things as on all sides I hear called foolish, and mummery.'

'There be among those who call themselves the godly, who will endure no mummery but of their own inventing. Cousin Thomas hath written a multitude of plays, but that he studied at Cambridge, and to good purpose, this book, which I was reading when you entered, bears good witness.'

'What is the book, father?'

'Stay, I will read thee a portion. The greater part is of learning rather than wisdom, the gathered opinions of the wise and good concerning things both high and strange; but I will read thee some verses bearing his own mind, which is indeed worthy to be set down with theirs.'

He read that wonderful poem ending the second Book of the Hierarchy, and having finished it looked at his son.

'I do not understand it, sir,' said Richard.

'I did not expect you would,' returned his father. 'Here, take the book, and read for thyself. If light should dawn upon the page, as thou readest, perhaps thou wilt understand what I now say, that I care but little for the bones concerning which king and parliament contend, but I do care that men, thou and I, my son, should be free to walk in any path whereon it may please God to draw us. Take the book, my son, and read again. But read no farther save with caution, for it dealeth with many things wherein old Thomas is too readily satisfied with hearsay for testimony.'

Richard took the small folio and carried it to his own chamber, where he read and partly understood the poem. But he was not ripe enough either in philosophy or religion for such meditations. Having executed his task, for as such he regarded it, he turned to look through the strange mixture of wisdom and credulity composing the volume. One tale after another, of witch, and demon, and magician, firmly believed and honestly recorded by his worthy relative, drew him on, until he sat forgetful of everything but the world of marvels before him, to none of which, however, did he accord a wider credence than sprung from the interest of the moment. He was roused by a noise of quarrel in the farmyard, towards which his window looked, and, laying aside reading, hastened out to learn the cause.

CHAPTER III

THE WITCH

It was a bright Autumn morning. A dry wind had been blowing all night through the shocks, and already some of the farmers had begun to carry to their barns the sheaves which had stood hopelessly dripping the day before. Ere Richard reached the yard, he saw, over the top of the wall, the first load of wheat-sheaves from the harvest-field, standing at the door of the barn, and high-uplifted thereon the figure of Faithful Stopchase, one of the men, a well-known frequenter of puritan assemblies all the country round, who was holding forth, and that with much freedom, in tones that sounded very like vituperation, if not malediction, against some one invisible. He soon found that the object of his wrath was a certain Welshwoman, named Rees, by her neighbours considered objectionable on the ground of witchcraft, against whom this much could with truth be urged, that she was so far from thinking it disreputable, that she took no pains to repudiate the imputation of it. Her dress, had it been judged by eyes of our day, would have been against her, but it was only old-fashioned, not even antiquated: common in Queen Elizabeth's time, it lingered still in remote country places, a gown of dark stuff, made with a long waist and short skirt over a huge farthingale; a ruff which stuck up and out, high and far, from her throat; and a conical Welsh hat invading the heavens. Stopchase, having descried her in the yard, had taken the opportunity of breaking out upon her in language as far removed from that of conventional politeness as his puritanical principles would permit. Doubtless he considered it a rebuking of Satan, but forgot that, although one of the godly, he could hardly on that ground lay claim to larger privilege in the use of bad language than the archangel Michael. For the old woman, although too prudent to reply, she scorned to flee, and stood regarding him fixedly. Richard sought to interfere and check the torrent of abuse, but it had already gathered so much head, that the man seemed even unaware of his attempt. Presently, however, he began to quail in the midst of his storming. The green eyes of the old woman, fixed upon him, seemed to be slowly fascinating him. At length, in the very midst of a volley of scriptural epithets, he fell suddenly silent, turned from her, and, with the fork on which he had been leaning, began to pitch the sheaves into the barn. The moment he turned his back, Goody Rees turned hers, and walked slowly away.

She had scarcely reached the yard gate, however, before the cow-boy, a delighted spectator and auditor of the affair, had loosed the fierce watch-dog, which flew after her. Fortunately Richard saw what took place, but the animal, which was generally chained up, did not heed his recall, and the poor woman had already felt his teeth, when Richard got him by the throat. She looked pale and frightened, but kept her composure wonderfully, and when Richard, who was prejudiced in her favour from having once heard Dorothy speak friendlily to her, expressed his great annoyance that she should have been so insulted on his father's premises, received his apologies with dignity and good faith. He dragged the dog back, rechained him, and was in the act of administering sound and righteous chastisement to the cow-boy, when Stopchase staggered, tumbled off the cart, and falling upon his head, lay motionless. Richard hurried to him, and finding his neck twisted and his head bent to one side, concluded he was killed. The woman who had accompanied him from the field stood for a moment uttering loud cries, then, suddenly bethinking herself, sped after the witch. Richard was soon satisfied he could do nothing for him.

Presently the woman came running back, followed at a more leisurely pace by Goody Rees, whose countenance was grave, and, even to the twitch about her mouth, inscrutable. She walked up to where the man lay, looked at him for a moment or two as if considering his case, then sat down on the ground beside him, and requested Richard to move him so that his head should lie on her lap. This done, she laid hold of it, with a hand on each ear, and pulled at his neck, at the same time turning his head in the right direction. There came a snap, and the neck was straight. She then began to stroke it with gentle yet firm hand. In a few moments he began to breathe. As soon as she saw his chest move, she called for a wisp of hay, and having shaped it a little, drew herself from under his head, substituting the hay. Then rising without a word she walked from the yard. Stopchase lay for a while, gradually coming to himself, then scrambled all at once to his feet, and staggered to his pitchfork, which lay where it had fallen. 'It is of the mercy of the Lord that I fell not upon the prongs of the pitchfork,' he said, as he slowly stooped and lifted it. He had no notion that he had lain more than a few seconds; and of the return of Goody Rees and her ministrations he knew nothing; while such an awe of herself and her influences had she left behind her, that neither the woman nor the cow-boy ventured to allude to her, and even Richard, influenced partly, no doubt, by late reading, was more inclined to think than speak about her. For the man himself, little knowing how close death had come to him, but inwardly reproached because of his passionate outbreak, he firmly believed that he had had a narrow escape from the net of the great fowler, whose decoy the old woman was, commissioned not only to cause his bodily death, but to work in him first such a frame of mind as should render his soul the lawful prey of the enemy.

CHAPTER IV

A CHAPTER OF FOOLS

The same afternoon, as it happened, a little company of rustics, who had just issued from the low hatch-door of the village inn, stood for a moment under the sign of the Crown and Mitre, which swung huskily creaking from the bough of an ancient thorn tree, then passed on to the road, and took their way together.

'Hope you then,' said one of them, as continuing their previous conversation, 'that we shall escape unhurt? It is a parlous business. Not as one of us is afeard as I knows on. But the old earl, he do have a most unregenerate temper, and you had better look to 't, my masters.'

'I tell thee, master Upstill, it's not the old earl as I'm afeard on, but the young lord. For thou knows as well as ere a one it be not without cause that men do call him a wizard, for a wizard he be, and that of the worst sort.'

'We shall be out again afore sundown, shannot we?' said another. 'That I trust.'

'Up to the which hour the High Court of Parliament assembled will have power to protect its own, eh, John Croning?'

'Nay, that I cannot tell. It be a parlous job, and for mine own part, whether for the love I bear to the truth, or the hatred I cherish toward the scarlet Antichrist, with her seven tails—'

'Tush, tush, John! Seven heads, man, and ten horns. Those are the numbers master Flowerdew read.'

'Nay, I know not for your horns; but for the rest I say seven tails. Did not honest master Flowerdew set forth unto us last meeting that the scarlet woman sat upon seven hills, eh? Have with you there, master Sycamore!'

'Well, for the sake of sound argument, I grant you. But we ha' got to do with no heads nor no tails, neither, save and except as you may say the sting is in the tail; and then, or I greatly mistake, it's not seven times seven as will serve to count the stings, come of the tails what may.'

'Very true,' said another; 'it be the stings and not the tails we want news of. But think you his lordship will yield them up without gainsaying to us the messengers of the High Parliament now assembled?'

'For mine own part,' said John Croning, 'though I fear it come of the old Adam yet left in me, I do count it a sorrowful thing that the earl should be such a vile recusant. He never fails with a friendly word, or it may be a jest, a foolish jest, but honest, for any one gentle or simple he may meet. More than once has he boarded me in that fashion. What do you think he said to me, now, one day as I was a mowin' of the grass in the court, close by the white horse that spout up the water high as a house from his nose-drills? Says he to me, for he come down the grand staircase, and steps out and spies me at the work with my old scythe, and come across to me, and says he, "Why, Thomas," says he, not knowin' of my name, "Why, Thomas," says he, "you look like old Time himself a mowing of us all down," says he. "For sure, my lord," says I, "your lordship reads it aright, for all flesh is grass, and all the glory of man is as the flower of the field." He look humble at that, for, great man as he be, his earthly tabernacle, though more than sizeable, is but a frail one, and that he do know. And says he, "Where did you read that, Thomas?" "I am not a larned man, please your lordship," says I, "and I cannot honestly say I read it nowheres, but I heerd the words from a book your lordship have had news of: they do call it the Holy Bible. But they tell me that they of your lordship's persuasion like it not." "You are very much mistaken there, Thomas," says he. "I read my Bible most days, only not the English Bible, which is full of errors, but the Latin, which is all as God gave it," says he. And thereby I had not where to answer withal.'

'I fear you proved a poor champion of the truth, master Croning.'

'Confess now, Cast-down Upstill, had he not both sun and wind of me, standing, so to say, on his own hearth-stone? Had it not been so, I could have called hard names with the best of you, though that is by rights the gift of the preachers of the truth. See how the good master Flowerdew excelleth therein, sprinkling them abroad from the watering-pot of the gospel. Verily, when my mind is too feeble to grasp his argument, my memory lays fast hold upon the hard names, and while I hold by them, I have it all in a nutshell.'

Fortified occasionally by a pottle of ale, and keeping their spirits constantly stirred by much talking, they had been all day occupied in searching the Catholic houses of the neighbourhood for arms. What authority they had for it never came to be clearly understood. Plainly they believed themselves possessed of all that was needful, or such men would never have dared it. As it was, they prosecuted it with such a bold front, that not until they were gone did it occur to some, who had yielded what arms they possessed, to question whether they had done wisely in acknowledging such fellows as parliamentary officials without demanding their warrant. Their day's gleanings up to this point, of swords and pikes, guns and pistols, they had left in charge of the host of the inn whence they had just issued, and were now bent on crowning their day's triumph with a supreme act of daring, the renown of which they enlarged in their own imaginations, while undermining the courage needful for its performance, by enhancing its terrors as they went.

At length two lofty hexagonal towers appeared, and the consciousness that the final test of their resolution drew nigh took immediate form in a fluttering at the heart, which, however, gave no outward sign but that of silence; and indeed they were still too full of the importance of unaccustomed authority to fear any contempt for it on the part of others.

It happened that at this moment Raglan Castle was full of merry-making upon occasion of the marriage of one of Lady Herbert's waiting-gentlewomen to an officer of the household; and in these festivities the earl of Worcester and all his guests were taking a part.

Among the numerous members of the household was one who, from being a turnspit, had risen, chiefly in virtue of an immovably lugubrious expression of countenance, to be the earl's fool. From this peculiarity his fellow-servants had given him the nickname of The Hangman; but the man himself had chosen the role of a puritan parson, as affording the best ground-work for the display of a humour suitable to the expression of countenance with which his mother had endowed him. That mother was Goody Rees, concerning whom, as already hinted, strange things were whispered. In the earlier part of his career the fool had not unfrequently found his mother's reputation a sufficient shelter from persecution; and indeed there might have been reason to suppose that it was for her son's sake she encouraged her own evil repute, a distinction involving considerable risk, seeing the time had not yet arrived when the disbelief in such powers was sufficiently advanced for the safety of those reported to possess them. In her turn, however, she ran a risk somewhat less than ordinary from the fact that her boy was a domestic in the family of one whose eldest son, the heir to the earldom, lay under a similar suspicion; for not a few of the household were far from satisfied that Lord Herbert's known occupations in the Yellow Tower were not principally ostensible, and that he and his man had nothing to do with the black art, or some other of the many regions of occult science in which the ambition after unlawful power may hopefully exercise itself.

Upon occasion of a family fete, merriment was in those days carried further, on the part of both masters and servants, than in the greatly altered relations and conditions of the present day would be desirable, or, indeed, possible. In this instance, the fun broke out in the arranging of a mock marriage between Thomas Rees, commonly called Tom Fool, and a young girl who served under the cook. Half the jest lay in the contrast between the long face of the bridegroom, both congenitally and wilfully miserable, and that of the bride, broad as a harvest moon, and rosy almost to purple. The bridegroom never smiled, and spoke with his jaws rather than his lips; while the bride seldom uttered a syllable without grinning from ear to ear, and displaying a marvellous appointment of huge and brilliant teeth. Entering solemnly into the joke, Tom expressed himself willing to marry the girl, but represented, as an insurmountable difficulty, that he had no clothes for the occasion. Thereupon the earl, drawing from his pocket his bunch of keys, directed him to go and take what he liked from his wardrobe. Now the earl was a man of large circumference, and the fool as lank in person as in countenance.

Tom took the keys and was some time gone, during which many conjectures were hazarded as to the style in which he would choose to appear. When he re-entered the great hall, where the company was assembled, the roar of laughter which followed his appearance made the glass of its great cupola ring again. For not merely was he dressed in the earl's beaver hat and satin cloak, splendid with plush and gold and silver lace, but he had indued a corresponding suit of his clothes as well, even to his silk stockings, garters, and roses, and with the help of many pillows and other such farcing, so filled the garments which otherwise had hung upon him like a shawl from a peg, and made of himself such a 'sweet creature of bombast' that, with ludicrous unlikeness of countenance, he bore in figure no distant resemblance to the earl himself.

Meantime Lady Elizabeth had been busy with the scullery-maid, whom she had attired in a splendid brocade of her grandmother's, with all suitable belongings of ruff, high collar, and lace wings, such as Queen Elizabeth is represented with in Oliver's portrait. Upon her appearance, a few minutes after Tom's, the laughter broke out afresh, in redoubled peals, and the merriment was at its height, when the warder of one of the gates entered and whispered in his master's ear the arrival of the bumpkins, and their mission announced, he informed his lordship, with all the importance and dignity they knew how to assume. The earl burst into a fresh laugh. But presently it quavered a little and ceased, while over the amusement still beaming on his countenance gathered a slight shade of anxiety, for who could tell what tempest such a mere whirling of straws might not forerun?

A few words of the warder's had reached Tom where he stood a little aside, his solemn countenance radiating disapproval of the tumultuous folly around him. He took three strides towards the earl.

'Wherein lieth the new jest?' he asked, with dignity.

'A set of country louts, my lord,' answered the earl, 'are at the gate, affirming the right of search in this your lordship's house of Raglan.'

'For what?'

'Arms, my lord.'

'And wherefore? On what ground?'

'On the ground that your lordship is a vile recusant, a papist, and therefore a traitor, no doubt, although they use not the word,' said the earl.

'I shall be round with them,' said Tom, embracing the assumed proportions in front of him, and turning to the door.

Ere the earl had time to conceive his intent, he had hurried from the hall, followed by fresh shouts of laughter. For he had forgotten to stuff himself behind, and, when the company caught sight of his back as he strode out, the tenuity of the foundation for such a 'huge hill of flesh' was absurd as Falstaff's ha'p'orth of bread to the 'intolerable deal of sack.'

But the next moment the earl had caught the intended joke, and although a trifle concerned about the affair, was of too mirth-loving a nature to interfere with Tom's project, the result of which would doubtless be highly satisfactory, at least to those not primarily concerned. He instantly called for silence, and explained to the assembly what he believed to be Tom Fool's intent, and as there was nothing to be seen from the hall, the windows of which were at a great height from the floor, and Tom's scheme would be fatally imperilled by the visible presence of spectators, from some at least of whom gravity of demeanour could not be expected, gave hasty instructions to several of his sons and daughters to disperse the company to upper windows having a view of one or the other court, for no one could tell where the fool's humour might find its principal arena. The next moment, in the plain dress of rough brownish cloth, which he always wore except upon state occasions, he followed the fool to the gate, where he found him talking through the wicket-grating to the rustics, who, having passed drawbridge and portcullises, of which neither the former had been raised nor the latter lowered for many years, now stood on the other side of the gate demanding admittance. In the parley, Tom Fool was imitating his master's voice and every one of the peculiarities of his speech to perfection, addressing them with extreme courtesy, as if he took them for gentlemen of no ordinary consideration, a point in his conception of his part which he never forgot throughout the whole business. To the dismay of his master he was even more than admitting, almost boasting, that there was an enormous quantity of weapons in the castle, sufficient at least to arm ten thousand horsemen! A prodigious statement, for, at the uttermost, there was not more than the tenth part of that amount, still a somewhat larger provision no doubt than the intruders had expected to find! The pseudo-earl went on to say that the armoury consisted of one strong room only, the door of which was so cunningly concealed and secured that no one but himself knew where it was, or if found could open it. But such he said was his respect to the will of the most august parliament, that he would himself conduct them to the said armoury, and deliver over upon the spot into their safe custody the whole mass of weapons to carry away with them. And thereupon he proceeded to open the gate.

By this time the door of the neighbouring guard-room was crowded with the heads of eager listeners, but the presence of the earl kept them quiet, and at a sign from him they drew back ere the men entered. The earl himself took a position where he would be covered by the opening wicket.

Tom received them into bodily presence with the notification that, having suspected their object, he had sent all his people out of the way, in order to avoid the least danger of a broil. Bowing to them with the utmost politeness as they entered, he requested them to step forward into the court while he closed the wicket behind them, but took the opportunity of whispering to one of the men just inside the door of the guardhouse, who, the moment Tom had led the rustics away, approached the earl, and told him what he had said.

'What can the rascal mean?' said the earl to himself; but he told the man to carry the fool's message exactly as he had received it, and quietly followed Tom and his companions, some of whom, conceiving fresh importance from the overstrained politeness with which they had been received, were now attempting a transformation of their usual loundering gait into a martial stride, with the result of a foolish strut, very unlike the dignified progress of the sham earl, whose weak back roused in them no suspicion, and who had taken care they should not see his face. Across the paved court, and through the hall to the inner court, Tom led them, and the earl followed.

The twilight was falling. The hall was empty of life, and filled with a sombre dusk, echoing to every step as they passed through it. They did not see the flash of eyes and glimmer of smiles from the minstrel's gallery, and the solitude, size, and gloom had, even on their dull natures, a palpable influence. The whole castle seemed deserted as they followed the false earl across the second court, with the true one stealing after them like a knave, little imagining that bright eyes were watching them from the curtains of every window like stars from the clear spaces and cloudy edges of heaven. To the north-west corner of the court he led them, and through a sculptured doorway up the straight wide ascent of stone called the grand staircase. At the top he turned to the right, along a dim corridor, from which he entered a suite of bedrooms and dressing-rooms, over whose black floors he led the trampling hob-nailed shoes without pity either for their polish or the labour of the housemaids in restoring it.

In this way he reached the stair in the bell-tower, ascending which he brought them into a narrow dark passage ending again in a downward stair, at the foot of which they found themselves in the long picture-gallery, having entered it in the recess of one of its large windows. At the other end of the gallery he crossed into the dining-room, then through an ante-chamber entered the drawing-room, where the ladies, apprised of their approach, kept still behind curtains and high chairs, until they had passed through, on their way to cross the archway of the main entrance, and through the library gain the region of household economy and cookery. Thither I will not drag my reader after them. Indeed the earl, who had been dogging them like a Fate, ever emerging on their track but never beheld, had already began to pay his part of the penalty of the joke in fatigue, for he was not only unwieldy in person, but far from robust, being very subject to gout. He owed his good spirits to a noble nature, and not to animal well-being. When they crossed from the picture-gallery to the dining-room, he went down the stair between, and into the oak-parlour adjoining the great hall. There he threw himself into an easy chair which always stood for him in the great bay window, looking over the moat to the huge keep of the castle, and commanding through its western light the stone bridge which crossed it. There he lay back at his ease, and, instructed by the message Tom had committed to the serjeant of the guard, waited the result.

As for his double, he went stalking on in front of his victims, never turning to show his face; he knew they would follow, were it but for the fear of being left alone. Close behind him they kept, scarce daring to whisper from growing awe of the vast place. The fumes of the beer had by this time evaporated, and the heavy obscurity which pervaded the whole building enhanced their growing apprehensions. On and on the fool led them, up and down, going and returning, but ever in new tracks, for the marvellous old place was interminably burrowed with connecting passages and communications of every sort, some of them the merest ducts which had to be all but crept through, and which would have certainly arrested the progress of the earl had he followed so far: no one about the place understood its "crenkles" so well as Tom. For the greater part of an hour he led them thus, until, having been on their legs the whole day, they were thoroughly wearied as well as awe-struck. At length, in a gloomy chamber, where one could not see the face of another, the pseudo-earl turned full upon them, and said in his most solemn tones:—

'Arrived thus far, my masters, it is borne in upon me with rebuke, that before undertaking to guide you to the armoury, I should have acquainted you with the strange fact that at times I am myself unable to find the place of which we are in search; and I begin to fear it is so now, and that we are at this moment the sport of a certain member of my family of whom it may be your worships have heard things not more strange than true. Against his machinations I am powerless. All that is left us is to go to him and entreat him to unsay his spells.'

A confused murmur of objections arose.

'Then your worships will remain here while I go to the Yellow Tower, and come to you again?' said the mock earl, making as if he would leave them.

But they crowded round him with earnest refusals to be abandoned; for in their very souls they felt the fact that they were upon enchanted ground and in the dark.

'Then follow me,' he said, and conducted them into the open air of the inner court, almost opposite the archway in its buildings leading to the stone bridge, whose gothic structure bestrid the moat of the keep.

For Raglan Castle had this peculiarity, that its keep was surrounded by a moat of its own, separating it from the rest of the castle, so that, save by bridge, no one within any more than without the walls could reach it. On to the bridge Tom led the way, followed by his dupes, now full in the view of the earl where he sat in his parlour window. When they had reached the centre of it, however, and glancing up at the awful bulk of stone towering above them, its walls strangely dented and furrowed, so as to such as they, might well suggest frightful means to wicked ends, they stood stock-still, refusing to go a step further; while their chief speaker, Upstill, emboldened by anger, fear, and the meek behaviour of the supposed earl, broke out in a torrent of arrogance, wherein his intention was to brandish the terrors of the High Parliament over the heads of his lordship of Worcester and all recusants. He had not got far, however, before a shrill whistle pierced the air, and the next instant arose a chaos of horrible, appalling, and harrowing noises, 'such a roaring,' in the words of their own report of the matter to the reverend master Flowerdew, 'as if the mouth of hell had been wide open, and all the devils conjured up', doubtless they meant by the arts of the wizard whose dwelling was that same tower of fearful fame before which they now stood. The skin-contracting chill of terror uplifted their hair. The mystery that enveloped the origin of the sounds gave them an unearthliness which froze the very fountains of their life, and rendered them incapable even of motion. They stared at each other with a ghastly observance, which descried no comfort, only like images of horror. 'Man's hand is not able to taste' how long they might have thus stood, nor 'his tongue to conceive' what the consequences might have been, had not a more healthy terror presently supervened. Across the tumult of sounds, like a fiercer flash through the flames of a furnace, shot a hideous, long-drawn yell, and the same instant came a man running at full speed through the archway from the court, casting terror-stricken glances behind him, and shouting with a voice half-choked to a shriek—

'Look to yourselves, my masters; the lions are got loose!'

All the world knew that ever since King James had set the fashion by taking so much pleasure in the lions at the Tower, strange beasts had been kept in the castle of Raglan.

The new terror broke the spell of the old, and the parliamentary commissioners fled. But which was the way from the castle? Which the path to the lions' den? In an agony of horrible dread, they rushed hither and thither about the court, where now the white horse, as steady as marble, should be when first they crossed it, was, to their excited vision, prancing wildly about the great basin from whose charmed circle he could not break, foaming, at the mouth, and casting huge water-jets from his nostrils into the perturbed air; while from the surface of the moat a great column of water shot up nearly as high as the citadel, whose return into the moat was like a tempest, and with all the elemental tumult was mingled the howling of wild beasts. The doors of the hall and the gates to the bowling green being shut, the poor wretches could not find their way out of the court, but ran from door to door like madmen, only to find all closed against them. From every window around the court, from the apartments of the waiting gentlewomen, from the picture-gallery, from the officers' rooms, eager and merry eyes looked down on the spot, themselves unseen and unsuspected, for all voices were hushed, and for anything the bumpkins heard or saw they might have been in a place deserted of men, and possessed only by evil spirits, whose pranks were now tormenting them. At last Upstill, who had fallen on the bridge at his first start, and had ever since been rushing about with a limp and a leap alternated, managed to open the door of the hall, and its eastern door having been left open, shot across and into the outer court, where he made for the gate, followed at varied distance by the rest of the routed commissioners of search, as each had discovered the way his forerunner fled. With trembling hands Upstill raised the latch of the wicket, and to his delight found it unlocked. He darted through, passed the twin portcullises, and was presently thundering over the drawbridge, which, trembling under his heavy steps, seemed on the point of rising to heave him back into the jaws of the lion, or, worse still, the clutches of the enchanter. Not one looked behind him, not even when, having passed through the white stone gate, also purposely left open for their escape, and rattled down the multitude of steps that told how deep was the moat they had just crossed, where the last of them nearly broke his neck by rolling almost from top to bottom, they reached the outermost, the brick gate, and so left the awful region of enchantment and feline fury commingled. Not until the castle was out of sight, and their leader had sunk senseless on the turf by the roadside, did they dare a backward look. The moment he came to himself they started again for home, at what poor speed they could make, and reached the Crown and Mitre in sad plight, where, however, they found some compensation in the pleasure of setting forth their adventures, with the heroic manner in which, although vanquished by the irresistible force of enchantment, they had yet brought off their forces without the loss of a single man. Their story spread over the country, enlarged and embellished at every fresh stage in its progress.

When the tale reached mother Rees, it filled her with fresh awe of the great magician, the renowned Lord Herbert. She little thought the whole affair was a jest of her own son's. Firmly believing in all kinds of magic and witchcraft, but as innocent of conscious dealing with the powers of ill as the whitest-winged angel betwixt earth's garret and heaven's threshold, she owed her evil repute amongst her neighbours to a rare therapeutic faculty, accompanied by a keen sympathetic instinct, which greatly sharpened her powers of observation in the quest after what was amiss; while her touch was so delicate, so informed with present mind, and came therefore into such rapport with any living organism, the secret of whose suffering it sought to discover, that sprained muscles, dislocated joints, and broken bones seemed at its soft approach to re-arrange their disturbed parts, and yield to the power of her composing will as to a re-ordering harmony. Add to this, that she understood more of the virtues of some herbs than any doctor in the parish, which, in the condition of general practice at the time, is not perhaps to say much, and that she firmly believed in the might of certain charms, and occasionally used them, and I have given reason enough why, while regarded by all with disapprobation, she should be by many both courted and feared. For her own part she had a leaning to the puritans, chiefly from respect to the memory of a good-hearted, weak, but intellectually gifted, and, therefore, admired husband; but the ridicule of her yet more gifted son had a good deal shaken this predilection, so that she now spent what powers of discrimination and choice she possessed solely upon persons, heedless of principles in themselves, and regarding them only in their vital results. Hence, it was a matter of absolute indifference to her which of the parties now dividing the country was in the right, or which should lose, which win, provided no personal evil befel the men or women for whom she cherished a preference. Like many another, she was hardly aware of the jurisdiction of conscience, save in respect of immediate personal relations.

CHAPTER V

ANIMADVERSIONS

From the time when the conversation recorded had in some measure dispelled the fog between them, Roger and Richard Heywood drew rapidly nearer to each other. The father had been but waiting until his son should begin to ask him questions, for watchfulness of himself and others had taught him how useless information is to those who have not first desired it, how poor in influence, how soon forgotten; and now that the fitting condition had presented itself, he was ready: with less of reserve than in the relation between them was common amongst the puritans, he began to pour his very soul into that of his son. All his influence went with that party which, holding that the natural flow of the reformation of the church from popery had stagnated in episcopacy, consisted chiefly of those who, in demanding the overthrow of that form of church government, sought to substitute for it what they called presbyterianism; but Mr. Heywood belonged to another division of it which, although less influential at present, was destined to come by and by to the front, in the strength of the conviction that to stop with presbyterianism was merely to change the name of the swamp, a party whose distinctive and animating spirit was the love of freedom, which indeed, degenerating into a passion among its inferior members, broke out, upon occasion, in the wildest vagaries of speech and doctrine, but on the other hand justified itself in its leaders, chief amongst whom were Milton and Cromwell, inasmuch as they accorded to the consciences of others the freedom they demanded for their own, the love of liberty with them not meaning merely the love of enjoying freedom, but that respect for the thing itself which renders a man incapable of violating it in another.

Roger Heywood was, in fact, already a pupil of Milton, whose anonymous pamphlet of 'Reformation touching Church Discipline' had already reached him, and opened with him the way for all his following works.

Richard, with whom my story has really to do, but for the understanding of whom it is necessary that the character and mental position of his father should in some measure be set forth, proved an apt pupil, and was soon possessed with such a passion for justice and liberty, as embodied in the political doctrines now presented for his acceptance, that it was impossible for him to understand how any honest man could be of a different mind. No youth, indeed, of simple and noble nature, as yet unmarred by any dominant phase of selfishness, could have failed to catch fire from the enthusiasm of such a father, an enthusiasm glowing yet restrained, wherein party spirit had a less share than principle, which, in relation to such a time, is to say much. Richard's heart swelled within him at the vistas of grandeur opened by his father's words, and swelled yet higher when he read to him passages from the pamphlet to which I have referred. It seemed to him, as to most young people under mental excitement, that he had but to tell the facts of the case to draw all men to his side, enlisting them in the army destined to sweep every form of tyranny, and especially spiritual usurpation and arrogance, from the face of the earth.

Being one who took everybody at the spoken word, Richard never thought of seeking Dorothy again at their former place of meeting. Nor, in the new enthusiasm born in him, did his thoughts for a good many days turn to her so often, or dwell so much upon her, as to cause any keen sense of their separation. The flood of new thoughts and feelings had transported him beyond the ignorant present. In truth, also, he was a little angry with Dorothy for showing a foolish preference for the church party, so plainly in the wrong was it! And what could SHE know about the question by his indifference to which she had been so scandalised, but to which he had been indifferent only until rightly informed thereon! If he had ever given her just cause to think him childish, certainly she should never apply the word to him again! If he could but see her, he would soon convince her, indeed he MUST see her, for the truth was not his to keep, but to share! It was his duty to acquaint her with the fact that the parliament was the army of God, fighting the great red dragon, one of whose seven heads was prelacy, the horn upon it the king, and Laud its crown. He wanted a stroll, he would take the path through the woods and the shrubbery to the old sun-dial. She would not be there, of course, but he would walk up the pleached alley and call at the house.

Reasoning thus within himself one day, he rose and went. But, as he approached the wood, Dorothy's great mastiff, which she had reared from a pup with her own hand, came leaping out to welcome him, and he was prepared to find her not far off.

When he entered the yew-circle, there she stood leaning on the dial, as if, like old Time, she too had gone to sleep there, and was dreaming ancient dreams over again. She did not move at the first sounds of his approach; and when at length, as he stood silent by her side, she lifted her head, but without looking at him, he saw the traces of tears on her cheeks. The heart of the youth smote him.

'Weeping, Dorothy?' he said.

'Yes,' she answered simply.

'I trust I am not the cause of your trouble, Dorothy?'

'You!' returned the girl quickly, and the colour rushed to her pale cheeks. 'No, indeed. How should you trouble me? My mother is ill.'

Considering his age, Richard was not much given to vanity, and it was something better that prevented him from feeling pleased at being thus exonerated: she looked so sweet and sad that the love which new interests had placed in abeyance returned in full tide. Even when a child, he had scarcely ever seen her in tears; it was to him a new aspect of her being.

'Dear Dorothy!' he said, 'I am very much grieved to learn this of your beautiful mother.'

'She IS beautiful,' responded the girl, and her voice was softer than he had ever heard it before; 'but she will die, and I shall be left alone.'

'No, Dorothy! that you shall never be,' exclaimed Richard, with a confidence bordering on presumption.

'Master Herbert is with her now,' resumed Dorothy, heedless of his words.

'You do not mean her life is even now in danger?' said Richard, in a tone of sudden awe.

'I hope not, but, indeed, I cannot tell. I left master Herbert comforting her with the assurance that she was taken away from the evil to come. "And I trust, madam," the dear old man went on to say, "that my departure will not long be delayed, for darkness will cover the earth, and gross darkness the people." Those were his very words.'

'Nay, nay!' said Richard, hastily; 'the good man is deceived; the people that sit in darkness shall see a great light.'

The girl looked at him with strange interrogation.

'Do not be angry, sweet Dorothy,' Richard went on. 'Old men may mistake as well as youths. As for the realm of England, the sun of righteousness will speedily arise thereon, for the dawn draws nigh; and master Herbert may be just as far deceived concerning your mother's condition, for she has been but sickly for a long time, and yet has survived many winters.'

Dorothy looked at him still, and was silent. At length she spoke, and her words came slowly and with weight.

'And what prophet's mantle, if I may make so bold, has fallen upon Richard Heywood, that the word in his mouth should outweigh that of an aged servant of the church? Can it be that the great light of which he speaks is Richard Heywood himself?'

'As master Herbert is a good man and a servant of God,' said Richard, coldly, stung by her sarcasm, but not choosing to reply to it, 'his word weighs mightily; but as a servant of the church his word is no weightier than my father's, who is also a minister of the true tabernacle, that wherein all who are kings over themselves are priests unto God, though truly he pretends to no prophecy beyond the understanding of the signs of the times.'

Dorothy saw that a wonderful change, such as had been incredible upon any but the witness of her own eyes and ears, had passed on her old playmate. He was in truth a boy no longer. Their relative position was no more what she had been of late accustomed to consider it. But with the change a gulf had begun to yawn between them.

'Alas, Richard!' she said, mistaking what he meant by the signs of the times, 'those who arrogate the gift of the Holy Ghost, while their sole inspiration is the presumption of their own hearts and an overweening contempt of authority, may well mistake signs of their own causing for signs from heaven. I but repeat the very words of good master Herbert.'

'I thought such swelling words hardly sounded like your own, Dorothy. But tell me, why should the persuasion of man or woman hang upon the words of a fellow-mortal? Is not the gift of the Spirit free to each who asks it? And are we not told that each must be fully persuaded in his own mind?'

'Nay, Richard, now I have thee! Hang you not by the word of your father, who is one, and despise the authority of the true church, which is many?'

'The true church were indeed an authority, but where shall we find it? Anyhow, the true church is one thing, and prelatical episcopacy another. But I have yet to learn what authority even the true church could have over a man's conscience.'

'You need to be reminded, Richard, that the Lord of the church gave power to his apostles to bind or loose.'

'I do not need to be so reminded, Dorothy, but I do not need to be shown first that that power was over men's consciences; and second, that it was transmitted to others by the apostles waiving the question as to the doubtful ordination of English prelates.'

Fire flashed from Dorothy's eyes.

'Richard Heywood,' she said, 'the demon of spiritual pride has already entered into you, and blown you up with a self-sufficiency which I never saw in you before, or I would never, never have companied with you, as I am now ashamed to think I have done so long, even to the danger of my soul's health.'

'In that case I may comfort myself, mistress Dorothy Vaughan,' said Richard, 'that you will no longer count me a boy! But do you then no longer desire that I should take one part OR the other and show myself a man? Am I man enough yet for the woman thou art, Dorothy? But, Dorothy,' he added, with sudden change of tone, for she had in anger turned to leave him, 'I love you dearly, and I am truly sorry if I have spoken so as to offend you. I came hither eager to share with you the great things I have learned since you left me with just contempt a fortnight ago.'

'Then it is I whose foolish words have cast you into the seat of the scorner! Alas! alas! my poor Richard! Never, never more, while you thus rebel against authority and revile sacred things, will I hold counsel with you.'

And again she turned to go.

'Dorothy!' cried the youth, turning pale with agony to find on the brink of what an abyss of loss his zeal had set him, 'wilt thou, then, never speak to me more, and I love thee as the daylight?'

'Never more till thou repent and turn. I will but give thee one piece of counsel, and then leave thee, if forever, that rests with thee. There has lately appeared, like the frog out of the mouth of the dragon, a certain tractate or treatise, small in bulk, but large with the wind of evil doctrine. Doubtless it will reach your father's house ere long, if it be not, as is more likely, already there, for it is the vile work of one they call a puritan, though where even the writer can vainly imagine the purity of such work to lie, let the pamphlet itself raise the question. Read the evil thing, or, I will not say read it, but glance the eye over it. It is styled "Animadversions upon—." Truly, I cannot recall the long-drawn title. It is filled, even as a toad with poison, so full of evil and scurrilous sayings against good men, rating and abusing them as the very off-scouring of the earth, that you cannot yet be so far gone in evil as not to be reclaimed by seeing whither such men and their inspiration would lead you. Farewell, Richard.'

With the words, and without a look, Dorothy, who had been standing sideways in act to go, swept up the pleached alley, her step so stately and her head so high that Richard, slowly as she walked away, dared not follow her, but stood 'like one forbid.' When she had vanished, and the light shone in full at the far end, he gave a great sigh and turned away, and the old dial was forsaken.

The scrap of title Dorothy had given was enough to enable Richard to recognise the pamphlet as one a copy of which his father had received only a few days before, and over the reading of which they had again and again laughed unrestrainedly. As he walked home he sought in vain to recall anything in it deserving of such reprobation as Dorothy had branded it withal. Had it been written on the other side no search would have been necessary, for party spirit (from which how could such a youth be free, when the greatest men of his time were deeply tainted?), while it blinds the eyes in one direction, makes them doubly keen in another. As it was, the abuse in the pamphlet referred to, appeared to him only warrantable indignation; and, the arrogance of an imperfect love leading him to utter desertion of his newly-adopted principles, he scorned as presumptuous that exercise of her own judgment on the part of Dorothy which had led to their separation, bitterly resenting the change in his playmate, who, now an angry woman, had decreed his degradation from the commonest privileges of friendship, until such time as he should abjure his convictions, become a renegade to the truth, and abandon the hope of resulting freedom which the strife of parties held out, an act of tyranny the reflection upon which raised such a swelling in his throat as he had never felt but once before, when a favourite foal got staked in trying to clear a fence. Having neither friend nor sister to whom to confess that he was in trouble, have confided it he could not in any case, seeing it involved blame of the woman his love for whom now first, when on the point of losing her forever, threatened to overmaster him, he wandered to the stables, which he found empty of men and nearly so of horses, half-involuntarily sought the stall of the mare his father had given him on his last birthday, laid his head on the neck bent round to greet him, and sighed a sore response to her soft, low, tremulous whinny.

As he stood thus, overcome by the bitter sense of wrong from the one he loved best in the world, something darkened the stable-door, and a voice he knew reached his ear. Mistaking the head she saw across an empty stall for that of one of the farm-servants, Goody Rees was calling aloud to know if he wanted a charm for the toothache.

Richard looked up.

'And what may your charm be, mistress Rees?' he asked.

'Aha! is it thou, young master?' returned the woman. 'Thou wilt marvel to see me about the place so soon again, but verily desired to know how that godly man, Faithful Stopchase, found himself after his fall.'

'Nay, mistress Rees, make no apology for coming amongst thy friends. I warrant thee against further rudeness of man or beast. I have taken them to task, and truly I will break his head who wags tongue against thee. As for Stopchase, he does well enough in all except owing thee thanks which he declines to pay. But for thy charm, good mistress Rees, what is it, tell me?'

She took a step inside the door, sent her small eyes peering first into every corner her sight could reach, and then said:

'Are we alone, we two, master Richard?'

'There's a cat in the next stall, mistress: if she can hear, she can't speak.'

'Don't be too sure of that, master Richard. Be there no one else?'

'Not a body; soul there may be, who knows?'

'I know there is none. I will tell thee my charm, or what else I may that thou would wish to know; for he is a true gentleman who will help a woman because she is a woman, be she as old and ugly as Goody Rees herself. Hearken, my pretty sir: it is the tooth of a corpse, drawn after he hath lain a se'en-night in the mould: wilt buy, my master? Or did not I see thee now asking comfort from thy horse for the—'

She paused a moment, peered narrowly at him from under lowered eyebrows, and went on:

'—heartache, eh, master Richard? Old eyes can see through velvet doublets.'

'All the world knows yours can see farther than other people's,' returned Richard. 'Heaven knows whence they have their sharpness. But suppose it were a heartache now, have you got e'er a charm to cure that?'

'The best of all charms, my young master, is a kiss from the maiden; and what would thou give me for the spell that should set her by thy side at the old dial, under a warm harvest moon, all the long hours 'twixt midnight and the crowing of the black cock, eh, my master? What wilt thou give me?'

'Not a brass farthing, if she came not of her own good will,' murmured Richard, turning towards his mare. 'But come, mistress Rees, you know you couldn't do it, even if you were the black witch the neighbours would have you, though I, for my part, will not hear a word against you, never since you set my poor old dog upon his legs again, though to be sure he will die one of these days, and that no one can help, dogs have such short lives, poor fools!'

'Thou knows not what old mother Rees can do. Tell me, young master, did she ever say and not do, eh, now?'

'You said you would cure my dog, and you did,' answered Richard.

'And I say now, if thou will, I will set thee and her together by the old dial to-morrow night, and it shall be a warm and moonlit night on purpose for ye, an ye will.'

'It were to no good purpose, mistress Rees, for we parted this day, and that forever, I much fear me,' said Richard with a deep sigh, but getting some little comfort even out of a witch's sympathy.

'Tut, tut, tut! Lovers' quarrels! Who knows not what they mean? Crying and kissing, crying and kissing, that's what they mean. Come now, what did thou and she quarrel about?'

The old woman, if not a witch, at least looked very like one, with her two hands resting on the wide round ledge of her farthingale, her head thrown back, and from under her peaked hat that pointed away behind, her two greenish eyes peering with a half-coaxing, yet sharp and probing gaze into those of the youth.

But how could he make a confidante of one like her? What could she understand of such questions as had raised the wall of partition betwixt him and Dorothy? Unwilling to offend her, however, he hesitated to give her offer a plain refusal, and turning away in silence, affected to have caught sight of something suspicious about his mare's near hock.

'I see, I see!' said the old woman grimly, but not ill-naturedly, and nodded her head, so that her hat described great arcs across the sky; 'thou art ashamed to confess that thou lovest thy father's whims more than thy lady's favours. Well, well! Such lovers are hardly for my trouble!'

But here came the voice of Mr. Heywood, calling his groom. She started, glanced around her as if seeking a covert, then peered from the door, and glided noiselessly out.

CHAPTER VI

PREPARATIONS

Great was the merriment in Raglan Castle over the discomfiture of the bumpkins, and many were the compliments Tom received in parlour, nursery, kitchen, guard-room, everywhere, on the success of his hastily-formed scheme for the chastisement of their presumption. The household had looked for a merry time on the occasion of the wedding, but had not expected such a full cup of delight as had been pressed out for them betwixt the self-importance of the overweening yokels and the inventive faculties of Tom Fool. All the evening, one standing in any open spot of the castle might have heard, now on the one, now on the other side, renewed bursts of merriment ripple the air; but as the still autumn night crept on, the intervals between grew longer and longer, until at length all sounds ceased, and silence took up her ancient reign, broken only by the occasional stamp of a horse or howl of a watch-dog.

But the earl, who, from simplicity of nature and peace of conscience combined, was perhaps better fitted for the enjoyment of the joke, in a time when such ludifications were not yet considered unsuitable to the dignity of the highest position, than any other member of his household, had, through it all, showed a countenance in which, although eyes, lips, and voice shared in the laughter, there yet lurked a thoughtful doubt concerning the result. For he knew that, in some shape or other, and that certainly not the true one, the affair would be spread over the country, where now prejudice against the Catholics was strong and dangerous in proportion to the unreason of those who cherished it. Now, also, it was becoming pretty plain that except the king yielded every prerogative, and became the puppet which the mingled pride and apprehension of the Parliament would have him, their differences must ere long be referred to the arbitration of the sword, in which case there was no shadow of doubt in the mind of the earl as to the part befitting a peer of the realm. The king was a protestant, but no less the king; and not this man, but his parents, had sinned in forsaking the church, of which sin their offspring had now to bear the penalty, reaping the whirlwind sprung from the stormy seeds by them sown. For what were the puritans but the lawfully-begotten children of the so called reformation, whose spirit they inherited, and in whose footsteps they so closely followed? In the midst of such reflections, dawned slowly in the mind of the devout old man the enchanting hope that perhaps he might be made the messenger of God to lead back to the true fold the wandering feet of his king. But, fail or speed in any result, so long as his castle held together, it should stand for the king. Faithful catholic as he was, the brave old man was English to the backbone.

And there was no time to lose. This visit of search, let it have originated how it might, and be as despicable in itself as it was ludicrous in its result, showed but too clearly how strong the current of popular feeling was setting against all the mounds of social distinction, and not kingly prerogative alone. What preparations might be needful, must be prudent.

That same night, then, long after the rest of the household had retired, three men took advantage of a fine half-moon to make a circuit of the castle, first along the counterscarp of the moat, and next along all accessible portions of the walls and battlements. They halted often, and, with much observation of the defences, held earnest talk together, sometimes eagerly contending rather than disputing, but far more often mutually suggesting and agreeing. At length one of them, whom the others called Caspar, retired, and the earl was left with his son Edward, Lord Herbert, the only person in the castle who had gone to neither window nor door to delight himself with the discomfiture of the parliamentary commissioners.

They entered the long picture gallery, faintly lighted from its large windows to the court, but chiefly from the oriel which formed the northern end of it, where they now sat down, the earl being, for the second time that night, weary. Behind them was a long dim line of portraits, broken only by the great chimney-piece supported by human figures, all of carved stone, and before them, nearly as dim, was the moon-massed landscape, a lovely view of the woodland, pasture, and red tilth to the northward of the castle.

They sat silent for a while, and the younger said:

'I fear you are fatigued, my lord. It is late for you to be out of bed; nature is mortal.'

'Thou sayest well; nature is mortal, my son. But therein lies the comfort, it cannot last. It were hard to say whether of the two houses stands the more in need of the hand of the maker.'

'Were it not for villanous saltpetre, my lord, the castle would hold out well enough.'

'And were it not for villanous gout, which is a traitor within it, I see not why this other should not hold out as long. Be sure, Herbert, I shall not render the keep for the taking of the outworks.'

'I fear,' said his son, wishing to change the subject, 'this part where we now are is the most liable to hurt from artillery.'

'Yes, but the ground in front is not such as they would readiest plant it upon,' said the earl. 'Do not let us forecast evil, only prepare for it.'

'We shall do our best, my lord, with your lordship's good counsel to guide us.'

'You shall lack nothing, Herbert, that either counsel or purse of mine may reach unto.'

'I thank your lordship, for much depends upon both. And so I fear will his majesty find, if it comes to the worst.'

A brief pause followed.

'Thinkest thou not, Herbert,' said the earl, slowly and thoughtfully, 'it ill suits that a subject should have and to spare, and his liege go begging?'

'My father is pleased to say so.'

'I am but evil pleased to say so. Bethink thee, son, what man can be pleased to part with his money? And while my king is poor, I must be rich for him. Thou wilt not accuse me, Herbert, after I am gone to the rest, that I wasted thy substance, lad?'

'So long as you still keep wherewithal to give, I shall be content, my lord.'

'Well, time will show. I but tell thee what runneth in my mind, for thou and I, Herbert, have bosomed no secrets. I will to bed. We must go the round again to-morrow with the sun to hold as a candle.'

The next day the same party made a similar circuit three times, in the morning, at noon, and in the evening, that the full light might uncover what the shadows had hid, and that the shadows might show what a perpendicular light could not reveal. There is all the difference as to discovery whether a thing is lying under the shadow of another, or casting one of its own.

After this came a review of the outer fortifications, if, indeed, they were worthy of the name, enclosing the gardens, the old tilting yard, now used as a bowling-green, the home-farmyard, and other such outlying portions under the stewardship of sir Ralph Blackstone and the governorship of Charles Somerset, the earl's youngest son. It was here that the most was wanted; and the next few days were chiefly spent in surveying these works, and drawing plans for their extension, strengthening, and connection, especially about the stables, armourer's shop, and smithy, where the building of new defences was almost immediately set on foot.

A thorough examination of the machinery of the various portcullises and drawbridges followed; next an overhauling of the bolts, chains, and other defences of the gates. Then came an inspection of the ordnance, from cannons down to drakes, through a gradation of names as uncouth to our ears, and as unknown to the artillery descended from them, as many of the Christian names of the puritans are to their descendants of the present day. At length, to conclude the inspection, Lord Herbert and the master of the armoury held consultation with the head armourer, and the mighty accumulation of weapons of all sorts was passed under the most rigid scrutiny; many of them were sent to the forge, and others carried to the ground-floor of the keep.

Presently, things began to look busy in a quiet way about the place. Men were at work blasting the rocks in a quarry not far off, whence laden carts went creeping to the castle; but this was oftener in the night. Some of them drove into the paved court, for here and there a buttress was wanted inside, and of the battlements not a few were weather-beaten and out of repair. These the earl would have let alone, on the ground that they were no longer more than ornamental, and therefore had better be repaired AFTER the siege, if such should befall, for the big guns would knock them about like cards; but Caspar reminded him that every time the ball from a cannon, culvering, or saker missed the parapet, it remained a sufficient bar to the bullet that might equally avail to carry off the defenceless gunner. The earl, however, although he yielded, maintained that the flying of the wall when struck was a more than counterbalancing danger.

The stock of provisions began to increase. The dry larder, which lay under the court, between the kitchen and buttery, was by degrees filled with gammons and flitches of bacon, well dried and smoked. Wheat, barley, oats, and pease were stored in the granary, and potatoes in a pit dug in the orchard.

Strange faces in the guard-room caused wonderings and questions amongst the women. The stables began to fill with horses, and 'more man' to go about the farmyard and outhouses.

CHAPTER VII

REFLECTIONS

Left alone with Lady, his mare, Richard could not help brooding, rather than pondering, over what the old woman had said. Not that for a moment he contemplated as a possibility the acceptance of the witch's offer. To come himself into any such close relations with her as that would imply, was in repulsiveness second only to the idea of subjecting Dorothy to her influences. For something to occupy his hands, that his mind might be restless at will, he gave his mare a careful currying, then an extra feed of oats, and then a gallop; after which it was time to go to bed.

I doubt if anything but the consciousness of crime will keep healthy youth awake, and as such consciousness is generally far from it, youth seldom counts the watches of the night. Richard soon fell fast asleep, and dreamed that his patron saint, alas for his protestantism! appeared to him, handed him a lance headed with a single flashing diamond, and told him to go and therewith kill the dragon. But just as he was asking the way to the dragon's den, that he might perform his behest, the saint vanished, and feeling the lance melting away in his grasp, he gradually woke to find it gone.

After a long talk with his father in the study, he was left to his own resources for the remainder of the day; and as it passed and the night drew on, the offer of the witch kept growing upon his imagination, and his longing to see Dorothy became stronger and stronger, until at last it was almost too intense to be borne. He had never before known such a possession, and was more than half inclined to attribute it to the arts of mother Rees.

His father was busy in his study below, writing letters, an employment which now occupied much of his time; and Richard sat alone in a chamber in the upper part of one of the many gables of the house, which he had occupied longer than he could remember. Its one small projecting lozenge-paned window looked towards Dorothy's home. Some years ago he had been able to see her window, from it through a gap in the trees, by favour of which, indeed, they had indulged in a system of communications by means of coloured flags, so satisfactory that Dorothy not only pressed into the service all the old frocks she could find, but got into trouble by cutting up one almost new for the enlargement of the somewhat limited scope of their telegraphy. In this window he now sat, sending his soul through the darkness, milky with the clouded light of half an old moon, towards the ancient sun-dial, where Time stood so still that sometimes Richard had known an hour there pass in a moment.

Never until now had he felt enmity in space: it had been hitherto rather as a bridge to bear him to Dorothy than a gulf to divide him from her presence; but now, through the interpenetrative power of feeling, their alienation had affected all around as well as within him, and space appeared as a solid enemy, and darkness as an unfriendly enchantress, each doing what it could to separate betwixt him and the being to whom his soul was drawn as, no, there was no AS for such drawing. No opposition of mere circumstances could have created the feeling; it was the sense of an inward separation taking form outwardly. For Richard was now but too well convinced that he had no power of persuasion equal to the task of making Dorothy see things as he saw them. The dividing influence of imperfect opposing goods is potent as that of warring good and evil, with this important difference, that the former is but for a season, and will one day bind as strongly as it parted, while the latter is essential, absolute, impassible, eternal.

To Dorothy, Richard seemed guilty of overweening arrogance and its attendant, presumption; she could not see the form ethereal to which he bowed. To Richard, Dorothy appeared the dupe of superstition; he could not see the god that dwelt within the idol. To Dorothy, Richard seemed to be one who gave the holy name of truth to nothing but the offspring of his own vain fancy. To Richard, Dorothy appeared one who so little loved the truth that she was ready to accept anything presented to her as such, by those who themselves loved the word more than the spirit, and the chrysalis of safety better than the wings of power. But it is only for a time that any good can to the good appear evil, and at this very moment, Nature, who in her blindness is stronger to bind than the farthest-seeing intellect to loose, was urging him into her presence; and the heart of Dorothy, notwithstanding her initiative in the separation, was leaning as lovingly, as sadly after the youth she had left alone with the defaced sun-dial, the symbol of Time's weariness. Had they, however, been permitted to meet as they would, the natural result of ever-renewed dissension would have been a thorough separation in heart, no heavenly twilights of loneliness giving time for the love which grows like the grass to recover from the scorching heat of intellectual jar and friction.

The waning moon at length peered warily from behind a bank of cloud, and her dim light melting through the darkness filled the night with a dream of the day. Richard was no more of a poet or dreamer of dreams than is any honest youth so long as love holds the bandage of custom away from his eyes. The poets are they who all their life long contrive to see over or through the bandage; but they would, I doubt, have but few readers, had not nature decreed that all youths and maidens shall, for a period, be it long or short, become aware that they too are of the race of the singers, shall, in the journey of their life, at least pass through the zone of song: some of them recognise it as the region of truth, and continue to believe in it still when it seems to have vanished from around them; others scoff as it disappears, and curse themselves for dupes. Through this zone Richard was now passing. Hence the moon wore to him a sorrowful face, and he felt a vague sympathy in her regard, that of one who was herself in trouble, half the light of her lord's countenance withdrawn. For science had not for him interfered with the shows of things by a partial revelation of their realities. He had not learned that the face of the moon is the face of a corpse-world; that the sadness upon it is the sadness of utter loss; that her light has in it no dissolved smile, is but the reflex from a lifeless mirror; that of all the orbs we know best she can have least to do with lovers' longings and losses, she alone having no love left in her, the cold cinder of a quenched world. Not an out-burnt cinder, though! she needs but to be cast again into the furnace of the sun.

As it was, Richard had gazed at her hardly for a minute when he found the tears running down his face, and starting up, ashamed of the unmanly weakness, hardly knew what he was doing before he found himself in the open air. From the hall clock came the first stroke of twelve as he closed the door behind him. It was the hour at which mother Rees had offered him a meeting with Dorothy; but it was assuredly with no expectation of seeing her that he turned his steps towards her dwelling.

CHAPTER VIII

AN ADVENTURE

When he reached the spot at which he usually turned off by a gap in the hedge to NEEDLE his way through the unpathed wood, he yielded to the impulses of memory and habit, and sought the yew-circle, where for some moments he stood by the dumb, disfeatured stone, which seemed to slumber in the moonlight, a monument slowly vanishing from above a vanished grave. Indeed it might well have been the grave of buried Time, for what fitter monument could he have than a mutilated sun-dial, what better enclosure than such a hedge of yews, and more suitable light than that of the dying moon? Or was it but that the heart of the youth, receiving these things as into a concave mirror, reprojected them into space, all shadowy with its own ghostliness and gloom? Close by the dial, like the dark way into regions where time is not, yawned the mouth of the pleached alley. Beyond that was her window, on which the moon must now be shining. He entered the alley, and walked softly towards the house. Suddenly, down the dark tunnel came rushing upon him Dorothy's mastiff, with a noise as of twenty soft feet, and a growl as if his throat had been full of teeth, changing to a boisterous welcome when he discovered who the stranger was. Fearful of disturbing the household, Richard soon quieted the dog, which was in the habit of obeying him almost as readily as his mistress, and, fearful of disturbing sleepers or watchers, approached the house like a thief. To gain a sight of Dorothy's window he had to pass that of the parlour, and then the porch, which he did on the grass, that his steps might be noiseless. But here the dog started from his heel, and bounded into the porch, leading after him the eyes of Richard, who thereupon saw what would have else remained undiscovered, two figures, namely, standing in its deep shadow. Judging it his part, as a friend of the family, to see who, at so late an hour, and so near the house, seemed thus to avoid discovery, Richard drew nearer, and the next moment saw that the door was open behind them, and that they were Dorothy and a young man.

'The gates will be shut,' said Dorothy.

'It is no matter; old Eccles will open to me at any hour,' was the answer.

'Still it were well you went without delay,' said Dorothy; and her voice trembled a little, for she had caught sight of Richard.

Now not only are anger and stupidity near of kin, but when a man whose mental movements are naturally deliberate, is suddenly spurred, he is in great danger of acting like a fool, and Richard did act like a fool. He strode up to the entrance of the porch, and said,

'Do you not hear the lady, sir? She tells you to go.'

A voice as cool and self-possessed as the other was hasty and perturbed, replied,

'I am much in the wrong, sir, if the lady do not turn the command upon yourself. Until you have obeyed it, she may perhaps see reason for withdrawing it in respect of me.'

Richard stepped into the porch, but Dorothy glided between them, and gently pushed him out.

'Richard Heywood!' she said.

'Whew!' interjected the stranger, softly.

'You can claim no right,' she went on, 'to be here at this hour. Pray go; you will disturb my mother.'

'Who is this man, then, whose right seems acknowledged?' asked Richard, in ill-suppressed fury.

'When you address me like a gentleman, such as I used to believe you—'

'May I presume to ask when you ceased to regard me as a gentleman, mistress Dorothy?'

'As soon as I found that you had learned to despise law and religion,' answered the girl. 'Such a one will hardly succeed in acting the part of a gentleman, even had he the blood of the Somersets in his veins.'

'I thank you, mistress Dorothy,' said the stranger, 'and will profit by the plain hint. Once more tell me to go, and I will obey.'

'He must go first,' returned Dorothy.

Richard had been standing as if stunned, but now with an effort recovered himself.

'I will wait for you,' he said, and turned away.

'For whom, sir?' asked Dorothy, indignantly.

'You have refused me the gentleman's name,' answered Richard: 'perhaps I may have the good fortune to persuade himself to be more obliging.'

'I shall not keep you waiting long,' said the young man significantly, as Richard walked away.

To do Richard justice, and greatly he needs it, I must make the remark that such had been the intimacy betwixt him and Dorothy, that he might well imagine himself acquainted with all the friends of her house. But the intimacy had been confined to the children; the heads of the two houses, although good neighbours, had not been drawn towards each other, and their mutual respect had not ripened into friendship. Hence many of the family and social relations of each were unknown to the other; and indeed both families led such a retired life that the children knew little of their own relatives even, and seldom spoke of any.

Lady Scudamore, the mother of the stranger, was first cousin to Lady Vaughan. They had been very intimate as girls, but had not met for years, hardly since the former married sir John, the son of one of King James's carpet-knights. Hearing of her cousin's illness, she had come to visit her at last, under the escort of her son. Taken with his new cousin, the youth had lingered and lingered; and in fact Dorothy had been unable to get rid of him before an hour strange for leave-taking in such a quiet and yet hospitable neighbourhood.

Richard took his stand on the side of the public road opposite the gate; but just ere Scudamore came, which was hardly a minute after, a cloud crept over the moon, and, as he happened to stand in a line with the bole of a tree, Scudamore did not catch sight of him. When he turned to walk along the road, Richard thought he avoided him, and, making a great stride or two after him, called aloud—

'Stop, sir, stop. You forget your appointments over easily, I think.'

'Oh, you ARE there!' said the youth, turning.

'I am glad you acknowledge my presence,' said Richard, not the better pleased with his new acquaintance that his speech and behaviour had an easy tone of superiority, which, if indefinably felt by the home-bred lad, was not therefore to be willingly accorded. His easy carriage, his light step, his still shoulders and lithe spine, indicated both birth and training.

'Just the night for a serenade,' he went on, heedless of Richard's remark, '—bright, but not too bright; cloudy, but not too cloudy.'

'Sir!' said Richard, amazed at his coolness.

'Oh, you want to quarrel with me!' returned the youth. 'But it takes two to fight as well as to kiss, and I will not make one to-night. I know who you are well enough, and have no quarrel with you, except indeed it be true, as indeed it must, for Dorothy tells me so, that you have turned roundhead as well as your father.'

'What right have you to speak so familiarly of mistress Dorothy?' said Richard.

'It occurs to me,' replied Scudamore, airily, 'that I had better ask you by what right you haunt her house at midnight. But I would not willingly cross you in cold blood. I wish you good a night, and better luck next time you go courting.'

The moon swam from behind a cloud, and her over ripe and fading light seemed to the eyes of Richard to gather upon the figure before him and there revive. The youth had on a doublet of some reddish colour, ill brought out by the moonlight, but its silver lace and the rapier hilt inlaid with silver shone the keener against it. A short cloak hung from his left shoulder, trimmed also with silver lace, and a little cataract of silver fringe fell from the edges of his short trousers into the wide tops of his boots, which were adorned with ruffles. He wore a large collar of lace, and cuffs of the same were folded back from his bare hands. A broad-brimmed beaver hat, its silver band fastened with a jewel holding a plume of willowy feathers, completed his attire, which he wore with just the slightest of a jaunty air. It was hardly the dress for a walk at midnight, but he had come in his mother's carriage, and had to go home without it.

Alas now for Richard's share in the freedom to which he had of late imagined himself devoted! No sooner had the words last spoken entered his ears than he was but a driven slave ready to rush into any quarrel with the man who spoke them. Ere he had gone three paces he had stepped in front of him.

'Whatever rights mistress Dorothy may have given you,' he said, 'she had none to transfer in respect of my father. What do you mean by calling him a roundhead?'

'Why, is he not one?' asked the youth, simply, keeping his ground, in spite of the unpleasant proximity of Richard's person. 'I am sorry to have wronged him, but I mistook him for a ringleader of the same name. I heartily beg your pardon.'

'You did not mistake,' said Richard stupidly.

'Then I did him no wrong,' rejoined the youth, and once more would have gone his way.

But Richard, angrier than ever at finding he had given him such an easy advantage, moved with his movement, and kept rudely in front of him, provoking a quarrel, in clownish fashion, it must be confessed.

'By heaven,' said Scudamore, 'if Dorothy had not begged me not to fight with you—,' and as he spoke he slipped suddenly past his antagonist, and walked swiftly away. Richard plunged after him, and seized him roughly by the shoulder. Instantaneously he wheeled on the very foot whence he was taking the next stride, and as he turned his rapier gleamed in the moonlight. The same moment it left his hand, he scarce knew how, and flew across the hedge. Richard, who was unarmed, had seized the blade, and, almost by one and the same movement of his wrist, wrenched the hilt from the grasp of his adversary, and flung the thing from him. Then closing with the cavalier, slighter and less skilled in such encounters, the roundhead almost instantly threw him upon the turf that bordered the road.

'Take that for drawing on an unarmed man,' he said.

No reply came. The youth lay stunned.

Then compassion woke in the heart of the angry Richard, and he hastened to his help. Ere he reached him, however, he made an attempt to rise, but only to stagger and fall again.

'Curse you for a roundhead!' he cried; 'you've twisted some of my tackle. I can't stand.'

'I'm sorry,' returned Richard, 'but why did you bare bilbo on a naked man? A right malignant you are!'

'Did I?' returned Scudamore. 'You laid hands on me so suddenly! I ask your pardon.'

Accepting the offered aid of Richard, he rose; but his right knee was so much hurt that he could not walk a step without great pain. Full of regret for the suffering he had caused, Richard lifted him in his arms, and seated him on a low wall of earth, which was all that here inclosed Lady Vaughan's shrubbery; then, breaking through the hedge on the opposite side of the way, presently returned with the rapier, and handed it to him. Scudamore accepted it courteously, with difficulty replaced it in its sheath, rose, and once more attempted to walk, but gave a groan, and would have fallen had not Richard caught him.

'The devil is in it!' he cried, with more annoyance than anger. 'If I am not in my place at my lord's breakfast to-morrow, there will be questioning. That I had leave to accompany my mother makes the mischief. If I had stole away, it would be another matter. It will be hard to bear rebuke, and no frolic.'

'Come home with me,' said Richard. 'My father will do his best to atone for the wrong done by his son.'

'Set foot across the threshold of a roundhead fanatic! In the way of hospitality! Not if the choice lay betwixt that and my coffin!' cried the cavalier.

'Then let me carry you back to Lady Vaughan's,' said Richard, with a torturing pang of jealousy, which only his sense of right, now thoroughly roused, enabled him to defy.

'I dare not. I should terrify my mother, and perhaps kill my cousin.'

'Your mother! your cousin!' cried Richard.

'Yes,' returned Scudamore; 'my mother is there, on a visit to her cousin Lady Vaughan.'

'Alas, I am more to blame than I knew!' said Richard.

'No,' Scudamore went on, heedless of Richard's lamentation. 'I must crawl back to Raglan as I may. If I get there before the morning, I shall be able to show reason why I should not wait upon my Lord at his breakfast.'

'You belong to the earl's household, then?' said Richard.

'Yes; and I fear I shall be grey-headed before I belong to anything else. He makes much of the ancient customs of the country: I would he would follow them. In the good old times I should have been a squire at least by now, if, indeed, I had not earned my spurs; but his lordship will never be content without me to hand him his buttered egg at breakfast, and fill his cup at dinner with his favourite claret. And so I am neither more nor less than a page, which rhymes with my age better than suits it. But the earl has a will of his own. He is a master worth serving though. And there is my Lady Elizabeth and my Lady Mary, not to mention my Lord Herbert! But,' he concluded, rubbing his injured knee with both hands, 'why do I prate of them to a roundhead?'

'Why indeed?' returned Richard. 'Are they not, the earl and all his people, traitors, and that of the worst? Are they not the enemies of the truth, worshippers of idols, bowing the knee to a woman, and kissing the very toes of an old man so in love with ignorance, that he tortures the philosopher who tells him the truth about the world and its motions?'

'Go on, master Roundhead! I can chastise you, and that you know. This cursed knee—'

'I will stand unarmed within your thrust, and never budge a foot,' said Richard. 'But no,' he added, 'I dare not, lest I should further injure one I have wronged already. Let there be a truce between us.'

'I am no papist,' returned Scudamore. 'I speak only as one of the earl's household, true men all. For them I cast the word in your teeth, you roundhead traitor! For myself I am of the English church.'

'It is but the wolf and the wolf's cub,' said. Richard. 'Prelatical episcopacy is but the old harlot veiled, or rather, forsooth, her bloody scarlet blackened in the sulphur fumes of her coming desolation.'

'Curse on, roundhead,' sighed the youth; 'I must crawl home.'

Once more he rose and made an effort to walk. But it was of no use: walk he could not.

'I must wait till the morning,' he said, 'when some Christian waggoner may be passing. Leave me in peace.'

'Nay, I am no such boor!' said Richard. 'Do you think you could ride?'

'I could try.'

'I will bring you the best mare in Gwent. But tell me your name, that I may know with whom I have the honour of a feud.'

'My name is Rowland Scudamore,' answered the youth. 'Yours I know already, and roundhead as you are, you have some smatch of honour in you.'

With an air of condescension he held out his hand, which his adversary, oppressed with a sense of the injury he had done him, did not refuse.

Richard hurried home, and to the stable, where he saddled his mare. But his father, who was still in his study, heard the sound of her hoofs in the paved yard, and met him as he led her out on the road, with an inquiry as to his destination at such an hour. Richard told him that he had had a quarrel with a certain young fellow of the name of Scudamore, a page of the earl of Worcester, whom he had met at Lady Vaughan's: and recounted the result.

'Was your quarrel a just one, my son?'

'No sir. I was in the wrong.'

'Then you are so far in the right now. And you are going to help him home?'

'Yes, sir.'

'Have you confessed yourself in the wrong?'

'Yes, sir.'

'Then go, my son, but beware of private quarrel in such a season of strife. This youth and thyself may meet some day in mortal conflict on the battle-field; and for my part, I know not how it may be with another, in such a case I would rather slay my friend than my enemy.'

Enlightened by the inward experience of the moment, Richard was able to understand and respond to the feeling. How different a sudden action flashed off the surface of a man's nature may be from that which, had time been given, would have unfolded itself from its depths!

Bare-headed, Roger Heywood walked beside his son as he led the mare to the spot where Scudamore perforce awaited his return. They found him stretched on the roadside, plucking handfuls of grass, and digging up the turf with his fingers, thus, and thus alone, betraying that he suffered. Mr. Heywood at first refrained from any offer of hospitality, believing he would be more inclined to accept it after he had proved the difficulty of riding, in which case a previous refusal might stand in the way. But although a slight groan escaped as they lifted him to the saddle, he gathered up the reins at once, and sat erect while they shortened the stirrup-leathers. Lady seemed to know what was required of her, and stood as still as a vaulting horse until Richard took the bridle to lead her away.

'I see!' said Scudamore; 'you can't trust me with your horse!'

'Not so, sir,' answered Mr. Heywood. 'We cannot trust the horse with you. It is quite impossible for you to ride so far alone. If you will go, you must submit to the attendance of my son, on which I am sorry to think you have so good a claim. But will you not yet change your mind and be our guest, for the night at least? We will send a messenger to the castle at earliest dawn.'

Scudamore declined the invitation, but with perfect courtesy, for there was that about Roger Heywood which rendered it impossible for any man who was himself a gentleman, whatever his judgment of him might be, to show him disrespect. And the moment the mare began to move, he felt no further inclination to object to Richard's company at her head, for he perceived that, should she prove in the least troublesome, it would be impossible for him to keep his seat. He did not suffer so much, however, as to lose all his good spirits, or fail in his part of a conversation composed chiefly of what we now call chaff, both of them for a time avoiding all such topics as might lead to dispute, the one from a sense of wrong already done, the other from a vague feeling that he was under the protection of the foregone injury.

'Have you known my cousin Dorothy long?' asked Scudamore.

'Longer than I can remember,' answered Richard.

'Then you must be more like brother and sister than lovers.'

'That, I fear, is her feeling,' replied Richard, honestly.

'You need not think of me as a rival,' said Scudamore. 'I never saw the young woman in my life before, and although anything of yours, being a roundhead's, is fair game—'

'Your humble servant, sir Cavalier!' interjected Richard. 'Pray use your pleasure.'

'I tell you plainly,' Scudamore went on, without heeding the interruption, 'though I admire my cousin, as I do any young woman, if she be but a shade beyond the passable—'

'The ape! The coxcomb!' said Richard to himself.

'I am not, therefore, dying for her love; and I give you this one honest warning that, though I would rather see mistress Dorothy in her winding-sheet than dame to a roundhead, I should be—yes, I MAY be a more dangerous rival in respect of your mare, than of any lady YOU are likely to set eyes upon.'

'What do you mean?' said Richard gruffly.

'I mean that, the king having at length resolved to be more of a monarch and less of a saint—'

'A saint!' echoed Richard, but the echo was rather a loud one, for it startled his mare and shook her rider.

'Don't shout like that!' cried the cavalier, with an oath. 'Saint or sinner, I care not. He is my king, and I am his soldier. But with this knee you have given me, I shall be fitter for garrison than field-duty, damn it.'

'You do not mean that his majesty has declared open war against the parliament?' exclaimed Richard.

'Faithless puritan, I do,' answered Scudamore. 'His majesty has at length, with reluctance, I am sorry to hear, taken up arms against his rebellious subjects. Land will be cheap by-and-by.'

'Many such rumours have reached us,' returned Richard, quietly. 'The king spares no threats; but for blows, well!'

'Insolent fanatic!' shouted Vaughan, 'I tell you his majesty is on his way from Scotland with an army of savages; and London has declared for the king.'

Richard and his mare simultaneously quickened their pace.

'Then it is time you were in bed, Mr Scudamore, for my mare and I will be wanted,' he cried. 'God be praised! I thank you for the good news. It makes me young again to hear it.'

'What the devil do you mean by jerking this cursed knee of mine so?' shouted Scudamore. 'Faith, you were young enough in all conscience already, you fool! You want to keep me in bed, as well as send me there! Well out of the way, you think! But I give you honest warning to look after your mare, for I vow I have fallen in love with her. She's worth three, at least, of your mistress Dorothies.'

'You talk like a Dutch boor,' said Richard.

'Saith an English lout,' retorted Scudamore. 'But, all things being lawful in love and war, not to mention hate and rebellion, this mare, if I am blessed with a chance, shall be, well, shall be translated.'

'You mean from Redware to Raglan.'

'Where she shall be entertained in a manner worthy of her, which is saying no little, if all her paces and points be equal to her walk and her crest.'

'I trust you will be more pitiful to my poor Lady,' said Richard, quietly. 'If all they say be true, Raglan stables are no place for a mare of her breeding.'

'What do you mean, roundhead?'

'Folk say your stables at Raglan are like other some Raglan matters, of the infernal sort.'

Scudamore was silent for a moment.

'Whether the stables be under the pavement or over the leads,' he returned at last, 'there are not a few in them as good as she, of which I hope to satisfy my Lady some day,' he added, patting the mare's neck.

'Wert thou not hurt already, I would pitch thee out of the saddle,' said Richard.

'Were I not hurt in the knee, thou couldst not,' said Scudamore.

'I need not lay hand upon thee. Wert thou as sound in limb as thou art in wind, thou wouldst feel thyself on the road ere thou knewest thou hadst taken leave of the saddle, did I but give the mare the sign she knows.'

'By God's grace,' said the cavalier, 'she shall be mine, and teach me the trick of it.'

Richard answered only with a grim laugh, and again, but more gently this time, quickened the mare's pace. Little more had passed between them when the six-sided towers of Raglan rose on their view.

Richard had, from childhood, been familiar with their aspect, especially that of the huge one called the Yellow Tower, but he had never yet been within the walls that encircled them. At any time during his life, almost up to the present hour, he might have entered without question, for the gates were seldom closed and never locked, the portcullises, sheathed in the wall above, hung moveless in their rusty chains, and the drawbridges spanned the moat from scarp to counterscarp, as if from the first their beams had rested there in solid masonry. And still, during the day, there was little sign of change, beyond an indefinable presence of busier life, even in the hush of the hot autumnal noon. But at night the drawbridges rose and the portcullises descended, each with its own peculiar creak, and jar, and scrape, setting the young rooks cawing in reply from every pinnacle and tree-top, never later than the last moment when the warder could see anything larger than a cat on the brow of the road this side the village. For who could tell when, or with what force at their command, the parliament might claim possession? And now another of the frequent reports had arrived, that the king had at length resorted to arms. It was altogether necessary for such as occupied a stronghold, unless willing to yield it to the first who demanded entrance, to keep watch and ward.

Admitted at the great brick gate, the outermost of all, and turning aside from the steps leading up to the white stone gate and main entrance beyond, with its drawbridge and double portcullis, Richard, by his companion's directions, led his mare to the left, and, rounding the moat of the citadel, sought the western gate of the castle, which seemed to shelter itself under the great bulk of the Yellow Tower, the cannon upon more than one of whose bastions closely commanded it, and made up for its inferiority in defence of its own.

Scudamore had scarcely called, ere the warder, who had been waked by the sound of the horse's feet, began to set the machinery of the portcullis in motion.

'What! wounded already, master Scudamore!' he cried, as they rode under the archway.

'Yes, Eccles,' answered Scudamore, '—wounded and taken prisoner, and brought home for ransom!'

As they spoke, Richard made use of his eyes, with a vague notion that some knowledge of the place might one day or other be of service, but it was little he could see. The moon was almost down, and her low light, prolific of shadows, shone straight in through the lifted portcullis, but in the gateway where they stood, there was nothing for her to show but the groined vault, the massy walls, and the huge iron-studded gate beyond.

'Curse you for a roundhead!' cried Scudamore, in the wrath engendered of a fierce twinge, as Heywood sought to help his lamed leg over the saddle.

'Dismount on this side then,' said Richard, regardless of the insult.

But the warder had caught the word.

'Roundhead!' he exclaimed.

Scudamore did not answer until he found himself safe on his feet, and by that time he had recovered his good manners.

'This is young Mr. Heywood of Redware,' he said, and moved towards the wicket, leaning on Richard's arm.

But the old warder stepped in front, and stood between them and the gate.

'Not a damned roundhead of the pack shall set foot across this door-sill, so long as I hold the gate,' he cried, with a fierce gesture of the right arm. And therewith he set his back to the wicket.

'Tut, tut, Eccles!' returned Scudamore impatiently. 'Good words are worth much, and cost little.'

'If the old dog bark, he gives counsel,' rejoined Eccles, immovable.

Heywood was amused, and stood silent, waiting the result. He had no particular wish to enter, and yet would have liked to see what could be seen of the court.

'Where the doorkeeper is a churl, what will folk say of the master of the house?' said Scudamore.

'They may say as they list; it will neither hurt him nor me,' said Eccles.

'Make haste, my good fellow, and let us through,' pleaded Scudamore. 'By Saint George! but my leg is in great pain. I fear the knee-cap is broken, in which case I shall not trouble thee much for a week of months.'

As he spoke, he stood leaning on Richard's arm, and behind them stood Lady, still as a horse of bronze.

'I will but drop the portcullis,' said the warder, 'and then I will carry thee to thy room in my arms. But not a cursed roundhead shall enter here, I swear.'

'Let us through at once,' said Scudamore, trying the imperative.

'Not if the earl himself gave the order,' persisted the man.

'Ho! ho! what is that you say? Let the gentlemen through,' cried a voice from somewhere.

The warder opened the wicket immediately, stepped inside, and held it open while they entered, nor uttered another word. But as soon as Richard had got Scudamore clear of the threshold, to which he lent not a helping finger, he stepped quietly out again, closed the wicket behind him, and taking Lady by the bridle, led her back over the bridge towards the bowling-green.

Scudamore had just time to whisper to Heywood, 'It is my master, the earl himself,' when the voice came again.

'What! wounded, Rowland? How is this? And who have you there?'

But that moment Richard heard the sound of his mare's hoofs on the bridge, and leaving Scudamore to answer for them both, bounded back to the wicket, darted through, and called her by name. Instantly she stood stock still, notwithstanding a vicious kick in the ribs from Eccles, not unseen of Heywood. Enraged at the fellow's insolence, he dealt him a sudden blow that stretched him at the mare's feet, vaulted into the saddle, and had reached the outer gate before he had recovered himself. The sleepy porter had just let him through, when the warder's signal to let no one out reached him. Richard turned with a laugh.

'When next you catch a roundhead,' he said, 'keep him;' and giving Lady the rein, galloped off, leaving the porter staring after him through the bars like a half-roused wild beast.

Not doubting the rumour of open hostilities, the warder's design had been to secure the mare, and pretend she had run away, for a good horse was now more precious than ever.

The earl's study was over the gate, and as he suffered much from gout and slept ill, he not unfrequently sought refuge in the night-watches with his friends Chaucer, Gower, and Shakspere.

Richard drew rein at the last point whence the castle would have been visible in the daytime. All he saw was a moving light. The walls whence it shone were one day to be as the shell around the kernel of his destiny.

CHAPTER IX

LOVE AND WAR

When Richard reached home and recounted the escape he had had, an imprecation, the first he had ever heard him utter, broke from his father's lips. With the indiscrimination of party spirit, he looked upon the warder's insolence and attempted robbery as the spirit and behaviour of his master, the earl being in fact as little capable of such conduct as Mr. Heywood himself.

Immediately after their early breakfast the next morning, he led his son to a chamber in the roof, of the very existence of which he had been ignorant, and there discovered to him good store of such armour of both kinds as was then in use, which for some years past he had been quietly collecting in view of the time—which, in the light of the last rumour, seemed to have at length arrived—when strength would have to decide the antagonism of opposed claims. Probably also it was in view of this time, seen from afar in silent approach, that, from the very moment when he took his education into his own hands, he had paid thorough attention to Richard's bodily as well as mental accomplishment, encouraging him in all manly sports, such as wrestling, boxing, and riding to hounds, with the more martial training of sword-exercises, with and without the target, and shooting with the carbine and the new-fashioned flint-lock pistols.

The rest of the morning Richard spent in choosing a headpiece, and mail plates for breast, back, neck, shoulders, arms, and thighs. The next thing was to set the village tailor at work upon a coat of that thick strong leather, dressed soft and pliant, which they called buff, to wear under his armour. After that came the proper equipment of Lady, and that of the twenty men whom his father expected to provide from amongst his own tenants, and for whom he had already a full provision of clothing and armour; they had to be determined on, conferred with, and fitted, one by one, so as to avoid drawing attention to the proceeding. Hence both Mr. Heywood and Richard had enough to do, and the more that Faithful Stopchase, on whom was their chief dependence, had not yet recovered sufficiently from the effects of his fall to be equal to the same exertion as formerly—of which he was the more impatient that he firmly believed he had been a special object of Satanic assault, because of the present value of his counsels, and the coming weight of his deeds on the side of the well-affected. Thus occupied, the weeks passed into months.

During this time Richard called again and again upon Dorothy, ostensibly to inquire after her mother. Only once, however, did she appear, when she gave him to understand she was so fully occupied, that, although obliged by his attention, he must not expect to see her again.

'But I will be honest, Richard,' she added, 'and let you know plainly that, were it otherwise in respect of my mother, I yet should not see you, for you and I have parted company, and are already so far asunder on different roads that I must bid you farewell at once while yet we can hear each other speak.'

There was no anger, only a cold sadness in her tone and manner, while her bearing was stately as towards one with whom she had never had intimacy. Even her sadness seemed to Richard to have respect to the hopeless condition of her mother's health, and not at all to the changed relation between him and her.

'I trust, at least, mistress Dorothy,' he said, with some bitterness, 'you will grant me the justice that what I do, I do with a good conscience. After all that has been betwixt us I ask for no more.'

'What more could the best of men ask for?'

'I, who am far from making any claim to rank with such—'

'I am glad to know it,' interjected Dorothy.

'—am yet capable of hoping that an eye at once keener and kinder than yours may see conscience at the very root of the actions which you, Dorothy, will doubtless most condemn.'

Was this the boy she had despised for indifference?

'Was it conscience drove you to sprain my cousin Rowland's knee?' she asked.

Richard was silent for a moment. The sting was too cruel.

'Pray hesitate not to say so, if such be your conviction,' added Dorothy.

'No,' replied Richard, recovering himself. 'I trust it is not such a serious matter as you say; but any how it was not conscience but jealousy and anger that drove me to that wrong.'

'Did you see the action such at the time?'

'No, surely; else I would not have been guilty of that for which I am truly sorry now.'

'Then, perhaps, the day will come when, looking back on what you do now, you will regard it with the like disapprobation. God grant it may!' she added, with a deep sigh.

'That can hardly be, mistress Dorothy. I am, in the matters to which you refer, under the influence of no passion, no jealousy, no self-seeking, no—'

'Perhaps a deeper search might discover in you each and all of the bosom-sins you so stoutly abjure,' interrupted Dorothy. 'But it is needless for you to defend yourself to me; I am not your judge.'

'So much the better for me!' returned Richard; 'I should else have an unjust as well as severe one. I, on my part, hope the day may come when you will find something to repent of in such harshness towards an old friend whom you choose to think in the wrong.'

'Richard Heywood, God is my witness it is no choice of mine. I have no choice: what else is there to think? I know well enough what you and your father are about. But there is nothing save my own conscience and my mother's love I would not part with to be able to believe you honourably right in your own eyes, not in mine, God forbid! That can never be, not until fair is foul and foul is fair.'

So saying, she held out her hand.

'God be between thee and me, Dorothy!' said Richard, with solemnity, as he took it in his.

He spoke with a voice that seemed to him far away and not his own. Until now he had never realized the idea of a final separation between him and Dorothy; and even now, he could hardly believe she was in earnest, but felt, rather, like a child whose nurse threatens to forsake him on the dark road, and who begins to weep only from the pitiful imagination of the thing, and not any actual fear of her carrying the threat into execution. The idea of retaining her love by ceasing to act on his convictions, the very possibility of it, had never crossed the horizon of his thoughts. Had it come to him as the merest intellectual notion, he would have perceived at once, of such a loyal stock did he come, and so loyal had he himself been to truth all his days, that to act upon her convictions instead of his own would have been to widen a gulf at least measurable, to one infinite and impassable.

She withdrew the hand which had solemnly pressed his, and left the room. For a moment he stood gazing after her. Even in that moment, the vague fear that she would not come again grew to a plain conviction, and forcibly repressing the misery that rose in bodily presence from his heart to his throat, he left the house, hurried down the pleached alley to the old sun-dial, threw himself on the grass under the yews, and wept and longed for war.

But war was not to be just yet. Autumn withered and sank into winter. The rain came down on the stubble, and the red cattle waded through red mire to and from their pasture; the skies grew pale above, and the earth grew bare beneath; the winds grew sharp and seemed unfriendly; the brooks ran foaming to the rivers, and the rivers ran roaring to the ocean. Then the earth dried a little, and the frost came, and swelled and hardened it; the snow fell and lay, vanished and came again. But even out of the depth of winter, quivered airs and hints of spring, until at last the mighty weakling was born. And all this time rumour beat the alarum of war, and men were growing harder and more determined on both sides, some from self-opinion, some from party spirit, some from prejudice, antipathy, animosity, some from sense of duty, mingled more and less with the alloys of impulse and advantage. But he who was most earnest on the one side was least aware that he who was most earnest on the other was honest as himself. To confess uprightness in one of the opposite party, seemed to most men to involve treachery to their own; or if they were driven to the confession, it was too often followed with an attempt at discrediting the noblest of human qualities.

The hearts of the two young people fared very much as the earth under the altered skies of winter, and behaved much as the divided nation. A sense of wrong endured kept both from feeling at first the full sorrow of their separation; and by the time that the tide of memory had flowed back and covered the rock of offence, they had got a little used to the dulness of a day from which its brightest hour had been blotted. Dorothy learned very soon to think of Richard as a prodigal brother beyond seas, and when they chanced to meet, which was but seldom, he was to her as a sad ghost in a dream. To Richard, on the other hand, she looked a lovely but scarce worshipful celestial, with merely might enough to hold his heart, swelling with a sense of wrong, in her hand, and squeeze it very hard. His consolation was that he suffered for the truth's sake, for to decline action upon such insight as he had had, was a thing as impossible as to alter the relations between the parts of a sphere. Dorothy longed for peace, and the return of the wandering chickens of the church to the shelter of her wings, to be led by her about the paled yard of obedience, picking up the barley of righteousness; Richard longed for the trumpet-blast of Liberty to call her sons together, to a war whose battles should never cease until men were free to worship God after the light he had lighted within them, and the dragon of priestly authority should breathe out his last fiery breath, no more to drive the feebler brethren to seek refuge in the house of hypocrisy.

At home Dorothy was under few influences except those of her mother, and, through his letters, of Mr. Matthew Herbert. Upon the former a lovely spiritual repose had long since descended. Her anxieties were only for her daughter, her hopes only for the world beyond the grave. The latter was a man of peace, who, having found in the ordinances of his church everything to aid and nothing to retard his spiritual development, had no conception of the nature of the puritanical opposition to its government and rites. Through neither could Dorothy come to any true idea of the questions which agitated the politics of both church and state. To her, the king was a kind of demigod, and every priest a fountain of truth. Her religion was the sedate and dutiful acceptance of obedient innocence, a thing of small account indeed where it is rooted only in sentiment and customary preference, but of inestimable value in such cases as hers, where action followed upon acceptance.

Richard, again, was under the quickening masterdom of a well-stored, active mind, a strong will, a judgment that sought to keep its balance even, and whose descended scale never rebounded, a conscience which, through all the mists of human judgment, eyed ever the blotted glimmer of some light beyond; and all these elements of power were gathered in his own father, in whom the customary sternness of the puritan parent had at length blossomed in confidence, a phase of love which, to such a mind as Richard's, was even more enchanting than tenderness. To be trusted by such a father, to feel his mind and soul present with him, acknowledging him a fit associate in great hopes and noble aims, was surely and ought to be, whatever the sentimentalist may say, some comfort for any sorrow a youth is capable of, such being in general only too lightly remediable. I wonder if any mere youth ever suffered, from a disappointment in love, half the sense of cureless pain which, with one protracted pang, gnaws at the heart of the avaricious old man who has dropt a sovereign into his draw-well.

But the relation of Dorothy and Richard, although ordinary in outward appearance, was of no common kind; and while these two thus fell apart from each other in their outer life, each judging the other insensible to the call of highest rectitude, neither of them knew how much his or her heart was confident of the other's integrity. In respect of them, the lovely simile, in Christabel, of the parted cliffs, may be carried a little farther, for, under the dreary sea flowing between them, the rock was one still. Such a faith may sometimes, perhaps often does, lie in the heart like a seed buried beyond the reach of the sun, thoroughly alive though giving no sign: to grow too soon might be to die. Things had indeed gone farther with Dorothy and Richard, but the lobes of their loves had never been fairly exposed to the sun and wind ere the swollen clods of winter again covered them.

Once, in the cold noon of a lovely day of frost, when the lightest step crackled with the breaking of multitudinous crystals, when the trees were fringed with furry white, and the old spider-webs glimmered like filigrane of fairy silver, they met on a lonely country-road. The sun shone red through depths of half-frozen vapour, and tinged the whiteness of death with a faint warmth of feeling and hope. Along the rough lane Richard walked reading what looked like a letter, but was a copy his father had procured of a poem still only in manuscript, the Lycidas of Milton. In the glow to which the alternating hot and cold winds of enthusiasm and bereavement had fanned the fiery particle within him, Richard was not only able to understand and enjoy the thought of which the poem was built, but was borne aloft on its sad yet hopeful melodies as upon wings of an upsoaring seraph. The flow of his feeling suddenly broken by an almost fierce desire to share with Dorothy the tenderness of the magic music of the stately monody, and then, ere the answering waves of her emotion had subsided, to whisper to her that the marvellous spell came from the heart of the same wonderful man from whose brain had issued, like Pallas from Jove's, what? Animadversions upon the Remonstrants Defence against Smectymnus, the pamphlet which had so roused all the abhorrence her nature was capable of, he lifted his head and saw her but a few paces from him. Dorothy caught a glimpse of a countenance radiant with feeling, and eyes flashing through a watery film of delight; her own eyes fell; she said, 'Good morning, Richard!' and passed him without deflecting an inch. The bird of song folded its wings and called in its shining; the sun lost half his red beams; the sprinkled seed pearls vanished, and ashes covered the earth; he folded the paper, laid it in the breast of his doublet, and walked home through the glittering meadows with a fresh hurt in his heart.

Dorothy's time and thoughts were all but occupied with the nursing of her mother, who, contrary to the expectation of her friends, outlived the winter, and revived as the spring drew on. She read much to her. Some of the best books had drifted into the house and settled there, but, although English printing was now nearly two centuries old, they were not many. We must not therefore imagine, however, that the two ladies were ill supplied with spiritual pabulum. There are few houses of the present day in which, though there be ten times as many books, there is so much strong food; if there was any lack, it was rather of diluents. Amongst those she read were Queen Elizabeth's Homilies, Hooker's Politie, Donne's Sermons, and George Herbert's Temple, to the dying lady only less dear than her New Testament.

But even with this last, it was only through sympathy with her mother that Dorothy could come into any contact. The gems of the mind, which alone could catch and reflect such light, lay as yet under the soil, and much ploughing and breaking of the clods was needful ere they could come largely to the surface. But happily for Dorothy, there were amongst the books a few of those precious little quartos of Shakspere, the first three books of the Faerie Queene, and the Countess of Pembroke's Arcadia, then much read, if we may judge from the fact that, although it was not published till after the death of Sidney, the eighth edition of it had now been nearly ten years in Lady Vaughan's possession.

Then there was in the drawing-room an old spinnet, sadly out of tune, on which she would yet, in spite of the occasional jar and shudder of respondent nerves, now and then play at a sitting all the little music she had learned, and with whose help she had sometimes even tried to find out an air for words that had taken her fancy.

Also, she had the house to look after, the live stock to see to, her dog to play with and teach, a few sad thoughts and memories to discipline, a call now and then from a neighbour, or a longer visit from some old friend of her mother's to receive, and the few cottagers on all that was left of the estate of Wyfern to care for; so that her time was tolerably filled up, and she felt little need of anything more to occupy at least her hours and days.

Meanwhile, through all nature's changes, through calm and tempest, rain and snow, through dull refusing winter, and the first passing visits of open-handed spring, the hearts of men were awaiting the outburst of the thunder, the blue peaks of whose cloud-built cells had long been visible on the horizon of the future. Every now and then they would start and listen, and ask each other was it the first growl of the storm, or but the rumbling of the wheels of the government. To the dwellers in Raglan Castle it seemed at least a stormy sign, of which the news reached them in the dull November weather, that the parliament had set a guard upon Worcester House in the Strand, and searched it for persons suspected of high treason, Lord Herbert, doubtless, first of all, the direction and strength of whose political drift, suspicious from the first because of his religious persuasion, could hardly be any longer doubtful to the most liberal of its members.

The news of the terrible insurrection of the catholics in Ireland followed.

Richard kept his armour bright, his mare in good fettle, himself and his men in thorough exercise, read and talked with his father, and waited, sometimes with patience, sometimes without.

At length, in the early spring, the king withdrew to York, and a body-guard of the gentlemen of the neighbourhood gathered around him. Richard renewed the flints of his carbine and pistols.

In April, the king, refused entrance into the town of Hull, proclaimed the governor a traitor. The parliament declared the proclamation a breach of its privileges. Richard got new girths.

The summer passed in various disputes. Towards its close the governor of Portsmouth declined to act upon a commission to organize the new levies of the parliament, and administered instead thereof an oath of allegiance to the garrison and inhabitants. Thereupon the place was besieged by Essex; the king proclaimed him a traitor, and the parliament retorted by declaring the royal proclamation a libel. Richard had his mare new-shod.

On a certain day in August, the royal standard, with the motto, 'Give to Caesar his due,' was set up at Nottingham. Richard mounted his mare, and taking leave of his father, led Stopchase and nineteen men more, all fairly mounted, to offer his services to the parliament, as represented by the earl of Essex.

CHAPTER X

DOROTHY'S REFUGE

With the decay of summer, Lady Vaughan began again to sink, and became at length so weak that Dorothy rarely left her room. The departure of Richard Heywood to join the rebels affected her deeply. The report of the utter rout of the parliamentary forces at Edgehill, lighted up her face for the last time with a glimmer of earthly gladness, which the very different news that followed speedily extinguished; and after that she declined more rapidly. Mrs. Rees told Dorothy that she would yield to the first frost. But she lingered many weeks. One morning she signed to her daughter to come nearer that she might speak to her.

'Dorothy,' she whispered, 'I wish much to see good Mr. Herbert. Prithee send for him. I know it is an evil time for him to travel, being an old man and feeble, but he will do his endeavour to come to me, I know, if but for my husband's sake, whom he loved like a brother. I cannot die in peace without first taking counsel with him how best to provide for the safety of my little ewe-lamb until these storms are overblown. Alas! alas! I did look to Richard Heywood—'

She could say no more.

'Do not take thought about the morrow for me any more than you would for yourself, madam,' said Dorothy. 'You know master Herbert says the one is as the other.'

She kissed her mother's hand as she spoke, then hastened from the room, and despatched a messenger to Llangattock.

Before the worthy man arrived, Lady Vaughan was speechless. By signs and looks, definite enough, and more eloquent than words, she committed Dorothy to his protection, and died.

Dorothy behaved with much calmness. She would not, in her mother's absence, act so as would have grieved her presence. Little passed between her and Mr. Herbert until the funeral was over. Then they talked of the future. Her guardian wished much to leave everything in charge of the old bailiff, and take her with him to Llangattock; but he hesitated a little because of the bad state of the roads in winter, much because of their danger in the troubled condition of affairs, and most of all because of the uncertain, indeed perilous position of the Episcopalian clergy, who might soon find themselves without a roof to shelter them. Fearing nothing for himself, he must yet, in arranging for Dorothy, contemplate the worst of threatening possibilities; and one thing was pretty certain, that matters must grow far worse before they could even begin to mend.

But they had more time for deliberation given them than they would willingly have taken. Mr. Herbert had caught cold while reading the funeral service, and was compelled to delay his return. The cold settled into a sort of low fever, and for many weeks he lay helpless. During this time the sudden affair at Brentford took place, after which the king, having lost by it far more than he had gained, withdrew to Oxford, anxious to re-open the treaty which the battle had closed.

The country was now in a sad state. Whichever party was uppermost in any district, sought to ruin all of the opposite faction. Robbery and plunder became common, and that not only on the track of armies or the route of smaller bodies of soldiers, for bands of mere marauders, taking up the cry of the faction that happened in any neighbourhood to have the ascendancy, plundered houses, robbed travellers, and were guilty of all sorts of violence. Hence it had become as perilous to stay at home in an unfortified house as to travel; and many were the terrors which during the winter tried the courage of the girl, and checked the recovery of the old man. At length one morning, after a midnight alarm, Mr. Herbert thus addressed Dorothy, as she waited upon him with his breakfast:

'It fears me much, my dear Dorothy, that the time will be long ere any but fortified places will be safe abodes. It is a question in my mind whether it would not be better to seek refuge for you—. But stay; let me suggest my proposal, rather than startle you with it in sudden form complete. You are related to the Somersets, are you not?'

'Yes—distantly.'

'Is the relationship recognized by them?'

'I cannot tell, sir. I do not even distinctly know what the relationship is. And assuredly, sir, you mean not to propose that I should seek safety from bodily peril with a household which is, to say the least, so unfriendly to the doctrines you and my blessed mother have always taught me! You cannot, or indeed, must you not have forgotten that they are papists?'

Dorothy had been educated in such a fear of the catholics, and such a profound disapproval of those of their doctrines rejected by the reformers of the church of England, as was only surpassed in intensity by her absolute abhorrence of the assumptions and negations of the puritans. These indeed roused in her a certain sense of disgust which she had never felt in respect of what were considered by her teachers the most erroneous doctrines of the catholics. But Mr. Herbert, although his prejudices were nearly as strong, and his opinions, if not more indigenous at least far better acclimatised than hers, had yet reaped this advantage of a longer life, that he was better able to atone his dislike of certain opinions with personal regard for those who held them, and therefore did not, like Dorothy, recoil from the idea of obligation to one of a different creed—provided always that creed was catholicism and not puritanism. For to the church of England, the catholics, in the presence of her more rampant foes, appeared harmless enough now.

He believed that the honourable feelings of Lord Worcester and his family would be hostile to any attempt to proselytize his ward. But as far as she was herself concerned, he trusted more to the strength of her prejudices than the rectitude of her convictions, honest as the girl was, to prevent her from being over-influenced by the change of spiritual atmosphere; for in proportion to the simplicity of her goodness must be her capacity for recognizing the goodness of others, catholics or not, and for being wrought upon by the virtue that went out from them. His hope was, that England would have again become the abode of peace, long ere any risk to her spiritual well-being should have been incurred by this mode of securing her bodily safety and comfort.

But there was another fact, in the absence of which he would have had far more hesitation in seeking for his ewe-lamb the protection of sheep, the guardians of whose spiritual fold had but too often proved wolves in sheep-dogs' clothing: within the last few days the news had reached him that an old friend named Bayly, a true man, a priest of the English church and a doctor of divinity, had taken up his abode in Raglan castle as one of the household, chaplain indeed, as report would have it, though that was hard of belief, save indeed it were for the sake of the protestants within its walls. However that might be, there was a true shepherd to whose care to entrust his lamb; and it was mainly on the strength of this consideration that he had concluded to make his proposal to Dorothy, namely, that she should seek shelter within the walls of Raglan castle until the storm should be so far over-blown, as to admit either of her going to Llangattock or returning to her own home. He now discussed the matter with her in full, and, notwithstanding her very natural repugnance to the scheme, such was Dorothy's confidence in her friend that she was easily persuaded of its wisdom. What the more inclined her to yield was, that Mr. Heywood had written her a letter, hardly the less unwelcome for the kindness of its tone, in which he offered her the shelter and hospitality of Redware 'until better days.'

'Better days!' exclaimed Dorothy with contempt. 'If such days as he would count better should ever arrive, his house is the last place where I would have them find me!'

She wrote a polite but cold refusal, and rejoiced in the hope that he would soon hear of her having sought and found refuge in Raglan with the friends of the king.

Meanwhile Mr. Herbert had opened communication with Dr. Bayly, had satisfied himself that he was still a true son of the church, and had solicited his friendly mediation towards the receiving of mistress Dorothy Vaughan into the family of the Marquis of Worcester, to the dignity of which title the earl had now been raised, the parliament, to be sure, declining to acknowledge the patent conferred by his majesty, but that was of no consequence in the estimation of those chiefly concerned.

On a certain spring morning, then, the snow still lying in the hollows of the hills, Thomas Bayly came to Wyfern to see his old friend Matthew Herbert. He was a courteous little man, with a courtesy librating on a knife-edge of deflection towards obsequiousness on the one hand and condescension on the other, for neither of which, however, was his friend Herbert an object. His eye was keen, and his forehead good, but his carriage inclined to the pompous, and his speech to the formal, ornate, and prolix. The shape of his mouth was honest, but the closure of the lips indicated self-importance. The greeting between them was simple and genuine, and ere they parted, Bayly had promised to do his best in representing the matter to the Marquis , his daughter-in-law, Lady Margaret, the wife of Lord Herbert, and his daughter, Lady Anne, who, although the most rigid catholic in the house, was already the doctor's special friend.

It would have been greatly unlike the Marquis or any of his family to refuse such a prayer. Had not their house been for centuries the abode of hospitality, the embodiment of shelter? On the mere representation of Dr. Bayly, and the fact of the relationship, which, although distant, was well enough known, within two days mistress Dorothy Vaughan received an invitation to enter the family of the Marquis , as one of the gentlewomen of Lady Margaret's suite. It was of course gratefully accepted, and as soon as Mr. Herbert thought himself sufficiently recovered to encounter the fatigues of travelling, he urged on the somewhat laggard preparations of Dorothy, that he might himself see her safely housed on his way to Llangattock, whither he was most anxious to return.

It was a lovely spring morning when they set out together on horseback for Raglan. The sun looked down like a young father upon his earth-mothered children, peeping out of their beds to greet him after the long winter night. The rooks were too busy to caw, dibbling deep in the soft red earth with their great beaks. The red cattle, flaked with white, spotted the clear fresh green of the meadows. The bare trees had a kind of glory about them, like old men waiting for their youth, which might come suddenly. A few slow clouds were drifting across the pale sky. A gentle wind was blowing over the wet fields, but when a cloud swept before the sun, it blew cold. The roads were bad, but their horses were used to such, and picked their way with the easy carefulness of experience. The winter might yet return for a season, but this day was of the spring and its promises. Earth and air, field and sky were full of peace. But the heart of England was troubled, troubled with passions both good and evil, with righteous indignation and unholy scorn, with the love of liberty and the joy of license, with ambition and aspiration.

No honest heart could yield long to the comforting of the fair world, knowing that some of her fairest fields would soon be crimsoned afresh with the blood of her children. But Dorothy's sadness was not all for her country in general. Had she put the question honestly to her heart, she must have confessed that even the loss of her mother had less to do with a certain weight upon it, which the loveliness of the spring day seemed to render heavier, than the rarely absent feeling rather than thought, that the playmate of her childhood, and the offered lover of her youth, had thrown himself with all the energy of dawning manhood into the quarrel of the lawless and self-glorifying. Nor was she altogether free from a sense of blame in the matter. Had she been less imperative in her mood and bearing, more ready to give than to require sympathy, but ah! she could not change the past, and the present was calling upon her.

At length the towers of Raglan appeared, and a pang of apprehension shot through her bosom. She was approaching the unknown. Like one on the verge of a second-sight, her history seemed for a moment about to reveal itself, where it lay, like a bird in its egg, within those massive walls, warded by those huge ascending towers. Brought up in a retirement that some would have counted loneliness, and although used to all gentle and refined ways, yet familiar with homeliness and simplicity of mode and ministration, she could not help feeling awed at the prospect of entering such a zone of rank and stateliness and observance as the household of the Marquis , who lived like a prince in expenditure, attendance, and ceremony. She knew little of the fashions of the day, and, like many modest young people, was afraid she might be guilty of some solecism which would make her appear ill-bred, or at least awkward. Since her mother left her, she had become aware of a timidity to which she had hitherto been a stranger. 'Ah!' she said to herself, 'if only my mother were with me!'

At length they reached the brick gate, were admitted within the outer wall, and following the course taken by Scudamore and Heywood, skirted the moat which enringed the huge blind citadel or keep, and arrived at the western gate. The portcullis rose to admit them, and they rode into the echoes of the vaulted gateway. Turning to congratulate Dorothy on their safe arrival, Mr. Herbert saw that she was pale and agitated.

'What ails my child?' he said in a low voice, for the warder was near.

'I feel as if entering a prison,' she replied, with a shiver.

'Is thy God the God of the grange and not of the castle?' returned the old man.

'But, sir,' said Dorothy, 'I have been accustomed to a liberty such as few have enjoyed, and these walls and towers—'

'Heed not the look of things,' interrupted her guardian. 'Believe in the Will that with a thought can turn the shadow of death into the morning, give gladness for weeping, and the garment of praise for the spirit of heaviness.'

CHAPTER XI

RAGLAN CASTLE

While he yet spoke, their horses, of their own accord, passed through the gate which Eccles had thrown wide to admit them, and carried them into the Fountain court. Here, indeed, was a change of aspect! All that Dorothy had hitherto contemplated was the side of the fortress which faced the world, frowning and defiant, although here and there on the point of breaking into a half smile, for the grim, suspicious, altogether repellent look of the old feudal castle had been gradually vanishing in the additions and alterations of more civilised times. But now they were in the heart of the building, and saw the face which the house of strength turned upon its own people. The spring sunshine filled half the court; over the rest lay the shadow of the huge keep, towering massive above the three-storied line of building which formed the side next it. Here was the true face of the Janus-building, full of eyes and mouths; for many bright windows looked down into the court, in some of which shone the smiling faces of children and ladies peeping out to see the visitors, whose arrival had been announced by the creaking chains of the portcullis; and by the doors issued and entered, here a lady in rich attire, there a gentlemen half in armour, and here again a serving man or maid. Nearly in the centre of the quadrangle, just outside the shadow of the keep, stood the giant horse, rearing in white marble, almost dazzling in the sunshine, from whose nostrils spouted the jets of water which gave its name to the court. Opposite the gate by which they entered was the little chapel, with its triple lancet windows, over which lay the picture-gallery with its large oriel lights. Far above their roof, ascended from behind that of the great hall, with its fine lantern window seated on the ridge. From the other court beyond the hall, that upon which the main entrance opened, came the sounds of heavy feet in intermittent but measured tread, the clanking of arms, and a returning voice of loud command: the troops of the garrison were being exercised on the slabs of the pitched court.

From each of the many doors opening into the court they had entered, a path, paved with coloured tiles, led straight through the finest of turf to the marble fountain in the centre, into whose shadowed basin the falling water seemed to carry captive as into a prison the sunlight it caught above. Its music as it fell made a lovely but strange and sad contrast with the martial sounds from beyond.

It was but a moment they had to note these things; eyes and ears gathered them all at once. Two of the warder's men already held their horses, while two other men, responsive to the warder's whistle, came running from the hall and helped them to dismount. Hardly had they reached the ground ere a man-servant came, who led the way to the left towards a porch of carved stone on the same side of the court. The door stood open, revealing a flight of stairs, rather steep, but wide and stately, going right up between two straight walls. At the top stood Lady Margaret's gentleman usher, Mr. Harcourt by name, who received them with much courtesy, and conducting them to a small room on the left of the landing, went to announce their arrival to Lady Margaret, to whose private parlour this was the antechamber. Returning in a moment, he led them into her presence.

She received them with a frankness which almost belied the stateliness of her demeanour. Through the haze of that reserve which a consciousness of dignity, whether true or false, so often generates, the genial courtesy of her Irish nature, for she was an O'Brien, daughter of the earl of Thomond, shone clear, and justified her Celtic origin.

'Welcome, cousin!' she said, holding out her hand while yet distant half the length of the room, across which, upborne on slow firm foot, she advanced with even, stately motion, 'And you also, reverend sir,' she went on, turning to Mr. Herbert. 'I am told we are indebted to you for this welcome addition to our family, how welcome none can tell but ladies shut up like ourselves.'

Dorothy was already almost at her ease, and the old clergyman soon found Lady Margaret so sensible and as well as courteous, prejudiced yet further in her favour, it must be confessed, by the pleasant pretence she made of claiming cousinship on the ground of the identity of her husband's title with his surname, that, ere he left the castle, liberal as he had believed himself, he was nevertheless astonished to find how much of friendship had in that brief space been engendered in his bosom towards a catholic lady whom he had never before seen.

Since the time of Elizabeth, when the fear and repugnance of the nation had been so greatly and justly excited by the apparent probability of a marriage betwixt their queen and the detested Philip of Spain, a considerable alteration had been gradually wrought in the feelings of a large portion of it in respect of their catholic countrymen, a fact which gave strength to the position of the puritans in asserting the essential identity of episcopalian with catholic politics. Almost forty years had elapsed since the Gunpowder Plot; the queen was a catholic; the episcopalian party was itself at length endangered by the extension and development of the very principles on which they had themselves broken away from the church of Rome; and the catholics were friendly to the government of the king, under which their condition was one of comfort if not influence, while under that of the parliament they had every reason to anticipate a revival of persecution. Not a few of them doubtless cherished the hope that this revelation of the true spirit of dissent would result in driving the king and his party back into the bosom of the church.

The king, on the other hand, while only too glad to receive what aid he might from the loyal families of the old religion, yet saw that much caution was necessary lest he should alienate the most earnest of his protestant friends by giving ground for the suspicion that he was inclined to purchase their co-operation by a return to the creed of his Scottish grandmother, Mary Stuart, and his English great-great-grand-mother, Margaret Tudor.

On the part of the clergy there had been for some time a considerable tendency, chiefly from the influence of Laud, to cultivate the same spirit which actuated the larger portion of the catholic priesthood; and although this had never led to retrograde movement in regard to their politics, the fact that both were accounted by a third party, and that far the most dangerous to either of the other two, as in spirit and object one and the same, naturally tended to produce a more indulgent regard of each other than had hitherto prevailed. And hence, in part, it was that it had become possible for episcopalian Dr. Bayly to be an inmate of Raglan Castle, and for good, protestant Matthew Herbert to seek refuge for his ward with good catholic Lady Margaret.

Eager to return to the duties of his parish, through his illness so long neglected, Mr. Herbert declined her ladyship's invitation to dinner, which, she assured him, consulting a watch that she wore in a ring on her little finger, must be all but ready, seeing it was now a quarter to eleven, and took his leave, accompanied by Dorothy's servant to bring back the horse, if indeed they should be fortunate enough to escape the requisition of both horses by one party or the other. At present, however, the king's affairs continued rather on the ascendant, and the name of the Marquis in that country was as yet a tower of strength. Dorothy's horse was included in the hospitality shown his mistress, and taken to the stables, under the mid-day shadow of the Library Tower.

As soon as the parson was gone, Lady Margaret touched a small silver bell which hung in a stand on the table beside her.

'Conduct mistress Dorothy Vaughan to her room, wait upon her there, and then attend her hither,' she said to the maid who answered it. 'I would request a little not unneedful haste, cousin,' she went on, 'for my Lord of Worcester is very precise in all matters of household order, and likes ill to see any one enter the dining-room after he is seated. It is his desire that you should dine at his table to-day. After this I must place you with the rest of my ladies, who dine in the housekeeper's room.'

'As you think proper, madam,' returned Dorothy, a little disappointed, but a little relieved also.

'The bell will ring presently,' said Lady Margaret, 'and a quarter of an hour thereafter we shall all be seated.'

She was herself already dressed, in a pale-blue satin, with full skirt and close-fitting, long-peaked boddice, fastened in front by several double clasps set with rubies; her shoulders were bare, and her sleeves looped up with large round star-like studs, set with diamonds, so that her arms also were bare to the elbows. Round her neck was a short string of large pearls.

'You take no long time to attire yourself, cousin,' said her ladyship, kindly, when Dorothy returned.

'Little time was needed, madam,' answered Dorothy; 'for me there is but one colour. I fear I shall show but a dull bird amidst the gay plumage of Raglan. But I could have better adorned myself had not I heard the bell ere I had begun, and feared to lose your ladyship's company, and in very deed make my first appearance before my Lord as a transgressor of the laws of his household.'

'You did well, cousin Dorothy; for everything goes by law and order here. All is reason and rhyme too in this house. My lord's father, although one of the best and kindest of men, is, as I said, somewhat precise, and will, as he says himself, be king in his own kingdom, thinking doubtless of one who is not such. I should not talk thus with you, cousin, were you like some young ladies I know; but there is that about you which pleases me greatly, and which I take to indicate discretion. When first I came to the house, not having been accustomed to so severe a punctuality, I gave my Lord no little annoyance; for, oftener than once or twice, I walked into his dining-room not only after grace had been said, but after the first course had been sent down to the hall-tables. My Lord took his revenge in calling me the wild Irishwoman.'

Here she laughed very sweetly.

'The only one,' she resumed, 'who does here as he will, is my husband. Even Lord Charles, who is governor of the castle, must be in his place to the moment; but for my husband—.'

The bell rang a second time. Lady Margaret rose, and taking Dorothy's arm, led her from the room into a long dim-lighted corridor. Arrived at the end of it, where a second passage met it at right angles, she stopped at a door facing them.

'I think we shall find my Lord of Worcester here,' she said in a whisper, as she knocked and waited a response. 'He is not here,' she said. 'He expects me to call on him as I pass. We must make haste.'

The second passage, in which were several curves and sharp turns, led them to a large room, nearly square, in which were two tables covered for about thirty. By the door and along the sides of the room were a good many gentlemen, some of them very plainly dressed, and others in gayer attire, amongst whom Dorothy, as they passed through, recognised her cousin Scudamore. Whether he saw and knew her she could not tell. Crossing a small antechamber they entered the drawing-room, where stood and sat talking a number of ladies and gentlemen, to some of whom Lady Margaret spoke and presented her cousin, greeting others with a familiar nod or smile, and yet others with a stately courtesy. Then she said,

'Ladies, I will lead the way to the dining-room. My Lord Marquis would the less willingly have us late that something detains himself.'

Those who dined in the Marquis 's room followed her. Scarcely had she reached the upper end of the table when the Marquis entered, followed by all his gentlemen, some of whom withdrew, their service over for the time, while others proceeded to wait upon him and his family, with any of the nobility who happened to be his guests at the first table.

'I am the laggard to-day, my lady,' he said, cheerily, as he bore his heavy person up the room towards her. 'Ah!' he went on, as Lady Margaret stepped forward to meet him, leading Dorothy by the hand, 'who is this sober young damsel under my wild Irishwoman's wing? Our young cousin Vaughan, doubtless, whose praises my worthy Dr. Bayly has been sounding in my ears?'

He held out his hand to Dorothy, and bade her welcome to Raglan.

The Marquis was a man of noble countenance, of the type we are ready to imagine peculiar to the great men of the time of queen Elizabeth. To this his unwieldy person did not correspond, although his movements were still far from being despoiled of that charm which naturally belonged to all that was his. Nor did his presence owe anything to his dress, which was of that long-haired coarse woollen stuff they called frieze, worn, probably, by not another nobleman in the country, and regarded as fitter for a yeoman. His eyes, though he was yet but sixty-five or so, were already hazy, and his voice was husky and a little broken, results of the constantly poor health and frequent suffering he had had for many years; but he carried it all 'with', to quote the prince of courtesy, sir Philip Sydney, 'with a right old man's grace, that will seem livelier than his age will afford him.'

The moment he entered, the sewer in the antechamber at the other end of the room had given a signal to one waiting at the head of the stair leading down to the hall, and his lordship was hardly seated, ere, although the kitchen was at the corner of the pitched court diagonally opposite, he bore the first dish into the room, followed by his assistants, laden each with another.

Lady Margaret made Dorothy sit down by her. A place on her other side was vacant.

'Where is this truant husband of thine, my lady?' asked the Marquis , as soon as Dr. Bayly had said grace. 'Know you whether he eats at all, or when, or where? It is now three days since he has filled his place at thy side, yet is he in the castle. Thou knowest, my lady, I deal not with him, who is so soon to sit in this chair, as with another, but I like it not. Know you what occupies him to day?'

'I do not, my lord,' answered Lady Margaret. 'I have had but one glimpse of him since the morning, and if he looks now as he looked then, I fear your lordship would be minded rather to drive him from your table than welcome him to a seat beside you.'

As she spoke, Lady Margaret caught a glimpse of a peculiar expression on Scudamore's face, where he stood behind his master's chair.

'Your page, my lord,' she said, 'seems to know something of him: if it pleased you to put him to the question—'

'Hey, Scudamore!' said the Marquis without turning his head; 'what have you seen of my Lord Herbert?'

'As much as could be seen of him, my lord,' answered Scudamore. 'He was new from the powder-mill, and his face and hands were as he had been blown three times up the hall chimney.'

'I would thou didst pay more heed to what is fitting, thou monkey, and knewest either place or time for thy foolish jests! It will be long ere thou soil one of thy white fingers for king or country,' said the Marquis , neither angrily nor merrily. 'Get another flask of claret,' he added, 'and keep thy wit for thy mates, boy.'

Dorothy cast one involuntary glance at her cousin. His face was red as fire, but, as it seemed to her, more with suppressed amusement than shame. She had not been much longer in the castle before she learned that, in the opinion of the household, the Marquis did his best, or worst rather, to ruin young Scudamore by indulgence. The judgment, however, was partly the product of jealousy, although doubtless the Marquis had in his case a little too much relaxed the bonds of discipline. The youth was bright and ready, and had as yet been found trustworthy; his wit was tolerable, and a certain gay naivete of speech and manner set off to the best advantage what there was of it; but his laughter was sometimes mischievous, and on the present occasion Dorothy could not rid herself of the suspicion that he was laughing in his sleeve at his master, which caused her to redden in her turn. Scudamore saw it, and had his own fancies concerning the phenomenon.

CHAPTER XII

THE TWO MARQUIS ES

Dinner over, Lady Margaret led Dorothy back to her parlour, and there proceeded to discover what accomplishments and capabilities she might possess. Finding she could embroider, play a little on the spinnet, sing a song, and read aloud both intelligibly and pleasantly, she came to the conclusion that the country-bred girl was an acquisition destined to grow greatly in value, should the day ever arrive—which heaven forbid! when they would have to settle down to the monotony of a protracted siege. Remarking, at length, that she looked weary, she sent her away to be mistress of her time till supper, at half-past five.

Weary in truth with her journey, but still more weary from the multitude and variety of objects, the talk, and the constant demand of the general strangeness upon her attention and one form or other of suitable response, Dorothy sought her chamber. But she scarcely remembered how to reach it. She knew it lay a floor higher, and easily found the stair up which she had followed her attendant, for it rose from the landing of the straight ascent by which she had entered the house. She could hardly go wrong either as to the passage at the top of it, leading back over the room she had just left below, but she could not tell which was her own door. Fearing to open the wrong one, she passed it and went on to the end of the corridor, which was very dimly lighted. There she came to an open door, through which she saw a small chamber, evidently not meant for habitation. She entered. A little light came in through a crossed loophole, sufficient to show her the bare walls, with the plaster sticking out between the stones, the huge beams above, and in the middle of the floor, opposite the loop-hole, a great arblast or cross-bow, with its strange machinery. She had never seen one before, but she knew enough to guess at once what it was. Through the loophole came a sweet breath of spring air, and she saw trees bending in the wind, heard their faint far-off rustle, and saw the green fields shining in the sun.

Partly from having been so much with Richard, her only playmate, who was of an ingenious and practical turn, a certain degree of interest in mechanical forms and modes had been developed in Dorothy, sufficient at least to render her unable to encounter such an implement without feeling a strong impulse to satisfy herself concerning its mechanism, its motion, and its action. Approaching it cautiously and curiously, as if it were a live thing, which might start up and fly from, or perhaps at her, for what she knew, she gazed at it for a few moments with eyes full of unuttered questions, then ventured to lay gentle hold upon what looked like a handle. To her dismay, a wheezy bang followed, which seemed to shake the tower. Whether she had discharged an arrow, or an iron bolt, or a stone, or indeed anything at all, she could not tell, for she had not got so far in her observations as to perceive even that the bow was bent. Her heart gave a scared flutter, and she started back, not merely terrified, but ashamed also that she should initiate her life in the castle with meddling and mischief, when a low gentle laugh behind her startled her yet more, and looking round with her heart in her throat, she perceived in the half-light of the place a man by the wall behind the arblast watching her. Her first impulse was to run, and the door was open; but she thought she owed an apology ere she retreated. What sort of person he was she could not tell, for there was not light enough to show a feature of his face.

'I ask your pardon,' she said; 'I fear I have done mischief.'

'Not the least,' returned the man, in a gentle voice, with a tone of amusement in it.

'I had never seen a great cross-bow,' Dorothy went on, anxious to excuse her meddling. 'I thought this must be one, but I was so stupid as not to perceive it was bent, and that that was the—the handle—or do you call it the trigger? by which you let it go.'

The man, who had at first taken her for one of the maids, had by this time discovered from her tone and speech that she was a lady.

'It is a clumsy old-fashioned thing,' he returned, 'but I shall not remove it until I can put something better in its place; and it would be a troublesome affair to get even a demiculverin up here, not to mention the bad neighbour it would be to the ladies'chambers. I was just making a small experiment with it on the force of springs. I believe I shall yet prove that much may be done with springs, more perhaps, and certainly at far less expense, than with gunpowder, which costs greatly, is very troublesome to make, occupies much space, and is always like an unstable, half-treacherous friend within the gates, to say nothing of the expense of cannon, ten times that of an engine of timber and springs. See what a strong chain your shot has broken! Shall I show you how the thing works?'

He spoke in a gentle, even rapid voice, a little hesitating now and then, more, through the greater part of this long utterance, as if he were thinking to himself than addressing another. Neither his tone nor manner were those of an underling, but Dorothy's startled nerves had communicated their tremor to her modesty, and with a gentle 'No, sir, I thank you; I must be gone,' she hurried away.

Daring now a little more for fear of worse, the first door she tried proved that of her own room, and it was with a considerable sense of relief, as well as with weariness and tremor, that she nestled herself into the high window-seat, and looked out into the quadrangle. The shadow of the citadel had gone to pay its afternoon visit to the other court, and that of the gateway was thrown upon the chapel, partly shrouding the white horse, whose watery music was now silent, but allowing one red ray, which entered by the iron grating above the solid gates, to fall on his head, and warm its cold whiteness with a tinge of delicate pink. The court was more still and silent than in the morning; only now and then would a figure pass from one door to another, along the side of the buildings, or by one of the tiled paths dividing the turf. A large peacock was slowly crossing the shadowed grass with a stately strut and rhythmic thrust of his green neck. The moment he came out into the sunlight, he spread his wheeled fan aloft, and slowly pirouetting, if the word can be allowed where two legs are needful, in the very acme of vanity, turned on all sides the quivering splendour of its hundred eyes, where blue and green burst in the ecstasy of their union into a vapour of gold, that the circle of the universe might see. And truly the bird's vanity had not misled his judgment: it was a sight to make the hearts of the angels throb out a dainty phrase or two more in the song of their thanksgiving. Some pigeons, white, and blue-grey, with a lovely mingling and interplay of metallic lustres on their feathery throats, but with none of that almost grotesque obtrusion of over-driven individuality of kind, in which the graciousness of common beauty is now sacrificed to the whim of the fashion the vulgar fancier initiates, picked up the crumbs under the windows of Lady Margaret's nursery, or flew hither and thither among the roofs with wapping and whiffling wing.

But still from the next court came many and various mingling noises. The sounds of drill had long ceased, but those of clanking hammers were heard the more clearly, now one, now two, now several together. The smaller, clearer one was that of the armourer, the others those of the great smithy, where the horse-shoes were made, the horses shod, the smaller pieces of ordnance repaired, locks and chains mended, bolts forged, and, in brief, every piece of metal about the castle, from the cook's skillet to the winches and chains of the drawbridges, set right, renewed, or replaced. The forges were far from where she sat, outside the farthest of the two courts, across which, and the great hall dividing them, the clink, clink, the clank, and the ringing clang, softened by distance and interposition, came musical to her ear. The armourer's hammer was the keener, the quicker, the less intermittent, and yet had the most variations of time and note, as he shifted the piece on his anvil, or changed breastplate for gorget, or greave for pauldron, or it might be sword for pike-head or halbert. Mingled with it came now and then the creak and squeak of the wooden wheel at the draw-well near the hall-door in the farther court, and the muffled splash of the bucket as it struck the water deep in the shaft. She even thought she could hear the drops dripping back from it as it slowly ascended, but that was fancy. Everywhere arose the auricular vapour, as it were, of action, undefined and indefinable, the hum of the human hive, compounded of all confluent noises, the chatter of the servants' hall and the nursery, the stamping of horses, the ringing of harness, the ripping of the chains of kenneled dogs, the hollow stamping of heavy boots, the lowing of cattle, with sounds besides so strange to the ears of Dorothy that they set her puzzling in vain to account for them; not to mention the chaff of the guard-rooms by the gates, and the scolding and clatter of the kitchen. This last, indeed, was audible only when the doors were open, for the walls of the kitchen, whether it was that the builders of it counted cookery second only to life, or that this had been judged, from the nature of the ground outside, the corner of all the enclosure most likely to be attacked, were far thicker than those of any of the other towers, with the one exception of the keep itself.

As she sat listening to these multitudinous exhalations of life around her, yet with a feeling of loneliness and a dim sense of captivity, from the consciousness that huge surrounding walls rose between her and the green fields, of which, from earliest memory, she had been as free as the birds and beetles, a white rabbit, escaped from the arms of its owner, little Mary Somerset, Lady Margaret's only child, a merry but delicate girl not yet three years old, suddenly darted like a flash of snow across the shadowy green, followed in hot haste a moment after by a fine-looking boy of thirteen and two younger girls, after whom toddled tiny Mary. Dorothy sat watching the pursuit, accompanied with sweet outcry and frolic laughter, when in a moment the sounds of their merriment changed to shrieks of terror, and she saw a huge mastiff come bounding she knew not whence, and rush straight at the rabbit, fierce and fast. When the little creature saw him, struck with terror it stopped dead, cowered on the sward, and was stock still. But Henry Somerset, who was but a few paces from it, reached it before the dog, and caught it up in his arms. The rush of the dog threw him down, and they rolled over and over, Henry holding fast the poor rabbit.

By this time Dorothy was half-way down the stair: the moment she caught sight of the dog she had flown to the rescue. When she issued from the porch at the foot of the grand staircase, Henry was up again, and running for the house with the rabbit yet safe in his arms, pursued by the mastiff. Evidently the dog had not harmed him, but he might get angry. The next moment she saw, to her joy and dismay both at once, that it was her own dog.

'Marquis ! Marquis !' she cried, calling him by his name.

He abandoned the pursuit at once, and went bounding to her. She took him by the back of the neck, and the displeasure manifest upon the countenance of his mistress made him cower at her feet, and wince from the open hand that threatened him. The same instant a lattice window over the gateway was flung open, and a voice said—

'Here I am. Who called me?'

Dorothy looked up. The children had vanished with their rescued darling. There was not a creature in the court but herself, and there was the Marquis , leaning half out of the window, and looking about.

'Who called me?' he repeated—angrily, Dorothy thought.

All at once the meaning of it flashed upon her, and she was confounded, ready to sink with annoyance. But she was not one to hesitate when a thing HAD to be done. Keeping her hold of the dog's neck, for his collar was gone, she dragged him half-way towards the gate, then turning up to the Marquis a face like a peony, replied—

'I am the culprit, my lord.'

'By St. George! you are a brave damsel, and there is no culpa that I know of, except on the part of that intruding cur.'

'And the cur's mistress, my lord. But, indeed, he is no cur, but a true mastiff.'

'What! is the animal thy property, fair cousin? He is more than I bargained for.'

'He is mine, my lord, but I left him chained when I set out from Wyfern this morning. That he got loose I confess I am not astonished, neither that he tracked me hither, for he has the eyes of a gaze-hound, and the nose of a bloodhound; but it amazes me to find him in the castle.'

'That must be inquired into,' said the Marquis .

'I am very sorry he has carried himself so ill, my lord. He has put me to great shame. But he hath more in him than mere brute, and understands when I beg you to pardon him. He misbehaved himself on purpose to be taken to me, for at home no one ever dares punish him but myself.'

The Marquis laughed.

'If you are so completely his mistress then, why did you call on me for help?'

'Pardon me, my lord; I did not so.'

'Why, I heard thee call me two or three times!'

'Alas, my lord! I called him Marquis when he was a pup. Everybody about Redware knows Marquis .'

The animal cocked his ears and started each time his name was uttered, and yet seemed to understand well enough that ALL the talk was about him and his misdeeds.

'Ah! ha!' said his lordship, with a twinkle in his eye, 'that begets complications. Two Marquis es in Raglan? Two kings in England! The thing cannot be. What is to be done?'

'I must take him back, my lord! I cannot send him, for he would not go. I dread they will not be able to hold him chained; in which evil case I fear me I shall have to go, my lord, and take the perils of the time as they come.'

'Not of necessity so, cousin, while you can choose between us; although I freely grant that a Marquis with four legs is to be preferred before a Marquis with only two. But what if you changed his name?'

'I fear it could not be done, my lord. He has been Marquis all his life.'

'And I have been Marquis only six months! Clearly he hath the better right—. But there would be constant mistakes between us, for I cannot bring myself to lay aside the honour his majesty hath conferred upon me, "which would be worn now in its newest gloss, not cast aside so soon," as master Shakspere says. Besides, it would be a slight to his majesty, and that must not be thought of—not for all the dogs in parliament or out of it. No—it would breed factions in the castle too. No; one of us two must die.'

'Then, indeed, I must go,' said Dorothy, her voice trembling as she spoke; for although the words of the Marquis were merry, she yet feared for her friend.

'Tut! tut! let the older Marquis die: he has enjoyed the title; I have not. Give him to Tom Fool: he will drown him in the moat. He shall be buried with honour, under his rival's favourite apple-tree in the orchard. What more could dog desire?'

'No, my lord,' answered Dorothy. 'Will you allow me to take my leave? If I only knew where to find my horse!'

'What! would you saddle him yourself, cousin Vaughan?'

'As well as e'er a knave in your lordship's stables. I am very sorry to displease you, but to my dog's death I cannot and will not consent. Pardon me, my lord.'

The last words brought with them a stifled sob, for she scarcely doubted any more that he was in earnest.

'It is assuredly not gratifying to a Marquis of the king's making to have one of a damsel's dubbing take the precedence of him. I fear you are a roundhead and hold by the parliament. But no, that cannot be, for you are willing to forsake your new cousin for your old dog. Nay, alas! it is your old cousin for your young dog. Puritan! puritan! Well, it cannot be helped. But what! you would ride home alone! Evil men are swarming, child. This sultry weather brings them out like flies.'

'I shall not be alone, my lord. Marquis will take good care of me.'

'Indeed, my Lord Marquis will pledge himself to nothing outside his own walls.'

'I meant the dog, my lord.'

'Ah! you see how awkward it is. However, as you will not choose between us, and to tell the truth, I am not yet quite prepared to die, we must needs encounter what is inevitable. I will send for one of the keepers to take him to the smithy, and get him a proper collar, one he can't slip like that he left at home, and a chain.'

'I must go with him myself, my lord. They will never manage him else.'

'What a demon you have brought into my peaceable house! Go with him, by all means. And mind you choose him a kennel yourself. You do not desire him in your chamber, do you, mistress?'

Dorothy secretly thought it would be the best place for him, but she was only too glad to have his life spared.

'No, my lord, I thank you,' she said. '—I thank your lordship with all my heart.'

The Marquis disappeared from the window. Presently young Scudamore came into the court from the staircase by the gate, and crossed to the hall, in a few minutes returning with the keeper. The man would have taken the dog by the neck to lead him away, but a certain form of canine curse, not loud but deep, and a warning word from Dorothy, made him withdraw his hand.

'Take care, Mr. Keeper,' she said, 'he is dangerous. I will go with him myself, if thou wilt show me whither.'

'As it please you, mistress,' answered the keeper, and led the way across the court.

'Have you not a word to throw at a poor cousin, mistress Dorothy?' said Rowland, when the man was a pace or two in advance.

'No, Mr. Scudamore,' answered Dorothy; 'not until we have first spoken in my Lord Worcester's or my Lady Margaret's presence.'

Scudamore fell behind, followed her a little way, and somewhere vanished.

Dorothy followed the keeper across the hall, the size of which, its height especially, and the splendour of its windows of stained glass, almost awed her; then across the next court to the foot of the Library Tower forming the south-east corner of it, near the two towers flanking the main entrance. Here a stair led down, through the wall, to a lower level outside, where were the carpenters' and all other workshops, the forges, the stables, and the farmyard buildings.

As it happened, when Dorothy entered the smithy, there was her own little horse being shod, and Marquis and he interchanged a whine and a whinny of salutation, while the men stared at the bright apparition of a young lady in their dingy regions. Having heard her business, the head-smith abandoned everything else to alter an iron collar, of which there were several lying about, to fit the mastiff, the presence of whose mistress proved entirely necessary. Dorothy had indeed to put it on him with her own hands, for at the sound of the chain attached to it he began to grow furious, growling fiercely. When the chain had been made fast with a staple driven into a strong kennel-post, and his mistress proceeded to take her leave of him, his growling changed to the most piteous whining; but when she actually left him there, he flew into a rage of indignant affection. After trying the strength of his chain, however, by three or four bounds, each so furious as to lay him sprawling on his back, he yielded to the inevitable, and sullenly crept into his kennel, while Dorothy walked back to the room which had already begun to seem to her a cell.

CHAPTER XIII

THE MAGICIAN'S VAULT

Dorothy went straight to Lady Margaret's parlour, and made her humble apology for the trouble and alarm her dog had occasioned. Lady Margaret assured her that the children were nothing the worse, not having been even much terrified, for the dog had not gone a hair's-breadth beyond rough play. Poor bunny was the only one concerned who had not yet recovered his equanimity. He did not seem positively hurt, she said, but as he would not eat the lovely clover under his nose where he lay in Molly's crib, it was clear that the circulation of his animal spirits had been too rudely checked. Thereupon Dorothy begged to be taken to the nursery, for, being familiar with all sorts of tame animals, she knew rabbits well. As she stood with the little creature in her arms, gently stroking its soft whiteness, the children gathered round her, and she bent herself to initiate a friendship with them, while doing her best to comfort and restore their favourite. Success in the latter object she found the readiest way to the former. Under the sweet galvanism of her stroking hand the rabbit was presently so much better that when she offered him a blade of the neglected clover, the equilateral triangle of his queer mouth was immediately set in motion, the trefoil vanished, and when he was once more placed in the crib he went on with his meal as if nothing had happened. The children were in ecstasies, and cousin Dorothy was from that moment popular and on the way to be something better.

When supper time came, Lady Margaret took her again to the dining-room, where there was much laughter over the story of the two Marquis es, Lord Worcester driving the joke in twenty different directions, but so kindly that Dorothy, instead of being disconcerted or even discomposed thereby, found herself emboldened to take a share in the merriment. When the company rose, Lady Margaret once more led her to her own room, where, working at her embroidery frame, she chatted with her pleasantly for some time. Dorothy would have been glad if she had set her work also, for she could ill brook doing nothing. Notwithstanding her quietness of demeanour, amounting at times to an appearance of immobility, her nature was really an active one, and it was hard for her to sit with her hands in her lap. Lady Margaret at length perceived her discomfort.

'I fear, my child, I am wearying you,' she said.

'It is only that I want something to do, madam,' said Dorothy.

'I have nothing at hand for you to-night,' returned Lady Margaret. 'Suppose we go and find my lord; I mean my own Lord Herbert. I have not seen him since we broke fast together, and you have not seen him at all. I am afraid he must think of leaving home again soon, he seems so anxious to get something or other finished.'

As she spoke, she pushed aside her frame, and telling Dorothy to go and fetch herself a cloak, went into the next room, whence she presently returned, wrapped in a hooded mantle. As soon as Dorothy came, she led her along the corridor to a small lobby whence a stair descended to the court, issuing close by the gate.

'I shall never learn my way about,' said Dorothy. 'If it were only the staircases, they are more than my memory will hold.'

Lady Margaret gave a merry little laugh.

'Harry set himself to count them the other day,' she said. 'I do not remember how many he made out altogether, but I know he said there were at least thirty stone ones.'

Dorothy's answer was an exclamation.

But she was not in the mood to dwell upon the mere arithmetic of vastness. Invaded by the vision of the mighty structure, its aspect rendered yet more imposing by the time which now suited with it, she forgot Lady Margaret's presence, and stood still to gaze.

The twilight had deepened half-way into night. There was no moon, and in the dusk the huge masses of building rose full of mystery and awe. Above the rest, the great towers on all sides seemed by indwelling might to soar into the regions of air. The pile stood there, the epitome of the story of an ancient race, the precipitate from its vanished life, a hard core that had gathered in the vaporous mass of history, the all of solid that remained to witness of the past.

She came again to herself with a start. Lady Margaret had stood quietly waiting for her mood to change. Dorothy apologised, but her mistress only smiled and said,

'I am in no haste, child. I like to see another impressed as I was when first I stood just where you stand now. Come, then, I will show you something different.'

She led the way along the southern side of the court until they came to the end of the chapel, opposite which an archway pierced the line of building, and revealed the mighty bulk of the citadel, the only portion of the castle, except the kitchen-tower, continuing impregnable to enlarged means of assault: gunpowder itself, as yet far from perfect in composition and make, and conditioned by clumsy, uncertain, and ill-adjustable artillery, was nearly powerless against walls more than ten feet in thickness.

I have already mentioned that one peculiarity of Raglan was a distinct moat surrounding its keep. Immediately from the outer end of the archway, a Gothic bridge of stone led across this thirty-foot moat to a narrow walk which encompassed the tower. The walk was itself encompassed and divided from the moat by a wall with six turrets at equal distances, surmounted by battlements. At one time the sole entrance to the tower had been by a drawbridge dropping across the walk to the end of the stone bridge, from an arched door in the wall, whose threshold was some ten or twelve feet from the ground; but another entrance had since been made on the level of the walk, and by it the two ladies now entered. Passing the foot of a great stone staircase, they came to the door of what had, before the opening of the lower entrance, been a vaulted cellar, probably at one time a dungeon, at a later period a place of storage, but now put to a very different use, and wearing a stranger aspect than it could ever have borne at any past period of its story, a look indeed of mystery inexplicable.

When Dorothy entered she found herself in a large place, the form of which she could ill distinguish in the dull light proceeding from the chinks about the closed doors of a huge furnace. The air was filled with gurglings and strange low groanings, as of some creature in dire pain. Dorothy had as good nerves as ever woman, yet she could not help some fright as she stood alone by the door and stared into the gloomy twilight into which her companion had advanced. As her eyes became used to the ruddy dusk, she could see better, but everywhere they lighted on shapes inexplicable, whose forms to the first questioning thought suggested instruments of torture; but cruel as some of them looked, they were almost too strange, contorted, fantastical for such. Still, the wood-cuts in a certain book she had been familiar with in childhood, commonly called Fox's Book of Martyrs, kept haunting her mind's eye, and were they not Papists into whose hands she had fallen? she said to herself, amused at the vagaries of her own involuntary suggestions.

Among the rest, one thing specially caught her attention, both from its size and its complicated strangeness. It was a huge wheel standing near the wall, supported between two strong uprights, some twelve or fifteen feet in diameter, with about fifty spokes, from every one of which hung a large weight. Its grotesque and threatful character was greatly increased by the mingling of its one substance with its many shadows on the wall behind it. So intent was she upon it that she started when Lady Margaret spoke.

'Why, mistress Dorothy!' she said, 'you look as if you had wandered into St. Anthony's cave! Here is my Lord Herbert to welcome his cousin.'

Beside her stood a man rather under the middle stature, but as his back was to the furnace this was about all Dorothy could discover of his appearance, save that he was in the garb of a workman, with bare head and arms, and held in his hand a long iron rod ending in a hook.

'Welcome, indeed, cousin Vaughan!' he said heartily, but without offering his hand, which in truth, although an honest, skilful, and well-fashioned hand, was at the present moment far from fit for a lady's touch.

There was something in his voice not altogether strange to Dorothy, but she could not tell of whom or what it reminded her.

'Are you come to take another lesson on the cross-bow?' he asked with a smile.

Then she knew he was the same she had met in the looped chamber beside the arblast. An occasional slight halt, not impediment, in his speech, was what had remained on her memory. Did he always dwell only in the dusky borders of the light?

Dorothy uttered a little 'Oh!' of surprise, but immediately recovering herself, said,

'I am sorry I did not know it was you, my lord. I might by this time have been capable of discharging bolt or arrow with good aim in defence of the castle.'

'It is not yet too late, I hope,' returned the workman-lord. 'I confess I was disappointed to find your curiosity went no further. I hoped I had at last found a Lady capable of some interest in pursuits like mine. For my Lady Margaret here, she cares not a straw for anything I do, and would rather have me keep my hands clean than discover the mechanism of the primum mobile!'

'Yes, in truth, Ned,' said his wife, 'I would rather have thee with fair hands in my sweet parlour, than toiling and moiling in this dirty dungeon, with no companion but that horrible fire-engine of thine, grunting and roaring all night long.'

'Why, what do you make of Caspar Kaltoff, my lady?'

'I make not much of him.'

'You misjudge his goodfellowship then.'

'Truly, I think not well of him: he always hath secrets with thee, and I like it not.'

'That they are secrets is thine own fault, Peggy. How can I teach thee my secrets if thou wilt not open thine ears to hear them?'

'I would your lordship would teach me!' said Dorothy. 'I might not be an apt pupil, but I should be both an eager and a humble one.'

'By St. Patrick! mistress Dorothy, but you go straight to steal my husband's heart from me. "Humble," forsooth! and "eager" too! Nay! nay! If I have no part in his brain, I can the less yield his heart.'

'What would be gladly learned would be gladly taught, cousin,' said Lord Herbert.

'There! there!' exclaimed Lady Margaret; 'I knew it would be so. You discharge your poor dull apprentice the moment you find a clever one!'

'And why not? I never was able to teach thee anything.'

'Ah, Ned, there you are unkind indeed!' said Lady Margaret, with something in her voice that suggested the water-springs were swelling.

'My shamrock of four!' said her husband in the tenderest tone, 'I but jested with thee. How shouldst thou be my pupil in anything I can teach? I am yours in all that is noble and good. I did not mean to vex you, sweet heart.'

''Tis gone again, Ned,' she answered, smiling. 'Give cousin Dorothy her first lesson.'

'It shall be that, then, to which I sought in vain to make thee listen this very morning, a certain great saying of my Lord of Verulam, mistress Dorothy. I had learnt it by heart that I might repeat it word for word to my lady, but she would none of it.'

'May I not hear it, madam?' said Dorothy.

'We will both hear it, Herbert, if you will pardon your foolish wife and admit her to grace.' And as she spoke she laid her hand on his sooty arm.

He answered her only with a smile, but such a one as sufficed.

'Listen then, ladies both,' he said. 'My Lord of Verulam, having quoted the words of Solomon, "The glory of God is to conceal a thing, but the glory of the king is to find it out," adds thus, of his own thought concerning them, "as if," says my lord, "according to the innocent play of children, the divine majesty took delight to hide his works, to the end to have them found out, and as if kings could not obtain a greater honour than to be God's playfellows in that game, considering the great commandment of wits and means, whereby nothing needeth to be hidden from them."'

'That was very well for my Lord of, what did'st thou call him, Ned?'

'Francis Bacon, Lord Verulam,' returned Herbert, with a queer smile.

'Very well for my Lord of Veryflam!' resumed Lady Margaret, with a mock, yet bewitching affectation of innocence and ignorance; 'but tell me had he? nay, I am sure he had not a wild Irishwoman sitting breaking her heart in her bower all day long for his company. He could never else have had the heart to say it. Mistress Dorothy,' she went on, 'take the counsel of a forsaken wife, and lay it to thy heart: never marry a man who loves lathes and pipes and wheels and water and fire, and I know not what. But do come in ere bed-time, Herbert, and I will sing thee the sweetest of English ditties, and make thee such a sack-posset as never could be made out of old Ireland any more than the song.'

But her husband that moment sprang from her side, and shouting 'Caspar! Caspar!' bounded to the furnace, reached up with his iron rod into the darkness over his head, caught something with the hooked end of it, and pulled hard. A man who from somewhere in the gloomy place had responded like a greyhound to his master's call, did the like on the other side. Instantly followed a fierce, protracted, sustained hiss, and in a moment the place was filled with a white cloud, whence issued still the hideous hiss, changing at length to a roar. Lady Margaret turned in terror, ran out of the keep, and fled across the bridge and through the archway before she slackened her pace. Dorothy followed, but more composedly, led by duty, not driven by terror, and indeed reluctantly forsaking a spot where was so much she did not understand.

They had fled from the infant roar of the 'first stock-father' of steam-engines, whose cradle was that feudal keep, eight centuries old.

That night Dorothy lay down weary enough. It seemed a month since she had been in her own bed at Wyfern, so many new and strange things had crowded into her house, hitherto so still. Every now and then the darkness heaved and rippled with some noise of the night. The stamping of horses, and the ringing of their halter chains, seemed very near her. She thought she heard the howl of Marquis from afar, and said to herself, 'The poor fellow cannot sleep! I must get my Lord to let me have him in my chamber.' Then she listened a while to the sweet flow of the water from the mouth of the white horse, which in general went on all night long. Suddenly came an awful sound, like a howl also, but such as never left the throat of dog. Again and again at intervals it came, with others like it but not the same, torturing the dark with a dismal fear. Dorothy had never heard the cry of a wild beast, but the suggestion that these might be such cries, and the recollection that she had heard such beasts were in Raglan Castle, came together to her mind. She was so weary, however, that worse noises than these could hardly have kept her awake; not even her weariness could prevent them from following her into her dreams.

CHAPTER XIV

SEVERAL PEOPLE

Lord Worcester had taken such a liking to Dorothy, partly at first because of the good store of merriment with which she and her mastiff had provided him, that he was disappointed when he found her place was not to be at his table but the housekeeper's. As he said himself, however, he did not meddle with women's matters, and indeed it would not do for Lady Margaret to show her so much favour above her other women, of whom at least one was her superior in rank, and all were relatives as well as herself.

Dorothy did not much relish their society, but she had not much of it except at meals, when, however, they always treated her as an interloper. Every day she saw more or less of Lady Margaret, and found in her such sweetness, if not quite evenness of temper, as well as gaiety of disposition, that she learned to admire as well as love her. Sometimes she had her to read to her, sometimes to work with her, and almost every day she made her practise a little on the harpsichord. Hence she not only improved rapidly in performance, but grew capable of receiving more and more delight from music. There was a fine little organ in the chapel, on which blind young Delaware, the son of the Marquis 's master of the horse, used to play delightfully; and although she never entered the place, she would stand outside listening to his music for an hour at a time in the twilight, or sometimes even after dark. For as yet she indulged without question all the habits of her hitherto free life, as far as was possible within the castle walls, and the outermost of these were of great circuit, enclosing lawns, shrubberies, wildernesses, flower and kitchen gardens, orchards, great fish-ponds, little lakes with fountains, islands, and summer-houses, not to mention the farmyard, and indeed a little park, in which were some of the finest trees upon the estate.

The gentlewomen with whom Dorothy was, by her position in the household, associated, were three in number. One was a rather elderly, rather plain, rather pious lady, who did not insist on her pretensions to either of the epithets. The second was a short, plump, round-faced, good-natured, smiling woman of sixty, excelling in fasts and mortifications, which somehow seemed to agree with her body as well as her soul. The third was only two or three years older than Dorothy, and was pretty, except when she began to speak, and then for a moment there was a strange discord in her features. She took a dislike to Dorothy, as she said herself, the instant she cast her eyes upon her. She could not bear that prim, set face, she said. The country-bred heifer evidently thought herself superior to everyone in the castle. She was persuaded the minx was a sly one, and would carry tales. So judged mistress Amanda Serafina Fuller, after her kind. Nor was it wonderful that, being such as she was, she should recoil with antipathy from one whose nature had a tendency to ripen over soon, and stunt its slow orbicular expansion to the premature and false completeness of a narrow and self-sufficing conscientiousness.

Doubtless if Dorothy had shown any marked acknowledgment of the precedency of their rights, any eagerness to conciliate the aborigines of the circle, the ladies would have been more friendly inclined; but while capable of endless love and veneration, there was little of the conciliatory in her nature. Hence Mrs. Doughty looked upon her with a rather stately, indifference, my Lady Broughton with a mild wish to save her poor, proud, protestant soul, and mistress Amanda Serafina said she hated her; but then ever since the Fall there has been a disproportion betwixt the feelings of young ladies and the language in which they represent them. Mrs. Doughty neglected her, and Dorothy did not know it; Lady Broughton said solemn things to her, and she never saw the point of them; but when mistress Amanda half closed her eyes and looked at her in snake-Geraldine fashion, she met her with a full, wide-orbed, questioning gaze, before which Amanda's eyes dropped, and she sank full fathom five towards the abyss of real hatred.

During the dinner hour, the three generally talked together in an impregnable manner, not that they were by any means bosom-friends, for two of them had never before united in anything except despising good, soft Lady Broughton. When they were altogether in their mistress's presence, they behaved to Dorothy and to each other with studious politeness.

The ladies Elizabeth and Anne, had their gentlewomen also, in all only three, however, who also ate at the housekeeper's table, but kept somewhat apart from the rest, yet were, in a distant way, friendly to Dorothy.

But hers, as we have seen, was a nature far more capable of attaching itself to a few than of pleasing many; and her heart went out to Lady Margaret, whom she would have come ere long to regard as a mother, had she not behaved to her more like an elder sister. Lady Margaret's own genuine behaviour had indeed little of the matronly in it; when her husband came into the room, she seemed to grow instantly younger, and her manner changed almost to that of a playful girl. It is true, Dorothy had been struck with the dignity of her manner amid all the frankness of her reception, but she soon found that, although her nature was full of all real dignities, that which belonged to her carriage never appeared in the society of those she loved, and was assumed only, like the thin shelter of a veil, in the presence of those whom she either knew or trusted less. Before her ladies, she never appeared without some restraint, manifest in a certain measuredness of movement, slowness of speech, and choice of phrase; but before a month was over, Dorothy was delighted to find that the reserve instantly vanished when she happened to be left alone with her.

She took an early opportunity of informing her mistress of the relationship between herself and Scudamore, stating that she knew little or nothing of him, having seen him only once before she came to the castle. The youth on his part took the first fitting opportunity of addressing her in Lady Margaret's presence, and soon they were known to be cousins all over the castle.

With Lady Margaret's help, Dorothy came to a tolerable understanding of Scudamore. Indeed her ladyship's judgment seemed but a development of her own feeling concerning him.

'Rowland is not a bad fellow,' she said, 'but I cannot fully understand whence he comes in such grace with my Lord Worcester. If it were my husband now, I should not marvel: he is so much occupied with things and engines, that he has as little time as natural inclination to doubt anyone who will only speak largely enough to satisfy his idea. But my Lord of Worcester knows well enough that seldom are two things more unlike than men and their words. Yet that is not what I mean to say of your cousin: he is no hypocrite, means not to be false, but has no rule of right in him so far as I can find. He is pleasant company; his gaiety, his quips, his readiness of retort, his courtesy and what not, make him a favourite; and my Lord hath in a manner reared him, which goes to explain much. He is quick yet indolent, good-natured but selfish, generous but counting enjoyment the first thing, though, to speak truth of him, I have never known him do a dishonourable action. But, in a word, the star of duty has not yet appeared above his horizon. Pardon me, Dorothy, if I am severe upon him. More or less I may misjudge him, but this is how I read him; and if you wonder that I should be able so to divide him, I have but to tell you that I should be unapt indeed if I had not yet learned of my husband to look into the heart of both men and things.'

'But, madam,' Dorothy ventured to say, 'have you not even now told me that from very goodness my Lord is easily betrayed?'

'Well replied, my child! It is true, but only while he has had no reason to mistrust. Let him once perceive ground for dissatisfaction or suspicion, and his eye is keen as light itself to penetrate and unravel.'

Such good qualities as Lady Margaret accorded her cousin were of a sort more fitted to please a less sedate and sober-minded damsel than Dorothy, who was fashioned rather after the model of a puritan than a royalist maiden. Pleased with his address and his behaviour to herself as she could hardly fail to be, she yet felt a lingering mistrust of him, which sprang quite as much from the immediate impression as from her mistress's judgment of him, for it always gave her a sense of not coming near the real man in him. There is one thing a hypocrite even can never do, and that is, hide the natural signs of his hypocrisy; and Rowland, who was no hypocrite, only a man not half so honourable as he chose to take himself for, could not conceal his unreality from the eyes of his simple country cousin. Little, however, did Dorothy herself suspect whence she had the idea, that it was her girlhood's converse with real, sturdy, honest, straight-forward, simple manhood, in the person of the youth of fiery temper, and obstinate, opinionated, sometimes even rude behaviour, whom she had chastised with terms of contemptuous rebuke, which had rendered her so soon capable of distinguishing between a profound and a shallow, a genuine and an unreal nature, even when the latter comprehended a certain power of fascination, active enough to be recognisable by most of the women in the castle.

Concerning this matter, it will suffice to say that Lord Worcester, who ruled his household with such authoritative wisdom that honest Dr. Bayly avers he never saw a better-ordered family, never saw a man drunk or heard an oath amongst his servants, all the time he was chaplain in the castle, would have been scandalized to know the freedoms his favourite indulged himself in, and regarded as privileged familiarities.

There was much coming and going of visitors, more now upon state business than matters of friendship or ceremony; and occasional solemn conferences were held in the Marquis 's private room, at which sometimes Lord John, who was a personal friend of the king's, and sometimes Lord Charles, the governor of the castle, with perhaps this or that officer of dignity in the household, would be present; but whoever was or was not present, Lord Herbert when at home was always there, sometimes alone with his father and commissioners from the king. His absences, however, had grown frequent now that his majesty had appointed him general of South Wales, and he had considerable forces under his command, mostly raised by himself, and maintained at his own and his father's expense.

It was some time after Dorothy had twice in one day met him darkling, before she saw him in the light, and was able to peruse his countenance, which she did carefully, with the mingled instinct and insight of curious and doubtful girlhood. He had come home from a journey, changed his clothes, and had some food; and now he appeared in his wife's parlour, to sun himself a little, he said. When he entered, Dorothy, who was seated at her mistress's embroidery frame, while she was herself busy mending some Flanders lace, rose to leave the room. But he prayed her to be seated, saying gayly,

'I would have you see, cousin, that I am no beast of prey that loves the darkness. I can endure the daylight. Come, my lady, have you nothing to amuse your soldier with? No good news to tell him? How is my little Molly?'

During the conjugal talk that followed, his cousin had good opportunity of making her observations. First she saw a fair, well-proportioned forehead, with eyes whose remarkable clearness looked as if it owed itself to the mingling of manly confidence with feminine trustfulness. They were dark, not very large, but rather prominent, and full of light. His nose was a little aquiline, and perfectly formed. A soft obedient moustache, brushed thoroughly aside, revealed right generous lips, about which hovered a certain sweetness ever ready to break into the blossom of a smile. That and a small tuft below was all the hair he wore upon his face. Rare conjunction, the whole of the countenance was remarkable both for symmetry and expression, the latter mainly a bright intelligence; and if, strangely enough, the predominant sweetness and delicacy at first suggested genius unsupported by practical faculty, there was a plentifulness and strength in the chin which helped to correct the suggestion, and with the brightness and prominence of the eyes and the radiance of the whole, to give a brave, almost bold look to a face which could hardly fail to remind those who knew them of the lovely verses of Matthew Raydon, describing that of sir Philip Sidney:

A sweet attractive kinde of grace,
A full assurance given by lookes,
Continuall comfort in a face,
The lineaments of Gospell-bookes;
I trowe that countenance cannot lie
Whose thoughts are legible in the eie.

Notwithstanding the disadvantages of the fashion, in the mechanical pursuits to which he had hitherto devoted his life, he wore, like Milton's Adam, his wavy hair down to his shoulders. In his youth, it had been thick and curling; now it was thinner and straighter, yet curled where it lay. His hands were small, with the taper fingers that indicate the artist, while his thumb was that of the artizan, square at the tip, with the first joint curved a good deal back. That they were hard and something discoloured was not for Dorothy to wonder at, when she remembered what she had both heard and seen of his occupations.

I may here mention that what aided Dorothy much in the interpretation of Lord Herbert's countenance and the understanding of his character, for it was not on this first observation of him that she could discover all I have now set down, and tended largely to the development of the immense reverence she conceived for him, was what she saw of his behaviour to his father one evening not long after, when, having been invited to the Marquis 's table, she sat nearly opposite him at supper. With a willing ear and ready smile for everyone who addressed him, notably courteous where all were courteous, he gave chief observance, amounting to an almost tender homage, to his father. His thoughts seemed to wait upon him with a fearless devotion. He listened intently to all his jokes, and laughed at them heartily, evidently enjoying them even when they were not very good; spoke to him with profound though easy respect; made haste to hand him whatever he seemed to want, preventing Scudamore; and indeed conducted himself like a dutiful youth, rather than a man over forty. Their confident behaviour, wherein the authority of the one and the submission of the other were acknowledged with co-relative love, was beautiful to behold.

When husband and wife had conferred for a while, the former stretched on a settee embroidered by the skilful hands of the latest-vanished countess, his mother, and the latter seated near him on a narrow tall-backed chair, mending her lace, there came a pause in their low-toned conversation, and his lordship looking up seemed anew to become aware of the presence of Dorothy.

'Well, cousin,' he said, 'how have you fared since we half-saw each other a fortnight ago?'

'I have fared well indeed, my lord, I thank you,' said Dorothy, 'as your lordship may judge, knowing whom I serve. In two short weeks my lady loads me with kindness enough to requite the loyalty of a life.'

'Look you, cousin, that I should believe such laudation of any less than an angel?' said his lordship with mock gravity.

'No, my lord,' answered Dorothy.

There was a moment's pause; then Lord Herbert laughed aloud.

'Excellent well, mistress Dorothy!' he cried. 'Thank your cousin, my lady, for a compliment worthy of an Irishwoman.'

'I thank you, Dorothy,' said her mistress; 'although, Irishwoman as I am, my Lord hath put me out of love with compliments.'

'When they are true and come unbidden, my lady,' said Dorothy.

'What! are there such compliments, cousin?' said Lord Herbert.

'There are birds of Paradise, my lord, though rarely encountered.'

'Birds of Paradise indeed! they alight not in this world. Birds of Paradise have no legs, they say.

'They need them not, my lord. Once alighted, they fly no more.'

'How is it then they alight so seldom?'

'Because men shoo them away. One flew now from my heart to seek my lady's, but your lordship frighted it.'

'And so it flew back to Paradise, eh, mistress Dorothy?' said Lord Herbert, smiling archly.

The supper bell rang, and instead of replying, Dorothy looked up for her dismissal.

'Go to supper, my lady,' said Lord Herbert. 'I have but just dined, and will see what Caspar is about.'

'I want no supper but my Herbert,' returned Lady Margaret. 'Thou wilt not go to that hateful workshop?'

'I have so little time at home now—'

'That you must spend it from your lady? Go to supper, Dorothy.'

CHAPTER XV

HUSBAND AND WIFE

'What an old-fashioned damsel it is!' said Lord Herbert when Dorothy had left the room.

'She has led a lonely life,' answered Lady Margaret, 'and has read a many old-fashioned books.'

'She seems a right companion for thee, Peggy, and I am glad of it, for I shall be much from thee, more and more, I fear, till this bitter weather be gone by.'

'Alas, Ned! hast thou not been more than much from me already? Thou wilt certainly be killed, though thou hast not yet a scratch on thy blessed body. I would it were over and all well!'

'So would I, and heartily, dear heart! In very truth I love fighting as little as thou. But it is a thing that hath to be done, though small honour will ever be mine therefrom, I greatly fear me. It is one of those affairs in which liking goes farther than goodwill, and as I say, I love it not, only to do my duty. Hence doubtless it comes that no luck attends me. God knows I fear nothing a man ought not to fear, he is my witness, but what good service of arms have I yet rendered my king? It is but thy face, Peggy, that draws the smile from me. My heart is heavy. See how my rascally Welsh yielded before Gloucester, when the rogue Waller stole a march upon them, and I must be from thence! Had I but been there instead of at Oxford, thinkest thou they would have laid down their arms nor struck a single blow? I like not killing, but I can kill, and I can be killed. Thou knowest, sweet wife, thy Ned would not run.'

'Holy mother!' exclaimed Lady Margaret.

'But I have no good luck at fighting,' he went on. 'And how again at Monmouth, the hare-hearts with which I had thought to garrison the place fled at the bare advent of that same parliament beagle, Waller! By St. George! it were easier to make an engine that should mow down a thousand brave men with one sweep of a scythe, and I could make it, than to put courage into the heart of one runaway rascal. It makes me mad to think how they have disgraced me!'

'But Monmouth is thine own again, Herbert!'

'Yes, thanks to the love they bear my father, not to my generalship! Thy husband is a poor soldier, Peggy: he cannot make soldiers.'

'Then why not leave the field to others, and labour at thy engines, love? If thou wilt, I tell thee what, I will doff my gown, and in wrapper and petticoat help thee, sweet. I will to it with bare arms like thine own.'

'Thou wouldst like Una make a sunshine in the shady place, Margaret. But no. Poor soldier as I am, I will do my best, even where good fortune fails me, and glory awaits not my coming. Thou knowest that at fourteen days' warning I brought four thousand foot and eight hundred horse again to the siege of Gloucester. It would ill befit my father's son to spare what he can when he is pouring out his wealth like water at the feet of his king. No, wife; the king shall not find me wanting, for in serving my king, I serve my God; and if I should fail, it may hold that an honest failure comes nigh enough a victory to be set down in the chronicles of the high countries. But in truth it presses on me sorely, and I am troubled at heart that I should be so given over to failure.'

'Never heed it, my lord. The sun comes out clear at last maugre all the region fogs.'

'Thanks, sweet heart! Things do look up a little in the main, and if the king had but a dozen more such friends as my Lord Marquis , they would soon be well. Why, my dove of comfort, wouldst thou believe it? I did this day, as I rode home to seek thy fair face, I did count up what sums he hath already spent for his liege; and indeed I could not recollect them all, but I summed up, of pounds already spent by him on his majesty's behalf, well towards a hundred and fifty thousand! And thou knowest the good man, that while he giveth generously like the great Giver, he giveth not carelessly, but hath respect to what he spendeth.'

'Thy father, Ned, is loyalty and generosity incarnate. If thou be but half so good a husband as thy father is a subject, I am a happy woman.'

'What! know'st thou not yet thy husband, Peggy?'

'In good soberness, though, Ned, surely the saints in heaven will never let such devotion fail of its end.'

'My father is but one, and the king's foes are many. So are his friends, but they are lukewarm compared to my father, the rich ones of them, I mean. Would to God I had not lost those seven great troop-horses that the pudding-fisted clothiers of Gloucester did rob me of! I need them sorely now. ! bought them with mine own, or rather with thine, sweet heart. I had been saving up the money for a carcanet for thy fair neck.'

'So my neck be fair in thine eyes, my lord, it may go bare and be well clad. I should, in sad earnest, be jealous of the pretty stones didst thou give my neck one look the more for their presence. Here! thou may'st sell these the next time thou goest London-wards.'

As she spoke, she put up her hand to unclasp her necklace of large pearls, but he laid his hand upon it, saying,

'Nay, Margaret, there is no need. My father is like the father in the parable: he hath enough and to spare. I did mean to have the money of him again, only as the vaunted horses never came, but were swallowed up of Gloucester, as Jonah of the whale, and have not yet been cast up again, I could not bring my tongue to ask him for it; and so thy neck is bare of emeralds, my dove.'

'Back and sides go bare, go bare,'

sang Lady Margaret with a merry laugh;

'Both foot and hand go cold;'

here she paused for a moment, and looked down with a shining thoughtfulness; then sang out clear and loud, with bold alteration of bishop Stills' drinking song,

'But, heart, God send thee love enough,
Of the new that will never be old.'

'Amen, my dove!'said Lord Herbert.

'Thou art in doleful dumps, Ned. If we had but a masque for thee, or a play, or even some jugglers with their balls!'

'Puh, Peggy! thou art masque and play both in one; and for thy jugglers, I trust I can juggle better at my own hand than any troop of them from furthest India. Sing me a song, sweet heart.'

'I will, my love,' answered Lady Margaret.

Rising, she went to the harpsichord, and sang, in sweet unaffected style, one of the songs of her native country, a merry ditty, with a breathing of sadness in the refrain of it, like a twilight wind in a bed of bulrushes.

'Thanks, my love,' said Lord Herbert, when she had finished. 'But I would I could tell its hidden purport; for I am one of those who think music none the worse for carrying with it an air of such sound as speaks to the brain as well as the heart.'

Lady Margaret gave a playful sigh.

'Thou hast one fault, my Edward, thou art a stranger to the tongue in which, through my old nurse's tales, I learned the language of love. I cannot call it my mother-tongue, but it is my love-tongue. Why, when thou art from me, I am loving thee in Irish all day long, and thou never knowest what my heart says to thee! It is a sad lack in thy all-completeness, dear heart. But, I bethink me, thy new cousin did sing a fair song in thy own tongue the other day, the which if thou canst understand one straw better than my Irish, I will learn it for thy sake, though truly it is Greek to me. I will send for her. Shall I?'

As she spoke she rose and rang the bell on the table, and a little page, in waiting in the antechamber, appeared, whom she sent to desire the attendance of mistress Dorothy Vaughan.

'Come, child,' said her mistress as she entered, 'I would have thee sing to my Lord the song that wandering harper taught thee.'

'Madam, I have learned of no wandering harper: your ladyship means mistress Amanda's Welsh song! shall I call her?' said Dorothy, disappointed.

'I mean thee, and thy song, thou green linnet!' rejoined Lady Margaret. 'What song was it of which I said to thee that the singer deserved, for his very song's sake, that whereof he made his moan? Whence thou hadst it, from harper or bagpiper, I care not.'

'Excuse me, madam, but why should I sing that you love not to hear?'

'It is not I would hear it, child, but I would have my Lord hear it. I would fain prove to him that there are songs in plain English, as he calls it, that have as little import, even to an English ear, as the plain truth-speaking Irish ditties which he will not understand. I say "WILL not," because our bards tell us that Irish was the language of Adam and Eve while yet in Paradise, and therefore he could by instinct understand it an' he would, even as the chickens understand their mother-tongue.'

'I will sing it at your desire, madam; but I fear the worse fault will lie in the singing.'

She seated herself at the harpsichord, and sang the following song with much feeling and simplicity. The refrain of the song, if it may be so called, instead of closing each stanza, preluded it.

O fair, O sweet, when I do look on thee,
In whom all joys so well agree,
Heart and soul do sing in me.
This you hear is not my tongue,
Which once said what I conceived,
For it was of use bereaved,
With a cruel answer stung.

No, though tongue to roof be cleaved,
Fearing lest he chastis'd be,
Heart and soul do sing in me.

O fair, O sweet, &c.
Just accord all music makes:
In thee just accord excelleth,
Where each part in such peace dwelleth,
One of other beauty takes.
Since then truth to all minds telleth
That in thee lives harmony,
Heart and soul do sing in me.

O fair, O sweet, &c.
They that heaven have known, do say
That whoso that grace obtaineth
To see what fair sight there reigneth,
Forced is to sing alway;
So then, since that heaven remaineth
In thy face, I plainly see,
Heart and soul do sing in me.

O fair, O sweet, &c.
Sweet, think not I am at ease,
For because my chief part singeth;
This song from death's sorrow springeth,
As to Swan in last disease;
For no dumbness nor death bringeth
Stay to true love's melody:
Heart and soul do sing in me.

'There!' cried Lady Margaret, with a merry laugh. 'What says the English song to my English husband?'

'It says much, Margaret,' returned Lord Herbert, who had been listening intently; 'it tells me to love you forever. What poet is he who wrote the song, mistress Dorothy? He is not of our day, that I can tell but too plainly. It is a good song, and saith much.'

'I found it near the end of the book called "The Countess of Pembroke's Arcadia,"' replied Dorothy.

'And I knew it not! Methought I had read all that man of men ever wrote,' said Lord Herbert. 'But I may have read it, and let it slip. But now that, by the help of the music and thy singing, cousin Dorothy, I am come to understand it, truly I shall forget it no more. Where got'st thou the music, pray?'

'It says in the book it was fitted to a certain Spanish tune, the name of which I knew not, and yet know not how to pronounce; but I had the look of the words in my head, and when I came upon some Spanish songs in an old chest at home, and, turning them over, saw those words, I knew I had found the tune to sir Philip's verses.'

'Tell me then, my lord, why you are pleased with the song,' said Lady Margaret, very quietly.

'Come, mistress Dorothy,' said Lord Herbert, 'repeat the song to my lady, slowly, line by line, and she will want no exposition thereon.'

When Dorothy had done as he requested, Lady Margaret put her arm round her husband's neck, laid her cheek to his, and said,

'I am a goose, Ned. It is a fair and sweet song. I thank you, Dorothy. You shall sing it to me another time when my Lord is away, and I shall love to think my Lord was ill content with me when I called it a foolish thing. But my Irish was a good song too, my lord.'

'Thy singing of it proves it, sweet heart. But come, my fair minstrel, thou hast earned a good guerdon: what shall I give thee in return for thy song?'

'A boon, a boon, my lord!' cried Dorothy.

'It is thine ere thou ask it,' returned his lordship, merrily following up the old-fashioned phrase with like formality.

'I must then tell my Lord what hath been in my foolish mind ever since my lady took me to the keep, and I saw his marvellous array of engines. I would gladly understand them, my lord. Who can fail to delight in such inventions as bring about that which before seemed impossible?'

Here came a little sigh with the thought of her old companion Richard, and the things they had together contrived. Already, on the mist of gathering time, a halo had begun to glimmer about his head, puritan, fanatic, blasphemer even, as she had called him.

Lord Herbert marked the soundless sigh.

'You shall not sigh in vain, mistress Dorothy,' he said, 'for anything I can give you. To one who loves inventions it is easy to explain them. I hoped you had a hankering that way when I saw you look so curiously at the cross-bow ere you discharged it.'

'Was it then charged, my lord?'

'Indeed, as it happened, it was. A great steel-headed arrow lay in the groove. I ought to have taken that away when I bent it. Some passing horseman may have carried it with him in the body of his plunging steed.'

'Oh, my lord!' cried Dorothy, aghast.

'Pray, do not be alarmed, cousin: I but jested. Had anything happened, we should have heard of it. It was not in the least likely. You will not be long in this house before you learn that we do not speak by the card here. We jest not a little. But in truth I was disappointed when I found your curiosity so easily allayed.'

'Indeed, my lord, it was not allayed, and is still unsatisfied. But I had no thought who it was offered me the knowledge I craved. Had I known, I should never have refused the lesson so courteously offered. But I was a stranger in the castle, and I thought, I feared I'

'You did even as prudence required, cousin Dorothy. A young maiden cannot be too chary of unbuckling her enchanted armour so long as the country is unknown to her. But it would be hard if she were to suffer for her modesty. You shall be welcome to my cave. I trust you will not find it as the cave of Trophonius to you. If I am not there, and it is not now as it has been, when you might have found me in it every day, and almost every hour of the day; but if I be not there, do not fear Caspar Kaltoff, who is a worthy man, and as my right hand to do the things my brain deviseth. I will speak to him of thee. He is full of trust and worthiness, and, although not of gentle blood, is sprung from a long race of artificers, the cloak of whose gathered skill seems to have fallen on him. He hath been in my service now for many years, but you will be the first lady, gentle cousin, who has ever in all that time wished us good speed in our endeavours. How few know,' he went on thoughtfully, after a pause, 'what a joy lies in making things obey thoughts! in calling out of the mind, as from the vasty-deep, and setting in visible presence before the bodily eye, that which till then had neither local habitation nor name! Some such marvels I have to show, for marvels I must call them, although it is my voice they have obeyed to come; and I never lose sight of the marvel even while amusing myself with the merest toy of my own invention.'

He paused, and Dorothy ventured to speak.

'I thank you, my lord, with all my heart. When have I leave to visit those marvels?'

'When you please. If I am not there, Caspar will be. If Caspar is not there, you will find the door open, for to enter that chamber without permission would be a breach of law such as not a soul in Raglan would dare be guilty of. And were it not so, there are few indeed in the place who would venture to set foot in it if I were absent, for it is not outside the castle walls only that I am looked upon as a magician. The armourer firmly believes that with a word uttered in my den there, I could make the weakest wall of the castle impregnable, but that it would be at too great a cost. If you come to-morrow morning you will find me almost certainly. But in case you should find neither of us, do not touch anything; be content with looking, for fear of mischance. Engines are as tickle to meddle with as incantations themselves.'

'If I know myself, you may trust me, my lord,' said Dorothy, to which he replied with a smile of confidence.

CHAPTER XVI

DOROTHY'S INITIATION

There was much about the castle itself to interest Dorothy. She had already begun the attempt to gather a clear notion of its many parts and their relations, but the knowledge of the building could not well advance more rapidly than her acquaintance with its inmates, for little was to be done from the outside alone, and she could not bear to be met in strange places by strange people. So that part of her education, I use the word advisedly, for to know all about the parts of an old building may do more for the education of minds of a certain stamp than the severest course of logic, must wait upon time and opportunity.

Every day, often twice, sometimes thrice, she would visit the stable-yard, and have an interview first with the chained Marquis , and then with her little horse. After that she would seldom miss looking in at the armourer's shop, and spending a few minutes in watching him at his work, so that she was soon familiar with all sorts of armour favoured in the castle. The blacksmiths' and the carpenters' shops were also an attraction to her, and it was not long before she knew all the artisans about the place. There were the farm and poultry yards too, with which kinds of place she was familiar, especially with their animals and all their ways. The very wild beasts in their dens in the solid basement of the kitchen tower, a panther, two leopards, an ounce, and a toothless old lion had already begun to know her a little, for she never went near their cages without carrying them something to eat. For all these visits there was plenty of room, lady Margaret never requiring much of her time in the early part of the day, and finding the reports she brought of what was going on always amusing. And now the orchards and gardens would soon be inviting, for the heart of the world was already sending up its blood to dye the apple blossoms.

But all the opportunities she yet had were less than was needful for the development of such a mind as Dorothy's, which, powerful in itself, needed to be roused, and was slow in its movements except when excited by a quick succession of objects, or the contact of a kindred but busier nature. It was lacking not only in generative, but in self-moving energy. Of self-sustaining force she had abundance.

There was a really fine library in the castle, to which she had free access, and whence, now and then, Lady Margaret would make her bring a book from which to read aloud, while she and her other ladies were at work; but books were not enough to rouse Dorothy, and when inclined to read she would return too exclusively to what she already knew, making little effort to extend her gleaning-ground.

From this fragment of analysis it will be seen that the new resource thus opened to her might prove of more consequence than, great as were her expectations from it, she was yet able to anticipate. But infinitely greater good than any knowledge of his mechanical triumphs could bring her, was on its way to Dorothy along the path of growing acquaintance with the noble-minded inventor himself.

The next morning, then, she was up before the sun, and, sitting at her window, awaited his arrival. The moment he shone upon the gilded cock of the bell tower, she rose and hastened out, eager to taste of the sweets promised her; stood a moment to gaze on the limpid stream ever flowing from the mouth of the white horse, and wonder whence that and the whale-spouts he so frequently sent aloft from his nostrils came; then passing through the archway and over the bridge, found herself at the magician's door. For a moment she hesitated: from within came such a tumult of hammering, that plainly it was of no use to knock, and she could not at once bring herself to enter unannounced and uninvited. But confidence in Lord Herbert soon aroused her courage, and gently she opened the door and peeped in. There he stood, in a linen frock that reached from his neck to his knees, already hard at work at a small anvil on a bench, while Caspar was still harder at work at a huge anvil on the ground in front of a forge. This, with the mighty bellows attached to it, occupied one of the six sides of the room, and the great roaring, hissing thing that had so frightened Lady Margaret, now silent and cold, occupied another. Neither of the men saw her. So she entered, closed the door, and approached Lord Herbert, but he continued unaware of her presence until she spoke. Then he ceased his hammering, turned, and greeted her with his usual smile of sincerity absolute.

'Are you always as true to your appointments, cousin?' he said, and resumed his hammering.

'It was hardly an appointment, my lord, and yet here I am,' said Dorothy.

'And you mean to infer that—?'

'An appointment is no slight matter, my lord, or one that admits of breaking.'

'Right,' returned his lordship, still hammering at the thin plate of whitish metal growing thinner and thinner under his blows. Dorothy glanced around her for a moment.

'I would not be troublesome, my lord,' she said; 'but would you tell me in a few words what it is you make here?'

'Had I three tongues, and thou three ears,' answered Lord Herbert, 'I could not. But look round thee, cousin, and when thou spiest the thing that draws thine eye more than another, ask me concerning that, and I will tell thee.'

Hardly had Dorothy, in obedience, cast her eyes about the place, ere they lighted on the same huge wheel which had before chiefly attracted her notice.

'What is that great wheel for, with such a number of weights hung to it?' she asked.

'For a memorial,' replied Lord Herbert, 'of the folly of the man who placeth his hopes in man. That wonderful engine; it is now nearly three years since I showed it to his blessed majesty in the Tower of London, also with him to the dukes of Richmond and Hamilton, and two extraordinary ambassadors besides, but of them all no man hath ever sought to look upon it again. It is a form of the Proteus-like perpetuum mobile, a most incredible thing if not seen.'

He then proceeded to show her how, as every spoke passed the highest point, the weight attached to it immediately hung a foot farther from the centre of the wheel, and as every spoke passed the lowest point, its weight returned a foot nearer to the centre, thus causing the leverage to be greater always on one and the same side of the wheel. Few of my readers will regret so much as myself that I am unable to give them the constructive explanation his lordship gave Dorothy as to the shifting of the weights. Whether she understood it or not, I cannot tell either, but that is of less consequence. Before she left the workshop that morning, she had learned that a thousand knowledges are needed to build up the pyramid on whose top alone will the bird of knowledge lay her new egg.

When he had finished his explanation, Lord Herbert returned to his work, leaving Dorothy again to her own observations. And now she would gladly have questioned him about the huge mass of brick and iron, which, now standing silent, cold, and motionless as death, had that night seemed alive with the fierce energy of flame, and yet sorely driven, sighing, and groaning, and furiously hissing; but as it was not now at work, she thought it would be better to wait an opportunity when it should be in the agony of its wrestle with whatever unseen enemy it coped withal. She did not know that, the first of its race, it was not quite equal to the task the magician had imposed upon it, but that its descendants would at length become capable of doing a thousand times as much, with the swinging joy of conscious might, with the pant of the giant, not the groan of the overtasked stripling urging his last effort.

She was standing by a chest, examining the strangely elaborate and mysterious-looking scutcheon of its lock, when his lordship's hammering ceased, and presently she found that he was by her side.

'That escutcheon is the best thing of the kind I have yet made,' he said. 'A humour I have, never to be contented to produce any invention the second time, without appearing refined. The lock and key of this are in themselves a marvel, for the little triangle screwed key weighs no more than a shilling, and yet it bolts and unbolts an hundred bolts through fifty staples round about the chest, and as many more from both sides and ends, and at the self-same time shall fasten it to a place beyond a man's natural strength to take it away. But the best thing is the escutcheon; for the owner of it, though a woman, may with her own delicate hand vary the ways of coming to open the lock ten millions of times, beyond the knowledge of the smith that made it, or of me who invented it. If a stranger open it, it setteth an alarm agoing, which the stranger cannot stop from running out; and besides, though none should be within hearing, yet it catcheth his hand, as a trap doth a fox; and though far from maiming him, yet it leaveth such a mark behind it, as will discover him if suspected; the escutcheon or lock plainly showing what moneys he hath taken out of the box to a farthing, and how many times opened since the owner hath been at it.'

He then showed her how to set it, left the chest open, and gave her the key off his bunch that she might use it more easily. Ere she returned it, she had made herself mistress of the escutcheon as far as the mere working of it was concerned, as she proved to the satisfaction of the inventor.

Her docility and quickness greatly pleased him. He opened a cabinet, and after a search in its drawers, took from it a little thing, in form and colour like a plum, which he gave her, telling her to eat it. She saw from his smile that there was something at the back of the playful request, and for a moment hesitated, but reading in his countenance that he wished her at least to make the attempt, she put it in her mouth.

She was gagged. She could neither open nor shut her mouth a hair's breadth, could neither laugh, cry out, nor make any noise beyond an ugly one she would not make twice. The tears came into her eyes, for her position was ludicrous, and she imagined that his lordship was making game of her. A girl less serious or more merry would have been moved only to laughter.

But Lord Herbert hastened to relieve her. On the application of a tiny key, fixed with a joint in a finger-ring, the little steel bolts it had thrown out in every direction returned within the plum, and he drew it from her mouth.

'You little fool!' he said, with indescribable sweetness, for he saw the tears in her eyes; 'did you think I would hurt you?'

'No, my lord; but I did fear you were going to make game of me. I could not have borne Caspar to see me so.'

'Alas, my poor child!' he rejoined, 'you have come to the wrong house if you cannot put up with a little chafing. There!' he added, putting the plum in her hand, 'it is an untoothsome thing, but the moment may come when you will find it useful enough to repay you for the annoyance of a smile that had in it ten times more friendship than merriment.'

'I ask your pardon, my lord,' said Dorothy, by this time blushing deep with shame of her mistrust and over-sensitiveness, and on the point of crying downright. But his lordship smiled so kindly that she took heart and smiled again.

He then showed her how to raise the key hid in the ring, and how to unlock the plum.

'Do not try it on yourself,' he said, as he put the ring on her finger; 'you might find that awkward.'

'Be sure I shall avoid it, my lord,' returned Dorothy.

'And do not let any one know you have such a thing,' he said, 'or that there is a key in your ring.'

'I will try not, my lord.'

The breakfast bell rang.

'If you will come again after supper,' he said, as he pulled off his linen frock, 'I will show you my fire-engine at work, and tell you all that is needful to the understanding thereof; only you must not publish it to the world,' he added, 'for I mean to make much gain by my invention.'

Dorothy promised, and they parted, Lord Herbert for the Marquis 's parlour, Dorothy for the housekeeper's room, and Caspar for the third table in the great hall.

After breakfast Dorothy practised with her plum until she could manage it with as much readiness as ease. She found that it was made of steel, and that the bolts it threw out upon the slightest pressure were so rounded and polished that they could not hurt, while nothing but the key would reduce them again within their former sheath.

VOLUME II

CHAPTER XVII

THE FIRE-ENGINE

As soon as supper was over in the housekeeper's room, Dorothy sped to the keep, where she found Caspar at work.

'My Lord is not yet from supper, mistress,' he said. 'Will it please you wait while he comes?'

Had it been till midnight, so long as there was a chance of his appearing, Dorothy would have waited. Caspar did his best to amuse her, and succeeded, showing her one curious thing after another, amongst the rest a watch that seemed to want no winding after being once set agoing, but was in fact wound up a little by every opening of the case to see the dial. All the while the fire-engine was at work on its mysterious task, with but now and then a moment's attention from Caspar, a billet of wood or a shovelful of sea-coal on the fire, a pull at a cord, or a hint from the hooked rod. The time went rapidly.

Twilight was over, Caspar had lighted his lamp, and the moon had risen, before Lord Herbert came.

'I am glad to find you have patience as well as punctuality in the catalogue of your virtues, mistress Dorothy,' he said as he entered. 'I too am punctual, and am therefore sorry to have failed now, but it is not my fault: I had to attend my father. For his sake pardon me.'

'It were but a small matter, my lord, even had it been uncompelled, to keep an idle girl waiting.'

'I think not so,' returned Lord Herbert. 'But come now, I will explain to you my wonderful fire-engine.'

As he spoke, he took her by the hand, and led her towards it. The creature blazed, groaned, and puffed, but there was no motion to be seen about it save that of the flames through the cracks in the door of the furnace, neither was there any clanking noise of metal. A great rushing sound somewhere in the distance, that seemed to belong to it, yet appeared too far off to have any connection with it.

'It is a noisy thing,' he said, as they stood before it, 'but when I make another, it shall do its work that thou wouldst not hear it outside the door. Now listen to me for a moment, cousin. Should it come to a siege and I not at Raglan, the wise man will always provide for the worst, Caspar will be wanted everywhere. Now this engine is essential to the health and comfort, if not to the absolute life of the castle, and there is no one at present capable of managing it save us two. A very little instruction, however, would enable any one to do so: will you undertake it, cousin, in case of need?'

'Make me assured that I can, and I will, my lord,' answered Dorothy.

'A good and sufficing answer,' returned his lordship, with a smile of satisfaction. 'First then,' he went on, 'I will show you wherein lies its necessity to the good of the castle. Come with me, cousin Dorothy.'

He led the way from the room, and began to ascend the stair which rose just outside it. Dorothy followed, winding up through the thickness of the wall. And now she could not hear the engine. As she went up, however, certain sounds of it came again, and grew louder till they seemed close to her ears, then gradually died away and once more ceased. But ever, as they ascended, the rushing sound which had seemed connected with it, although so distant, drew nearer and nearer, until, having surmounted three of the five lofty stories of the building, they could scarcely hear each other speak for the roar of water, falling in intermittent jets. At last they came out on the top of the wall, with nothing between them and the moat below but the battlemented parapet, and behold! the mighty tower was roofed with water: a little tarn filled all the space within the surrounding walk. It undulated in the moonlight like a subsiding storm, and beat the encircling banks. For into its depths shot rather than poured a great volume of water from a huge orifice in the wall, and the roar and the rush were tremendous. It was like the birth of a river, bounding at once from its mountain rock, and the sound of its fall indicated the great depth of the water into which it plunged. Solid indeed must be the walls that sustained the outpush of such a weight of water!

'You see now, cousin, what yon fire-souled slave below is labouring at,' said his lordship. 'His task is to fill this cistern, and that he can in a few hours; and yet, such a slave is he, a child who understands his fetters and the joints of his bones can guide him at will.'

'But, my lord,' questioned Dorothy, 'is there not water here to supply the castle for months? And there is the draw-well in the pitched court besides.'

'Enough, I grant you,' he replied, 'for the mere necessities of life. But what would come of its pleasures? Would not the beleaguered ladies miss the bounty of the marble horse? Whence comes the water he gives so freely that he needeth not to drink himself? He would thirst indeed but for my water-commanding fiend below. Or how would the birds fare, were the fountains on the islands dry in the hot summer? And what would the children say if he ceased to spout? And how would my lord's tables fare, with the armed men besetting every gate, the fish-ponds dry, and the fish rotting in the sun? See you, mistress Dorothy? And for the draw-well, know you not wherein lies the good of a tower stronger than all the rest? Is it not built for final retreat, the rest of the castle being at length in the hands of the enemy? Where then is your draw-well?'

'But this tower, large as it is, could not receive those now within the walls of the castle,' said Dorothy.

'They will be fewer ere its shelter is needful.'

It was his tone quite as much as the words that drove a sudden sickness to the heart of the girl: for one moment she knew what siege and battle meant. But she recovered herself with a strong effort, and escaped from the thought by another question.

'And whence comes all this water, my lord?' she said, for she was one who would ask until she knew all that concerned her.

'Have you not chanced to observe a well in my workshop below, on the left-hand side of the door, not far from the great chest?'

'I have observed it, my lord.'

'That is a very deep well, with a powerful spring. Large pipes lead from all but the very bottom of that to my fire-engine. The fuller the well, the more rapid the flow into the cistern, for the shallower the water, the more labour falls to my giant. He is finding it harder work now. But you see the cistern is nearly full.'

'Forgive me, my lord, if I am troubling you,' said Dorothy, about to ask another question.

'I delight in the questions of the docile,' said his lordship. 'They are the little children of wisdom. There! that might be out of the book of Ecclesiasticus,' he added, with a merry laugh. 'I might pass that off on Dr. Bayly for my father's: he hath already begun to gather my father's sayings into a book, as I have discovered. But, prithee, cousin, let not my father know of it.'

'Fear not me, my lord,' returned Dorothy. 'Having no secrets of my own to house, it were evil indeed to turn my friends' out of doors.'

'Why, that also would do for Dr. Bayly! Well said, Dorothy! Now for thy next question.'

'It is this, my lord: having such a well in your foundations, whence the need of such a cistern on your roof? I mean now as regards the provision of the keep itself in case of ultimate resort.'

'In coming to deal with a place of such strength as this,' replied his lordship, '—I mean the keep whereon we now stand, not the castle, which, alas! hath many weak points, the enemy would assuredly change the siege into a blockade; that is, he would try to starve instead of fire us out; and, procuring information sufficiently to the point, would be like enough to dig deep and cut the water-veins which supply that well; and thereafter all would depend on the cistern. From the moment therefore when the first signs of siege appear, it will be wisdom and duty on the part of the person in charge to keep it constantly full, full as a cup to the health of the king. I trust however that such will be the good success of his majesty's arms that the worst will only have to be provided against, not encountered. But there is more in it yet. Come hither, cousin. Look down through this battlement upon the moat. You see the moon in it? No? That is because it is covered so thick with weeds. When you go down, mark how low it is. There is little defence in the moat that a boy might wade through. I have allowed it to get shallow in order to try upon its sides a new cement I have lately discovered; but weeks and weeks have passed, and I have never found the leisure, and now I am sure I never shall until this rebellion is crushed. It is time I filled it. Pray look down upon it, cousin. In summer it will be full of the loveliest white water-lilies, though now you can see nothing but green weeds.'

He had left her side and gone a few paces away, but kept on speaking.

'One strange thing I can tell you about them, cousin, the roots of that whitest of flowers make a fine black dye! What apophthegm founded upon that, thinkest thou, my father would drop for Dr Bayly?'

'You perplex me much, my lord,' said Dorothy. 'I cannot at all perceive your lordship's drift.'

'Lay a hand on each side of the battlement where you now stand; lean through it and look down. Hold fast and fear nothing.' Dorothy did as she was desired, and thus supported gazed upon the moat below, where it lay a mere ditch at the foot of the lofty wall.

'My lord, I see nothing,' she said, turning to him, as she thought; but he had vanished.

Again she looked at the moat, and then her eyes wandered away over the castle. The two courts and their many roofs, even those of all the towers, except only the lofty watch-tower on the western side, lay bare beneath her, in bright moonlight, flecked and blotted with shadows, all wondrous in shape and black as Erebus.

Suddenly, she knew not whence, arose a frightful roaring, a hollow bellowing, a pent-up rumbling. Seized by a vague terror, she clung to the parapet and trembled. But even the great wall beneath her, solid as the earth itself, seemed to tremble under her feet, as with some inward commotion or dismay. The next moment the water in the moat appeared to rush swiftly upwards, in wild uproar, fiercely confused, and covered with foam and spray. To her bewildered eyes, it seemed to heap itself up, wave upon furious wave, to reach the spot where she stood, greedy to engulf her. For an instant she fancied the storming billows pouring over the edge of the battlement, and started back in such momentary agony as we suffer in dreams. Then, by a sudden rectification of her vision, she perceived that what she saw was in reality a multitude of fountain jets rushing high towards their parent-cistern, but far-failing ere they reached it. The roar of their onset was mingled with the despairing tumult of their defeat, and both with the deep tumble and wallowing splash of the water from the fire-engine, which grew louder and louder as the surface of the water in the reservoir sank. The uproar ceased as suddenly as it had commenced, but the moat mirrored a thousand moons in the agitated waters which had overwhelmed its mantle of weeds.

'You see now,' said Lord Herbert, rejoining her while still she gazed, 'how necessary the cistern is to the keep? Without it, the few poor springs in the moat would but sustain it as you saw it. From here I can fill it to the brim.'

'I see,' answered Dorothy. 'But would not a simple overflow serve, carried from the well through the wall?'

'It would, were there no other advantages with which this mode harmonised. I must mention one thing more, which I was almost forgetting, and which I cannot well show you to-night, namely, that I can use this water not only as a means of defence in the moat, but as an engine of offence also against any one setting unlawful or hostile foot upon the stone bridge over it. I can, when I please, turn that bridge, the same by which you cross to come here, into a rushing aqueduct, and with a torrent of water sweep from it a whole company of invaders.'

'But would they not have only to wait until the cistern was empty?'

'As soon and so long as the bridge is clear, the outflow ceases. One sweep, and my water-broom would stop, and the rubbish lie sprawling under the arch, or half-way over the court. And more still,' he added with emphasis: 'I COULD make it boiling!'

'But your lordship would not?' faltered Dorothy.

'That might depend,' he answered with a smile. Then changing his tone in absolute and impressive seriousness, 'But this is all nothing but child's play,' he said, 'compared with what is involved in the matter of this reservoir. The real origin of it was its needfulness to the perfecting of my fire-engine.'

'Pardon me, my lord, but it seems to me that without the cistern there would be no need for the engine. How should you want or how could you use the unhandsome thing? Then how should the cistern be necessary to the engine?'

'Handsome is that handsome does,' returned his lordship. 'Truly, cousin Dorothy, you speak well, but you must learn to hear better. I did not say that the cistern existed for the sake of the engine, but for the sake of the perfecting of the engine. Cousin Dorothy, I will give you the largest possible proof of my confidence in you, by not only explaining to you the working of my fire-engine, but acquainting you, only you must not betray me!'

'I, in my turn,' said Dorothy, 'will give your lordship, if not the strongest, yet a very strong proof of my confidence: I promise to keep your secret before knowing what it is.'

'Thanks, cousin. Listen then: That engine is a mingling of discovery and invention such as hath never had its equal since first the mechanical powers were brought to the light. For this shall be as a soul to animate those, all and each, lever, screw, pulley, wheel, and axle, what you will. No engine of mightiest force ever for defence or assault invented, let it be by Archimedes himself, but could by my fire-engine be rendered tenfold more mighty for safety or for destruction, although as yet I have applied it only to the blissful operation of lifting water, thus removing the curse of it where it is a curse, and carrying it where the parched soil cries for its help to unfold the treasures of its thirsty bosom. My fire-engine shall yet uplift the nation of England above the heads of all richest and most powerful nations on the face of the whole earth. For when the troubles of this rebellion are over, which press so heavily on his majesty and all loyal subjects, compelling even a peaceful man like myself to forsake invention for war, and the workman's frock which I love, for the armour which I love not, when peace shall smile again on the country, and I shall have time to perfect the work of my hands, I shall present it to my royal master, a magical supremacy of power, which shall for ever raise him and his royal progeny above all use or need of subsidies, ship-money, benevolences, or taxes of whatever sort or name, to rule his kingdom as independent of his subjects in reality as he is in right; for this water-commanding engine, which God hath given me to make, shall be the source of such wealth as no accountant can calculate. For herewith may marsh-land be thoroughly drained, or dry land perfectly watered; great cities kept sweet and wholesome; mines rid of the water gathering from springs therein, so as he may enrich himself withal; houses be served plentifully on every stage; and gardens in the dryest summer beautified and comforted with fountains. Which engine when I found that it was in the power of my hands to do, as well as of my heart to conceive that it might be done, I did kneel down and give humble thanks from the bottom of my heart to the omnipotent God whose mercies are fathomless, for his vouchsafing me an insight into so great a secret of nature and so beneficial to all mankind as this my engine.'

With all her devotion to the king, and all her hatred and contempt of the parliament and the puritans, Dorothy could not help a doubt whether such independence might be altogether good either for the king himself or the people thus subjected to his will. But the farther doubt did not occur to her whether a pre-eminence gained chiefly by wealth was one to be on any grounds desired for the nation, or, setting that aside, was one which carried a single element favourable to perpetuity.

All this time they had been standing on the top of the keep, with the moonlight around them, and in their ears the noise of the water flowing from the dungeon well into the sky-roofed cistern. But now it came in diminished flow.

'It is the earth that fails in giving, not my engine in taking,' said Lord Herbert as he turned to lead the way down the winding stair. Ever as they went, the noise of the water grew fainter and the noise of the engine grew louder, but just as they stepped from the stair, it gave a failing stroke or two, and ceased. A dense white cloud met them as they entered the vault.

'Stopped for the night, Caspar?' said his lordship.

'Yes, my lord; the well is nearly out.'

'Let it sleep,' returned his master; 'like a man's heart it will fill in the night. Thank God for the night and darkness and sleep, in which good things draw nigh like God's thieves, and steal themselves in, water into wells, and peace and hope and courage into the minds of men. Is it not so, my cousin?'

Dorothy did not answer in words, but she looked up in his face with a reverence in her eyes that showed she understood him. And this was one of the idolatrous catholics! It was neither the first nor the last of many lessons she had to receive, in order to learn that a man may be right although the creed for which he is and ought to be ready to die, may contain much that is wrong. Alas! that so few, even of such men, ever reflect, that it is the element common to all the creeds which gives its central value to each.

'I cannot show you the working of the engine to-night,' said Lord Herbert. 'Caspar has decreed otherwise.'

'I can soon set her agoing again, my lord,' said Caspar.

'No, no. We must to the powder-mill, Caspar. Mistress Dorothy will come again to-morrow, and you must yourself explain to her the working and management of it, for I shall be away. And do not fear to trust my cousin, Caspar, although she be a soft-handed lady. Let her have the brute's halter in her own hold.'

Filled with gratitude for the trust he reposed in her, Dorothy took her leave, and the two workmen immediately abandoned their shop for the night, leaving the door wide open behind them to let out the vapours of the fire-engine, in the confidence that no unlicensed foot would dare to cross the threshold, and betook themselves to the powder-mill, where they continued at work the greater part of the night.

His lordship was unfavourable to the storing of powder because of the danger, seeing they could, on his calculation, from the materials lying ready for mixing, in one week prepare enough to keep all the ordnance on the castle walls busy for two. But indeed he had not such a high opinion of gunpowder but that he believed engines for projection, more powerful as well as less expensive, could be constructed, after the fashion of ballista or catapult, by the use of a mode he had discovered of immeasurably increasing the strength of springs, so that stones of a hundredweight might be thrown into a city from a quarter of a mile's distance without any noise audible to those within. It was this device he was brooding over when Dorothy came upon him by the arblast. Nor did the conviction arise from any prejudice against fire-arms, for he had, among many other wonderful things of the sort, in cannons, sakers, harquebusses, muskets, musquetoons, and all kinds, invented a pistol to discharge a dozen times with one loading, and without so much as new priming being once requisite, or the possessor having to change it out of one hand into the other, or stop his horse.

One who had happened to see Lord Herbert as he went about within his father's walls, busy yet unhasting, earnest yet cheerful, rapid in all his movements yet perfectly composed, would hardly have imagined that a day at a time, or perhaps two, was all he was now able to spend there, days which were to him as breathing-holes in the ice to the wintered fishes. For not merely did he give himself to the enlisting of large numbers of men, but commanded both horse and foot, meeting all expenses from his own pocket, or with the assistance of his father. A few months before the period at which my story has arrived, he had in eight days raised six regiments, fortified Monmouth and Chepstow, and garrisoned half-a-dozen smaller but yet important places. About a hundred noblemen and gentlemen whom he had enrolled as a troop of life-guards, he furnished with the horses and arms which they were unable to provide with sufficient haste for themselves. So prominent indeed were his services on behalf of the king, that his father was uneasy because of the jealousy and hate it would certainly rouse in the minds of some of his majesty's well-wishers, a just presentiment, as his son had too good reason to acknowledge after he had spent a million of money, besides the labour and thought and dangerous endeavour of years, in the king's service.

CHAPTER XVIII

MOONLIGHT AND APPLE-BLOSSOMS

The next morning, immediately after breakfast, Lord Herbert set out for Chepstow first and then Monmouth, both which places belonged to his father, and were principal sources of his great wealth.

Still, amid the rush of the changeful tides of war around them, and the rumour of battle filling the air, all was peaceful within the defences of Raglan, and its towers looked abroad over a quiet country, where the cattle fed and the green wheat grew. On the far outskirts of vision, indeed, a smoke might be seen at times from the watch-tower, and across the air would come the dull boom of a great gun from one of the fortresses, at which Lady Margaret's cheek would turn pale; but, although every day something was done to strengthen the castle, although masons were at work here and there about the walls like bees, and Caspar Kaltoff was busy in all directions, now mounting fresh guns, now repairing steel cross-bows, now getting out of the armoury the queerest oldest-fashioned engines to place wherever available points could be found, there was no hurry and no confusion, and indeed so little appearance of unusual activity, that an unmilitary stranger might have passed a week in the castle without discovering that preparations for defence were actively going on. All around them the buds were creeping out, uncurling, spreading abroad, straightening themselves, smoothing out the creases of their unfolding, and breathing the air of heaven, in some way very pleasant to creatures with roots as well as to creatures with legs. The apple-blossoms came out, and the orchard was lovely as with an upward-driven storm of roseate snow. Ladies were oftener seen passing through the gates and walking in the gardens, where the fountains had begun to play, and the swans and ducks on the lakes felt the return of spring in every fibre of their webby feet and cold scaly legs.

And Dorothy sat as it were at the spring-head of the waters, for, through her dominion over the fire-engine, she had become the naiad of Raglan. The same hour in which Lord Herbert departed she went to Kaltoff, and was by him instructed in its mysteries. On the third day after, so entirely was the Dutchman satisfied with her understanding and management of it, that he gave up to her the whole water-business. And now, as I say, she sat at the source of all the streams and fountains of the place, and governed them all. The horse of marble spouted and ceased at her will, but in general she let the stream from his mouth flow all day long. Every water-cock on the great tower was subject to her. From the urn of her pleasure the cistern was daily filled, and from the summit of defence her flood went pouring into the moat around its feet, until it mantled to the brim, turning the weeds into a cold shadowy pavement of green for a foil to its pellucid depth. She understood all the secrets of the aqueous catapult, at which its contriver had little more than hinted on that memorable night when he disclosed so much, and believed she could arrange it for action without assistance. At the same time her new responsibilities required but a portion of her leisure, and Lady Margaret was not the less pleased with the wise-headed girl, whose manners and mental ways were such a contrast to her own, that her husband considered her fit to be put in charge of his darling invention. But Dorothy kept silence concerning the trust to all but her mistress, who, on her part, was prudent enough to avoid any allusion which might raise yet higher the jealousy of her associates, by whom she was already regarded as supplanting them in the favour of their mistress.

One lovely evening in May, the moon at the full, the air warm yet fresh, the apple-blossoms at their largest, with as yet no spot upon their fair skin, and the nightingales singing out of their very bones, the season, the hour, the blossoms, and the moon had invaded every chamber in the castle, seized every heart of both man and beast, and turned all into one congregation of which the nightingales were the priests. The cocks were crowing as if it had been the dawn itself instead of its ghost they saw; the dogs were howling, but whether that was from love or hate of the moon, I cannot tell; the pigeons were cooing; the peacock had turned his train into a paralune, understanding well that the carnival could not be complete without him and his; and the wild beasts were restless, uttering a short yell now and then, at least aware that something was going on. All the inhabitants of the castle were out of doors, the ladies and gentlemen in groups here and there about the gardens and lawns and islands, and the domestics, and such of the garrison as were not on duty, wandering hither and thither where they pleased, careful only not to intrude on their superiors.

Lady Margaret was walking with her step-son Henry on a lawn under the northern window of the picture-gallery, and there the ladies Elizabeth and Anne joined them, the former a cheerful woman, endowed with a large share of her father's genial temperament; joke or jest would moult no feather in Lady Elizabeth's keeping; the latter quiet, sincere, and reverent. The Marquis himself, notwithstanding a slight attack of the gout, had hobbled on his stick to a chair set for him on the same lawn. Beside him sat Lady Mary, younger than the other two, and specially devoted to her father.

Their gentlewomen were also out, flitting in groups that now and then mingled and changed. Rowland Scudamore joined Lady Margaret's people, and in a moment Lady Broughton was laughing merrily. But mistress Doughty walked on with straight neck, as if there were nobody but herself in heaven or on the earth, although mortals were merry by her side, and nightingales singing themselves to death over her head. Behind them came Amanda Serafina, with her eyes on her feet, and the corners of her pretty mouth drawn down in contempt of nobody in particular. Now and then Scudamore, when satisfied with his own pretty wit, would throw a glance behind him, and she, somehow or other, would, without change of muscle, let him know that she had heard him. This group sauntered into the orchard.

After them came Dorothy with Dr Bayly, talking of their common friend Mr. Matthew Herbert, and following them into the orchard, wandered about among the trees, under the curdled moonlight of the apple-blossoms, amid the challenges and responses of five or six nightingales, that sang as if their bodies had dwindled under the sublimating influences of music, until, with more than cherubic denudation, their sum of being was reduced to a soul and a throat.

Moonlight, apple-blossoms, nightingales, with the souls of men and women for mirrors and reflectors! The picture is for the musician not the painter, either him of words or him of colours. It was like a lovely show in the land of dreams, even to the living souls that moved in and made part of it. The earth is older now, colder at the heart, a little nearer to the fate of cold-hearted things, which is to be slaves and serve without love; but she has still the same moonlight, the same apple-blossoms, the same nightingales, and we have the same hearts, and so can understand it. But, alas! how differently should we come in amongst the accessories of such a picture! For we men at least are all but given over to ugliness, and, artistically considered, even vulgarity, in the matter of dress, wherein they, of all generations of English men and women, were too easily supreme both as to form and colour. Hence, while they are an admiration to us, we shall be but a laughter to those that come behind us, and that whether their fashions be better than ours or no, for nothing is so ridiculous as ugliness out of date. The glimmer of gold and silver, the glitter of polished steel, the flashing of jewels, and the flowing of plumes, went well. But, so canopied with loveliness, so besung with winged passion, so clothed that even with the heavenly delicacies enrounding them they blended harmoniously, their moonlit orchard was an island beat by the waves of war, its air would quiver and throb by fits, shaken with the roar of cannon, and might soon gleam around them with the whirring sweep of the troopers' broad blades; while all throughout the land, the hateful demon of party spirit tore wide into gashes the wounds first made by conscience in the best, and by prejudice in the good.

The elder ladies had floated away together between the mossy stems, under the canopies of blossoms; Rowland had fallen behind and joined the waiting Amanda, and the two were now flitting about like moths in the moonshine; Dorothy and Dr. Bayly had halted in an open spot, like a moonlight impluvium, the divine talking eagerly to the maiden, and the maiden looking up at the moon, and heeding the nightingales more than the divine.

'CAN they be English nightingales?' said Dorothy thoughtfully.

The doctor was bewildered for a moment. He had been talking about himself, not the nightingales, but he recovered himself like a gentleman.

'Assuredly, mistress Dorothy,' he replied; 'this is the land of their birth. Hither they come again when the winter is over.'

'Yes; they take no part in our troubles. They will not sing to comfort our hearts in the cold; but give them warmth enough, and they sing as careless of battle-fields and dead men as if they were but moonlight and apple-blossoms.'

'Is it not better so?' returned the divine after a moment's thought. 'How would it be if everything in nature but re-echoed our moan?'

Dorothy looked at the little man, and was in her turn a moment silent.

'Then,' she said, 'we must see in these birds and blossoms, and that great blossom in the sky, so many prophets of a peaceful time and a better country, sent to remind us that we pass away and go to them.'

'Nay, my dear mistress Dorothy!' returned the all but obsequious doctor; 'such thoughts do not well befit your age, or rather, I would say, your youth. Life is before you, and life is good. These evil times will go by, the king shall have his own again, the fanatics will be scourged as they deserve, and the church will rise like the phoenix from the ashes of her purification.'

'But how many will lie out in the fields all the year long, yet never see blossoms or hear nightingales more!' said Dorothy.

'Such will have died martyrs,' rejoined the doctor.

'On both sides?' suggested Dorothy.

Again for a moment the good man stood checked. He had not even thought of the dead on the other side.

'That cannot be,' he said. And Dorothy looked up again at the moon.

But she listened no more to the songs of the nightingales, and they left the orchard together in silence.

'Come, Rowland, we must not be found here alone,' said Amanda, who saw them go. 'But tell me one thing first: is mistress Dorothy Vaughan indeed your cousin?'

'She is indeed. Her mother and mine were cousins german—sisters' children.'

'I thought it could not be a near cousinship. You are not alike at all. Hear me, Rowland, but let it die in your ear—I love not mistress Dorothy.'

'And the reason, lovely hater? "Is not the maiden fair to see?" as the old song says. I do not mean that she is fair as some are fair, but she will pass; she offends not.'

'She is fair enough, not beautiful, not even pleasing; but, to be just, the demure look she puts on may bear the fault of that. Rowland, I would not speak evil of any one, but your cousin is a hypocrite. She is false at heart, and she hates me. Trust me, she but bides her time to let me know it, and you too, my Rowland.'

'I am sure you mistake her, Amanda,' said Scudamore. 'Her looks are but modest, and her words but shy, for she came hither from a lonely house. I believe she is honest and good.'

'Seest thou not then how that she makes friends with none but her betters? Already hath she wound herself around my lady's heart, forsooth! and now she pays her court to the puffing chaplain! Hast thou never observed, my Rowland, how oft she crosses the bridge to the yellow tower? What seeks she there? Old Kaltoff, the Dutchman, it can hardly be. I know she thinks to curry with my Lord by pretending to love locks and screws and pistols and such like. "But why should she haunt the place when my Lord is not there?" you will ask. Her pretence will hold the better for it, no doubt, and Caspar will report concerning her. And if she pleases my Lord well, who knows but he may give her a pair of watches to hang at her ears, or a box that Paracelsus himself could not open without the secret as well as the key? I have heard of both such. They say my Lord hath twenty cartloads of quite as wonderful things in that vault he calls his workshop. Hast thou never marked the huge cabinet of black inlaid with silver, that stands by the wall, fitter indeed for my lady's chamber than such a foul place?'

'I have seen it,' answered Scudamore.

'I warrant me it hath store of gewgaws fit for a duchess.'

'Like enough,' assented Rowland.

'If mistress Dorothy were to find the way through my lord's favour into that cabinet, truly it were nothing to thee or me, Rowland.'

'Assuredly not. It would be my lord's own business.'

'Once upon a time I was sent to carry my young Lady Raven thither, to see my Lord earn his bread, as said my lady: and what should my Lord but give her no less than a ball of silver which, thrown into a vessel of water at any moment would plainly tell by how much it rose above the top, the very hour and minute of the day or night, as well and truly as the castle-clock itself. Tell me not, Rowland, that the damsel hath no design in it. Her looks betoken a better wisdom. Doth she not, I ask your honesty, far more resemble a nose-pinched puritan than a loyal maiden?'

Thus amongst the apple-blossoms talked Amanda Serafina.

'Prithee, be not too severe with my cousin, Amanda,' pleaded Scudamore. 'She is much too sober to please my fancy, but wherefore should I for that hate her? And if she hath something the look of a long-faced fanatic, thou must think, she hath but now, as it were, lost her mother.'

'But now! And I never knew mine! Ah, Rowland, how lonely is the world!'

'Lovely Amanda!' said Rowland.

So they passed from the orchard and parted, fearful of being missed.

How should such a pair do, but after its kind? Life was dull without love-making, so they made it. And the more they made, the more they wanted to make, until casual encounters would no longer serve their turn.

CHAPTER XIX

THE ENCHANTED CHAIR

In the castle things went on much the same, nor did the gathering tumult without wake more than an echo within. Yet a cloud slowly deepened upon the brow of the Marquis , and a look of disquiet, to be explained neither by the more frequent returns of his gout, nor by the more lengthened absences of his favourite son. In his judgment the king was losing ground, not only in England but in the deeper England of its men. Lady Margaret also, for all her natural good spirits and light-heartedness, showed a more continuous anxiety than was to be accounted for by her lord's absences and the dangers he had to encounter: little Molly, the treasure of her heart next to her lord, had never been other than a delicate child, but now had begun to show signs of worse than weakness of constitution, and the heart of the mother was perpetually brooding over the ever-present idea of her sickly darling.

But she always did her endeavour to clear the sky of her countenance before sitting down with her father-in-law at the dinner-table, where still the Marquis had his jest almost as regularly as his claret, although varying more in quality and quantity both, now teasing his son Charles about the holes in his pasteboard, as he styled the castle walls; now his daughter Anne about a design, he and no one else attributed to her, of turning protestant and marrying Dr. Bayly; now Dr. Bayly about his having been discovered blowing the organ in the chapel at high mass, as he said; for when no new joke was at hand he was fain to content himself with falling back upon old ones. The first of these mentioned was founded on the fact, as undeniable as deplorable, of the weakness of many portions of the defences, to remedy which, as far as might be, was for the present Lord Charles's chief endeavour, wherein he had the best possible adviser, engineer, superintendent, and workman, all in the person of Caspar Kaltoff. The second jest of the Marquis was a pure invention upon the liking of Lady Anne for the company and conversation of the worthy chaplain. The last mentioned was but an exaggeration of the following fact.

One evening the doctor came upon young Delaware, loitering about the door of the chapel, with as disconsolate a look as his lovely sightless face was ever seen to wear, and, inquiring what was amiss with him, learned that he could find no one to blow the organ bellows for him. The youth had for years, boy as he still was, found the main solace of his blindness in the chapel-organ, upon which he would have played from morning to night could he have got any one to blow as long. The doctor, then, finding the poor boy panting for music like the hart for the water-brooks, but with no Jacob to roll the stone from the well's mouth that he might water the flocks of his thirsty thoughts, made willing proffer of his own exertions to blow the bellows of the organ, so long as the somewhat wheezy bellows of his body would submit to the task.

By degrees however the good doctor had become so absorbed in the sounds that rushed, now wailing, now jubilant, now tender as a twilight wind, now imperious as the voice of the war-tempest, from the fingers of the raptured boy, that the reading of the first vesper-psalm had commenced while he was yet watching the slow rising index, in the expectation that the organist was about to resume. The voice of his Irish brother-chaplain, Sir Toby Mathews, roused him from his reverie of delight, and as one ashamed he stole away through the door that led from the little organ loft into the minstrel's gallery in the great hall, and so escaped the catholic service, but not the Marquis 's roasting. Whether the music had any share in the fact that the good man died a good catholic at last, I leave to the speculation of who list.

Lady Margaret continued unchangingly kind to Dorothy; and the tireless efforts of the girl to amuse and please poor little Molly, whom the growing warmth of the season seemed to have no power to revive, awoke the deep gratitude of a mother. This, as well as her husband's absences, may have had something to do with the interest she began to take in the engine of which Dorothy had assumed the charge, for which she had always hitherto expressed a special dislike, professing to regard it as her rival in the affections of her husband, but after which she would now inquire as Dorothy's baby, and even listen with patience to her expositions of its wonderful construction and capabilities. Ere long Dorothy had a tale to tell her in connection with the engine, which, although simple and uneventful enough, she yet found considerably more interesting, as involving a good deal of at least mental adventure on the part of her young cousin.

One evening, after playing with little Molly for an hour, then putting her to bed and standing by her crib until she fell asleep, Dorothy ran to see to her other baby; for the cistern had fallen rather lower than she thought well, and she was going to fill it. She found Caspar had lighted the furnace as she had requested; she set the engine going, and it soon warmed to its work.

The place was hot, and Dorothy was tired. But where in that wide and not over-clean place should she find anything fitter than a grindstone to sit upon? Never yet, through all her acquaintance with the workshop, had she once seated herself in it. Looking about, however, she soon espied, almost hidden in the corner of a recess behind the furnace, what seemed an ordinary chair, such as stood in the great hall for the use of the family when anything special was going on there. With some trouble she got it out, dusted it, and set it as far from the furnace as might be, consistently with watching the motions of the engine. But the moment she sat down in it, she was caught and pinned so fast that she could scarcely stir hand or foot, and could no more leave it again than if she had been paralyzed in every limb. One scream she uttered of mingled indignation and terror, fancying herself seized by human arms; but when she found herself only in the power of one of her cousin's curiosities, she speedily quieted herself and rested in peace, for Caspar always paid a visit to the workshop the last thing before going to bed. The pressure of the springs that had closed the trap did not hurt her in the least, she was indeed hardly sensible of it; but when she made the least attempt to stir, the thing showed itself immovably locked, and she had too much confidence in the workmanship of her cousin and Caspar to dream of attempting to open it: that she knew must be impossible. The worst that threatened her was that the engine might require some attention before the hour, or perhaps two, which must elapse ere Caspar came would be over, and she did not know what the consequences might be.

As it happened, however, something either in the powder-mill or about the defences detained Caspar far beyond his usual hour for retiring, and the sultriness of the weather having caused him a headache, he represented to himself that, with mistress Dorothy tending the engine, who knew where and would be sure to find him upon the least occasion, there could be no harm in his going to bed without paying his usual precautionary visit to the keep.

So Dorothy sat, and waited in vain. The last drops of the day trickled down the side of the world, the night filled the crystal globe from its bottom of rock to its cover of blue aether, and the red glow of the furnace was all that lighted the place. She waited and waited in her mind; but Caspar did not come. She began to feel miserable. The furnace fire sank, and the rush of the water grew slower and slower, and ceased. Caspar did not come. The fire sank lower and lower, its red eye dimmed, darkened, went out. Still Caspar did not come. Faint fears began to gather about poor Dorothy's heart. It was clear at last that there she must be all the night long, and who could tell how far into the morning? It was good the night was warm, but it would be very dreary. And then to be fixed in one position for so long! The thought of it grew in misery faster than the thing itself. The greater torment lies always in the foreboding. She felt almost as if she were buried alive. Having their hands tied even, is enough to drive strong men almost crazy. Nor, firm of heart as she was, did no evils of a more undefined and less resistible character claim a share in her fast-rising apprehensions; she began to discover that she too was assailable by the terror of the night, although she had not hitherto been aware of it, no one knowing what may lie unhatched in his mind, waiting the concurrence of vital conditions.

But Dorothy was better able to bear up under such assaults than thousands who believe nothing of many a hideous marvel commonly accepted in her day; and anyhow the unavoidable must be encountered, if not with indifference, yet with what courage may be found responsive to the call of the will. So, with all her energy, a larger store than she knew, she braced herself to endure. As to any attempt to make herself heard, she knew from the first that was of doubtful result, and now must certainly be of no avail when all but the warders were asleep. But to spend the night thus was a far less evil than to be discovered by the staring domestics, and exposed to the open merriment of her friends, and the hidden mockery of her enemies. As to Caspar, she was certain of his silence. So she sat on, like the lady in Comus, 'in stony fetters fixed and motionless;' only, as she said to herself, there was no attendant spirit to summon Caspar, who alone could take the part of Sabrina, and 'unlock the clasping charm.' Little did Dorothy think, as in her dreary imprisonment she recalled that marvellous embodiment of unified strength and tenderness, as yet unacknowledged of its author, that it was the work of the same detestable fanatic who wrote those appalling 'Animadversions, &c.'

She grew chilly and cramped. The night passed very slowly. She dozed and woke, and dozed again. At last, from very weariness of both soul and body, she fell into a troubled sleep, from which she woke suddenly with the sound in her ears of voices whispering. The confidence of Lord Herbert, both in the evil renown of his wizard cave and the character of his father's household, seemed mistaken. Still the subdued manner of their conversation appeared to indicate it was not without some awe that the speakers, whoever they were, had ventured within the forbidden precincts; their whispers, indeed, were so low that she could not say of either voice whether it belonged to man or woman. Her first idea was to deliver herself from the unpleasantness of her enforced espial by the utterance of some frightful cry such as would at the same time punish with the pains of terror their fool-hardy intrusion. But the spur of the moment was seldom indeed so sharp with Dorothy as to drive her to act without reflection, and a moment showed her that such persons being in the Marquis 's household as would meet in the middle of the night, and on prohibited ground, apparently for the sake of avoiding discovery, and even then talked in whispers, he had a right to know who they were: to act from her own feelings merely would be to fail in loyalty to the head of the house. Who could tell what might not be involved in it? For was it not thus that conspiracy and treason walked? And any alarm given them now might destroy every chance of their discovery. She compelled herself therefore to absolute stillness, immeasurably wretched, with but one comfort, no small one, however, although negative, that their words continued inaudible, a fact which doubtless saved much dispute betwixt her propriety and her loyalty.

Long time their talk lasted. Every now and then they would start and listen, so Dorothy interpreted sudden silence and broken renewals. The genius of the place, although braved, had yet his terrors. At length she heard something like a half-conquered yawn, and soon after the voices ceased.

Again a weary time, and once more she fell asleep. She woke in the grey of the morning, and after yet two long hours, but of more hopeful waiting, she heard Caspar's welcome footsteps, and summoned all her strength to avoid breaking down on his entrance. His first look of amazement she tried to answer with a smile, but at the expression of pitiful dismay which followed when another glance had revealed the cause of her presence, she burst into tears. The honest man was full of compunctious distress at the sight of the suffering his breach of custom had so cruelly prolonged.

'And I haf bin slap in mine bed!' he exclaimed with horror at the contrast.

Had she been his daughter and his mistress both in one, he could not have treated her with greater respect or tenderness. Of course he set about relieving her at once, but this was by no means such an easy matter as Dorothy had expected. For the key of the chair was in the black cabinet; the black cabinet was secured with one of Lord Herbert's marvellous locks; the key of that lock was in Lord Herbert's pocket, and Lord Herbert was either in bed at Chepstow or Monmouth or Usk or Caerlyon, or on horseback somewhere else, nobody in Raglan knew where. But Caspar lost no time in unavailing moan. He proceeded at once to light a fire on his forge hearth, and in the course of a few minutes had fashioned a pick-lock, by means of which, after several trials and alterations, at length came the welcome sound of the yielding bolts, and Dorothy rose from the terrible chair. But so benumbed were all her limbs that she escaped being relocked in it only by the quick interposition of Caspar's arms. He led her about like a child, until at length she found them sufficiently restored to adventure the journey to her chamber, and thither she slowly crept. Few of the household were yet astir, and she met no one. When she was covered up in bed, then first she knew how cold she was, and felt as if she should never be warm again.

At last she fell asleep, and slept long and soundly. Her maid went to call her, but finding it difficult to wake her, left her asleep, and did not return until breakfast was over. Then finding her still asleep she became a little anxious, and meeting mistress Amanda, told her she was afraid mistress Dorothy was ill. But mistress Amanda was herself sleepy and cross, and gave her a sharp answer, whereupon the girl went to Lady Broughton. She, however, being on her way to morning mass, for it was Sunday, told her to let mistress Dorothy have her sleep out.

The noise of horses' hoofs upon the paving of the stone court roused her, and then in came the sounds of the organ from the chapel. She rose confounded, and hurrying to the window drew back the curtain. The same moment Lord Herbert walked from the hall into the fountain-court in riding dress, followed by some forty or fifty officers, the noise of whose armour and feet and voices dispelled at once the dim Sabbath feeling that hung vapour-like about the place. They gathered around the white horse, leaning or sitting on the marble basin, some talking in eager groups, others folding their arms in silence, listening, or lost heedless in their own thoughts, while their leader entered the staircase door at the right-hand corner of the western gate, the nearest way to his wife's apartment of the building.

Now Dorothy had gone to sleep in perplexity, and all through her dreams had been trying to answer the question what course she should take with regard to the nocturnal intrusion. If she told Lady Margaret she could but go with it to the Marquis , and he was but just recovering from an attack of the gout, and ought not to be troubled except it were absolutely necessary. Was it, or was it not, necessary? Or was there no one else to whom she might with propriety betake herself in her doubt, Lord Charles or Dr. Bayly? But here now was Lord Herbert come back, and doubt there was none any more. She dressed herself in tremulous haste, and hurried to Lady Margaret's room, where she hoped to see him. No one was there, and she tried the nursery, but finding only Molly and her attendant, returned to the parlour, and there seated herself to wait, supposing Lady Margaret and he had gone together to morning service.

They had really gone to the oak parlour, whither the Marquis generally made his first move after an attack that had confined him to his room; for in the large window of that parlour, occupying nearly the whole side of it towards the moat, he generally sat when well enough to be about and take cognizance of what was going on; and there they now found him.

'Welcome home, Herbert!' he said, kindly, holding out his hand. 'And how does my wild Irishwoman this morning? Crying her eyes out because her husband is come back, eh? But, Herbert, lad, whence is all that noise of spurs and scabbards, and in the fountain court, too? I heard them go clanking and clattering through the hall like a torrent of steel! Here I sit, a poor gouty old man, deserted of my children and servants, all gone to church, to serve a better Master, not a page or a maid left me to send out to see and bring me word what is the occasion thereof! I was on the point of hobbling to the door myself when you came.'

'Being on my way to the forest of Dean, my lord, and coming round by Raglan to inquire after you and my lady, I did bring with me some of my officers to dine and drink your lordship's health on our way.'

'You shall all be welcome, though I fear I shall not make one,' said the Marquis , with a grimace, for just then he had a twinge of the gout.

'I am sorry to see you suffer, sir,' said his son.

'Man is born unto trouble as the sparks fly upward,' returned the Marquis, giving a kick with the leg which contained his inheritance; and then came a pause, during which Lady Margaret left the room.

'My lord,' said Herbert at length, with embarrassment, and forcing himself to speak, 'I am sorry to trouble you again, after all the money, enough to build this castle from the foundations—'

'Ah! ha!' interjected the Marquis, but Lord Herbert went on—

'which you have already spent on behalf of the king, my master, but—'

'YOUR master, Herbert!' said the Marquis, testily. 'Well?'

'I must have some more money for his pressing necessities.' In his self-compulsion he had stumbled upon the wrong word.

'MUST you?' cried the Marquis angrily. 'Pray take it.'

And drawing the keys of his treasury from the pocket of his frieze coat, he threw them down on the table before him. Lord Herbert reddened like a girl, and looked as much abashed as if he had been caught in something of which he was ashamed. One moment he stood thus, then said,

'Sir, the word was out before I was aware. I do not intend to put it into force. I pray will you put up your key again?'

'Truly, son,' replied the Marquis, still testily, but in a milder tone, 'I shall think my keys not safe in my pocket whilst you have so many swords by your side; nor that I have the command of my house whilst you have so many officers in it; nor that I am at my own disposal, whilst you have so many commanders.'

'My lord,' replied Herbert, 'I do not intend that they shall stay in the castle; I mean they shall be gone.'

'I pray, let them. And have care that MUST do not stay behind,' said the Marquis. 'But let them have their dinner first, lad.'

Lord Herbert bowed, and left the room. Thereupon, in the presence of Lady Margaret, who just then re-entered, good Dr. Bayly, who, unperceived by Lord Herbert in his pre-occupation, had been present during the interview, stepped up to the Marquis and said:

'My good lord, the honourable confidence your lordship has reposed in me boldens me to do my duty as, in part at least, your lordship's humble spiritual adviser.'

'Thou shouldst want no boldening to do thy duty, doctor,' said the Marquis, making a wry face.

'May I then beg of your lordship to consider whether you have not been more severe with your noble son than the occasion demanded, seeing not only was the word uttered by a lapse of the tongue, but yourself heard my Lord express much sorrow for the overslip?'

'What!' said Lady Herbert, something merrily, but looking in the face of her father-in-law with a little anxious questioning in her eyes, 'has my Lord been falling out with my Ned?'

'Hark ye, daughter!' answered the Marquis , his face beaming with restored good-humour, for the twinge in his toe had abated, 'and you too, my good chaplain! if my son be dejected, I can raise him when I please; but it is a question, if he should once take a head, whether I could bring him lower when I list. Ned was not wont to use such courtship to me, and I believe he intended a better word for his father; but MUST was for the king.'

Returning to her own room, Lady Margaret found Dorothy waiting for her.

'Well, my little lig-a-bed!' she said sweetly, 'what is amiss with thee? Thou lookest but soberly.'

'I am well, madam; and that I look soberly,' said Dorothy, 'you will not wonder when I tell you wherefore. But first, if it please you, I would pray for my lord's presence, that he too may know all.'

'Holy mother! what is the matter, child?' cried Lady Margaret, of late easily fluttered. 'Is it my Lord Herbert you mean, or my Lord of Worcester?'

'My Lord Herbert, my lady. I dread lest he should be gone ere I have found a time to tell him.'

'He rides again after dinner,' said Lady Margaret.

'Then, dear my lady, if you would keep me from great doubt and disquiet, let me have the ear of my Lord for a few moments.'

Lady Margaret rang for her page, and sent him to find his master and request his presence in her parlour.

Within five minutes Lord Herbert was with them, and within five more, Dorothy had ended her tale of the night, uninterrupted save by Lady Margaret's exclamations of sympathy.

'And now, my lord, what am I to do?' she asked in conclusion.

Lord Herbert made no answer for a few moments, but walked up and down the room. Dorothy thought he looked angry as well as troubled. He burst at length into a laugh, however, and said merrily,

'I have it, ladies! I see how we may save my father much annoyance without concealment, for nothing must be concealed from him that in any way concerns the house. But the annoyance arising from any direct attempt at discovering the wrongdoers would be endless, and its failure almost certain. But now, as I would plan it, instead of trouble my father shall have laughter, and instead of annoyance such a jest as may make him good amends for the wrong done him by the breach of his household laws. Caspar has explained to you all concerning the water-works, I believe, cousin?'

'All, my lord. I may without presumption affirm that I can, so long as there arises no mishap, with my own hand govern them all. Caspar has for many weeks left everything to me, save indeed the lighting of the furnace-fire.'

'That is as I would have it, cousin. So soon then as it is dark this evening, you will together, you and Caspar, set the springs which lie under the first stone of the paving of the bridge. Thereafter, as you know, the first foot set upon it will drop the drawbridge to the stone bridge, and the same instant convert the two into an aqueduct, filled with a rushing torrent from the reservoir, which will sweep the intruders away. Before they shall have either gathered their discomfited wits or raised their prostrate bones, my father will be out upon them, nor shall they find shelter for their shame ere every soul in the castle has witnessed their disgrace.'

'I had thought of the plan, my lord; but I dreaded the punishment might be too severe, not knowing what the water might do upon them.'

'There will be no danger to life, and little to limb,' said his lordship. 'The torrent will cease flowing the moment they are swept from the bridge. But they shall be both bruised and shamed; and,' added his lordship, with an oath such as seldom crossed his lips, 'in such times as these, they will well deserve what shall befall them. Intruding hounds! But you must take heed, cousin Dorothy, that you forget not that you have yourself done. Should you have occasion to go on the bridge after setting your vermin-trap, you must not omit to place your feet precisely where Caspar will show you, else you will have to ride a watery horse half-way, mayhap to the marble one, except indeed he throw you from his back against the chapel-door.'

When her husband talked in long sentences, as he was not unfrequently given to do, Lady Margaret, even when their sequences were not very clear, seldom interrupted him: she had learned that she gained more by letting him talk on; for however circuitous the route he might take, he never forgot where he was going. He might obscure his object, but there it always was. He was now again walking up and down the room, and, perceiving that he had not yet arranged all to his satisfaction, she watched him with merriment in her Irish eyes, and waited.

'I have it!' he cried again. 'It shall be so, and my father shall thus have immediate notice. The nights are weekly growing warmer, and he will not therein be tempted to his hurt. Our trusty and well-beloved cousin Dorothy, we herewith, in presence of our liege and lovely lady, appoint thee our deputy during our absence. No one but thyself hath a right to cross the bridge after dark, save Caspar and the governor, whom with my father I shall inform and warn concerning what is to be done. But I will myself adjust the escape, so that the torrent shall not fall too powerful; Caspar must connect it with the drawbridge, whose fall will then open it. And pray remind him to see first that all the hinges and joints concerned be well greased, that it may fall instantly.'

So saying, he left the room, and sought out Caspar, with whom he contrived the ringing of a bell in the Marquis 's chamber by the drawbridge in its fall, the arrangement for which Caspar was to carry out that same evening after dark. He next sought his father, and told him and his brother Charles the whole story; nor did he find himself wrong in his expectation that the prospect of so good a jest would go far to console the Marquis for the annoyance of finding that his household was not quite such a pattern one as he had supposed. That there was anything of conspiracy or treachery involved, he did not for a moment believe.

After dinner, while the horses were brought out, Lord Herbert went again to his wife's room. There was little Molly waiting to bid him good-bye, and she sat upon his knee until it was time for him to go. The child's looks made his heart sad, and his wife could not restrain her tears when she saw him gaze upon her so mournfully. It was with a heavy heart that, when the moment of departure came, he rose, gave her into her mother's arms, clasped them both in one embrace, and hurried from the room. He ought to be a noble king for whom such men and women make such sacrifices.

To witness such devotion on the part of personages to whom she looked up with such respect and confidence, would have been in itself more than sufficient to secure for its object the unquestioning partisanship of Dorothy; partisan already, it raised her prejudice to a degree of worship which greatly narrowed what she took for one of the widest gulfs separating her from the creed of her friends. The favourite dogma of the school-master-king, the offspring of his pride and weakness, had found fitting soil in Dorothy. When, in the natural growth of the confidence reposed in her by her protectors, she came to have some idea of the immensity of the sums spent by them on behalf of his son, had, indeed, ere the close of another year read the king's own handwriting and signature in acknowledgment of a debt of a quarter of a million, she took it only as an additional sign, for additional proof there was no room, of their ever admirable devotion to his divine right. That the Marquis and his son were catholics served but to glorify the right to which a hostile faith yielded such practical homage.

Immediately after nightfall she repaired to Caspar, and between them everything was speedily arranged for the carrying out of Lord Herbert's counter-plot.

But night after night passed, and the bell in the Marquis 's room remained voiceless.

CHAPTER XX

MOLLY AND THE WHITE HORSE

Meantime Lord Herbert came and went. There was fighting here and fighting there, castles taken, defended, re-taken, here a little success and there a worse loss, now on this side and now on that; but still, to say the best, the king's affairs made little progress; and for Mary Somerset, her body and soul made progress in opposite directions.

There was a strange pleasant mixture of sweet fretfulness and trusting appeal in her. Children suffer less because they feel that all is right when father or mother is with them; grown people from whom this faith has vanished ere it has led them to its original fact, may well be miserable in their sicknesses.

She lay moaning one night in her crib, when suddenly she opened her eyes and saw her mother's hand pressed to her forehead. She was imitative, like most children, and had some very old-fashioned ways of speech.

'Have you got a headache, madam?' she asked.

'Yes, my Molly,' answered her mother.

'Then you will go to mother Mary. She will take you on her knee, madam. Mothers is for headaches. Oh me! my headache, madam!'

The poor mother turned away. It was more than she could bear alone. Dorothy entered the room, and she rose and left it, that she might go to mother Mary as the child had said.

Dorothy's cares were divided between the duties of naiad and nursemaid, for the child clung to her as to no one else except her mother. The thing that pleased her best was to see the two whale-like spouts rise suddenly from the nostrils of the great white horse, curve away from each other aloft in the air, and fall back into the basin on each side of him. 'See horse spout,' she would say moanfully; and that instant, if Dorothy was not present, a messenger would be despatched to her. On a bright day this would happen repeatedly. For the sake of renewing her delight, the instant she turned from it, satisfied for the moment, the fountain ceased to play, and the horse remained spoutless, awaiting the revival of the darling's desire; for she was not content to see him spouting: she must see him spout. Then again she would be carried forth to the verge of the marble basin, and gazing up at the rearing animal would say, in a tone daintily wavering betwixt entreaty and command, 'Spout, horse, spout,' and Dorothy, looking down from the far-off summit of the tower, and distinguishing by the attitude of the child the moment when she uttered her desire, would instantly, with one turn of her hand, send the captive water shooting down its dark channel to reascend in sunny freedom.

If little Mary Somerset was counted a strange child, the wisdom with which she was wise is no more unnatural because few possess it, than the death of such is premature because they are yet children. They are small fruits whose ripening has outstripped their growth. Of such there are some who, by the hot-house assiduities of their friends, heating them with sulphurous stoves, and watering them with subacid solutions, ripen into insufferable prigs. For them and for their families it is well that Death the gardener should speedily remove them into the open air. But there are others who, ripening from natural, that is divine causes and influences, are the daintiest little men and women, gentle in the utmost peevishness of their lassitude, generous to share the gifts they most prize, and divinely childlike in their repentances. Their falling from the stalk is but the passing from the arms of their mothers into those of, God knows whom, which is more than enough.

The chief part of little Molly's religious lessons, I do not mean training, consisted in a prayer or two in rhyme, and a few verses of the kind then in use among catholics. Here is a prayer which her nurse taught her, as old, I take it, as Chaucer's time at least:—

Hail be thou, Mary, that high sittest in throne!
I beseech thee, sweet lady, grant me my boon
Jesus to love and dread, and my life to amend soon,
And bring me to that bliss that never shall be done.

And here are some verses quite as old, which her mother taught her. I give them believing that in understanding and coming nearer to our fathers and mothers who are dead, we understand and come nearer to our brothers and sisters who are alive. I change nothing but the spelling, and a few of the forms of the words.

Jesu, Lord, that madest me,
And with thy blessed blood hast bought,
Forgive that I have grieved thee
With word, with will, and eke with thought.

Jesu, for thy wounds' smart,
On feet and on thine hands two,
Make me meek and low of heart,
And thee to love as I should do.

Jesu, grant me mine asking,
Perfect patience in my disease,
And never may I do that thing
That should thee in any wise displease.

Jesu, most comfort for to see
Of thy saints every one,
Comfort them that careful be,
And help them that be woe-begone.

Jesu, keep them that be good,
And amend them that have grieved thee,
And send them fruits of early food,
As each man needeth in his degree.

Jesu, that art, without lies,
Almighty God in trinity,
Cease these wars, and send us peace
With lasting love and charity.

Jesu, that art the ghostly stone
Of all holy church in middle-earth,
Bring thy folds and flocks in one,
And rule them rightly with one herd.

Jesu, for thy blissful blood,
Bring, if thou wilt, those souls to bliss
From whom I have had any good,
And spare that they have done amiss.

This old-fashioned hymn Lady Margaret had learned from her grandmother, who was an Englishwoman of the pale. She also had learned it from her grandmother.

One day, by some accident, Dorothy had not reached her post of naiad before Molly arrived in presence of her idol, the white horse, her usual application to which was thence for the moment in vain. Having waited about three seconds in perfect patience, she turned her head slowly round, and gazed in her nurse's countenance with large questioning eyes, but said nothing. Then she turned again to the horse. Presently a smile broke over her face, and she cried in the tone of one who had made a great discovery,

'Horse has ears of stone: he cannot hear, Molly.'

Instantly thereupon she turned her face up to the sky, and said,

'Dear holy Mary, tell horse to spout.'

That moment up into the sun shot the two jets. Molly clapped her little hands with delight and cried,

'Thanks, dear holy Mary! I knowed thou would do it for Molly. Thanks, madam!'

The nurse told the story to her mistress, and she to Dorothy. It set both of them feeling, and Dorothy thinking besides.

'It cannot be,' she thought, 'but that a child's prayer will reach its goal, even should she turn her face to the west or the north instead of up to the heavens! A prayer somewhat differs from a bolt or a bullet.'

'How you protestants CAN live without a woman to pray to!' said Lady Margaret.

'Her son Jesus never refused to hear a woman, and I see not wherefore I should go to his mother, madam,' said Dorothy, bravely.

'Thou and I will not quarrel, Dorothy,' returned Lady Margaret sweetly; 'for sure am I that would please neither the one nor the other of them.'

Dorothy kissed her hand, and the subject dropped.

After that, Molly never asked the horse to spout, or if she happened to do so, would correct herself instantly, and turn her request to the mother Mary. Nor did the horse ever fail to spout, notwithstanding an evil thought which arose in the protestant part of Dorothy's mind, the temptation, namely, to try the effect upon Molly of a second failure. All the rest of her being on the instant turned so violently protestant against the suggestion, that no parley with it was possible, and the conscience of her intellect cowered before the conscience of her heart.

It was from this fancy of the child's for the spouting of the horse that it came to be known in the castle that mistress Dorothy was ruler of Raglan waters. In Lord Herbert's absence not a person in the place but she and Caspar understood their management, and except Lady Margaret, the Marquis , and Lord Charles, no one besides even knew of the existence of such a contrivance as the water-shoot or artificial cataract.

Every night Dorothy and Caspar together set the springs of it, and every morning Caspar detached the lever connecting the stone with the drawbridge.

CHAPTER XXI

THE DAMSEL WHICH FELL SICK

From within the great fortress, like the rough husk whence the green lobe of a living tree was about to break forth, a lovely child-soul, that knew neither of war nor ambition, knew indeed almost nothing save love and pain, was gently rising as from the tomb. The bonds of the earthly life that had for ever conferred upon it the rights and privileges of humanity were giving way, and little, white-faced, big-eyed Molly was leaving father and mother and grandfather and spouting horse and all, to find, what? To find what she wanted, and wait a little for what she loved.

One sultry evening in the second week of June, the weather had again got inside the inhabitants of the castle, forming different combinations according to the local atmosphere it found in each. Clouds had been slowly steaming up all day from several sides of the horizon, and as the sun went down, they met in the zenith. Not a wing seemed to be abroad under heaven, so still was the region of storms. The air was hot and heavy and hard to breathe, whether from lack of life, or too much of it, oppressing the narrow and weak recipients thereof, as the sun oppresses and extinguishes earthly fires, I at least cannot say. It was weather that made SOME dogs bite their masters, made most of the maids quarrelsome, and all the men but one or two more or less sullen, made Dorothy sad, Molly long after she knew not what, her mother weep, her grandfather feel himself growing old, and the hearts of all the lovers, within and without the castle, throb for the comfort of each other's lonely society. The fish lay still in the ponds, the pigeons sat motionless on the roof-ridges, and the fountains did not play; for Dorothy's heart was so heavy about Molly, that she had forgotten them.

The Marquis , fond of all his grandchildren, had never taken special notice of Molly beyond what she naturally claimed as youngest. But when it appeared that she was one of the spring-flowers of the human family, so soon withdrawing thither whence they come, he found that she began to pull at his heart, not merely with the attraction betwixt childhood and age, in which there is more than the poets have yet sung, but with the dearness which the growing shadow of death gives to all upon whom it gathers. The eyes of the child seemed to nestle into his bosom. Every morning he paid her a visit, and every morning it was clear that little Molly's big heart had been waiting for him. The young as well as the old recognize that they belong to each other, despite the unwelcome intervention of wrinkles and baldness and toothlessness. Molly's eyes brightened when she heard his steps at the door, and ere he had come within her sight, where she lay half-dressed on her mother's bed, tented in its tall carved posts and curtains of embroidered silk, the figures on which gave her so much trouble all the half-delirious night long, her arms would be stretched out to him, and the words would be trembling on her lips, 'Prithee, tell me a tale, sir.'

'Which tale wouldst thou have, my Molly?' the grandsire would say: it was the regular form of each day's fresh salutation; and the little one would answer, 'Of the good Jesu,' generally adding, 'and of the damsel which fell sick and died.'

Torn as the country was, all the good grandparents, catholic and protestant, royalist and puritan, told their children the same tales about the same man; and I suspect there was more then than there is now of that kind of oral teaching, for which any amount of books written for children is a sadly poor substitute.

Although Molly asked oftenest for the tale of the damsel who came alive again at the word of the man who knew all about death, she did not limit her desires to the repetition of what she knew already; and in order to keep his treasure supplied with things new as well as old, the Marquis went the oftener to his Latin bible to refresh his memory for Molly's use, and was in both ways, in receiving and in giving, a gainer. When the old man came thus to pour out his wealth to the child, Lady Margaret then first became aware what a depth both of religious knowledge and feeling there was in her father-in-law. Neither sir Toby Mathews, nor Dr. Bayly, who also visited her at times, ever, with the torch of their talk, lighted the lamps behind those great eyes, whose glass was growing dull with the vapours from the grave; but her grandfather's voice, the moment he began to speak to her of the good Jesu, brought her soul to its windows.

This sultry evening Molly was restless. 'Madam! madam!' she kept calling to her mother, for, like so many of such children, her manners and modes of speech resembled those of grown people, 'What wouldst thou, chicken?' her mother would ask. 'Madam, I know not,' the child would answer. Twenty times in an hour, as the evening went on, almost the same words would pass between them. At length, once more, 'Madam! madam!' cried the child. 'What would my heart's treasure?' said the mother; and Molly answered, 'Madam, I would see the white horse spout.'

With a glance and sign to her mistress. Dorothy rose and crept from the room, crossed the court and the moat, and dragged her heavy heart up the long stair to the top of the keep. Arrived there, she looked down through a battlement, and fixed her eyes on a certain window, whence presently she caught the wave of a signal-handkerchief.

At the open window stood Lady Margaret with Molly in her arms. The night was so warm that the child could take no hurt; and indeed what could hurt her, with the nameless fever-moth within, fretting a passage for the new winged body which, in the pains of a second birth, struggled to break from its dying chrysalis.

'Now, Molly, tell the horse to spout,' said Lady Margaret, with such well-simulated cheerfulness as only mothers can put on with hearts ready to break.

'Mother Mary, tell the horse to spout,' said Molly; and up went the watery parabolas.

The old flame of delight flushed the child's cheek, like the flush in the heart of a white rose. But it died almost instantly, and murmuring, 'Thanks, good madam!' whether to mother Mary or mother Margaret little mattered, Molly turned towards the bed, and her mother knew at her heart that the child sought her last sleep, as we call it, God forgive us our little faith! 'Madam!' panted the child, as she laid her down. 'Darling?' said the mother. 'Madam, I would see my Lord Marquis .' 'I will send and ask him to come.' 'Let Robert say that Molly is going, going, where is Molly going, madam?' 'Going to mother Mary, child,' answered Lady Margaret, choking back the sobs that would have kept the tears company. 'And the good Jesu?' 'Yes.'—'And the good God over all?' 'Yes, yes.' 'I want to tell my Lord Marquis . Pray, madam, let him come, and quickly.'

His lordship entered, pale and panting. He knew the end was approaching. Molly stretched out to him one hand instead of two, as if her hold upon earth were half yielded. He sat down by the bedside, and wiped his forehead with a sigh.

'Thee tired too, Marquis ?' asked the odd little love-bird.

'Yes, I am tired, my Molly. Thou seest I am so fat.'

'Shall I ask the good mother, when I go to her, to make thee spare like Molly?'

'No, Molly, thou need'st not trouble her about that. Ask her to make me good.'

'Would it then be easier to make thee good than to make thee spare, Marquis ?'

'No, child—much harder, alas!'

'Then why—?' began Molly; but the Marquis perceiving her thought, made haste to prevent it, for her breath was coming quick and weak.

'But it is so much better worth doing, you see. If she makes me good, she will have another in heaven to be good to.'

'Then I know she will. But I will ask her. Mother Mary has so many to mind, she might be forgetting.'

After this she lay very quiet with her hand in his. All the windows of the room were open, and from the chapel came the mellow sounds of the organ. Delaware had captured Tom Fool and got him to blow the bellows, and through the heavy air the music surged in. Molly was dozing a little, and she spoke as one that speaks in a dream.

'The white horse is spouting music,' she said. 'Look! See how it goes up to mother Mary. She twists it round her distaff and spins it with her spindle. See, Marquis , see! Spout, horse, spout.'

She lay silent again for a long time. The old man sat holding her hand; her mother sat on the farther side of the bed, leaning against one of the foot-posts, and watching the white face of her darling with eyes in which love ruled distraction. Dorothy sat in one of the window-seats, and listened to the music, which still came surging in, for still the fool blew the bellows, and the blind youth struck the keys. And still the clouds gathered overhead and sunk towards the earth; and still the horse, which Dorothy had left spouting, threw up his twin-fountain, whose musical plash in the basin as it fell mingled with the sounds of the organ.

'What is it?' said Molly, waking up. 'My head doth not ache, and my heart doth not beat, and I am not affrighted. What is it? I am not tired. Marquis , are you no longer tired? Ah, now I know! He cometh! He is here! Marquis , the good Jesu wants Molly's hand. Let him have it, Marquis . He is lifting me up. I am quite well—quite—'

The sentence remained broken. The hand which the Marquis had yielded, with the awe of one in bodily presence of the Holy, and which he saw raised as if in the grasp of one invisible, fell back on the bed, and little Molly was quite well.

But she left sick hearts behind. The mother threw herself on the bed, and wailed aloud. The Marquis burst into tears, left the room, and sought his study. Mechanically he took his Confessio Amantis, and sat down, but never opened it; rose again and took his Shakespere, opened it, but could not read; rose once more, took his Vulgate, and read:

'Quid turbamini, et ploratis? puella non est mortua, sed dormit.'

He laid that book also down, fell on his knees, and prayed for her who was not dead but sleeping.

Dorothy, filled with awe, rather from the presence of the mother of the dead than death itself, and feeling that the mother would rather be alone with her dead, also left the room, and sought her chamber, where she threw herself upon the bed. All was still save the plashing of the fountain, for the music from the chapel had ceased.

The storm burst in a glare and a peal. The rain fell in straight lines and huge drops, which came faster and faster, drowning the noise of the fountain, till the sound of it on the many roofs of the place was like the trampling of an army of horsemen, and every spout was gurgling musically with full throat. The one court was filled with a clashing upon its pavement, and the other with a soft singing upon its grass, with which mingled a sound as of little castanets from the broad leaves of the water-lilies in the moat. Ever and anon came the lightning, and the great bass of the thunder to fill up the psalm.

At the first thunderclap Lady Margaret fell on her knees and prayed in an agony for the little soul that had gone forth into the midst of the storm. Like many women she had a horror of lightning and thunder, and it never came into her mind that she who had so loved to see the horse spout was far more likely to be revelling in the elemental tumult, with all the added ecstasy of new-born freedom and health, than to be trembling like her mortal mother below.

Dorothy was not afraid, but she was heavy and weary; the thunder seemed to stun her and the lightning to take the power of motion from the shut eyelids through which it shone. She lay without moving, and at length fell fast asleep.

To the Marquis alone of the mourners the storm came as a relief to his overcharged spirit. He had again opened his New Testament, and tried to read; but if the truths which alone can comfort are not at such a time present to the spirit, the words that embody them will seldom be of much avail. When the thunder burst he closed the book and went to the window, flung it wide, and looked out into the court. Like a tide from the plains of innocent heaven through the sultry passionate air of the world, came the coolness to his brow and heart. Oxygen, ozone, nitrogen, water, carbonic acid, is it? Doubtless and other things, perhaps, which chemistry cannot detect. Nevertheless, give its parts what names you will, its whole is yet the wind of the living God to the bodies of men, his spirit to their spirits, his breath to their hearts. When I learn that there is no primal intent, only chance, in the unspeakable joy that it gives, I shall cease to believe in poetry, in music, in woman, in God. Nay, I must have already ceased to believe in God ere I could believe that the wind that bloweth where it listeth is free because God hath forgotten it, and that it bears from him no message to me.

CHAPTER XXII

THE CATARACT

In the midst of a great psalm, on the geyser column of which his spirit was borne heavenward, young Delaware all of a sudden found the keys dumb beneath his helpless fingers: the bellows was empty, the singing thing dead. He called aloud, and his voice echoed through the empty chapel, but no living response came back. Tom Fool had grown weary and forsaken him. Disappointed and baffled, he rose and left the chapel, not immediately from the organ loft, by a door and a few upward steps through the wall to the minstrels' gallery, as he had entered, but by the south door into the court, his readiest way to reach the rooms he occupied with his father, near the Marquis 's study. Hardly another door in either court was ever made fast except this one, which, merely in self-administered flattery of his own consequence, the conceited sacristan who assumed charge of the key, always locked at night. But there was no reason why Delaware should pay any respect to this, or hesitate to remove the bar securing one-half of the door, without which the lock retained no hold.

Although Tom had indeed deserted his post, the organist was mistaken as to the cause and mode of his desertion: oppressed like everyone else with the sultriness of the night, he had fallen fast asleep, leaning against the organ. The thunder only waked him sufficiently to render him capable of slipping from the stool on which he had lazily seated himself as he worked the lever of the bellows, and stretching himself at full length upon the floor; while the coolness that by degrees filled the air as the rain kept pouring, made his sleep sweeter and deeper. He lay and snored till midnight.

A bell rang in the Marquis 's chamber.

It was one of his lordship's smaller economic maxims that in every house, and the larger the house the more necessary its observance, the master thereof should have his private rooms as far apart from each other as might, with due respect to general fitness, be arranged for, in order that, to use his own figure, he might spread his skirts the wider over the place, and chiefly the part occupied by his own family and immediate attendants, thereby to give himself, without paying more attention to such matters than he could afford, a better chance of coming upon the trace of anything that happened to be going amiss. 'For,' he said, 'let a man have ever so many responsible persons about him, the final responsibility of his affairs yet returns upon himself.' Hence, while his bedroom was close to the main entrance, that is the gate to the stone court, the room he chose for retirement and study was over the western gate, that of the fountain-court, nearly a whole side of the double quadrangle away from his bedroom, and still farther from the library, which was on the other side of the main entrance, whence, notwithstanding, he would himself, gout permitting, always fetch any book he wanted. It was, therefore, no wonder that, being now in his study, the Marquis , although it rang loud, never heard the bell which Caspar had hung in his bedchamber. He was, however, at the moment, looking from a window which commanded the very spot, namely, the mouth of the archway, towards which the bell would have drawn his attention.

The night was still, the rain was over, and although the moon was clouded, there was light enough to recognise a known figure in any part of the court, except the shadowed recess where the door of the chapel and the archway faced each other, and the door of the hall stood at right angles to both.

Came a great clang that echoed loud through the court, followed by the roar of water. It sounded as if a captive river had broken loose, and grown suddenly frantic with freedom. The Marquis could not help starting violently, for his nerves were a good deal shaken. The same instant, ere there was time for a single conjecture, a torrent, visible by the light of its foam, shot from the archway, hurled itself against the chapel door, and vanished. Sad and startled as he was, Lord Worcester, requiring no explanation of the phenomenon now that it was completed, laughed aloud and hurried from the room.

When he had screwed his unwieldy form to the bottom of the stair, and came out into the court, there was Tom Fool flying across the turf in mortal terror, his face white as another moon, and his hair standing on end, visibly in the dull moonshine.

His terror had either deafened him, or paralysed the nerves of his obedience, for the first call of his master was insufficient to stop him. At the second, however, he halted, turned mechanically, went to him trembling, and stood before him speechless. But when the Marquis , to satisfy himself that he was really as dry as he seemed, laid his hand on his arm, the touch brought him to himself, and, assisted by his master's questions, he was able to tell how he had fallen asleep in the chapel, had waked but a minute ago, had left it by the minstrels' gallery, had reached the floor of the hall, and was approaching the western door, which was open, in order to cross the court to his lodging near the watch-tower, when a hellish explosion, followed by the most frightful roaring, mingled with shrieks and demoniacal laughter, arrested him; and the same instant, through the open door, he saw, as plainly as he now saw his noble master, a torrent rush from the archway, full of dim figures, wallowing and shouting. The same moment they all vanished, and the flood poured into the hall, wetting him to the knees, and almost carrying him off his legs.

Here the Marquis professed profound astonishment, remarking that the water must indeed have been thickened with devils to be able to lay hold of Tom's legs.

'Then,' pursued Tom, reviving a little, 'I summoned up all my courage—'

'No great feat,' said the Marquis .

But Tom went on unabashed.

'I summoned up the whole of my courage,' he repeated, 'stepped out of the hall, carefully examined the ground, looked through the archway, saw nothing, and was walking slowly across the court to my lodging, pondering with myself whether to call my Lord governor or sir Toby Mathews, when I heard your lordship call me.'

'Tom! Tom! thou liest,' said the Marquis . 'Thou wast running as if all the devils in hell had been at thy heels.'

Tom turned deadly pale, a fresh access of terror overcoming his new-born hardihood.

'Who were they, thinkest thou, whom thou sawest in the water, Tom?' resumed his master. 'For what didst thou take them?'

Tom shook his head with an awful significance, looked behind him, and said nothing.

Perceiving there was no more to be got out of him, the Marquis sent him to bed. He went off shivering and shaking. Three times ere he reached the watch-tower his face gleamed white over his shoulder as he went. The next day he did not appear. He thought himself he was doomed, but his illness was only the prostration following upon terror.

In the version of the story which he gave his fellow-servants, he doubtless mingled the after visions of his bed with what he had when half-awake seen and heard through the mists of his startled imagination. His tale was this, that he saw the moat swell and rise, boil over in a mass, and tumble into the court as full of devils as it could hold, swimming in it, floating on it, riding it aloft as if it had been a horse; that in a moment they had all vanished again, and that he had not a doubt the castle was now swarming with them, in fact, he had heard them all the night long.

The Marquis walked up to the archway, saw nothing save the grim wall of the keep, impassive as granite crag, and the ground wet a long way towards the white horse; and never doubting he had lost his chance by taking Tom for the culprit, contented himself with the reflection that, whoever the night-walkers were, they had received both a fright and a ducking, and betook himself to bed, where, falling asleep at length, he saw little Molly in the arms of mother Mary, who, presently changing to his own Lady Anne that left him about a year before little Molly came, held out a hand to him to help him up beside them, whereupon the bubble sleep, unable to hold the swelling of his gladness, burst, and he woke just as the first rays of the sun smote the gilded cock on the bell-tower.

The noise of the falling drawbridge and the out-rushing water had roused Dorothy also, with most of the lighter sleepers in the castle; but when she and all the rest whose windows were to the fountain court, ran to them and looked out, they saw nothing but the flight of Tom Fool across the turf, its arrest by his master, and their following conference. The moon had broken through the clouds, and there was no mistaking either of their persons.

Meantime, inside the chapel door stood Amanda and Rowland, both dripping, and one of them crying as well. Thither, as into a safe harbour, the sudden flood had cast them; and it indicated no small amount of ready faculty in Scudamore that, half-stunned as he was, he yet had the sense, almost ere he knew where he was, to put up the long bar that secured the door.

All the time that the Marquis was drawing his story from Tom, they stood trembling, in great bewilderment yet very sensible misery, bruised, drenched, and horribly frightened, more even at what might be than by what had been. There was only one question, but that was hard to answer: what were they to do next? Amanda could contribute nothing towards its solution, for tears and reproaches resolve no enigmas. There were many ways of issue, whereof Rowland knew several; but their watery trail, if soon enough followed, would be their ruin as certainly as Hop-o'-my-Thumb's pebbles were safety to himself and his brothers. He stood therefore the very bond slave of perplexity, 'and, like a neutral to his will and matter, did nothing.'

Presently they heard the approaching step of the Marquis , which every one in the castle knew. It stopped within a few feet of them, and through the thick door they could hear his short asthmatic breathing.

They kept as still as their trembling, and the mad beating of their hearts, would permit. Amanda was nearly out of her senses, and thought her heart was beating against the door, and not against her own ribs. But the Marquis never thought of the chapel, having at once concluded that they had fled through the open hall. Had he not, however, been so weary and sad and listless, he would probably have found them, for he would at least have crossed the hall to look into the next court, and, the moon now shining brightly, the absence of all track on the floor where the traces of the brief inundation ceased, would have surely indicated the direction in which they had sought refuge.

The acme of terror happily endured but a moment. The sound of his departing footsteps took the ghoul from their hearts; they began to breathe, and to hope that the danger was gone. But they waited long ere at last they ventured, like wild animals overtaken by the daylight, to creep out of their shelter and steal back like shadows, but separately, Amanda first, and Scudamore some slow minutes after, to their different quarters. The tracks they could not help leaving in-doors were dried up before the morning.

Rowland had greater reason to fear discovery than anyone else in the castle, save one, would in like circumstances have had, and that one was his bedfellow in the ante-chamber to his master's bedroom. Through this room his lordship had to pass to reach his own; but so far was he from suspecting Rowland, or indeed any gentleman of his retinue, that he never glanced in the direction of his bed, and so could not discover that he was absent from it. Had Rowland but caught a glimpse of his own figure as he sneaked into that room five minutes after the Marquis had passed through it, believing his master was still in his study, where he had left his candles burning, he could hardly for some time have had his usual success in regarding himself as a fine gentleman.

Amanda Serafina did not show herself for several days. A bad cold in her head luckily afforded sufficient pretext for the concealment of a bad bruise upon her cheek. Other bruises she had also, but they, although more severe, were of less consequence.

For a whole fortnight the lovers never dared exchange a word.

In the morning the Marquis was in no mood to set any inquiry on foot. His little lamb had vanished from his fold, and he was sad and lonely. Had it been otherwise, possibly the shabby doublet in which Scudamore stood behind his chair the next morning, might have set him thinking; but as it was, it fell in so well with the gloom in which his own spirit shrouded everything, that he never even marked the change, and ere long Rowland began to feel himself safe.

CHAPTER XXIII

AMANDA - DOROTHY - LORD HERBERT

So also did Amanda; but not the less did she cherish feelings of revenge against her whom she more than suspected of having been the contriver of her harmful discomfiture. She felt certain that Dorothy had laid the snare into which they had fallen, with the hope if not the certainty of catching just themselves two in it, and she read in her, therefore, jealousy and cruelty as well as coldness and treachery. Rowland on the other hand was inclined to attribute the mishap to the displeasure of Lord Herbert, whose supernatural acquirements, he thought, had enabled him both to discover and punish their intrusion. Amanda, nevertheless, kept her own opinion, and made herself henceforth all eyes and ears for Dorothy, hoping ever to find a chance of retaliating, if not in kind yet in plentiful measure of vengeance. Dorothy's odd ways, lawless movements, and what the rest of the ladies counted her vulgar tastes, had for some time been the subject of remark to the gossiping portion of the castle community; and it seemed to Amanda that in watching and discovering what she was about when she supposed herself safe from the eyes of her equals and superiors, lay her best chance of finding a mode of requital. Nor was she satisfied with observation, but kept her mind busy on the trail, now of one, now of another vague-bodied revenge.

The charge of low tastes was founded upon the fact that there was not an artisan about the castle, from Caspar downwards, whom Dorothy did not know and address by his name; but her detractors, in drawing their conclusions from it, never thought of finding any related significance in another fact, namely, that there was not a single animal either, of consequence enough to have a name, which did not know by it. There were very few of the animals indeed which did not know her in return, if not by her name, yet by her voice or her presence, some of them even by her foot or her hand. She would wander about the farmyard and stables for an hour at a time, visiting all that were there, and specially her little horse, which she had long, oh, so long ago! named Dick, nor had taken his name from him any more than from Marquis .

The charge of lawlessness in her movements was founded on another fact as well, namely, that she was often seen in the court after dusk, and that not merely in running across to the keep, as she would be doing at all hours, but loitering about, in full view of the windows. It was not denied that this took place only when the organ was playing, but then who played the organ? Was not the poor afflicted boy, barring the blank of his eyes, beautiful as an angel? And was not mistress Dorothy too deep to be fathomed? And so the tattling streams flowed on, and the ears of mistress Amanda willingly listened to their music, nor did she disdain herself to contribute to the reservoir in which those of the castle whose souls thirsted after the minutiae of live biography, accumulated their stores of fact and fiction, conjecture and falsehood.

Lord Herbert came home to bury his little one, and all that was left behind of her was borne to the church of St. Cadocus, the parish church of Raglan, and there laid beside the Marquis 's father and mother. He remained with them a fortnight, and his presence was much needed to lighten the heavy gloom that had settled over both his wife and his father.

As if it were not enough to bury the bodies of the departed, there are many, and the Marquis and his daughter-in-law were of the number, who in a sense seek to bury their souls as well, making a graveyard of their own spirits, and laying the stone of silence over the memory of the dead. Such never speak of them but when compelled, and then almost as if to utter their names were an act of impiety. Not In Memoriam but In Oblivionem should be the inscription upon the tombs they raise. The memory that forsakes the sunlight, like the fishes in the underground river, loses its eyes; the cloud of its grief carries no rainbow; behind the veil of its twin-future burns no lamp fringing its edges with the light of hope. I can better, however, understand the hopelessness of the hopeless than their calmness along with it. Surely they must be upheld by the presence within them of that very immortality, against whose aurora they shut to their doors, then mourn as if there were no such thing.

Radiant as she was by nature, Lady Margaret, when sorrow came, could do little towards her own support. The Marquis said to himself, 'I am growing old, and cannot smile at grief so well as once on a day. Sorrow is a hawk more fell than I had thought.' The name of little Molly was never mentioned between them. But sudden floods of tears were the signs of the mother's remembrance; and the outbreak of ambushed sighs, which he would make haste to attribute to the gout, the signs of the grandfather's.

Dorothy, too, belonged in tendency to the class of the unspeaking. Her nature was not a bright one. Her spirit's day was evenly, softly lucent, like one of those clouded calm grey mornings of summer, which seem more likely to end in rain than sunshine.

Lord Herbert was of a very different temperament. He had hope enough in his one single nature to serve the whole castle, if only it could have been shared. The veil between him and the future glowed as if on fire with mere radiance, and about to vanish in flame. It was not that he more than one of the rest imagined he could see through it. For him it was enough that beyond it lay the luminous. His eyes, to those that looked on him, were lighted with its reflex.

Such as he, are, by those who love them not, misjudged as shallow. Depth to some is indicated by gloom, and affection by a persistent brooding, as if there were no homage to the past of love save sighs and tears. When they meet a man whose eyes shine, whose step is light, on whose lips hovers a smile, they shake their heads and say, 'There goes one who has never loved, and who therefore knows not sorrow.' And the man is one of those over whom death has no power; whom time nor space can part from those he loves; who lives in the future more than in the past! Has not his being ever been for the sake of that which was yet to come? Is not his being now for the sake of that which it shall be? Has he not infinitely more to do with the great future than the little past? The Past has descended into hell, is even now ascending glorified, and will, in returning cycle, ever and again greet our faith as the more and yet more radiant Future.

But even Lord Herbert had his moments of sad longing after his dainty Molly. Such moments, however, came to him, not when he was at home with his wife, but when he rode alone by his troops on a night march, or when, upon the eve of an expected battle, he sought sleep that he might fight the better on the morrow.

CHAPTER XXIV

THE GREAT MOGUL

One evening, Tom Fool, and a groom, his particular friend, were taking their pastime after a somewhat selfish fashion, by no means newly discovered in the castle, that of teasing the wild beasts. There was one in particular, a panther, which, in a special dislike to grimaces, had discovered a special capacity for being teased. Betwixt two of the bars of his cage, therefore, Tom was busy presenting him with one hideous puritanical face after another, in full expectation of a satisfactory outburst of feline rancour. But to their disappointment, the panther on this occasion seemed to have resolved upon a dignified resistance to temptation, and had withdrawn in sultry displeasure to the back of his cage, where he lay sideways, deigning to turn neither his back nor his face towards the inferior animal, at whom to cast but one glance, he knew, would be to ruin his grand Oriental sulks, and fly at the hideous ape-visage insulting him in his prison. It was tiresome of the brute. Tom Fool grew more daring and threw little stones at him, but the panther seemed only to grow the more imperturbable, and to heed his missiles as little as his grimaces.

At length, proceeding from bad to worse, as is always the way with fools, born or made, Tom betook himself to stronger measures.

The cages of the wild beasts were in the basement of the kitchen tower, with a little semicircular yard of their own before them. They were solid stone vaults, with open fronts grated with huge iron bars, our ancestors, whatever were their faults, did not err in the direction of flimsiness. Between two of these bars, then, Tom, having procured a long pole, proceeded to poke at the beast; but he soon found that the pole thickened too rapidly towards the end he held, to pass through the bars far enough to reach him. Thereupon, in utter fool-hardiness, backed by the groom, he undid the door a little way, and, his companion undertaking to prevent it from opening too far, pushed in the pole till it went right in the creature's face. One hideous yell, and neither of them knew what was occurring till they saw the tail of the panther disappearing over the six-foot wall that separated the cages from the stableyard. Tom fled at once for the stair leading up to the stone-court, while the groom, whose training had given him a better courage, now supplemented by the horror of possible consequences, ran to warn the stablemen and get help to recapture the animal.

The uproariest tumult of maddest barking which immediately arose from the chained dogs, entered the ears of all in the castle, at least every one possessed of dog-sympathies, and penetrated even those of the rather deaf host of the White Horse in Raglan village. Dorothy, sitting in her room, of course, heard it, and hearing it, equally of course, hurried to see what was the matter. The Marquis heard it where he sat in his study, but was in no such young haste as Dorothy: it was only after a little, when he found the noise increase, and certain other sounds mingle with it, that he rose in some anxiety and went to discover the cause.

Halfway across the stone court, Dorothy met Tom running, and the moment she saw his face, knew that something serious had happened.

'Get indoors, mistress,' he said, almost rudely, 'the devil is to pay down in the yard.' and ran on. 'Shut your door, master cook,' she heard him cry as he ran. 'The Great Mogul is out.'

And as she ran too, she heard the door of the kitchen close with a great bang.

But Dorothy was not running after the fool, or making for any door but that at the bottom of the library tower; for the first terror that crossed her mind was the possible fate of Dick, and the first comfort that followed, the thought of Marquis ; so she was running straight for the stable-yard, where the dogs, to judge by the way they tore their throats with barking, seemed frantic with rage.

No doubt the panther, when he cleared the wall, hoped exultant to find himself in the savage forest, instead of which he came down on the top of a pump, fell on the stones, and the same instant was caught in a hurricane of canine hate. A little hurt and a good deal frightened, for he had not endured such long captivity without debasement, he glared around him with sneaking enquiry. But the walls were lofty and he saw no gate, and feeling unequal at the moment to the necessary spring, he crept almost like a snake under what covert seemed readiest, and disappeared, just as the groom entering by a door in one of the walls began to look about for him in a style wherein caution predominated. Seeing no trace of him, and concluding that, as he had expected, the clamour of the dogs had driven him further, he went on, crossing the yard to find the men, whose voices he heard on the green at the back of the rick-yard, when suddenly he found that his arm was both broken and torn. The sight of the blood completed the mischief, and he fell down in a swoon.

Meantime Dorothy had reached the same door in the wall of the stableyard, and peeping in saw nothing but the dogs raging and RUGGING at their chains as if they would drag the earth itself after them to reach the enemy. She was one of those on whose wits, usually sedate in their motions, all sorts of excitement, danger amongst the rest, operate favourably. When she specially noticed the fury of Marquis , the same moment she perceived the danger in which he, that was, all the dogs, would be, if the panther should attack them one by one on the chain; not one of them had a chance. With the thought, she sped across the space between her and Marquis , who, I really cannot say WHICH concerning such a dog, was fortunately not very far from the door. Feeling him a little safer now that she stood by his side, she resumed her ocular search for the panther, or any further sign of his proximity, but with one hand on the dog's collar, ready in an instant to seize it with both, and unclasp it.

Nor had she to look long, for all the dogs were straining their chains in one direction, and all their lines converged upon a little dark shed, where stood a cart: under the cart, between its lower shafts, she caught a doubtful luminousness, as if the dark while yet dark had begun to throb with coming light. This presently seemed to resolve itself, and she saw, vaguely but with conviction, two huge lamping cat-eyes. I will not say she felt no fear, but she was not terrified, for she had great confidence in Marquis . One moment she stood bethinking herself, and one glance she threw at the spot where her mastiff's chain was attached to his collar: she would fain have had him keep the latter to defend his neck and throat: but alas! it was as she knew well enough before, the one was riveted to the other, and the two must go together.

And now first, as she raised her head from the momentary inspection, she saw the groom lying on the ground within a few yards of the shed. Her first thought was that the panther had killed him, but ere a second had time to rise in her mind, she saw the terrible animal creeping out from under the cart, with his chin on the ground, like the great cat he was, and making for the man.

The brute had got the better of his fall, and finding he was not pursued, the barking of the dogs, to which in moderation he was sufficiently accustomed, had ceased to confuse him, he had recovered his awful self, and was now scenting prey. Had the man made a single movement he would have been upon him like lightning; but the few moments he took in creeping towards him, gave Dorothy all the time she needed. With resolute, though trembling hands, she undid Marquis 's collar.

The instant he was free, the fine animal went at the panther straight and fast like a bolt from a cross-bow. But Dorothy loved him too well to lose a moment in sending even a glance after him. Leaving him to his work, she flew to hers, which lay at the next kennel, that of an Irish wolf-hound, whose curling lip showed his long teeth to the very root, and whose fury had redoubled at the sight of his rival shooting past him free for the fight. So wildly did he strain upon his collar, that she found it took all her strength to unclasp it. In a much shorter time, however, than she fancied, O'Brien too was on the panther, and the sounds of cano-feline battle seemed to fill every cranny of her brain.

But now she heard the welcome cries of men and clatter of weapons. Some, alarmed by Tom Fool, came rushing from the guard-rooms down the stair, and others, chiefly farm-servants and grooms, who had heard the frightful news from two that were in the yard when the panther bounded over the wall, were approaching from the opposite side, armed with scythes and pitchforks, the former more dangerous to their bearers than to the beast.

Dorothy, into whom, girl as she was, either Bellona or Diana, or both, had entered, was now thoroughly excited by the conflict she ruled, although she had not wasted a moment in watching it. Having just undone the collar of the fourth dog, she was hounding him on with a cry, little needed, as she flew to let go the fifth, a small bull-terrier, mad with rage and jealousy, when the crowd swept between her and her game. The beast was captured, and the dogs taken off him, ere the terrier had had a taste or Dorothy a glimpse of the battle.

As the men with cart-ropes dragged the panther away, terribly torn by the teeth of the dogs, and Tom Fool was following them, with his hands in his pockets, looking sheepish because of the share he had had in letting him loose, and the share he had not had in securing him again, Dorothy was looking about for her friend Marquis . All at once he came bounding up to her, and, exultant in the sense of accomplished duty, leaped up against her, at once turning her into a sanguineous object frightful to behold; for his wounds were bad, although none of them were serious except one in his throat. This upon examination she found so severe that to replace his collar was out of the question. Telling him therefore to follow her, in the confidence that she might now ask for him what she would, she left the yard, went up the stair, and was crossing the stone court with the trusty fellow behind her, making a red track all the way, when out of the hall came the Marquis , looking a little frightened. He started when he saw her, and turned pale, but perceiving instantly from her look that, notwithstanding the condition of her garments, she was unhurt, he cast a glance at her now rather disreputable-looking attendant, and said,

'I told you so, mistress Dorothy! Now I understand! It is that precious mastiff of yours, and no panther of mine, that has been making this uproar in my quiet house! Nay, but he looks evil enough for any devil's work! Prithee keep him off me.'

He drew back, for the dog, not liking the tone in which he addressed his mistress, had taken a step nearer to him.

'My lord,' said Dorothy, as she laid hold of the animal, for the first and only time in her life a little inclined to be angry with her benefactor, 'you do my poor Marquis wrong. At the risk of his own life he has just saved your lordship's groom, Shafto, from being torn in pieces by the Great Mogul.'

While she spoke, some of those of the garrison who had been engaged in securing the animal came up into the court, and attracted the Marquis 's attraction by their approach, which, in the relaxation of discipline consequent on excitement, was rather tumultuous. At their head was Lord Charles, who had led them to the capture, and without whose ruling presence the enemy would not have been re-caged in twice the time. As they drew near, and saw Dorothy stand in battle-plight, with her dog beside her, even in their lord's presence they could not resist the impulse to cheer her. Annoyed at their breach of manners, the Marquis had not however committed himself to displeasure ere he spied a joke:

'I told you so, mistress Dorothy!' he said again. 'That rival of mine has, as I feared, already made a party against me. You see how my own knaves, before my very face, cheer my enemy! I presume, my lord,' he went on, turning to the mastiff, and removing his hat, 'it will be my wisdom to resign castle and title at once, and so forestall deposition.'

Marquis replied with a growl, and amidst subdued yet merry laughter, Lord Charles hastened to enlighten his father.

'My lord,' he said, 'the dog has done nobly as ever dog, and deserves reward, not mockery, which it is plain he understands, and likes not. But it was not the mastiff, it was his fair mistress I and my men presumed on saluting in your lordship's presence. No dog ever yet shook off collar of Cranford's forging; nor is Marquis the only dog that merits your lordship's acknowledgment: O'Brien and Tom Fool, the lurcher, I mean, seconded him bravely, and perhaps Strafford did best of all.'

'Prithee, now, take me with thee,' said the Marquis . 'Was, or was not the Great Mogul forth of his cage?'

'Indeed he was, my lord, and might be now in the fields but for cousin Vaughan there by your side.'

The Marquis turned and looked at her, but in his astonishment said nothing, and Lord Charles went on.

'When we got into the yard, there was the Great Mogul with three dogs upon him, and mistress Dorothy uncollaring Tom Fool and hounding him at the devilish brute; while poor Shafto, just waking up, lay on the stones, about three yards off the combat. It was the finest thing I ever saw, my lord.'

The Marquis turned again to Dorothy, and stared without speech or motion.

'Mean you—?' he said at length, addressing Lord Charles, but still staring at Dorothy; 'Mean you—?' he said again, half stammering, and still staring.

'I mean, my lord,' answered his son, 'that mistress Dorothy, with self-shown courage, and equal judgment as to time and order of attack, when Tom Fool had fled, and poor Shafto, already evil torn, had swooned from loss of blood, came to the rescue, stood her ground, and loosed dog after dog, her own first, upon the animal. And, by heaven! it is all owing to her that he is already secured and carried back to his cage, nor any great harm done save to the groom and the dogs, of which poor Strafford hath a hind leg crushed by the jaws of the beast, and must be killed.'

'He shall live,' cried the Marquis , 'as long as he hath legs enough to eat and sleep with. Mistress Dorothy,' he went on, turning to her once more, 'what is thy request? It shall be performed even to the half of—of my Marquis ate.'

'My lord,' returned Dorothy, 'it is a small deed I have strewn to gather such weighty thanks.'

'Be honest as well as brave, mistress. Mock me no modesty.' said the Marquis a little roughly.

'Indeed, my lord, I but spoke as I deemed. The thing HAD to be done, and I did but do it. Had there been room to doubt, and I had yet done well, then truly I might have earned your lordship's thanks. But good my lord, do not therefore recall the word spoken,' she added hurriedly, 'but grant me my boon. Your lordship sees my poor dog can endure no collar: let him therefore be my chamber-fellow until his throat be healed, when I shall again submit him to your lordship's mandate.'

'What you will, cousin. He is a noble fellow, and hath a right noble mistress.'

'Will you then, my Lord Charles, order a bucket of water to be drawn for me, that I may wash his wounds ere I take him to my chamber?'

Ten men at the word flew to the draw-well, but Lord Charles ordered them all back to the guard-room, except two whom he sent to fetch a tub. With his own hands he then drew three bucketfuls of water, which he poured into the tub, and by the side of the well, in the open paved court, Dorothy washed her four-legged hero, and then retired with him, to do a like office for herself.

The Marquis stood for some time in the gathering dusk, looking on, and smiling to see how the sullen animal allowed his mistress to handle even his wounds without a whine, not to say a growl, at the pain she must have caused him.

'I see, I see!' he said at length, 'I have no chance with a rival like that!' and turning away he walked slowly into the oak parlour, threw himself down in his great chair, and sat there, gazing at the eyeless face of the keep, but thinking all the time of the courage and patience of his rival, the mastiff.

'God made us both,' he said at length, 'and he can grant me patience as well as him;' and so saying he went to bed.

His washing over, the dog showed himself much exhausted, and it was with hanging head he followed his mistress up the grand staircase and the second spiral one that led yet higher to her chamber. Thither presently came Lady Elizabeth, carrying a cushion and a deerskin for him to lie upon, and it was with much apparent satisfaction that the wounded and wearied animal, having followed his tail but one turn, dropped like a log on his well-earned couch.

The night was hot, and Dorothy fell asleep with her door wide open.

In the morning Marquis was nowhere to be found. Dorothy searched for him everywhere, but in vain.

'It is because you mocked him, my lord,' said the governor to his father at breakfast. 'I doubt not he said to himself, "If I AM a dog, my Lord need not have mocked me, for I could not help it, and I did my duty."'

'I would make him an apology,' returned the Marquis , 'an' I had but the opportunity. Truly it were evil minded knowingly to offer insult to any being capable of so regarding it. But, Charles, I bethink me: didst ever learn how our friend got into the castle? It was assuredly thy part to discover that secret.'

'No, my lord. It hath never been found out in so far as I know.'

'That is an unworthy answer, Lord Charles. As governor of the castle, you ought to have had the matter thoroughly searched into.'

'I will see to it now, my lord,' said the governor, rising.

'Do, my lad,' returned his father.

And Lord Charles did inquire; but not a ray of light did he succeed in letting in upon the mystery. The inquiry might, however, have lasted longer and been more successful, had not Lord Herbert just then come home, with the welcome news of the death of Hampden, from a wound received in attacking prince Rupert at Chalgrove. He brought news also of prince Maurice's brave fight at Bath, and Lord Wilmot's victory over sir William Waller at Devizes, which latter, Lord Herbert confessed, yielded him some personal satisfaction, seeing he owed Waller more grudges than as a Christian he had well known how to manage: now he was able to bear him a less bitter animosity. The queen, too, had reached Oxford, bringing large reinforcement to her husband, and prince Rupert had taken Bristol, castle and all. Things were looking mighty hopeful, Lord Herbert was radiant, and Lady Margaret, for the first time since Molly's death, was merry. The castle was illuminated, and Marquis forgotten by all but Dorothy.

CHAPTER XXV

RICHARD HEYWOOD

So things looked ill for the puritans in general, and Richard Heywood had his full portion in the distribution of the evils allotted them. Following Lord Fairfax, he had shared his defeat by the Marquis of Newcastle on Atherton moor, where of his score of men he lost five, and was, along with his mare, pretty severely wounded. Hence it had become absolutely necessary for both of them, if they were to render good service at any near future, that they should have rest and tending. Towards the middle of July, therefore, Richard, followed by Stopchase, and several others of his men who had also been wounded and were in need of nursing, rode up to his father's door. Lady was taken off to her own stall, and Richard was led into the house by his father, without a word of tenderness, but with eyes and hands that waited and tended like those of a mother.

Roger Heywood was troubled in heart at the aspect of affairs. There was now a strong peace-party in the parliament, and to him peace and ruin seemed the same thing. If the parliament should now listen to overtures of accommodation, all for which he and those with whom he chiefly sympathised had striven, was in the greatest peril, and might be, if not irrecoverably lost, at least lost sight of, perhaps for a century. The thing that mainly comforted him in his anxiety was that his son had showed himself worthy, not merely in the matter of personal courage, which he took as a thing of course in a Heywood, but in his understanding of and spiritual relation to the questions really at issue, not those only which filled the mouths of men. For the best men and the weightiest questions are never seen in the forefront of the battle of their time, save by "larger other eyes than ours."

But now, from his wounds, as he thought, and the depression belonging to the haunting sense of defeat, a doubt had come to life in Richard's mind, which, because it was born IN weakness, he very pardonably looked upon as born OF weakness, and therefore regarded as itself weak and cowardly, whereas his mood had been but the condition that favoured its development. It came and came again, maugre all his self-recrimination because of it: what was all this fighting for? It was well indeed that nor king nor bishop should interfere with a man's rights, either in matters of taxation or worship, but the war could set nothing right either betwixt him and his neighbour, or betwixt him and his God.

There was in the mind of Richard, innate, but more rapidly developed since his breach with Dorothy, a strong tendency towards the supernatural, I mean by the word that which neither any one of the senses nor all of them together, can reveal. He was one of those young men, few, yet to be found in all ages of the world's history, who, in health and good earthly hope, and without any marked poetic or metaphysical tendency, yet know in their nature the need of conscious communion with the source of that nature, truly the veriest absurdity if there be no God, but as certainly the most absolute necessity of conscious existence if there be a first life from whom our life is born.

'Am I not free now?' he said to himself, as he lay on his bed in his own gable of the many-nooked house; 'Am I not free to worship God as I please? Who will interfere with me? Who can prevent me? As to form and ceremony, what are they, or what is the absence of them, to the worship in which my soul seeks to go forth? What the better shall I be when all this is over, even if the best of our party carry the day? Will Cromwell rend for me the heavy curtain, which, ever as I lift up my heart, seems to come rolling down between me and him whom I call my God? If I could pass within that curtain, what would Charles, or Laud, or Newcastle, or the mighty Cromwell himself and all his Ironsides be to me? Am I not on the wrong road for the high peak?'

But then he thought of others, of the oppressed and the superstitious, of injustice done and not endured, not wrapt in the pearly antidote of patience, but rankling in the soul; of priests who, knowing not God, substituted ceremonies for prayer, and led the seeking heart afar from its goal, and said that his arm could at least fight for the truth in others, if only his heart could fight for the truth in himself. No; he would go on as he had begun; for, might it not be the part of him who could take the form of an angel of light when he would deceive, to make use of inward truths, which might well be the strength of his own soul, to withdraw him from the duties he owed to others, and cause the heart of devotion to paralyze the arm of battle? Besides, was he not now in a low physical condition, and therefore the less likely to judge truly with regard to affairs of active outer life? His business plainly was to gain strength of body, that the fumes of weakness might no longer cloud his brain, and that, if he had to die for the truth, whether in others or in himself, he might die in power, like the blast of an exploding mine, and not like the flame of an expiring lamp. And certainly, as his body grew stronger, and the impulses to action, so powerful in all healthy youth, returned, his doubts grew weaker, and he became more and more satisfied that he had been in the right path.

Lady outstripped her master in the race for health, and after a few days had oats and barley in a profusion which, although far from careless, might well have seemed to her unlimited. Twice every day, sometimes oftener, Richard went to see her, and envied the rapidity of her recovery from the weakness which scanty rations, loss of blood, and the inflammation of her wounds had caused. Had there been any immediate call for his services, however, that would have brought his strength with it. Had the struggle been still going on upon the fields of battle instead of in the houses of words, he would have been well in half the time. But Waller and Essex were almost without an army between them, and were at bitter strife with each other, while the peace-party seemed likely to carry everything before them, women themselves presenting a petition for peace, and some of them using threats to support it.

At length, chiefly through the exertions of the presbyterian preachers and the common council of the city of London, the peace-party was defeated, and a vigorous levying and pressing of troops began anew. So the hour had come for Richard to mount. His men were all in health and spirits, and their vacancies had been filled up. Lady was frolicsome, and Richard was perfectly well.

The day before they were to start he took the mare out for a gallop across the fields. Never had he known her so full of life. She rushed at hedge and ditch as if they had been squares of royalist infantry. Her madness woke the fervour of battle in Richard's own veins, and as they swept along together, it grew until he felt like one of the Arabs of old, flashing to the harvest field of God, where the corn to be reaped was the lives of infidels, and the ears to be gleaned were the heads of the fallen. That night he scarcely slept for eagerness to be gone.

Waking early from what little sleep he had had, he dressed and armed himself hurriedly, and ran to the stables, where already his men were bustling about getting their horses ready for departure.

Lady had a loose box for herself, and thither straight her master went, wondering as he opened the door of it that he did not hear usual morning welcome. The place was empty. He called Stopchase.

'Where is my mare?' he said. 'Surely no one has been fool enough to take her to the water just as we are going to start.'

Stopchase stood and stared without reply, then turned and left the stable, but came back almost immediately, looking horribly scared. Lady was nowhere to be seen or heard. Richard rushed hither and thither, storming. Not a man about the place could give him a word of enlightenment. All knew she was in that box the night before; none knew when she left it or where she was now.

He ran to his father, but all his father could see or say was no more than was plain to every one: the mare had been carried off in the night, and that with a skill worthy of a professional horse-thief.

What now was the poor fellow to do? If I were to tell the truth, namely, that he wept, so courageous are the very cowards of this century that they would sneer at him; but I do tell it notwithstanding, for I have little regard to the opinion of any man who sneers. Whatever he may or may not have been as a man, Richard felt but half a soldier without his mare, and, his country calling him, oppressed humanity crying aloud for his sword and arm, his men waiting for him, and Lady gone, what was he to do?

'Never heed, Dick, my boy,' said his father. It was the first time since he had put on man's attire that he had called him Dick, 'Thou shalt have my Oliver. He is a horse of good courage, as thou knowest, and twice the weight of thy little mare.'

'Ah, father! you do not know Lady so well as I. Not Cromwell's best horse could comfort me for her. I MUST find her. Give me leave, sir; I must go and think. I cannot mount and ride, and leave her I know not where. Go I will, if it be on a broomstick, but this morning I ride not. Let the men put up their horses, Stopchase, and break their fast.'

'It is a wile of the enemy,' said Stopchase. 'Truly, it were no marvel to me were the good mare at this moment eating her oats in the very stall where we have even but now in vain sought her. I will go and search for her with my hands.'

'Verily,' said Mr. Heywood with a smile, 'to fear the devil is not to run from him! How much of her hay hath she eaten, Stopchase?' he added, as the man returned with disconsolate look.

'About a bottle, sir,' answered Stopchase, rather indefinitely; but the conclusion drawn was, that she had been taken very soon after the house was quiet.

The fact was, that since the return of their soldiers, poor watch had been kept by the people of Redware. Increase of confidence had led to carelessness. Mr. Heywood afterwards made inquiry, and had small reason to be satisfied with what he discovered.

'The thief must have been one who knew the place,' said Faithful.

'Why dost thou think so?' asked his master.

'How swooped he else so quietly upon the best animal, sir?' returned the man.

'She was in the place of honour,' answered Mr. Heywood.

'Scudamore!' said Richard to himself. It might be no light, only a flash in his brain. But that even was precious in the utter darkness.

'Sir,' he said, turning to his father, 'I would I had a plan of Raglan stables.'

'What wouldst thou an' thou hadst, my son?' asked Mr. Heywood.

'Nay, sir, that wants thinking. But I believe my poor mare is at this moment in one of those vaults they tell us of.'

'It may be, my son. It is reported that the earl hath of late been generous in giving of horses. Poor soldiers the king will find them that fight for horses, or titles either. Such will never stand before them that fight for the truth, in the love thereof! Eh, Richard?'

'Truly, sir, I know not,' answered his son, disconsolately. 'I hope I love the truth, and I think so doth Stopchase, after his kind; and yet were we of those that fled from Atherton moor.'

'Thou didst not flee until thou couldst no more, my son. It asketh greater courage of some men to flee when the hour of flight hath come, for they would rather fight on to the death than allow, if but to their own souls, that they are foiled. But a man may flee in faith as well as fight in faith, my son, and each is good in its season. There is a time for all things under the sun. In the end, when the end cometh, we shall see how it hath all gone. When, then, wilt thou ride?'

'To-morrow, an' it please you, sir. I should fight but evil with the knowledge that I had left my best battle-friend in the hands of the Philistines, nor sent even a cry after her.'

'What boots it, Richard? If she be within Raglan walls, they yield her not again. Bide thy time; and when thou meetest thy foe on thy friend's back, woe betide him!'

'Amen, sir!' said Richard. 'But with your leave I will not go to-day. I give you my promise I will go to-morrow.'

'Be it so, then. Stopchase, let the men be ready at this hour on the morrow. The rest of the day is their own.'

So saying, Roger Heywood turned away, in no small distress, although he concealed it, both at the loss of the mare and his son's grief over it. Betaking himself to his study, he plunged himself straightway deep in the comfort of the last born and longest named of Milton's tracts.

The moment he was gone, Richard, who had now made up his mind as to his first procedure, sent Stopchase away, saddled Oliver, rode slowly out of the yard, and struck across the fields. After a half-hour's ride he stopped at a lonely cottage at the foot of a rock on the banks of the Usk. There he dismounted, and having fastened his horse to the little gate in front, entered a small garden full of sweet-smelling herbs mingled with a few flowers, and going up to the door, knocked, and then lifted the latch.

CHAPTER XXVI

THE WITCH'S COTTAGE

Richard was met on the threshold by mistress Rees, in the same old-fashioned dress, all but the hat, which I have already described. On her head she wore a widow's cap, with large crown, thick frill, and black ribbon encircling it between them. She welcomed him with the kindness almost of an old nurse, and led the way to the one chair in the room, beside the hearth, where a fire of peat was smouldering rather than burning beneath the griddle, on which she was cooking oat-cake. The cottage was clean and tidy. From the smoky rafters hung many bunches of dried herbs, which she used partly for medicines, partly for charms.

To herself, the line dividing these uses was not very clearly discernible.

'I am in trouble, mistress Rees,' said Richard, as he seated himself.

'Most men do be in trouble most times, master Heywood,' returned the old woman. 'Dost find thou hast taken the wrong part, eh? There be no need to tell what aileth thee. 'Tis a bit easier to cast off a maiden than to forget her, eh?'

'No, mistress Rees. I came not to trouble thee concerning what is past and gone,' said Richard with a sigh. 'It is a taste of thy knowledge I want rather than of thy skill.'

'What skill I have is honest,' said the old woman.

'Far be it from thee to say otherwise, mother Rees. But I need it not now. Tell me, hast thou not been once and again within the great gates of Raglan castle?'

'Yes, my son, oftener than I can tell thee,' answered the old woman. 'It is but a se'night agone that I sat a talking with my son Thomas Rees in the chimney corner of Raglan kitchen, after the supper was served and the cook at rest. It was there my lad was turnspit once upon a time, for as great a man as he is now with my Lord and all the household. Those were hard times after my good man left me, master Heywood. But the cream will to the top, and there is my son now, who but he in kitchen and hall? Well, of all places in the mortal world, that Raglan passes!'

'They tell strange things of the stables there, mistress Rees: know you aught of them?'

'Strange things, master? They tell nought but good of the stables that tell the truth. As to the armoury, now, well it is not for such as mother Rees to tell tales out of school.'

'What I heard, and wanted to ask thee about, mother, was that they are under ground. Thinkest thou horses can fare well under ground? Thou knowest a horse as well as a dog, mother.'

Ere she replied, the old woman took her cake from the griddle, and laid it on a wooden platter, then caught up a three-legged stool, set it down by Richard, seated herself at his knee, and assumed the look of mystery wherewith she was in the habit of garnishing every bit of knowledge, real or fancied, which it pleased her to communicate.

'Hear me, and hold thy peace, master Richard Heywood,' she said. 'As good horses as ever stamped in Redware stables go down into Raglan vaults; but yet they eat their oats and their barley, and when they lift their heads they look out to the ends of the world. Whether it be by the skill of the mason or of such as the hidden art of my Lord Herbert knows best how to compel, let them say that list to make foes where it were safer to have friends. But this I am free to tell thee, that in the pitched court, betwixt the antechamber to my lord's parlour that hath its windows to the moat, and the great bay window of the hall that looks into that court, there goeth a descent, as it seemeth of stairs only; but to him that knoweth how to pull a certain tricker, as of an harquebus or musquetoon, the whole thing turneth around, and straightway from a stair passeth into an easy matter of a sloping way by the which horses go up and down. And Thomas he telleth me also that at the further end of the vaults to which it leads, the which vaults pass under the Marquis 's oak parlour, and under all the breadth of the fountain court, as they do call the other court of the castle, thou wilt come to a great iron door in the foundations of one of the towers, in which my Lord hath contrived stabling for a hundred and more horses, and that, mark my words, my son, not in any vault or underground dungeon, but in the uppermost chamber of all.'

'And how do they get up there, mother?' asked Richard, who listened with all his ears.

'Why, they go round and round, and ever the rounder the higher, as a fly might crawl up a corkscrew. And there is a stair also in the same screw, as it were, my Thomas do tell me, by which the people of the house do go up and down, and know nothing of the way for the horses within, neither of the stalls at the top of the tower, where they stand and see the country. Yet do they often marvel at the sounds of their hoofs, and their harness, and their cries, and their chumping of their corn. And that is how Raglan can send forth so many horseman for the use of the king. But alack, master Heywood! is it for a wise woman like myself to forget that thou art of the other part, and that these are secrets of state which scarce another in the castle but my son Thomas knoweth aught concerning! What will become of me that I have told them to a Heywood, being, as is well known, myself no more of a royalist than another?'

And she regarded him a little anxiously.

'What should it signify, mother," said Richard, 'so long as neither you nor I believe a word of it? Horses go up a tower to bed forsooth! Yet for the matter of that, I will engage to ride my mare up any corkscrew wide enough to turn her forelock and tail in, ay, and down again too, which is another business with most horses. But come now, mother Rees, confess this all a fable of thine own contriving to make a mock of a farm-bred lad like me.'

'In good sooth, master Heywood,' answered the old woman, 'I tell the tale as 'twas told to me. I avouch it not for certain, knowing that my son Thomas hath a seething brain and loveth a joke passing well, nor heedeth greatly upon whom he putteth it, whether his master or his mother; but for the stair by the great hall window, that stair have I seen with mine own eyes, though for the horses to come and go thereby, that truly have I not seen. And for the rest I only say it may well be, for there is nothing of it all which the wise man, my Lord Herbert, could not with a word, and that a light one for him to speak, though truly another might be torn to pieces in saying it.'

'I would I might see the place!' murmured Richard.

'An' it were not thou art such a—! But it boots not talking, master Heywood. Thou art too well known for a puritan, roundhead they call thee; and thou hast given them and theirs too many hard knocks, my son, to look they should be willing to let thee gaze on the wonders of their great house. Else, being that I am a friend to thee and thine, I would gladly—. But, as I say, it boots nothing, although I have a son, who being more of the king's part than I am—.'

'Hast thou not then art enough, mother, to set me within Raglan walls for an hour or two after midnight? I ask no more,' said Richard, who, although he was but leading the way to quite another proposal, nor desired aid of art black or white, yet could not help a little tremor at making the bare suggestion of the unhallowed idea.

'An' I had, I dared not use it,' answered the old woman; 'for is not my Lord Herbert there? Were it not for him—well—. But I dare not, as I say, for his art is stronger than mine, and from his knowledge I could hide nothing. And I dare not for thy sake either, my young master. Once inside those walls of stone, those gates of oak, and those portcullises of iron, and thou comes not out alive again, I warrant thee.'

'I should like to try once, though,' said Richard. 'Couldst thou not disguise me, mother Rees, and send me with a message to thy son?'

'I tell thee, young master, I dare not,' answered the old woman, with utmost solemnity. 'And if I did, thy speech would presently bewray thee.'

'I would then I knew that part of the wall a man might scramble over in the dark,' said Richard.

'Thinks thou my Lord Marquis hath been fortifying his castle for two years that a young Heywood, even if he be one of the godly, and have long legs to boot, should make a vaulting horse of it? I know but one knows the way over Raglan walls, and thou wilt hardly persuade him to tell thee,' said mother Rees, with a grim chuckle.

As she spoke she rose, and went towards her sleeping chamber. Then first Richard became aware that for some time he had been hearing a scratching and whining. She opened the door, and out ran a wretched-looking dog, huge and gaunt, with the red marks of recent wounds all over his body, and his neck swathed in a discoloured bandage. He went straight to Richard, and began fawning upon him and licking his hands. Miserable and most disreputable as he looked, he recognised in him Dorothy's mastiff.

'My poor Marquis !' he said, 'what evil hath then befallen thee? What would thy mistress say to see thee thus?'

Marquis whined and wagged his tail as if he understood every word he said, and Richard was stung to the heart at the sight of his apparently forlorn condition.

'Hath thy mistress then forsaken thee too, Marquis ?' he said, and from fellow-feeling could have taken the dog in his arms.

'I think not so,' said mistress Rees. 'He hath been with her in the castle ever since she went there.'

'Poor fellow, how thou art torn!' said Richard. 'What animal of thine own size could have brought thee into such a plight? Or can it be that thou hast found a bigger? But that thou hast beaten him I am well assured.'

Marquis wagged an affirmative.

'Fangs of biggest dog in Gwent never tore him like that, master Heywood. Heark'ee now. He cannot tell his tale, so I must tell thee all I know of the matter. I was over to Raglan village three nights agone, to get me a bottle of strong waters from mine host of the White Horse, for the distilling of certain of my herbs good for inward disorders, when he told me that about an hour before there had come from the way of the castle all of a sudden the most terrible noise that ever human ears were pierced withal, as if every devil in hell of dog or cat kind had broken loose, and fierce battle was waging between them in the Yellow Tower. I said little, but had my own fears for my Lord Herbert, and came home sad and slow and went to bed. Now what should wake me the next morning, just as daylight broke the neck of the darkness, but a pitiful whining and obstinate scratching at my door! And who should it be but that same lovely little lapdog of my young mistress now standing by thy knee! But had thou seen him then, master Richard! It was the devil's hackles he had been through! Such a torn dishclout of a dog thou never did see! I understood it all in a moment. He had made one in the fight, and whether he had had the better or the worse of it, like a wise dog as he always was, he knew where to find what would serve his turn, and so when the house was quiet, off he came to old mother Rees to be plaistered and physicked. But what perplexes my old brain is, how, at that hour of the night, for to reach my door when he did, and him hardly able to stand when I let him in, it must have been dead night when he left, it do perplex me, I say, to think how at that time of the night he got out of that prison, watched as it is both night and day by them that sleep not.'

'He couldn't have come over the wall?' suggested Richard.

'Had thou seen him, thou would not make that the question.'

'Then he must have come through or under it; there are but three ways,' said Richard to himself. 'He's a big dog,' he added aloud, regarding him thoughtfully as he patted his sullen affectionate head. 'He's a big dog,' he repeated.

'I think a'most he be the biggest dog I ever saw,' assented mistress Rees.

'I would I were less about the shoulders,' said Richard.

'Who ever heard a man worth his mess of pottage wish him such a wish as that, master Heywood! What would mistress Dorothy say to hear thee? I warrant me she findeth no fault with the breadth of thy shoulders.'

'I am less in the compass than I was before the last fight,' he went on, without heeding his hostess, and as if he talked to the dog, who stood with his chin on his knee, looking up in his face. 'Where thou, Marquis , canst walk, I doubt not to creep; but if thou must creep, what then is left for me? Yet how couldst thou creep with such wounds in thy throat and belly, my poor Marquis ?'

The dog whined, and moved all his feet, one after the other, but without taking his chin off Richard's knee.

'Hast seen thy mistress, little Dick, Marquis ?' asked Richard.

Again the dog whined, moved his feet, and turned his head towards the door. But whether it was that he understood the question, or only that he recognised the name of his friend, who could tell?

'Will thou take me to Dick, Marquis ?'

The dog turned and walked to the door, then stood and looked back, as if waiting for Richard to open it and follow him.

'No, Marquis , we must not go before night,' said Richard.

The dog returned slowly to his knee, and again laid his chin upon it.

'What will the dog do next, thinkest thou, mother, when he finds himself well again, I mean? Will he run from thee?' said Richard.

'He would be like neither dog nor man I ever knew, did he not,' returned the old woman. 'He will for sure go back where he got his hurts, to revenge them if he may, for that is the custom also with both dogs and men.'

'Couldst thou make sure of him that he run not away till I come again at night, mother?'

'Certain I can, my son. I will shut him up whence he will not break so long as he hears me nigh him.'

'Do so then an' thou lovest me, mother Rees, and I will be here with the first of the darkness.'

'An' I love thee, master Richard? Nay, but I do love thy good face and thy true words, be thou puritan or roundhead, or fanatic, or what evil name soever the wicked fashion of the times granteth to men to call thee.'

'Hark in thine ear then, mother: I will call no names; but they of Raglan have, as I truly believe, stolen from me my Lady.'

'Nay, nay, master Richard,' interrupted mistress Rees; 'did I not tell thee with my own mouth that she went of her own free will, and in the company of the reverend sir Matthew Herbert?'

.

'Alas! thou goest not with me, mother Rees. I meant not mistress Dorothy. She is lost to me indeed; but so also is my poor mare, which was stolen last night from Redware stables as the watchers slept.'

'Alack-a-day!' cried goody Rees, holding up her hands in sore trouble for her friend. 'But what then dreams thou of doing? Not surely, before all the saints in heaven, will thou adventure thy body within Raglan walls? But I speak like a fool. Thou canst not.'

'This good dog,' said Richard, stroking Marquis , 'must, as thou thyself plainly seest, have found some way of leaving Raglan without the knowledge or will of its warders. Where he gat him forth, will he not get him in again? And where dog can go, man may at least endeavour to follow. Mayhap he hath for himself scratched a way, as many dogs will.'

'But, for the love of God, master Heywood, what would thou do inside that stone cage? Thy mare, be she, as thou hast often vaunted her to me, the first for courage and wisdom and strength and fleetness of all mares created, be her fore feet like a man's hands and her heart like a woman's heart, as thou sayest, yet cannot she overleap Raglan walls; and thinks thou they will raise portcullis and open gate and drop drawbridge to let thee and her ride forth in peace? It were a fool's errand, my young master, and nowise befitting thy young wisdom.'

'What I shall do, when I am length within the walls, I cannot tell thee, mother. Nor have I ever yet known much good in forecasting. To have to think, when the hour is come, of what thou didst before resolve, instead of setting thyself to understand what is around thee, and perchance the whole matter different from what thou had imagined, is to stand like Lazarus bound hand and foot in thine own graveclothes. It will be given me to meet what comes; or if not, who will bar me from meeting what follows?'

'Master Heywood,' cried goody Rees, drawing herself with rebuke, 'for a man that is born of a woman to talk so wisely and so foolishly both in a breath! But,' she added, with a change of tone, 'I know better than bar the path to a Heywood. An' he will, he will. And thou hast been vilely used, my young master. I will do what I can to help thee to thine own, and no more, no more than thine own. Hark in thine ear now. But first swear to me by the holy cross, puritan as thou art, that thou wilt make no other use of what I tell thee but to free thy stolen mare. I know thou may be trusted even with the secret that would slay thine enemy. But I must have thy oath notwithstanding thereto.'

'I will not swear by the cross, which was never holy, for thereby was the Holy slain. I will not swear at all, mother Rees. I will pledge thee the word of a man who fears God, that I will in no way dishonourable make use of that which thou tellest me. An' that suffice not, I will go without thy help, trusting in God, who never made that mare to carry the enemy of the truth into the battle.'

'But what an' thou should take the staff of strife to measure thy doings withal? That may then seem honourable, done to an enemy, which thou would scorn to do to one of thine own part, even if he wronged thee.'

'Nay, mother; but I will do nothing THOU wouldst think dishonourable, that I promise thee. I will use what thou tellest me for no manner of hurt to my Lord of Worcester or aught that is his. But Lady is not his, and her will I carry, if I may, from Raglan stables back to Redware.'

'I am content. Hearken then, my son. Raglan watchword for the rest of the month is—ST. GEORGE AND ST. PATRICK! May it stand thee in good stead.'

'I thank thee, mother, with all my heart,' said Richard, rising jubilant. 'Now shut up the dog, and let me go. One day it may lie in my power to requite thee.'

'Thou hast requited me beforehand, master Heywood. Old mother Rees never forgets. I would have done well by thee with the maiden, an' thou would but have hearkened to my words. But the day may yet come. Go now, and return with the last of the twilight. Come hither, Marquis .'

The dog obeyed, and she shut him again in her chamber.

CHAPTER XXVII

THE MOAT OF THE KEEP

Richard left the cottage, and mounted Oliver. To pass the time and indulge a mournful memory, he rode round by Wyfern. When he reached home, he found that his father had gone to pay a visit some miles off. He went to his own room, cast himself on his bed, and tried to think. But his birds would not come at his call, or coming would but perch for a moment, and again fly. As he lay thus, his eyes fell on his cousin, old Thomas Heywood's little folio, lying on the window seat where he had left it two years ago, and straightway his fluttering birds alighting there, he thought how the book had been lying unopened all the months, while he had been passing through so many changes and commotions. How still had the room been around it, how silent the sunshine and the snow, while he had inhabited tumult—tumult in his heart, tumult in his ears, tumult of sorrows, of vain longings, of tongues and of swords! Where was the gain to him? Was he nearer to that centre of peace, which the book, as it lay there so still, seemed to his eyes to typify? The maiden loved from childhood had left him for a foolish king and a phantom-church: had he been himself pursuing anything better? He had been fighting for the truth: had he then gained her? where was she? what was she if not a living thing in the heart? Would the wielding of the sword in its name ever embody an abstraction, call it from the vasty deep of metaphysics up into self-conscious existence in the essence of a man's own vitality? Was not the question still, how, of all loves, to grasp the thing his soul thirsted after?

To many a sermon, cleric and lay, had he listened since he left that volume there, in church, in barn, in the open field, but the religion which seemed to fill all the horizon of these preachers' vision, was to him little better than another tumult of words; while, far beyond all the tumults, hung still, in the vast of thought unarrived, unembodied, that something without a shape, yet bearing a name around which hovered a vague light as of something dimly understood, after which, in every moment of inbreaking silence, his soul straightway began to thirst. And if the Truth was not to be found in his own heart, could he think that the blows by which he had not gained her had yet given her? that through means of the tumult he had helped to arouse in her name and for her sake, but in which he had never caught a sight of her beauteous form, she now sat radiantly smiling in any one human soul where she sat not before?

Or should he say it was Freedom for which he had fought? Was he then one whit more free in the reality of his being than he had been before? Or had ever a battle wherein he had perilled his own life, striking for liberty, conveyed that liberty into a single human heart? Was there one soul the freer within, from the nearer presence of that freedom which would have a man endure the heaviest wrong, rather than inflict the lightest? He could not tell, but he greatly doubted.

His thought went wandering away, and vision after vision, now of war and now of love, now of earthly victory and now of what seemed unattainable felicity, arose and passed before him, filling its place. At length it came back: he would glance again into his cousin Thomas's book. He had but to stretch out his hand to take it, for his bed was close by the window. Opening it at random, he came upon this passage:

And as the Mill, that circumgyreth fast,
Refuseth nothing that therein is cast,
But whatsoever is to it assign'd
Gladly receives and willing is to grynd,
But if the violence be with nothing fed,
It wasts itselfe: e'en so the heart mis-led,
Still turning round, unstable as the Ocean,
Never at rest, but in continuall Motion,
Sleepe or awake, is still in agitation
Of some presentment in th' imagination.

If to the Mill-stone you shall cast in Sand,
It troubles them, and makes them at a stand;
If Pitch, it chokes them; or if Chaffe let fall,
They are employ'd, but to no use at all.
So, bitter thoughts molest, uncleane thoughts staine
And spot the Heart; while those idle and vaine
Weare it, and to no purpose. For when 'tis
Drowsie and carelesse of the future blisse,
And to implore Heav'n's aid, it doth imply
How far is it remote from the most High.
For whilst our Hearts on Terrhen things we place,
There cannot be least hope of Divine grace.

'Just such a mill is my mind,' he said to himself. 'But can I suppose that to sit down and read all day like a monk, would bring me nearer to the thing I want?'

He turned over the volume half thinking, half brooding.

'I will look again,' he thought, 'at the verses which that day my father gave me to read. Truly I did not well understand them.'

Once more he read the poem through. It closed with these lines:

So far this LIGHT the Raies extends,
As that no place IT comprehends.
So deepe this SOUND, that though it speake,
It cannot by a Sence so weake
Be entertain'd. A REDOLENT GRACE
The Aire blowes not from place to place.
A pleasant TASTE, of that delight
It doth confound all appetite.
A strict EMBRACE, not felt, yet leaves
That vertue, where it takes it cleaves.
This LIGHT, this SOUND, this SAVOURING GRACE,
This TASTEFULL SWEET, this STRICT EMBRACE,
No PLACE containes, no EYE can see,

My GOD is; and there's none but Hee.

'I HAVE gained something,' he crie aloud. 'I understand it now, at least I think I do. What if, in fighting for the truth as men say, the doors of a man's own heart should at length fly open for her entrance! What if the understanding of that which is uttered concerning her, be a sign that she herself draweth nigh! Then I will go on. And that I may go on, I must recover my mare.'

Honestly, however, he could not quite justify the scheme. All the efforts of his imagination, as he rode home, to bring his judgment to the same side with itself, had failed, and he had been driven to confess the project a foolhardy one. But, on the other hand, had he not had a leading thitherward? Whence else the sudden conviction that Scudamore had taken her, and the burning desire to seek her in Raglan stables? And had he not heard mighty arguments from the lips of the most favoured preachers in the army for an unquestioning compliance with leadings? Nay, had he not had more than a leading? Was it not a sign to encourage him, even a pledge of happy result, that, within an hour of it, and in consequence of his first step in partial compliance with it, he had come upon the only creature capable of conducting him into the robber's hold? And had he not at the same time learned the Raglan password? He WOULD go.

He rose, and descending the little creaking stair of black oak that led from his room to the next storey, sought his father's study, where he wrote a letter informing him of his intended attempt, and the means to its accomplishment that had been already vouchsafed him. The rest of his time, after eating his dinner, he spent in making overshoes for his mare out of an old buff jerkin. As soon as the twilight began to fall, he set out on foot for the witch's cottage.

When he arrived, he found her expecting him, but prepared with no hearty welcome.

'I had liefer by much thee had not come so pat upon thy promise, master Heywood. Then I might have looked to move thee from thy purpose, for truly I like it not. But thou will never bring an old woman into trouble, master Richard?'

'Or a young one either, if I can help it Mother Rees,' answered Richard. 'But come now, thou must trust me, and tell me all I want to know.'

He drew from his pocket paper and pencil, and began to put to her question after question as to the courts and the various buildings forming them, with their chief doors and windows, and ever as she gave him an answer, he added its purport to the rough plan he was drawing of the place.

'Listen to me, Master Heywood,' said the old woman at length after a long, silence, during which he had been pondering over his paper. 'An' thou get once into the fountain court thou will know where thee is by the marble horse that stands in the middle of it. Turn then thy back to the horse, with the yellow tower above thee upon thy right hand, and thee will be facing the great hall. On the other side of the hall is the pitched court with its great gate and double portcullis and drawbridge. Nearly at thy back, but to thy right hand, will lie the gate to the bowling-green. At which of these gates does thee think to lead out thy mare?'

'An' I pass at all, mother, it will be on her back, not at her head.'

'Thou wilt not pass, my son. Be counselled. To thy mare, thou wilt but lose thyself.'

Richard heard her as though he heard her not.

'At what hour doth the moon rise, mistress Rees?' he asked.

'What would thou with the moon?" she returned. "Is not she the enemy of him who roves for plunder? Shines she not that the thief may be shaken out of the earth?'

'I am not thief enough to steal in the dark, mother. How shall I tell without her help where I am or whither I go?'

'She will be half way to the top of her hill by midnight.'

'An' thou speak by the card, then is it time that Marquis and I were going.'

'Here, take thee some fern-seed in thy pouch, that thou may walk invisible,' said the old woman. 'If thee chance to be an hungred, then eat thereof,' she added, as she transferred something from her pocket to his.

She called the dog and opened the chamber door. Out came Marquis , walked to Richard, and stood looking up in his face as if he knew perfectly that his business was to accompany him. Richard bade the old woman good night, and stepped from the cottage.

No sooner was he in the darkness with the dog, than, fearing he might lose sight of him, he tied his handkerchief round the dog's neck, and fastened to it the thong of his riding whip, the sole weapon he had brought with him, and so they walked together, Marquis pulling Richard on. Ere long the moon rose, and the country dawned into the dim creation of the light.

On and on they trudged, Marquis pulling at his leash as if he had been a blind man's dog, and on and on beside them crept their shadows, flattened out into strange distortion upon the road. But when they had come within about two miles of Raglan, whether it was that the sense of proximity to his mistress grew strong in him, or that he scented the Great Mogul, as the horse the battle from afar, Marquis began to grow restless, and to sniff about on one side of the way. When at length they had by a narrow bridge crossed a brook, the dog insisted on leaving the road and going down into the meadow to the left. Richard made small resistance, and that only for experiment upon the animal's determination. Across field after field his guide led him, until, but for the great keep towering dimly up into the moonlit sky, he could hardly have even conjectured where he was. But he was well satisfied, for, ever as they came out of copse or hollow, there was the huge thing in the sky, nearer than before.

At last he was able to descry a short stretch of the castle rampart, past which, away to the westward, the dog was pulling, along a rough cart-track through a field. This he presently found to be a quarry road, and straight into the quarry the dog went, pulling eagerly; but Richard was compelled to follow with caution, for the ground was rough and broken, and the moon cast black misleading shadows. Towards the blackest of these the dog led, and entered a hollow way. Richard went straight after him, guarding his head with his arm, lest he might meet a sudden descent of the roof, and lengthening his leash to the utmost, that he might have timely warning of any descent of the floor.

It was a very rough tunnel, the intent of which will afterwards appear, forming part of one of Lord Herbert's later contrivances for the safety of the castle; but so well had Mr. Salisbury, the surveyor, managed, that not one of the men employed upon it had an idea that they were doing more than working the quarry for the repair of the fortifications.

From the darkness, and the cautious rate at which he had to proceed, holding back the dog who tugged hard at the whip, Richard could not even hazard a conjecture as to the distance they had advanced, when he heard the noise of a small runnel of water, which seemed from the sound to make abrupt descent from some little height. He had gone but a few paces further when the handle of the whip received a great upward pull and was left loose in his grasp: the dog was away, leaving his handkerchief at the end of the thong. So now he had to guide himself, and began to feel about him. He seemed at first to have come to the end of the passage, for he could touch both sides of it by stretching out his arms, and in front a tiny stream of water came down the face of the rough rock; but what then had become of Marquis ? The answer seemed plain: the water must come from somewhere, and doubtless its channel had spare room enough for the dog to pass thither. He felt up the rock, and found that, at about the height of his head, the water came over an obtuse angle. Climbing a foot or two, he discovered that the opening whence it issued was large enough for him to enter.

Only one who has at some time passed where lengthened creeping was necessary, will know how Richard felt, with water under him, pitch-darkness about him, and the rock within an inch or two of his body all round. By and by the slope became steeper and the ascent more difficult. The air grew very close, and he began to fear he should be stifled. Then came a hot breath, and a pair of eyes gleamed a foot or two from his face. Had he then followed into the den of the animal by which poor Marquis had been so frightfully torn? But no: it was Marquis himself waiting for him!

'Go on, Marquis ,' he said, with a sigh of relief.

The dog obeyed, and in another moment a waft of cool air came in. Presently a glimmer of light appeared. The opening through which it entered was a little higher than his horizontally posed head, and looked alarmingly narrow.

But as he crept nearer it grew wider, and when he came under it he found it large enough to let him through. When cautiously he poked up his head, there was the huge mass of the keep towering blank above him! On a level with his eyes, the broad, lilied waters of the moat lay betwixt him and the citadel.

Marquis had brought him to the one neglected, therefore forgotten, and thence undefended spot of the whole building. Before the well was sunk in the keep, the supply of water to the moat had been far more bountiful, and provision for a free overflow was necessary. For some reason, probably for the mere sake of facility in the construction, the passage for the superfluous water had been made larger than needful at the end next the moat. About midway to its outlet, however, a mere drain-mouth in a swampy hollow in the middle of a field, it had narrowed to a third of the compass. But the quarriers had cut across it above the point of contraction; and no danger of access occurring to Lord Herbert or Mr. Salisbury, while they found a certain service in the tiny waterfall, they had left it as it was.

CHAPTER XXVIII

RAGLAN STABLES

The passage for the overflow of the water of the moat was under the sunk walk which, reaching from the gate of the stone court round to the gate of the fountain court, enclosed the keep and its moat, looping them on as it were to the side of the double quadrangle of the castle. The only way out of this passage, at whose entrance Richard now found himself, was into the moat. As quietly therefore as he could, he got through the opening and into the water, amongst the lilies, where, much impeded by their tangling roots, which caused him many a submergence, but with a moon in her second quarter over his head to light him, he swam gently along. As he looked up from the water, however, to the huge crag-like tower over his head, the soft moonlight smoothing the rigour but bringing out all the wasteness of the grim blank, it seemed a hopeless attempt he had undertaken. Not the less did he keep his eye on the tower-side of the moat, and had not swum far before he caught sight of the little stair, which, enclosed in one of the six small round bastions encircling it, led up from the moat to the walk immediately around the citadel. The foot of this stair was, strangely enough, one of the only two points in the defence of the moat not absolutely commanded from either one or the other of the two gates of the castle. The top of the stair, however, was visible from one extreme point over the western gate, and the moment Richard, finding the small thick iron-studded door open, put his head out of the bastion, he caught sight of a warder far away, against the moonlit sky. All of the castle except the spot where that man stood, was hidden by the near bulk of the keep. He drew back, and sat down on the top of the stair, to think and let the water run from his clothes. When he issued, it was again on all-fours. He had, however, only to creep an inch or two to the right to be covered by one of the angles of the tower.

But this shelter was merely momentary, for he must go round the tower in search of some way to reach the courts beyond; and no sooner had he passed the next angle than he found himself within sight of one of the towers of the main entrance. Dropping once more on his hands and knees he crept slowly along, as close as he could squeeze to the root of the wall, and when he rounded the next angle, was in the shadow of the keep, while he had but to cross the walk to be covered by the parapet on the edge of the moat. This he did, and having crept round the curve of the next bastion, was just beginning to fear lest he should find only a lifted drawbridge, and have to take to the water again, when he came to the stone bridge.

It was well for him that Dorothy and Caspar had now omitted the setting of their water-trap, otherwise he would have entered the fountain court in a manner unfavourable to his project. As it was, he got over in safety, never ceasing his slow crawl until he found himself in the archway. Here he stood up, straightened his limbs, went through a few gymnastics, as silent as energetic, to send the blood through his chilled veins, and the next moment was again on the move.

Peering from the mouth of the archway, he saw to his left the fountain court, with the gleaming head of the great horse rising out of the sea of shadow into the moonlight, and knew where he was. Next he discovered close to him on his right an open door into a dim space, and knew that he was looking into the great hall. Opposite the door glimmered the large bay window of which Mrs. Rees had spoken.

There was now a point to be ascertained ere he could determine at which of the two gates he should attempt his exit, a question which, up to the said point, he had thoroughly considered on his way.

The stables opened upon the pitched court, and in that court was the main entrance: naturally that was the one to be used. But in front of it was a great flight of steps, the whole depth of the ditch, with the marble gate at the foot of them; and not knowing the carriageway, he feared both suspicion and loss of time, where a single moment might be all that divided failure from success. Also at this gate were a double portcullis and drawbridge, the working of whose machinery took time, and of all things a quick execution was essential, seeing that at any moment sleeping suspicion might awake, and find enough to keep her so. At the other gate there was but one portcullis and no drawbridge, while from it he perfectly knew the way to the brick gate. Clearly this was the preferable for his attempt. There was but one point to cast in the other scale, namely, that, if old Eccles were still the warder of it, there would be danger of his recognition in respect both of himself and his mare. But, on the other hand, he thought he could turn to account his knowledge of the fact that the Marquis 's room was over it. So here the scale had settled to rebound no more, except indeed he should now discover any difficulty in passing from the stone court in which lay the MOUTH of the stables, to the fountain court in which stood the preferable gate. This question he must now settle, for once on horseback there must be no deliberation.

One way at least there must be, through the hall: the hall must be accessible from both courts. He pulled off his shoes, and stepped softly in. Through the high window immediately over the huge fireplace, a little moonlight fell on the northern gable-wall, turning the minstrels' gallery into an aerial bridge to some strange region of loveliness, and in the shadow under it he found at once the door he sought, standing open but dark under a deep porch.

Issuing and gliding along by the side of the hall and round the great bay window, he came to the stair indicated by Mrs. Rees, and descending a little way, stood and listened: plainly enough to his practised ear, what the old woman had represented as the underground passage to the airiest of stables, was itself full of horses. To go down amongst these in the dark, and in ignorance of the construction of the stable, was somewhat perilous; but he had not come there to avoid risk. Step by step he stole softly down, and, arrived at the bottom, seated himself on the last, to wait until his eyes should get so far accustomed to the darkness as to distinguish the poor difference between the faint dusk sinking down the stair and the absolute murk. A little further on, he could descry two or three grated openings into the fountain court, but by them nothing could enter beyond the faintest reflection of moonlight from the windows between the grand staircase and the bell tower.

As soon as his eyes had grown capable of using what light there was, which however was scarcely sufficient to render him the smallest service, Richard began to whistle, very softly, a certain tune well known to Lady, one he always whistled when he fed or curried her himself. He had not got more than half through it, when a low drowsy whinny made reply from the depths of the darkness before him, and the heart of Richard leaped in his bosom for joy. He ceased a moment, then whistled again. Again came the response, but this time, although still soft and low, free from all the woolliness of sleep. Once more he whistled, and once more came the answer. Certain at length of the direction, he dropped on his hands and knees, and crawled carefully along for a few yards, then stopped, whistled again, and listened. After a few more calls and responses, he found himself at Lady's heels, which had begun to move restlessly. He crept into the stall beside her, spoke to her in a whisper, got upon his feet, caressed her, told her to be quiet, and, pulling her buff shoes from his pockets, drew them over her hoofs, and tied them securely about her pasterns. Then with one stroke of his knife he cut her halter, hitched the end round her neck, and telling her to follow him, walked softly through the stable and up the stair. She followed like a cat, though not without some noise, to whose echoes Richard's bosom seemed the beaten drum. The moment her back was level, he flung himself upon it, and rode straight through the porch and into the hall.

But here at length he was overtaken by the consequences of having an ally unequal to the emergency. Marquis , who had doubtless been occupied with his friends in the stable yard, came bounding up into the court just as Richard threw himself on the back of his mare. At the sight of Lady, whom he knew so well, with her master on her back, a vision of older and happier times, the poor animal forgot himself utterly, rushed through the hall like a whirlwind, and burst into a tempest of barking in the middle of the fountain court, whether to rouse his mistress, or but to relieve his own heart, matters little to my tale. There was not a moment to lose, and Richard rode out of the hall and made for the gate.

CHAPTER XXIX

THE APPARITION

The voice of her lost Marquis , which even in her dreams she could attribute to none but him, roused Dorothy at once. She sprang from her bed, flew to the window, and flung it wide. That same moment, from the shadows about the hall-door, came forth a man on horseback, and rode along the tiled path to the fountain, where never had hoof of horse before trod. Stranger still, the tramp sounded far away, and woke no echo in the echo-haunted place. A phantom surely, horse and man! As they drew nearer where she stared with wide eyes, the head of the rider rose out of the shadow into the moonlight, and she recognised the face of Richard, very white and still, though not, as she supposed, with the whiteness and stillness of a spectre, but with the concentration of eagerness and watchful resolution. The same moment she recognised Lady. She trembled from head to foot. What could it mean but that beyond a doubt they were both dead, slain in battle, and that Richard had come to pay her a last visit ere he left the world. On they came. Her heart swelled up into her throat, and the effort to queen it over herself, and neither shriek nor drop on the floor, was like struggling to support a falling wall. When the spectre reached the marble fountain, he gave a little start, drew bridle, and seemed to become aware that he had taken a wrong path, looked keenly around him, and instead of continuing his advance towards her window, turned in the direction of the gate. One thing was clear, that whether ghostly or mortal, whether already dead or only on the way to death, the apparition was regardless of her presence. A pang of disappointment shot through her bosom, and for the moment quenched her sense of relief from terror. With it sank the typhoon of her emotion, and she became able to note how draggled and soiled his garments were, how his hair clung about his temples, and that for all accoutrement his mare had but a halter. Yet Richard sat erect and proud, and Lady stepped like a mare full of life and vigour. And there was Marquis , not cowering or howling as dogs do in spectral presence, but madly bounding and barking as if in uncontrollable jubilation!

The acme of her bewilderment was reached when the phantom came under the Marquis 's study-window, and she heard it call aloud, in a voice which undoubtedly came from corporeal throat, and that throat Richard's, ringing of the morning and the sunrise and the wind that shakes the wheat, anything rather than of the tomb:

'Ho, master Eccles!' it cried; 'when? when? Must my lord's business cool while thou rubbest thy sleepy eyes awake? What, I say! When? Yes, my lord, I will punctually attend to your lordship's orders. Expect me back within the hour.'

The last words were uttered in a much lower tone, with the respect due to him he seemed addressing, but quite loud enough to be distinctly heard by Eccles or anyone else in the court.

Dorothy leaned from her window, and looked sideways to the gate, expecting to see the Marquis bending over his window-sill, and talking to Richard. But his window was close shut, nor was there any light behind it.

A minute or two passed, during which she heard the combined discords of the rising portcullis. Then out came Eccles, slow and sleepy.

'By St. George and St. Patrick!' cried Richard, 'why keep'st thou six legs here standing idle? Is thy master's business nothing to thee?'

Eccles looked up at him. He was coming to his senses.

'Thou rides in strange graith on my lord's business,' he said, as he put the key in the lock.

'What is that to thee? Open the gate. And make haste. If it please my Lord that I ride thus to escape eyes that else might see further than thine, keen as they are, master Eccles, it is nothing to thee.'

The lock clanged, the gate swung open, and Richard rode through.

By this time a process of doubt and reasoning, rapid as only thought can be, had produced in the mind of Dorothy the conviction that there was something wrong. By what authority was Richard riding from Raglan with muffled hoofs between midnight and morning? His speech to the Marquis was plainly a pretence, and doubtless that to Eccles was equally false. To allow him to pass unchallenged would be treason against both her host and her king.

'Eccles! Eccles!' she cried, her voice ringing clear through the court, 'let not that man pass.'

'He gave the word, mistress,' said Eccles, in dull response.

'Stop him, I say,' cried Dorothy again, with energy almost frantic, as she heard the gate swing to heavily. 'Thou shalt be held to account.'

'He gave the word.'

'He's a true man, mistress,' returned Eccles, in tone of self-justification. 'Heard you not my Lord Marquis give him his last orders from his window?'

'There was no Marquis at the window. Stop him, I say.'

'He's gone,' said Eccles quietly, but with waking uneasiness.

'Run after him,' Dorothy almost screamed.

'Stop him at the gate. It is young Heywood of Redware, one of the busiest of the roundheads.'

Eccles was already running and shouting and whistling. She heard his feet resounding from the bridge. With trembling hands she flung a cloak about her, and sped bare-footed down the grand staircase and along the north side of the court to the bell-tower, where she seized the rope of the alarm-bell, and pulled with all her strength. A horrid clangour tore the stillness of the night, re-echoed with yelping response from the multitudinous buildings around. Window after window flew open, head after head was popped out, amongst the first that of the Marquis, shouting to know what was amiss. But the question found no answer. The courts began to fill. Some said the castle was on fire; others, that the wild beasts were all out; others, that Waller and Cromwell had scaled the rampart, and were now storming the gates; others, that Eccles had turned traitor and admitted the enemy. In a few moments all was outcry and confusion. Both courts and the great hall were swarming with men and women and children, in every possible stage of attire. The main entrance was crowded with a tumult of soldiery, and scouts were rushing to different stations of outlook, when the cry reached them that the western gate was open, the portcullis up, and the guard gone.

The moment Richard was clear of the portcullis, he set off at a sharp trot for the brick gate, and had almost reached it when he became aware that he was pursued. He had heard the voice of Dorothy as he rode out, and knew to whom he owed it. But yet there was a chance. Rousing the porter with such a noisy reveillee as drowned in his sleepy ears the cries of the warder and those that followed him, he gave the watchword, and the huge key was just turning in the wards when the clang of the alarm-bell suddenly racked the air. The porter stayed his hand, and stood listening.

'Open the gate,' said Richard in authoritative tone.

'I will know first, master—' began the man.

'Dost not hear the bell?' cried Richard. 'How long wilt thou endanger the castle by thy dulness?'

'I shall know first,' repeated the man deliberately, 'what that bell—'

Ere he could finish the sentence, the butt of Richard's whip had laid him along the threshold of the gate. Richard flung himself from his horse, and turned the key. But his enemies were now close at hand, Eccles and the men of his guard. If the porter had but fallen the other way! Ere he could drag aside his senseless body and open the gate, they were upon him with blows and curses. But the puritan's blood was up, and with the heavy handle of his whip he had felled one and wounded another ere he was himself stretched on the ground with a sword-cut in the head.

CHAPTER XXX

RICHARD AND THE MARQUIS

A very few strokes of the brazen-tongued clamourer had been enough to wake the whole castle. Dorothy flew back to her chamber, and hurrying on her clothes, descended again to the court. It was already in full commotion. The western gate stood open, with the portcullis beyond it high in the wall, and there she took her stand, waiting the return of Eccles and his men.

Presently Lord Charles came through the hall from the stone court, and seeing the gate open, called aloud in anger to know what it meant. Receiving no reply, he ran with an oath to drop the portcullis.

'Is there a mutiny amongst the rascals?' he cried.

'There is no cause for dread, my lord,' said Dorothy from the shadow of the gateway.

'How know you that, fair mistress?' returned Lord Charles, who knew her voice. 'You must not inspire us with too much of your spare courage. That would be to make us fool-hardy.'

'Indeed, there is nothing to fear, my lord,' persisted Dorothy. 'The warder and his men have but this moment rushed out after one on horseback, whom they had let pass with too little question. They are ten to one,' added Dorothy with a shudder, as the sounds of the fray came up from below.

'If there is then no cause of fear, cousin, why look you so pale?' asked Lord Charles, for the gleam of a torch had fallen on Dorothy's face.

'I think I hear them returning, doubtless with a prisoner,' said Dorothy, and stood with her face turned aside, looking anxiously through the gateway and along the bridge. She had obeyed her conscience, and had now to fight her heart, which unreasonable member of the community would insist on hoping that her efforts had been foiled. But in a minute more came the gathering noise of returning footsteps, and presently Lady's head appeared over the crown of the bridge; then rose Eccles, leading her in grim silence; and next came Richard, pale and bleeding, betwixt two men, each holding him by an arm; the rest of the guard crowded behind. As they entered the court, Richard caught sight of Dorothy, and his face shone into a wan smile, to which her rebellious heart responded with a terrible pang.

The voice of Lord Charles reached them from the other side of the court.

'Bring the prisoner to the hall,' it cried.

Eccles led the mare away, and the rest took Richard to the hall, which now began to be lighted up, and was soon in a blaze of candles all about the dais. When Dorothy entered, it was crowded with household and garrison, but the Marquis , who was tardy at dressing, had not yet appeared. Presently, however, he walked slowly in from the door at the back of the dais, breathing hard, and seated himself heavily in the great chair. Dorothy placed herself near the door, where she could see the prisoner.

Lady Mary entered and seated herself beside her father.

'What meaneth all this tumult?' the Marquis began. 'Who rang the alarum-bell?'

'I did, my lord,' answered Dorothy in a trembling voice.

'Thou, mistress Dorothy!' exclaimed the Marquis . 'Then I doubt not thou hadst good reason for so doing. Prithee what was the reason? Verily it seems thou wast sent hither to be the guardian of my house!'

'It was not I, my lord, gave the first alarm, but—' She hesitated, then added, 'my poor Marquis .'

'Not so poor for a Marquis , cousin Dorothy, as to be called the poor Marquis . Why dost thou call me poor?'

'My lord, I mean my dog.'

'The truth will still lie—between me and thy dog,' said the Marquis . 'But come now, instruct me. Who is this prisoner, and how comes he here?'

'He be young Mr. Heywood of Redware, my lord, and a pestilent roundhead,' answered one of his captors.

'Who knows him?'

A moment's silence followed. Then came Dorothy's voice again.

'I do, my lord.'

'Tell me, then, all thou knowest from the beginning, cousin,' said the Marquis .

'I was roused by the barking of my dog,' Dorothy began.

'How came HE hither again?'

'My lord, I know not.'

''Tis passing strange. See to it, Lord Charles. Go on, mistress Dorothy.'

'I heard my dog bark in the court, my lord, and looking from my window saw Mr. Heywood riding through on horseback. Ere I could recover from my astonishment, he had passed the gate, and then I rang the alarm-bell,' said Dorothy briefly.

'Who opened the gate for him?'

'I did, my lord,' said Eccles. 'He made me believe he was talking to your lordship at the study window.'

'Ha! a cunning fox!' said the Marquis . 'And then?'

'And then mistress Dorothy fell out upon me—'

'Let thy tongue wag civilly, Eccles.'

'He speaks true, my lord,' said Dorothy. 'I did fall out upon him, for he was but half awake, and I knew not what mischief might be at hand.'

'Eccles is obliged to you, cousin. And so the lady brought you to your senses in time to catch him?'

'Yes, my lord.'

'How comes he wounded? He was but one to a score.'

'My lord, he would else have killed us all.'

'He was armed then?'

Eccles was silent.

'Was he armed?' repeated the Marquis .

'He had a heavy whip, my lord.'

'H'm!' said the Marquis , and turned to the prisoner.

'Is thy name Heywood, sirrah?' he asked.

'My lord, if you treat me as a clown, you shall have but clown's manners of me; I will not answer.'

''Fore heaven!' exclaimed the Marquis , 'our squires would rule the roast.'

'He that doth right, Marquis or squire, will one day rule, my lord,' said Richard.

''Tis well said,' returned the Marquis . 'I ask your pardon, Mr. Heywood. In times like these a man must be excused for occasionally dropping his manners.'

'Assuredly, my lord, when he stoops to recover them so gracefully as doth the Marquis of Worcester.'

'What, then, would'st thou in my house at midnight, Mr. Heywood?' asked the Marquis courteously.

'Nothing save mine own, my lord. I came but to look for a stolen mare.'

'What! thou takest Raglan for a den of thieves?'

'I found the mare in your lordship's stable.'

'How then came the mare in my stable?'

'That is not a question for me to answer, my lord.'

'Doubtless thou didst lose her in battle against thy sovereign.'

'She was in Redware stable last night, my lord.'

'Which of you, knaves, stole the gentleman's mare?' cried the Marquis . 'But, Mr. Heywood, there can be no theft upon a rebel. He is by nature an outlaw, and his life and goods forfeit to the king.'

'He will hardly yield the point, my lord. So long as Might, the sword, is in the hand of Right, the—'

'Of Right, the roundhead, I suppose you mean,' interrupted the Marquis . 'Who carried off Mr. Heywood's mare?' he repeated, rising, and looking abroad on the crowd.

'Tom Fool,' answered a voice from the obscure distance.

A buzz of suppressed laughter followed, which as instantly ceased, for the Marquis looked angrily around.

'Stand forth, Tom Fool,' he said.

Through the crowd came Tom, and stood before the dais, looking frightened and sheepish.

'Sure I am, Tom, thou didst never go to steal a mare of thine own notion: who went with thee?' said the Marquis .

'Mr. Scudamore, my lord,' answered Tom.

'Ha, Rowland! Art thou there?' cried his lordship.

'I gave him fair warning two years ago, my lord, and the king wants horses,' said Scudamore cunningly.

'Rowland, I like not such warfare. Yet can the roundheads say nought against it, who would filch kingdom from king and church from bishops,' said the Marquis , turning again to Heywood.

'As they from the pope, my lord,' rejoined Richard.

'True,' answered the Marquis ; 'but the bishops are the fairer thieves, and may one day be brought to reason and restitution.'

'As I trust your lordship will in respect of my mare.'

'Nay, that can hardly be. She shall to Gloucester to the king. I would not have sent to Redware to fetch her, but finding thee and her in my house at midnight, it would be plain treason to set such enemies at liberty. What! hast thou fought against his majesty? Thou art scored like an old buckler!'

Richard had started on his adventure very thinly clad, for he had expected to find all possible freedom of muscle necessary, and indeed could not in his buff coat have entered the castle. In the scuffle at the gate, his garment had been torn open, and the eye of the Marquis had fallen on the scar of a great wound on his chest, barely healed.

'What age art thou?' he went on, finding Richard made no answer.

'One and twenty, my lord—almost.'

'And what wilt thou be by the time thou art one and thirty, an' I'll let thee go,' said the Marquis thoughtfully.

'Dust and ashes, my lord, most likely. Faith, I care not.'

As he spoke he glanced at Dorothy, but she was looking on the ground.

'Nay, nay!' said the Marquis feelingly. 'These are, but wild and hurling words for a fine young fellow like thee. Long ere thou be a man, the king will have his own again, and all will be well. Come, promise me thou wilt never more bear arms against his majesty, and I will set thee and thy mare at liberty the moment thou shalt have eaten thy breakfast.'

'Not to save ten lives, my lord, would I give such a promise.'

'Roundhead hypocrite!' cried the Marquis , frowning to hide the gleam of satisfaction he felt breaking from his eyes. 'What will thy father say when he hears thou liest deep in Raglan dungeon?'

'He will thank heaven that I lie there a free man instead of walking abroad a slave,' answered Richard.

''Fore heaven!' said the Marquis , and was silent for a moment. 'Owest thou then thy king NOTHING, boy?' he resumed.

'I owe the truth everything,' answered Richard.

'The truth!' echoed the Marquis .

'Now speaks my Lord Worcester like my Lord Pilate,' said Richard.

'Hold thy peace, boy,' returned the Marquis sternly. 'Thy godly parents have ill taught thee thy manners. How knowest thou what was in my thought when I did but repeat after thee the sacred word thou didst misuse?'

'My lord, I was wrong, and I beg your lordship's pardon. But an' your lordship were standing here with your head half beaten in, and your clothes—'

Here Richard bethought himself, and was silent.

'Tell me then how gat'st thou in, lunatic,' said the Marquis, not unkindly, 'and thou shalt straight to bed.'

'My lord,' returned Richard, 'you have taken my mare, and taken my liberty, but the devil is in it if you take my secret.'

'I would thy mare had been poisoned ere she drew thee hither on such a fool's errand! I want neither thee nor thy mare, and yet I may not let you go!'

'A moment more, and it had been an exploit, and no fool's errand, my lord.'

'Then the fool's cap would have been thine, Eccles. How camest thou to let him out? Thou a warder, and ope gate and up portcullis 'twixt waking and sleeping!'

'Had he wanted in, my lord, it would have been different,' said Eccles. 'But he only wanted out, and gave the watchword.'

'Where got'st thou the watchword, Mr. Heywood?'

'I will tell thee what I gave for it, my lord. More I will not.'

'What gavest thou then?'

'My word that I would work neither thee nor thine any hurt withal, my lord.'

'Then there are traitors within my gates!' cried the Marquis.

'Truly, that I know not, my lord,' answered Richard.

'Prithee tell me how them gat thee into my house, Mr. Heywood? It were but neighbourly.'

'It were but neighbourly, my lord, to hang young Scudamore and Tom Fool for thieves.'

'Tell me how thou gat hold of the watchword, good boy, and I will set thee free, and give thee thy mare again.'

'I will not, my lord.'

'Then the devil take thee!' said the Marquis, rising.

The same moment Richard reeled, and but for the men about him, would have fallen heavily.

Dorothy darted forward, but could not come near him for the crowd.

'My Lord Charles,' cried the Marquis , 'see the poor fellow taken care of. Let him sleep, and perchance on the morrow he will listen to reason. Mistress Watson will see to his hurts. I would to God he were on our side! I like him well.'

The men took him up and followed Lord Charles to the housekeeper's apartment, where they laid him on a bed in a little turret, and left him, still insensible, to her care, with injunctions to turn the key in the lock if she went from the chamber but for a moment. 'For who can tell,' thought Lord Charles, greatly perplexed, 'but as he came he may go?'

Some of the household had followed them, and several of the women would gladly have stayed, but Mrs. Watson sent all away. Gradually the crowd dispersed. The tumult ceased; the household retired. The castle grew still, and most of its inhabitants fell asleep again.

'A damned hot-livered roundhead coxcomb!' said Lord Worcester to himself, pacing his room. 'These pelting cockerel squires and yeomen nowadays go strutting and crowing as if all the yard were theirs! We shall see how far this heat will carry the rogue! I doubt not the boy would tell everything than see his mare whipped. He's a fine fellow, and it were a thousand pities he turned coward and gave in. But the affair is not mine; it is the king's majesty's. Would to God the rascal were of our side! He's the right old English breed. A few such were very welcome, if only to show some of our dainty young lordlings of yesterday what breed can do. But an ass-foal it is! To run his neck into a halter, and set honest people in mortal doubt whether to pull the end or no!

How on earth did he ever dream of carrying off a horse out of the very courts of Raglan castle! And yet, by saint George! he would have done it too, but for that brave wench of a Vaughan! What a couple the two would make! They'd give us a race of Arthurs and Orlandos between them. God be praised there are such left in England! And yet the rogue is but a pestilent roundhead, the more's the pity! Those coward rascals need never have mauled him like that. Yet had the blow gone a little deeper it had been a mighty gain to our side. Out he shall not go till the war be over! It would be downright treason.'

So ran the thoughts of the Marquis as he paced his chamber. But at length he lay down once more, and sought refuge in sleep.

CHAPTER XXXI

THE SLEEPLESS

There were more than the Marquis left awake and thinking; amongst the rest one who ought to have been asleep, for the thoughts that kept her awake were evil thoughts.

Amanda Serafina Fuller was a twig or leaf upon one of many decaying branches, which yet drew what life they had from an ancient genealogical tree. Property gone, but the sense of high birth swollen to a vice, the one thought in her mother's mind, ever since she grew capable of looking upon the social world in its relation to herself, had been how, with stinted resources, to make the false impression of plentiful ease. For one of the most disappointing things in high descent is, that the descent is occasionally into depths of meanness. Some who are proudest of their lineage, instead of finding therein a spur to nobility of thought and action, find in it only a necessity for prostrating themselves with the more abject humiliation at the footstool of Mammon, to be admitted into the penetralia of which foul god's favours, they will hasten to mingle the blood of their pure descent with that of the very kennels, yellow with the gold to which a noble man, if poor as Jesus himself, would loathe to be indebted for a meal. In 'the high countries' there will be a finding of levels more appalling than strange.

Hence Amanda had been born and brought up in falsehood, had been all her life witness to a straining after the untrue so energetic, as to assume the appearance of conscience; while such was the tenor and spirit of the remarks she was constantly hearing, that she grew up with the ingrained undisputed idea that she and her mother, whom she had only known as a widow, had been wronged, spoiled indeed of their lawful rights, by a combination of their rich relatives; whereas in truth they had been the objects of very considerable generosity, which they resented the more that it had been chiefly exercised by such of the family as could least easily afford it, yet accepted in their hearts, if not in their words, as their natural right. The intercession through which Amanda had been received into Lady Margaret's household, was the contribution towards their maintenance of one of their richer connections: the Marquis himself, although distantly related, not having previously been aware of their existence.

But Amanda felt degraded by her position, and was unaware that to herself alone she owed the degradation: she had not yet learned that the only service which can degrade is that which is unwillingly rendered. To be paid for such, is degradation in its very essence. Every one who grumbles at his position as degrading, yet accepts the wages thereof, brands himself a slave.

The evil tendencies which she had inherited, had then been nourished in her from her very birth, chief of these envy, and a strong tendency to dislike. Mean herself, she was full of suspicions with regard to others, and found much pleasure in penetrating what she took to be disguise, and laying bare the despicable motives which her own character enabled her either to discover or imagine, and which, in other people, she hated. Moderately good people have no idea of the vileness of which their own nature is capable, or which has been developed in not a few who pass as respectable persons, and have not yet been accused either of theft or poisoning. Such as St. Paul alone can fully understand the abyss of moral misery from which the in-dwelling spirit of God has raised them.

The one redeeming element in Amanda was her love to her mother, but inasmuch as it was isolated and self-reflected, their mutual attachment partook of the nature of a cultivated selfishness, and had lost much of its primal grace. The remaining chance for such a woman, so to speak, seems, that she should either fall in love with a worthy man, if that be still possible to her, or, by her own conduct, be brought into dismal and incontrovertible disgrace.

She had stood in the hall within a few yards of Dorothy, and had intently watched her face all the time Richard was before the Marquis . But not because she watched the field of their play was Amanda able to read the heart whence ascended those strangely alternating lights and shadows. She had, by her own confession, conceived a strong dislike to Dorothy the moment she saw her, and without love there can be no understanding. Hate will sharpen observation to the point of microscopic vision, affording opportunity for many a shrewd guess, and revealing facts for the construction of the cleverest and falsest theories, but will leave the observer as blind as any bat to the scope of the whole, or the meaning of the parts which can be understood only from the whole; for love alone can interpret.

As she gazed on the signs of conflicting emotion in Dorothy's changes of colour and expression, Amanda came quickly enough to the conclusion that nothing would account for them but the assumption that the sly puritanical minx was in love with the handsome young roundhead. How else could the deathly pallor of her countenance while she fixed her eyes wide and unmoving upon his face, and the flush that ever and anon swept its red shadow over the pallor as she cast them on the ground at some brave word from the lips of the canting psalm-singer, be in the least intelligible? Then came the difficulty: how in that case was her share in his capture to be explained? But here Amanda felt herself in her own province, and before the Marquis rose, had constructed a very clever theory, in which exercise of ingenuity, however, unluckily for its truth, she had taken for granted that Dorothy's nature corresponded to her own, and reasoned freely from the character of the one to the conduct of the other. This was her theory: Dorothy had expected Richard, and contrived his admission. His presence betrayed by the mastiff, and his departure challenged by the warder, she had flown instantly to the alarm-bell, to screen herself in any case, and to secure the chance, if he should be taken, of liberating him without suspicion under cover of the credit of his capture. The theory was a bold one, but then it accounted for all the points, amongst the rest, how he had got the password and why he would not tell, and was indeed in the fineness of its invention equally worthy of both the heart and the intellect of the theorist.

Nor were mistress Fuller's resolves behind her conclusions in merit: of all times since first she had learned to mistrust her, this night must Dorothy be watched; and it was with a gush of exultation over her own acuteness that she saw her follow the men who bore Richard from the hall.

If Dorothy knew more of her own feelings than she who watched her, she was far less confident that she understood them. Indeed she found them strangely complicated, and as difficult to control as to understand, while she stood gazing on the youth who through her found himself helpless and wounded in the hands of his enemies. He was all in the wrong, no doubt, a rebel against his king, and an apostate from the church of his country; but he was the same Richard with whom she had played all her childhood, whom her mother had loved, and between whom and herself had never fallen shadow before that cast by the sudden outblaze of the star of childish preference into the sun of youthful love. And was it not when the very mother of shadows, the blackness of darkness itself, swept between them and separated them forever, that first she knew how much she had loved him? What if not with the love that could listen entranced to its own echo! love of child or love of maiden, Dorothy never asked herself which it had been, or which it was now. She was not given to self-dissection. The cruel fingers of analysis had never pulled her flower to pieces, had never rubbed the bloom from the sun-dyed glow of her feelings. But now she could not help the vaporous rise of a question: all was over, for Richard had taken the path of presumption, rebellion, and violence, how then came it that her heart beat with such a strange delight at every answer he made to the expostulations or enticements of the Marquis ? How was it that his approval of the intruder, not the less evident that it was unspoken, made her heart swell with pride and satisfaction, causing her to forget the rude rebellion housed within the form whose youth alone prevented it from looking grand in her eyes?

For the moment her heart had the better of—her conscience, shall I say? Yes, of that part of her conscience, I will allow, which had grown weak by the wandering of its roots into the poor soil of opinion. In the delight which the manliness of the young fanatic awoke in her, she even forgot the dull pain which had been gnawing at her heart ever since first she saw the blood streaming down his face as he passed her in the gateway. But when at length he fell fainting in the arms of his captors, and the fear that she had slain him writhed sickening through her heart, it was with a grim struggle indeed that she kept silent and conscious. The voice of the Marquis , committing him to the care of mistress Watson instead of the rough ministrations of the guard, came with the power of a welcome restorative, and she hastened after his bearers to satisfy herself that the housekeeper was made understand that he was carried to her at the Marquis 's behest. She then retired to her own chamber, passing in the corridor Amanda, whose room was in the same quarter, with a salute careless from weariness and pre-occupation.

The moment her head was on her pillow the great fight began, on that only battle-field of which all others are but outer types and pictures, upon which the thoughts of the same spirit are the combatants, accusing and excusing one another.

She had done her duty, but what a remorseless thing that duty was! She did not, she could not, repent that she had done it, but her heart WOULD complain that she had had it to do. To her, as to Hamlet, it was a cursed spite. She had not yet learned the mystery of her relation to the Eternal, whose nature in his children it is that first shows itself in the feeling of duty. Her religion had not as yet been shaken, to test whether it was of the things that remain or of those that pass. It is easy for a simple nature to hold by what it has been taught, so long as out of that faith springs no demand of bitter obedience; but when the very hiding place of life begins to be laid bare under the scalpel of the law, when the heart must forego its love, when conscience seems at war with kindness, and duty at strife with reason, then most good people, let their devotion to what they call their religion be what it may, prove themselves, although generally without recognising the fact, very much of pagans after all. And good reason why! For are they not devoted to their church or their religion tenfold more than to the living Love, the father of their spirits? and what else is that, be the church or religion what it will, but paganism? Gentle and strong at once as Dorothy was, she was not yet capable of knowing that, however like it may look to a hardship, no duty can be other than a privilege. Nor was it any wonder if she did not perceive that she was already rewarded for the doing of the painful task, at the memory of which her heart ached and rebelled, by the fresh outburst in that same troubled heart of the half-choked spring of her love to the playmate of her childhood. Had it fallen, as she would have judged so much fairer, to some one else of the many in the populous place to defeat Richard's intent and secure his person, she would have both suffered and loved less. The love, I repeat, was the reward of the duty done.

For a long time she tossed sleepless, for what she had just passed through had so thoroughly possessed her imagination that, ever as her wearied brain was sinking under the waves of sleep, up rose the face of Richard from its depths, deathlike, with matted curls and bloodstained brow, and drove her again ashore on the rocks of wakefulness. By and by the form of her suffering changed, and then instead of the face of Richard it was his voice, ever as she reached the point of oblivion, calling aloud for help in a tone of mingled entreaty and reproach, until at last she could no longer resist the impression that she was warned to go and save him from some impending evil. This once admitted, not for a moment would she delay response. She rose, threw on a dressing-gown, and set out in the dim light of the breaking day to find again the room into which she had seen him carried.

There was yet another in the house who could not sleep, and that was Tom Fool. He had a strong suspicion that Richard had learned the watchword from his mother, who, like most people desirous of a reputation for superior knowledge, was always looking out for scraps and orts of peculiar information. In such persons an imagination after its kind has considerable play, and when mother Rees had succeeded, without much difficulty on her own, or sense of risk on her son's part, in drawing from him the watchword of the week, she was aware in herself of a huge accession of importance; she felt as if she had been intrusted with the keys of the main entrance, and trod her clay floor as if the fate of Raglan was hid in her bosom, and the great pile rested in safety under the shadow of her wings. But her imagined gain was likely to prove her son's loss; for, as he reasoned with himself, would Mr. Heywood, now that he knew him for the thief of his mare, persist, upon reflection, in refusing to betray his mother? If not, then the fault would at once be traced to him, with the result at the very least, of disgraceful expulsion from the Marquis 's service. Almost any other risk would be preferable.

But he had yet another ground for uneasiness. He knew well his mother's attachment to young Mr. Heywood, and had taken care she should have no suspicion of the way he was going after leaving her the night he told her the watchword; for such was his belief in her possession of supernatural powers, that he feared the punishment she would certainly inflict for the wrong done to Richard, should it come to her knowledge, even more than the wrath of the Marquis . For both of these weighty reasons therefore he must try what could be done to strengthen Richard in his silence, and was prepared with an offer, or promise at least, of assistance in making his escape.

As soon as the house was once more quiet, he got up, and, thoroughly acquainted with the "crenkles" of it, took his way through dusk and dark, through narrow passage and wide chamber, without encountering the slightest risk of being heard or seen, until at last he stood, breathless with anxiety and terror, at the door of the turret-chamber, and laid his ear against it.

CHAPTER XXXII

THE TURRET CHAMBER

When mistress Watson had, as gently as if she had been his mother, bound up Richard's wounded head, she gave him a composing draught, and sat down by his bedside. But as soon as she saw it begin to take effect, she withdrew, in the certainty that he would not move for some hours at least. Although he did fall asleep, however, Richard's mind was too restless and anxious to yield itself to the natural influence of the potion. He had given his word to his father that he would ride on the morrow; the morrow had come, and here he was! Hence the condition which the drug superinduced was rather that of dreaming than sleep, the more valuable element, repose, having little place in the result.

The key was in the lock, and Tom Fool as he listened softly turned it, then lifted the latch, peeped in, and entered. Richard started to his elbow, and stared wildly about him. Tom made him an anxious sign, and, fevered as he was and but half awake, Richard, whether he understood it or not, anyhow kept silence, while Tom Fool approached the bed, and began to talk rapidly in a low voice, trembling with apprehension. It was some time, however, before Richard began to comprehend even a fragment here and there of what he was saying. When at length he had gathered this much, that his visitor was running no small risk in coming to him, and was in mortal dread of discovery, he needed but the disclosure of who he was, which presently followed, to spring upon him and seize him by the throat with a gripe that rendered it impossible for him to cry out, had he been so minded.

'Master, master!' he gurgled, 'let me go. I will swear any oath you please—'

'And break it any moment YOU please,' returned Richard through his set teeth, and caught with his other hand the coverlid, dragged it from the bed, and, twisting it first round his face, flung the remainder about his body; then, threatening to knock his brains out if he made the least noise, proceeded to tie him up in it with his garters and its own corners. No sound escaped poor Tom beyond a continuous mumbled entreaty through its folds. Richard laid him on the floor, pulled all the bedding upon the top of him, and gliding out, closed the door, but, to Tom's unspeakable relief, as his ears, agonizedly listening, assured him, did not lock it behind him.

Tom's sole anxiety was now to get back to his garret unseen, and nothing was farther from his thoughts than giving the alarm. The moment Richard was out of hearing, out of sight he had been for some stifling minutes, he devoted his energies to getting clear of his entanglement, which he did not find very difficult; then stepping softly from the chamber, he crept with a heavy heart back as he had come through a labyrinth of by-ways.

About half an hour after, Dorothy came gliding through the house, making a long circuit of corridors. Gladly would she have avoided passing Amanda's door, and involuntarily held her breath as she approached it, stepping as lightly as a thief. But alas! nothing save incorporeity could have availed her. The moment she had passed, out peeped Amanda and crept after her barefooted, saw her to her joy enter the chamber and close the door behind her, then 'like a tiger of the wood,' made one noiseless bound, turned the key, and sped back to her own chamber, with the feeling of Mark Antony when he said, 'Now let it work!'

Dorothy was startled by a slight click, but concluded at once that it was nothing but a further fall of the latch, and was glad it was no louder. The same moment she saw, by the dim rushlight, the signs of struggle which the room presented, and discovered that Richard was gone. Her first emotion was an undefined agony: they had murdered him, or carried him off to a dungeon! There were the bedclothes in a tumbled heap upon the floor! And, yes, it was blood with which they were marked! Sickening at the thought, and forgetting all about her own situation, she sank on the chair by the bedside.

Knowing the castle as she did, a very little reflection convinced her that if he had met with violence it must have been in attempting to escape; and if he had made the attempt, might he not have succeeded? There had certainly been no fresh alarm given. But upon this consoling supposition followed instantly the pang of the question: what was now required of her? The same hard thing as before? Ought she not again to give the alarm, that the poor wounded boy might be recaptured? Alas! had not evil enough already befallen him at her hand? And if she did, horrible thought! what account could she give this time of her discovery? What indeed but the truth? And to what vile comments would not the confession of her secret visit in the first grey of the dawn to the chamber of the prisoner expose her? Would it not naturally rouse such suspicion as any modest woman must shudder to face, if but for the one moment between utterance and refutation. And what refutation could there be for her, so long as the fact remained? If he had escaped, the alarm would serve no good end, and her shame could be spared; but he might be hiding somewhere about the castle, and she must choose between treachery to the Marquis , was it? on the one hand, and renewed hurt, wrong, perhaps, to Richard, coupled with the bitterest disgrace to herself, on the other. To weigh such a question impartially was impossible; for in the one alternative no hurt would befall the Marquis , while from the other her very soul recoiled sickening. Thus tortured, she sat motionless in the very den of the dragon, the one moment vainly endeavouring to rouse up her courage and look her duty in the face that she might know with certainty what it was; the next, feeling her whole nature rise rebellious against the fate that demanded such a sacrifice. Ought she to be thus punished for an intent of the purest humanity?

There came a lull, and with the lull a sense of her position: she sat in the very, jaws of slander! Any moment mistress Watson or another might enter and find her there, and what then more natural or irrefutable than the accusation of having liberated him? She sprang to her feet, and darted to the door. It was locked!

Her first thought was relief: she had no longer to decide; her second, that she was a prisoner, till, horror of horrors! the soldiers of the guard came to seek Richard and found her, or stern mistress Watson appeared, grim as one of the Fates; or, perhaps, if Richard had been carried away, until she was compelled by hunger and misery to call aloud for release. But no! she would rather die. Now in this case, now in that, her thoughts pursued the horrible possibilities, one or other of which was inevitable, through all the windings of the torture of anticipation, until for a time she must have lost consciousness, for she had no recollection of falling where she found herself, on the heap in the middle of the floor. The gray heartless dawn had begun to peer in through the dull green glass that closed the one loophole. It grew and grew, and its growth was the approach of the grinning demon of shame. The nearer a man can arrive to the knowledge of such feelings as hers is the conviction that he never can comprehend them. The cruel light seemed gathering its strength to publish her shame to the universe. Blameless as she was, she would have gladly accepted death in escape from the misery that every moment grew nearer. Now and then a faint glimmer of comfort reached her in the thought that at least the escape of Richard, if he had escaped, was thus ensured, and that without any blame to her. And perhaps mistress Watson would be merciful, only she too had her obligations, and as housekeeper was severely responsible. And even if she should prove pitiful, there was the locking of the door! It followed so quickly, that someone must have seen her enter, and wittingly snared her, believing most likely that she was not alone in the chamber.

The terrible bolt at length slid back in the lock, gently, yet with tearing sound; mistress Watson entered, stood, stared. Before her sat Dorothy by the side of the bedstead, in her dressing-gown, her hair about her neck, her face like the moon at sunrise, and her eyelids red and swollen with weeping. She stood speechless, staring first at the disconsolate maiden, and then at the disorder of the room. The prisoner was nowhere. What her thoughts were, I must only imagine. That she should stare and be bewildered, finding Dorothy where she had left Richard, was at least natural.

The moment Dorothy found herself face to face with her doom, her presence of mind returned. The blood rushed from her heart to her brain. She rose, and ere the astonished matron, who stood before her erect, high-nosed, and open-mouthed like Michael Angelo's Clotho, could find utterance, said,

'Mistress Watson, I swear to you by the soul of my mother, that although all seeming is against me, W—'

'Where is the young rebel?' interrupted mistress Watson sternly.

'I know not,' answered Dorothy. 'When first I entered the chamber, he had already gone.'

'And what then hadst thou to do entering it?' asked the housekeeper, in a tone that did Dorothy good by angering her.

Mistress Watson was a kind soul in reality, but few natures can resist the debasing influence of a sudden sense of superiority. Besides, was not the young gentlewoman in great wrong, and therefore before her must she not personify an awful Purity?

'That I will tell to none but my Lord Marquis ,' answered Dorothy, with sudden resolve.

'Oh, by all means, mistress! but an' thou think to lead him by the nose while I be in Raglan—'

'Shall I inform his lordship in what high opinion his housekeeper holds him?' said Dorothy. 'It seems to me he will hardly savour it.'

'It would be an ill turn to do me, but my Lord Marquis did never heed a tale-bearer.'

'Then will he not heed the tale thou wouldst yield him concerning me.'

'What tale should I yield him but that I find—thee here and the prisoner gone?'

'The tale I read in thy face and thy voice. Thou lookest and talkest as if I were a false woman.'

'Verily to my eyes the thing looketh ill.'

'It would look ill to any eyes, and therefore I need kind eyes to read, and just ears to hear my tale. I tell thee this is a matter for my lord, and if thou spread any report in the castle ere his lordship hear it, whatever evil springs therefrom it will lie at thy door.'

'My life! what dost take me for, mistress Dorothy? My age and holding deserves some consideration at thy hands! Am I one to go tattling about the courts forsooth?'

'Pardon me, madam, but a maiden's good name may be as precious to Dorothy Vaughan as a matron's respectability to mistress Watson. An' you had left me with that look on your face, and had but spoken my name to it, someone would have guessed ten times more than you know, or I either for that gear.'

'I must tell the truth,' said mistress Watson, relenting a little.

'Thou must, or I will tell it for thee but to the Marquis . Thou shalt be there to hear, and if, after that, thou tell it to another, then hast thou no mother's heart in thee.'

Dorothy gave way at last and burst into tears. Mistress Watson was touched.

'Nay, child, I would do thee no wrong,' she rejoined. 'Get thee to bed. I must rouse the guard to go look for the prisoner, but I will say nothing of thee to any but my Lord Marquis . When he is dressed and in his study, I will come for thee myself.'

Dorothy thanked her warmly, and betook herself to her chamber, considerably relieved.

CHAPTER XXXIII

JUDGE GOUT

Dorothy had hardly reached her room when the castle was once more astir. The rush of the guard across the stone court, the clang of opening lattices, and the voices that called from out-shot heads, again filled her ears, but she never once peeped from her window. A moment, and the news was all over the castle that the prisoner had escaped.

Lord Charles went at once to his father's room. The old man woke instantly. He had but just laid his hand on his mane, not mounted the shadowy steed, and was ill pleased to be already, and the second time, startled back to conscious weariness. When he heard the bad tidings he was silent for a few moments.

'I would Herbert were at home, Charles, to stop this rat-hole for me,' he said at length. 'Let the roundhead go, I care not. I had but half a right to hold him, and he deserves his freedom. But what a governor art thou, my lord? Prithee, dost know the rents in thine own hose, who knowest not when thy gingerbread bulwarks gape? Find me out this rat-hole, I say, or I will depose thee and send for thy brother John, whom the king can ill spare.'

'Have patience with me, father,' said Lord Charles gently. 'I am more ashamed than thou art angry.'

'Thou know'st I did but jest, my son. But in truth an' thou find it not I will send for Lord Herbert. If he find what thou canst not, that will be no disgrace to thee. But find it we must.'

'Think you not, my lord, it were best set mistress Dorothy on the search? She hath a wondrous gift of discovery.'

'A good thought, Charles! I will even do as thou sayest. But search the castle first, from vane to dungeon, that we may be assured the roundhead hath indeed vanished.'

As he spoke the Marquis turned him round, to search the wide gray fields again for the shadowy horse that roamed them tetherless. But the steed would not come to his call; he grew chilly and asthmatic, tossed to and fro, and began to dread an attack of the gout.

The sun rose higher; the hive of men and women was astir once more; the clatter of the day's work and the buzz of the day's talk began, and nothing was in anybody's mouth but the escape of the prisoner. His capture and trial were already of the past, forgotten for the time in the nearer astonishment. Lord Charles went searching, questioning, peering about everywhere, but could find neither prisoner nor the traitorous hole.

Meantime mistress Watson was not a little anxious until she should have revealed what she knew to the Marquis, for the prisoner was in her charge when he disappeared. In the course of the morning Lord Charles came to her apartment to question her, but she begged to be excused, because of a certain disclosure she was not at liberty to make to any but his father. Lord Charles, whom she had known from his boyhood, readily yielded, and mistress Watson, five minutes after he had left his room, followed the Marquis to his study, whither it was his custom always to repair before breakfast. He was looking pale from the trouble of the night, which had resulted in unmistakeable symptoms of the gout, listened to all she had to tell him without comment, looked grave, and told her to fetch mistress Dorothy. As soon as she was gone, he called Scudamore from the antechamber, and sent him to request Lord Charles's presence. He came at once, and was there when Dorothy entered.

She was very white and worn, and her eyes were heavily downcast. Her face wore that expression so much resembling guilt, which indicates the misery the most innocent feel the most under the consciousness of suspicion. At the sight of Lord Charles, she crimsoned: it was one thing to confess to the Marquis, and quite another to do so in the presence of his son.

The Marquis sat with one leg on a stool, already in the gradually contracting gripe of his ghoulish enemy. Before Dorothy could recover from the annoyance of finding Lord Charles present, or open her mouth to beg for a more private interview, he addressed her abruptly.

'Our young rebel friend hath escaped, it seems, mistress Dorothy!' he said, gently but coldly, looking her full in the eyes, with searching gaze and hard expression.

'I am glad to hear it, my lord,' returned Dorothy, with a sudden influx of courage, coming, as the wind blows, she knew not whence.

'Ha!' said the Marquis, quickly; 'then is it news to thee, mistress Dorothy?'

His lip, as it seemed to Dorothy, curled into a mocking smile; but the gout might have been in it.

'Indeed it is news, my lord. I hoped it might be so, I confess, but I knew not that so it was.'

'What, mistress Dorothy! knewest thou not that the young thief was gone?'

'I knew that Richard Heywood was gone from his chamber, whether from the castle I knew not. He was no thief, my lord. Your lordship's page and fool were the thieves.'

'Cousin, I hardly know myself in the change I find in thee! Truly, a marvellous change! In the dark night thou takest a roundhead prisoner; in the gray of the morning thou settest him free again! Hath one visit to his chamber so wrought upon thee? To an old man it seemeth less than maidenly.'

Again a burning blush overspread poor Dorothy's countenance. But she governed herself, and spoke bravely, although she could not keep her voice from trembling.

'My lord,' she said, 'Richard Heywood was my playmate. We were as brother and sister, for our fathers' lands bordered each other.'

'Thou didst say nothing of these things last night?'

'My lord! Before the whole hall? Besides, what mattered it? All was over long ago, and I had done my part against him.'

'Fell you out together then?'

'What need is there for your lordship to ask? Thou seest him of the one part, and me of the other.'

'And from loving thou didst fall to hating?'

'God forbid, my lord! I but do my part against him.'

'For the which thou hadst a noble opportunity unsought, raising the hue and cry upon him within his enemy's walls!'

'I would to God, my lord, it had not fallen to me.'

'Thinking better of it, therefore, and repenting of thy harshness, thou didst seek his chamber in the night to tell him so? I would fain know how a maiden reasoneth with herself when she doth such things.'

'Not so, my lord. I will tell you all. I could not sleep for thinking of my wounded playmate. And as to what he had done, after it became clear that he sought but his own, and meant no hair's-breadth of harm to your lordship, I confess the matter looked not the same.'

'Therefore you would make him amends and undo what you had done? You had caught the bird, and had therefore a right to free the bird when you would? All well, mistress Dorothy, had he been indeed a bird! But being a man, and in thy friend's house, I doubt thy logic. The thing had passed from thy hands into mine, young mistress,' said the Marquis , into the ball of whose foot the gout that moment ran its unicorn-horn.

'I did not set him free, my lord. When I entered the prison-chamber, he was already gone.'

'Thou hadst the will and didst it not! Is there yet another in my house who had the will and did it?' cried the Marquis , who, although more than annoyed that she should have so committed herself, yet was willing to give such scope to a lover, that if she had but confessed she had liberated him, he would have pardoned her heartily. He did not yet know how incapable Dorothy was of a lie.

'But, my lord, i had not the will to set him free,' she said.

'Wherefore then didst go to him?'

'My lord, he was sorely wounded, and I had seen him fall fainting,' said Dorothy, repressing her tears with much ado.

'And thou didst go to comfort him?'

Dorothy was silent.

'How camest thou locked into his room? Tell me that, mistress.'

'Your lordship knows as much of that as I do. Indeed, I have been sorely punished for a little fault.'

'Thou dost confess the fault then?'

'If it WAS a fault to visit him who was sick and in prison, my lord.'

The Marquis was silent for a whole minute.

'And thou canst not tell how he gat him forth of the walls? Must I believe him to be forth of them, my lord?' he said, turning to his son.

'I cannot imagine him within them, my lord, after such search as we have made.'

'Still,' returned the Marquis , the acuteness of whose wits had not been swallowed up by that of the gout, 'so long as thou canst not tell how he gat forth, I may doubt whether he be forth. If the manner of his exit be acknowledged hidden, wherefore not the place of his refuge? Mistress Dorothy,' he continued, altogether averse to the supposition of treachery amongst his people, 'thou art bound by all obligations of loyalty and shelter and truth, to tell what thou knowest. An' thou do not, thou art a traitor to the house, yea to thy king, for when the worst comes, and this his castle is besieged, much harm may be wrought by that secret passage, yea, it may be taken thereby.'

'You say true, my lord: I should indeed be so bound, an' I knew what my Lord would have me disclose.'

'One may be bound and remain bound,' said the Marquis , spying prevarication. 'Now the thing is over, and the youth safe, all I ask of thee, and surely it is not much, is but to bar the door against his return, except indeed thou didst from the first contrive so to meet thy roundhead lover in my loyal house. Then indeed it were too much to require of thee! Ah ha! mistress Dorothy, the little blind god is a rascally deceiver. He is but blind nor' nor' west. He playeth hoodman, and peepeth over his bandage.'

'My lord, you wrong me much,' said Dorothy, and burst into tears, while once more the red lava of the human centre rushed over her neck and brow. 'I did think that I had done enough both for my Lord of Worcester and against Richard Heywood, and I did hope that he had escaped: there lies the worst I can lay to my charge even in thought, my lord, and I trust it is no more than may be found pardonable.'

'It sets an ill example to my quiet house if the ladies therein go anights to the gentlemen's chambers.'

'My lord, you are cruel,' said Dorothy.

'Not a soul in the house knows it but myself, my lord,' said mistress Watson.

'Hold there, my good woman! Whose hand was it turned the key upon her? More than thou must know thereof. Hear me, mistress Dorothy: I would be heart-loath to quarrel with thee, and in all honesty I am glad thy lover—'

'He is no lover of mine, my lord! At least—'

'Be he what he may, he is a fine fellow, and I am glad he hath escaped. Do thou but find out for my Lord Charles here the cursed rat-hole by which he goes and comes, and I will gladly forgive thee all the trouble thou hast brought into my sober house. For truly never hath been in my day such confusion and uproar therein as since thou camest hither, and thy dog and thy lover and thy lover's mare followed thee.'

'Alas, my lord! if I were fortunate enough to find it, what would you but say I found it where I knew well to look for it?'

'Find it, and I promise thee I will never say word on the matter again. Thou art a good girl, and thou do venture a hair too far for a lover. The still ones are always the worst, mistress Watson.'

'My lord! my lord!' cried Dorothy, but ended not, for his lordship gave a louder cry. His face was contorted with anguish, and he writhed under the tiger fangs of the gout.

'Go away,' he shouted, 'or I shall disgrace my manhood before women, God help me!'

'I trust thee will bear me no malice,' said the housekeeper, as they walked in the direction of Dorothy's chamber.

'You did but your duty,' said Dorothy quietly.

'I will do all I can for thee,' continued mistress Watson, mounted again, if not on her high horse then on her palfrey, by her master's behaviour to the poor girl—'if thou but confess to me how thou didst contrive the young gentleman's escape, and wherefore he locked the door upon thee.'

At the moment they were close to Dorothy's room; her answer to the impertinence was to walk in and shut the door; and mistress Watson was thenceforward entirely satisfied of her guilt.

CHAPTER XXXIV

And now was an evil time for Dorothy. She retired to her chamber more than disheartened by Lord Worcester's behaviour to her, vexed with herself for doing what she would have been more vexed with herself for having left undone, feeling wronged, lonely, and disgraced, conscious of honesty, yet ashamed to show herself and all for the sake of a presumptuous boy, whose opinions were a disgust to her and his actions a horror! Yet not only did she not repent of what she had done, but, fact as strange as natural, began, with mingled pleasure and annoyance, to feel her heart drawn towards the fanatic as the only one left her in the world capable of doing her justice, that was, of understanding her. She thus unknowingly made a step towards the discovery that it is infinitely better to think wrong and to act right upon that wrong thinking, than it is to think right and not to do as that thinking requires of us. In the former case the man's house, if not built upon the rock, at least has the rock beneath it; in the latter, it is founded on nothing but sand. The former man may be a Saul of Tarsus, the latter a Judas Iscariot. He who acts right will soon think right; he who acts wrong will soon think wrong. Any two persons acting faithfully upon opposite convictions, are divided but by a bowing wall; any two, in belief most harmonious, who do not act upon it, are divided by infinite gulfs of the blackness of darkness, across which neither ever beholds the real self of the other.

Dorothy ought to have gone at once to Lady Margaret and told her all; but she naturally and rightly shrank from what might seem an appeal to the daughter against the judgment of her father; neither could she dare hope that, if she did, her judgment would not be against her also. Her feelings were now in danger of being turned back upon herself, and growing bitter; for a lasting sense of injury is, of the human moods, one of the least favourable to sweetness and growth. There was no one to whom she could turn. Had good Dr. Bayly been at home but he was away on some important mission from his lordship to the king: and indeed she could scarcely have looked for refuge from such misery as hers in the judgment of the rather priggish old-bachelor ecclesiastic. Gladly would she have forsaken the castle, and returned to all the dangers and fears of her lonely home; but that would be to yield to a lie, to flee from the devil instead of facing him, and with her own hand to fix the imputed smirch upon her forehead, exposing herself besides to the suspicion of having fled to join her lover, and cast in her lot with his amongst the traitors. Besides, she had been left by Lord Herbert in charge of his fire-engine and the water of the castle, which trust she could not abandon. Whatever might be yet to come of it, she must stay and encounter it, and would in the meantime set herself to discover, if she might, the secret pathway by which dog and man came and went at their pleasure. This she owed her friends, even at the risk, in case of success, of confirming the Marquis 's worst suspicions.

She was not altogether wrong in her unconscious judgment of Lady Margaret. Her nature was such as, its nobility tinctured with romance, rendered her perfectly capable of understanding either of the two halves of Dorothy's behaviour, but was not sufficient to the reception and understanding of the two parts together. That is, she could have understood the heroic capture of her former lover, or she could have understood her going to visit him in his trouble, and even, what Dorothy was incapable of, his release; but she was not yet equal to understanding how she should set herself so against a man, even to his wounding and capture, whom she loved so much as, immediately thereupon, to dare the loss of her good name by going to his chamber, so placing herself in the power of a man she had injured, as well as running a great risk of discovery on the part of her friends. Hence she was quite prepared to accept the solution of her strange conduct, which by and by, it was hard to say how, came to be offered and received all over the castle, that Dorothy first admitted, then captured, and finally released the handsome young roundhead.

Her first impressions of the affair, Lady Margaret received from Lord Charles, who was certainly prejudiced against Dorothy, and no doubt jealous of the relation of the fine young rebel to a loyal maiden of Raglan; while the suspicion, almost belief, that she knew and would not reveal the flaw in his castle, the idea of which had begun to haunt him like some spot in his own body of which pain made him unnaturally conscious, annoyed him more and more. To do him justice, I must not omit to mention that he never made a communication on the matter to any but his sister-in-law, who would however have certainly had a more kindly as well as exculpatory feeling towards Dorothy, had she first heard the truth from her own lips.

For some little time, not perceiving the difficulties in her way, and perhaps from unlikeness not understanding the disinclination of such a girl to self-defence, Lady Margaret continued to expect a visit from her, with excuse at least, if not confession and apology upon her lips, and was hurt by her silence as much as offended by her behaviour. She was yet more annoyed, when they first met, that, notwithstanding her evident suffering, she wore such an air of reticence, and thence she both regarded and addressed her coldly; so that Dorothy was confirmed in her disinclination to confide in her. Besides, as she said to herself, she had nothing to tell but what she had already told; everything depended on the interpretation accorded to the facts, and the right interpretation was just the one thing she had found herself unable to convey. If her friends did not, she could not justify herself.

She tried hard to behave as she ought, for, conscious how much appearances were against her, she felt it would be unjust to allow her affection towards her mistress to be in the least shaken by her treatment of her, and was if possible more submissive and eager in her service than before. But in this she was every now and then rudely checked by the fear that Lady Margaret would take it as the endeavour of guilt to win favour; and, do what she would, instead of getting closer to her, she felt every time they met, that the hedge of separation which had sprung up between them had in the interval grown thicker. By degrees the mistress had assumed towards the poor girl that impervious manner of self-contained dignity, which, according to her who wears it, is the carriage either of a wing-bound angel, the gait of a stork, or the hobble of a crab.

Of a different kind was the change which now began to take place towards her on the part of another member of the household.

While she had been intent upon Richard as he stood before the Marquis , not Amanda only but another as well had been intent upon her. Poor creature as Scudamore yet was, he possessed, besides no small generosity of nature, a good deal of surface sympathy, and a ready interest in the shows of humanity. Hence as he stood regarding now the face of the prisoner and now that of Dorothy, whom he knew for old friends, he could not help noticing that every phase of the prisoner, so to speak, might be read on Dorothy. He was too shallow to attribute this to anything more than the interest she must feel in the results of the exploit she had performed. The mere suggestion of what had afforded such wide ground for speculation on the part of Amanda, was to Scudamore rendered impossible by the meeting of two things, the fact that the only time he had seen them together, Richard was very plainly out of favour, and now the all-important share Dorothy had had in his capture. But the longer he looked, the more he found himself attracted by the rich changefulness of expression on a countenance usually very still. He surmised little of the conflict of emotions that sent it to the surface, had to construct no theory to calm the restlessness of intellectual curiosity, discovered no secret feeding of the flame from behind. Yet the flame itself drew him as the candle draws the moth. Emotion in the face of a woman was enough to attract Scudamore; the prettier the face, the stronger the attraction, but the source or character of the emotion mattered nothing to him: he asked no questions any more than the moth, but circled the flame. In a word, Dorothy had now all at once become to him interesting.

As soon as she found a safe opportunity, Amanda told him of Dorothy's being found in the turret chamber, a fact she pretended to have heard in confidence from mistress Watson, concealing her own part in it. But as Amanda spoke, Dorothy became to Rowland twice as interesting as ever Amanda had been. There was a real romance about the girl, he thought. And then she LOOKED so quiet! He never thought of defending her or playing the true part of a cousin. Amanda might think of her as she pleased: Rowland was content. Had he cared ever so much more for her judgment than he did, it would have been all the same. How far Dorothy had been right or wrong in visiting Heywood, he did not even conjecture, not to say consider. It was enough that she who had been to him like the blank in the centre of the African map, was now a region of marvels and possibilities, vague but not the less interesting, or the less worthy of beholding the interest she had awaked. As to her loving the roundhead fellow, that would not stand long in the way.

In this period then of gloom and wretchedness, Dorothy became aware of a certain increase of attention on the part of her cousin. This she attributed to kindness generated of pity. But to accept it, and so confess that she needed it, would have been to place herself too much on a level with one whom she did not respect, while at the same time it would confirm him in whatever probably mistaken grounds he had for offering it. She therefore met his advances kindly but coldly, a treatment under which his feelings towards her began to ripen into something a little deeper and more genuine.

During the next ten days or so, Dorothy could not help feeling that she was regarded by almost every one in the castle as in disgrace, and that deservedly. The most unpleasant proof she had of this was the behaviour of the female servants, some of them assuming airs of injured innocence, others of offensive familiarity in her presence, while only one, a kitchen-maid she seldom saw, Tom Fool's bride in the marriage-jest, showed her the same respect as formerly. This girl came to her one night in her room, and with tears in her eyes besought permission to carry her meals thither, that she might be spared eating with the rude ladies, as in her indignation she called them. But Dorothy saw that to forsake mistress Watson's table would be to fly the field, and therefore, hateful as it was to meet the looks of those around it, she did so with unvailed lids and an enforced dignity which made itself felt. But the effort was as exhausting as painful, and the reflex of shame, felt as shame in spite of innocence, was eating into her heart. In vain she said to herself that she was guiltless; in vain she folded herself round in the cloak of her former composure; the consciousness that, to say the least of it, she was regarded as a young woman of questionable refinement, weighed down her very eyelids as she crossed the court.

But she was not left utterly forsaken; she had still one refuge, the workshop, where Caspar Kaltoff wrought like an 'artificial god;' for the worthy German altered his manner to her not a whit, but continued to behave with the mingled kindness of a father and devotion of a servant. His respect and trustful sympathy showed, without word said, that he, if no other, believed nothing to her disadvantage, but was as much her humble friend as ever; and to the hitherto self-reliant damsel, the blessedness of human sympathy, embodied in the looks and tones of the hard-handed mechanic, brought such healing and such schooling together, that for a long time she never said her prayers by her bedside without thanking God for Caspar Kaltoff.

Ere long her worn look, thin cheek, and weary eye began to work on the heart of Lady Margaret, and she relented in spirit towards the favourite of her husband, whose anticipated disappointment in her had sharpened the arrows of her resentment. But to the watery dawn of favour which followed, the poor girl could not throw wide her windows, knowing it arose from no change in Lady Margaret's judgment concerning her: she could not as a culprit accept what had been as a culprit withdrawn from her. The conviction burned in her heart like cold fire, that, but for compassion upon the desolate state of an orphan, she would have been at once dismissed from the castle. Sometimes she ventured to think that if Lord Herbert had been at home, all this would not have happened; but now what could she expect other than that on his return he would regard her and treat her in the same way as his wife and father and brother?

CHAPTER XXXV

THE DELIVERER

But she found some relief in applying her mind to the task which Lord Worcester had set her; and many a night as she tossed sleepless on her bed, would she turn from the thoughts that tortured her, to brood upon the castle, and invent if she might some new possible way, however difficult, of getting out of it unseen: and many a morning after the night thus spent, would she hasten, ere the household was astir, to examine some spot which had occurred to her as perhaps containing the secret she sought. One time it was a chimney that might have door and stair concealed within it; another, the stables, where she examined every stall in the hope of finding a trap to an underground way. Had anyone else been in question but Richard, the traitor, the roundhead, she might have imagined an associate within the walls, in which case farther solution would not have been for her; but somehow, she did not make it clear to herself how, she could not entertain the idea in connection with Richard. Besides, in brooding over everything, it had grown plain to her that both Richard and Marquis had that night been through the moat.

Some who caught sight of her in the early dawn, wandering about and peering here and there, thought that she was losing her senses; others more ingenious in the thinking of evil, imagined she sought to impress the household with a notion of her innocence by pretending a search for the concealed flaw in the defences.

Ever since she had been put in charge of the water-works, she had been in the habit of lingering a little on the roof of the keep as often as occasion took her thither, for she delighted in the far outlook on the open country which it afforded; and perhaps it was a proof of the general healthiness of her nature that now in her misery, instead of shutting herself up in her own chamber, she oftener sought the walk around the reservoir, looking abroad in shadowy hope of some lurking deliverance, like captive lady in the stronghold of evil knight. On one of these occasions, in the first of the twilight, she was leaning over one of the battlements looking down upon the moat and its white and yellow blossoms and great green leaves, and feeling very desolate. Her young life seemed to have crumbled down upon her and crushed her heart, and all for one gentle imprudence.

'Oh my mother!' she murmured, 'an' thou couldst hear me, thou wouldst help me an' thou couldst. Thy poor Dorothy is sorely sad and forsaken, and she knows no way of escape. Oh my mother, hear me!'

As she spoke, she looked away from the moat to the sky, and spread out her arms in the pain of her petition.

There was a step behind her.

'What! what! My little protestant praying to the naughty saints! That will never do.'

Dorothy had turned with a great start, and stood speechless and trembling before Lord Herbert.

'My poor child!' he said, holding out both his hands, and taking those which Dorothy did not offer, 'did I startle thee then so much? I am truly sorry. I heard but thy last words; be not afraid of thy secret. But what hath come to thee? Thou art white and thin, there are tears on thy face, and it seems as thou wert not so glad to see me as I thought thou wouldst have been. What is amiss? I hope thou art not sick, but plainly thou art ill at ease! Go not yet after my Molly, cousin, for truly we need thee here yet a while.'

'Would i might go to Molly, my lord!' said Dorothy. 'Molly would believe me.'

'Thou need'st not go to Molly for that, cousin. I will believe thee. Only tell me what thou wouldst have me believe, and I will believe it. What! think'st thou I am not magician enough to know whom to believe and whom not? Fye, fye, mistress! Thou, on thy part, wilt not put faith in thy cousin Herbert!'

His kind words were to her as the voice of him that calleth for the waters of the sea that he may pour them out on the face of the earth. The poor girl burst into a passion of weeping, fell on her knees before him, and holding up her clasped hands, cried out in a voice of sob-choked agony, for she was not used to tears, and it was to her a rending of the heart to weep—

'Save me, save me, my lord! I have no friend in the world who can help me but thee.'

'No friend! What meanest thou, Dorothy?' said Lord Herbert, taking her two clasped hands between his. 'There is my Margaret and my father!'

'Alas, my lord! they mean well by me, but they do not believe me; and if your lordship believe me no more than they, I must go from Raglan. Yet believing me, I know not how you could any more help me.'

'Dorothy, my child, I can do nothing till thou take me with thee. I cannot even comfort thee.'

'Your lordship is weary,' said Dorothy, rising and wiping her eyes. 'You cannot yet have eaten since you came. Go, my lord, and hear my tale first from them that believe me not. They will assure you of nothing that is not true, only they understand it not, and wrong me in their conjectures. Let my Lady Margaret tell it you, my lord, and then if you have yet faith enough in me to send for me, I will come and answer all you ask. If you send not for me, I will ride from Raglan to-morrow.'

'It shall be as thou sayest, Dorothy. An' it be not fit for the judge to hear both sides of the tale, or an' it boots the innocent which side he first heareth, then were he no better judge than good king James, of blessed memory, when he was so sore astonished to find both sides in the right.'

'A king, my lord, and judge foolishly!'

'A king, my damsel, and judged merrily. But fear me not; I trust in God to judge fairly even betwixt friend and foe, and I doubt not it will be now to the lightening of thy trouble, my poor storm-beaten dove.'

It startled Dorothy with a gladness that stung like pain, to hear the word he never used but to his wife thus flit from his lips in the tenderness of his pity, and alight like the dove itself upon her head. She thanked him with her whole soul, and was silent.

'I will send hither to thee, my child, when I require thy presence; and when I send come straight to my lady's parlour.'

Dorothy bowed her head, but could not speak, and Lord Herbert walked quickly from her. She heard him run down the stair almost with the headlong speed of his boy Henry.

Half an hour passed slowly, then Lady Margaret's page came lightly up the steps, bearing the request that she would favour his mistress with her presence. She rose from the battlement where she had seated herself to watch the moon, already far up in the heavens, as she brightened through the gathering dusk, and followed him with beating heart.

When she entered the parlour, where as yet no candles had been lighted, she saw and knew nothing till she found herself clasped to a bosom heaving with emotion.

'Forgive me, Dorothy,' sobbed Lady Margaret. 'I have done thee wrong. But thou wilt love me yet again, wilt thou not, Dorothy?'

'Madam! madam!' was all Dorothy could answer, kissing her hands.

Lady Margaret led her to her husband, who kissed her on the forehead, and seated her betwixt himself and his wife; and for a space there was silence. Then at last said Dorothy:

'Tell me, madam, how is it that I find myself once more in the garden of your favour? How know you that I am not all unworthy thereof?'

'My Lord tells me so,' returned Lady Margaret simply.

'And whence doth my Lord know it?' asked Dorothy, turning to Lord Herbert.

''An' thou be not satisfied of thine own innocence, Dorothy, I will ask thee a few questions. Listen to thine answers, and judge. How came the young puritan into the castle that night? But stay: we must have candles, for how can I, the judge, or my lady, the jury, see into the heart of the prisoner save through the window of her face?'

Dorothy laughed, her first laugh since the evil fog had ascended and swathed her. Lady Margaret rang the bell on her table. Candles were brought from where they stood ready in the ante-chamber, and as soon as they began to burn clear, Lord Herbert repeated his question.

'My lord,' answered Dorothy, 'I look to you to tell me so much, for before God I know not.'

'Nay, child! thou need'st not buttress thy words with an oath,' said his lordship. 'Thy fair eyes are worth a thousand oaths. But to the question: tell me wherefore didst thou not let the young man go when first thou spied him? Wherefore didst ring the alarm-bell? Thou sawest he was upon his own mare, for thou knewest her, didst thou not?'

'I did, my lord; but he had no business there, and I was of my Lord Worcester's household. Here I am not Dorothy Vaughan, but my lady's gentlewoman.'

'Then why didst thou go to his room thereafter? Didst thou not know it for the most perilous adventure maiden could undergo?'

'Perilous it hath indeed proved, my lord.'

'And might have proved worse than perilous.'

'No, my lord. Other danger was none where Richard was,' returned Dorothy with vehemence.

'It beareth a look as if mayhap thou dost or mightst one day love the young man!' said Lord Herbert in slow pondering tone.

'My spirit hath of late been driven to hold him company, my lord. It seemed that, save Caspar, I had no friend left but him. God help me! it were a fearful thing to love a fanatic! But I will resist the devil.'

'Truly we are in lack of a few such devils on what we count the honest side, Dorothy!' said Lord Herbert, laughing. 'Not every man that thinks the other way is a rogue or a fool. But thou hast not told me why thou didst run the heavy risk of seeking him in the night.'

'I could not rest for thinking of him, my lord, with that terrible wound in the head I had as good as given him, and from whose effects I had last seen him lie as one dead. He was my playmate, and my mother loved him.'

Here poor Dorothy broke down and wept, but recovered herself with an effort, and proceeded.

'I kept starting awake, seeing him thus at one time, and at another hearing him utter my name as if entreating me to go to him, until at last I believed that I was called.'

'Called by whom, Dorothy?'

'I thought, I thought, my lord, it might be the same that called Samuel, who had opened my ears to hear Richard's voice.'

'And it was indeed therefore thou didst go?'

'I think so, my lord. I am sure, at least, but for that I would not have gone. Yet surely I mistook, for see what hath come of it,' she added, turning to Lady Margaret.

'We must not judge from one consequence where there are a thousand yet to follow,' said his lordship. '—And thou sayest, when thou didst enter the room thou didst find no one there?'

'I say so, my lord, and it is true.'

'That I know as well as thou. What then didst thou think of the matter?'

'I was filled with fear, my lord, when I saw the bedclothes all in a heap on the floor, but upon reflection I hoped that he had had the better in the struggle, and had escaped; for now at least he could do no harm in Raglan, I thought. But when I found the door was locked, I dare hardly think of that, my lord; it makes me tremble yet.'

'Now, who thinkest thou in thy heart did lock the door upon thee?'

'Might it not have been Satan himself, my lord?'

'Nay, I cannot tell what might or might not be where such a one is so plainly concerned. But I believe he was only acting in his usual fashion, which, as a matter of course, must be his worst, I mean through the heart and hands of someone in the house who would bring thee into trouble.'

'I would it were the other way, my lord.'

'So would I heartily. In his own person I fear him not a whit. But hast thou no suspicion of any one owing thee a grudge, who might be glad on such opportunity to pay it thee with interest?'

'I must confess I have, my lord; but I beg of your lordship not to question me on the matter further, for it reaches only to suspicion. I know nothing, and might, if I uttered a word, be guilty of grievous wrong. Pardon me, my lord.'

Lord Herbert looked hard at his wife. Lady Margaret dropped her head.

'Thou art right, indeed, my good cousin!' he said, turning again to Dorothy; 'for that would be to do by another as thou sufferest so sorely from others doing by thee. I must send my brains about and make a discovery or two for myself. It is well I have a few days to spend at home. And now to the first part of the business in hand. Hast thou any special way of calling thy dog? It is a moonlit night, I believe.'

He rose and went to the window, over which hung a heavy curtain of Flemish tapestry.

'It is a three-quarter old moon, my lord,' said Dorothy, 'and very bright. I did use to call my dog with a whistle my mother gave me when I was a child.'

'Canst thou lay thy hand upon it? Hast thou it with thee in Raglan?'

'I have it in my hand now, my lord.'

'What then with the moon and thy whistle, I think we shall not fail.'

'Hast lost thy wits, Ned?' said his wife. 'Or what fiend wouldst thou raise to-night?'

'I would lay one rather,' returned Lord Herbert. 'But first I would discover this same perilous fault in the armour of my house. Is thy genet still in thy control, Dorothy?'

'I have no reason to think otherwise, my lord. The frolicker he, the merrier ever was I.'

'Darest thou ride him alone in the moonlight, outside the walls.'

'I dare anything on Dick's back, that Dick can do, my lord.'

'Doth thy dog know Caspar, in friendly fashion, I mean?'

'Caspar is the only one in the castle he is quite friendly with, my lord.'

'Then is all as I would have it. And now I will tell thee what I would not have: I would not have a soul in the place but my lady here know that I am searching with thee after this dog-and-man hole. Therefore I will saddle thy little horse for thee myself, and—'

'No, no, my lord!' interrupted Dorothy. 'That I can do.'

'So much the better for thee. But I am no boor, fair damsel. Then shalt thou mount and ride him forth, and Marquis thy mastiff shall see thee go from the yard. Then will I mount the keep, and from that point of vantage look down upon the two courts, while Caspar goes to stand by thy dog. Thou shalt ride slowly along for a minute or two, until these preparations shall have been made; then shalt thou blow thy whistle, and set off at a gallop to round the castle, still ever and anon blowing thy whistle; by which means, if I should fail to see thy Marquis leave the castle, thou mayest perchance discover at least from which side of the castle he comes to thee.'

Dorothy sprang to her feet.

'I am ready, my lord,' she said.

'And so am I, my maiden,' returned Lord Herbert, rising. 'Wilt go to the top of the keep, wife, and grant me the light of eyes in aid of the moonshine? I will come thither presently.'

'Thou shalt find me there, Ned, I promise thee. Mother Mary speed thy quest?'

CHAPTER XXXVI

THE DISCOVERY

All was done as had been arranged. Lord Herbert saddled Dick, not unaided of Dorothy, lifted her to his back, and led her to the gate, in full vision of Marquis , who went wild at the sight, and threatened to pull down kennel and all in his endeavours to follow them. Lord Herbert himself opened the yard gate, for the horses had already been suppered, and the men were in bed. He then walked by her side down to the brick gate. A moment there, and she was free and alone, with the wide green fields and the yellow moonlight all about her.

She had some difficulty in making Dick go slowly, quietly she could not, for the first minute or two, as Lord Herbert had directed. He had had but little exercise of late, and moved as if his four legs felt like wings. Dorothy had ridden him very little since she came to the castle, but being very handy, Lord Charles had used him, and one of the grooms had always taken him to ride messages. He had notwithstanding had but little of the pleasure of speed for a long time, and when Dorothy at length gave him the rein, he flew as if every member of his body from tail to ears and eyelids had been an engine of propulsion. But Dorothy had more wings than Dick. Her whole being was full of wings. It was a small thing that she had not had a right gallop since she left Wyfern; the strength she had been putting forth to bear the Atlas burden that night lifted from her soul, was now left free to upbear her, and she seemed in spirit to soar aloft into the regions of aether. With her horse under her, the moon over her, "the wind of their own speed" around them, and her heart beating with a joy such as she had never known, she could hardly help doubting sometimes for a moment whether she was not out in one of those delightful dreams of liberty and motion which had so frequently visited her sleep since she came to Raglan. Three shrill whistles she had blown, about a hundred yards from the gate, had heard the eager crowded bark of her dog in answer, and then Dick went flying over the fields like a water-bird over the lake, that scratches its smooth surface with its feet as it flies. Around the rampart they went. The still night was jubilant around them as they flew. The stars shone as if they knew all about her joy, that the shadow of guilt had been lifted from her, and that to her the world again was fair. She felt as the freed Psyche must feel when she drops the clay, and lo! the whole chrysalid world, which had hitherto hung as a clog at her foot, fast by the inexorable chain our blindness calls gravitation, has dropped from her with the clay, and the universe is her own.

At intervals she blew her whistle, and ever kept her keen eyes and ears awake, looking and listening before and behind, in the hope of hearing her dog, or seeing him come bounding through the moonlight.

Meantime Lord Herbert and his wife had taken their stand on the top of the great tower, and were looking down, the lady into the stone court, and her husband into the grass one. Dorothy's shrill whistle came once, twice, and just as it began to sound a third time,

'Here he comes!' cried Lady Margaret.

A black shadow went from the foot of the library tower, tearing across the moonlight to the hall door, where it vanished. But in vain Lord Herbert kept his eyes on the fountain court, in the hope of its reappearance there. Presently they heard a heavy plunge in the water on the other side of the keep, and running round, saw plainly, the moat there lying broad in the moonlight, a little black object making its way across it. Through the obstructing floats of water-lily-leaves, it held steadily over to the other side. There for a moment they saw the whole body of the animal, as he scrambled out of the water up against the steep side of the moat, when suddenly, and most unaccountably to Lady Margaret, he disappeared.

'I have it!' cried Lord Herbert. 'What an ass I was not to think of it before! Come down with me, my dove, and I will show thee. Dorothy's Marquis hath got into the drain of the moat! He is a large dog, and beyond a doubt that is where the young roundhead entered. Who could have dreamed of such a thing! I had no thought it was such a size.'

Dorothy, having made the circuit, and arrived again at the brick gate, found Lord Herbert waiting there, and pulled up.

'I have seen nothing of him, my lord,' she said, as he came to her side. 'Shall I ride round once more?'

'Do, prithee, for I see thou dost enjoy it. But we have already learned all we want to know, so far as goeth to the security of the castle. There is but one Marquis in Raglan, and he is, I believe, in the oak parlour.'

'You saw my Marquis make his exit then, my lord?'

'My lady and I both saw him.'

'What then can have become of him? We went very fast, and I suppose he gave up the chase in despair.'

'Thou wilt find him the second round. But stay, I will get a horse and go with thee.'

Dorothy went within the gate, and Lord Herbert ran back to the stables. In a few minutes he was by her side again, and together they rode around the huge nest. The moon was glorious, with a few large white clouds around her, like great mirrors hung up to catch and reflect her light. The stars were few, and doubtful near the moon, but shone like diamonds in the dark spaces between the clouds. The rugged fortress lay swathed in the softness of the creamy light. No noise broke the stillness, save the dull drum-beat of their horses' hoofs on the turf, or their cymbal-clatter where they crossed a road, and the occasional shrill call from Dorothy's whistle.

On all sides the green fields, cow-cropped, divided by hedge-rows, and spotted with trees, single and in clumps, came close to the castle walls, except in one or two places where the corner of a red ploughed field came wedging in. All was so quiet and so soft that the gaunt old walls looked as if, having at first with harsh intrusion forced their way up into the sweet realm of air from the stony regions of the earth beneath, by slow degrees, yet long since, they had suffered an air change, and been charmed and gentled into harmony with soft winds and odours and moonlight. To Dorothy it seemed as if peace itself had taken form in the feathery weight that filled the flaky air; and as her horse galloped along, flying like a bird over ditch and mound, her own heart so light that her body seemed to float above the saddle rather than rest upon it, she felt like a soul which, having been dragged to hell by a lurking fiend, a good and strong angel was bearing aloft into bliss. Few delights can equal the mere presence of one whom we trust utterly.

No mastiff came to Dorothy's whistle, and having finished their round, they rode back to the stables, put up their horses, and rejoined Lady Margaret, where she was still pacing the sunk walk around the moat. There Lord Herbert showed Dorothy where her dog vanished, comforting her with the assurance that nothing should be altered before the faithful animal returned, as doubtless he would the moment he despaired of finding her in the open country.

Lord Herbert said nothing to his father that night lest he should spoil his rest, for he was yet far from well, but finding him a good deal better the next morning, he laid open the whole matter to him according to his convictions concerning Dorothy and her behaviour, ending with the words: 'That maiden, my lord, hath truth enough in her heart to serve the whole castle, an' if it might be but shared. To doubt her is to wrong the very light. I fear there are not many maidens in England who would have the courage and honesty, necessary both, to act as she hath done.'

The Marquis listened attentively, and when Lord Herbert had ended, sat a few moments in silence; then, for all answer, said,

'Go and fetch her, my lad.'

When Dorothy entered—

'Come hither, maiden,' he said from his chair. 'Wilt thou kiss an old man who hath wronged thee, for so my son hath taught me?'

Dorothy stooped, and he kissed her on both cheeks, with the tears in his eyes.

'Thou shalt dine at my table,' he said, 'an' thy mistress will permit thee, as I doubt not she will when I ask her, until, thou art weary of our dull company. Hear me, cousin Dorothy: an' thou wilt go with us to mass next Sunday, thou shalt sit on one side of me and thy mistress on the other, and all the castle shall see thee there, and shall know that thou art our dear cousin, mistress Dorothy Vaughan, and shall do thee honour.'

'I thank you, my lord, with all my heart,' said Dorothy, with troubled look, 'but, may I then speak without offence to your lordship, where my heart knoweth nought but honour, love, and obedience?'

'Speak what thou wilt, so it be what thou would'st,' answered the Marquis .

'Then pardon me, my lord, that which would have made my mother sad, and would make my good master Herbert sorry that he brought me hither. He would fear I had forsaken the church of my fathers.'

'And returned to the church of thy grandfathers, eh, mistress Dorothy? And wherefore, then, should that weigh so much with thee, so long as thou wert no traitor to our blessed Lord?'

'But should I be no traitor, sir, an' I served him not with my best?'

'Thou hast nothing better than thy heart to give him, and nothing worse will serve his turn; and that we two have offered where I would have thee offer thine, and I trust, Herbert, the offering hath not lain unaccepted.'

'I trust not, my lord,' responded Herbert.

'But, my lord,' said Dorothy, with hot cheek and trembling voice, 'if I brought it him upon a dish which I believed to be of brass, when I had one of silver in the house, would it avail with him that your lordship knew the dish to be no brass, but the finest of gold? I should be unworthy of your lordship's favour, if, to be replaced in the honour of men, I did that which needed the pardon of God.'

'I told thee so, sir!' cried Lord Herbert, who had been listening with radiant countenance.

'Thou art a good girl, Dorothy,' said the Marquis . 'Verily I spoke but to try thee, and I thank God thou hast stood the trial, and answered aright. Now am I sure of thee; and I will no more doubt thee, not if I wake in the night and find thee standing over me with a drawn dagger like Judith. An' my worthy Bayly had been at home, perchance this had not happened; but forgive me, Dorothy, for the gout is the sting of the devil's own tail, and driveth men mad. Verily, it seemeth now as if I could never have behaved to thee as I have done. Why, one might say the foolish fat old man was jealous of the handsome young puritan! The wheel will come round, Dorothy. One day thou wilt marry him.'

'Never, my lord,' exclaimed Dorothy with vehemence.

'And when thou dost,' the Marquis went on, 'all I beg of thee is, that on thy wedding day thou whisper thy bridegroom: "My Lord of Worcester told me so;" and therewith thou shalt have my blessing, whether I be down here in Raglan, or up the great stair with little Molly.'

Dorothy was silent. The Marquis held out his hand. She kissed it, left the room, and flew to the top of the keep.

CHAPTER XXXVII

THE HOROSCOPE

Ere the next day was over, it was understood throughout the castle that Lord Herbert was constructing a horoscope, not that there were many in the place who understood what a horoscope really was, or had any knowledge of the modes of that astrology in whose results they firmly believed; yet Kaltoff having been seen carrying several mysterious-looking instruments to the top of the library tower, the word was presently in everybody's mouth. Nor were the lovers of marvel likely to be disappointed, for no sooner was the sun down than there was Lord Herbert, his head in an outlandish Persian hat, visible over the parapet from the stone-court, while from some of the higher windows in the grass-court might be seen through a battlement his long flowing gown of a golden tint, wrought with hieroglyphics in blue. Now he would stand for a while gazing up into the heavens, now would be shifting and adjusting this or that instrument, then peering along or through it, and then re-arranging it, or kneeling and drawing lines, now circular, now straight, upon a sheet of paper spread flat on the roof of the tower. There he still was when the household retired to rest, and there, in the grey dawn, his wife, waking up and peeping from her window, saw him still, against the cold sky, pacing the roof with bent head and thoughtful demeanour. In the morning he was gone, and no one but Lady Margaret saw him during the whole of the following day. Nor indeed could any but herself or Caspar have found him, for the tale Tom Fool told the rustics of a magically concealed armoury had been suggested by a rumour current in the house, believed by all without any proof, and yet not the less a fact, that Lord Herbert had a chamber of which none of the domestics knew door or window, or even the locality. That recourse should have been had to spells and incantations for its concealment, however, as was also commonly accepted, would have seemed trouble unnecessary to anyone who knew the mechanical means his lordship had employed for the purpose. The touch of a pin on a certain spot in one of the bookcases in the library, admitted him to a wooden stair which, with the aid of Caspar, he had constructed in an ancient disused chimney, and which led down to a small chamber in the roof of a sort of porch built over the stair from the stone-court to the stables. There was no other access to it, and the place had never been used, nor had any window but one which they had constructed in the roof so cunningly as to attract no notice. All the household supposed the hidden chamber, whose existence was unquestioned, to be in the great tower, somewhere near the workshop.

In this place he kept his books of alchemy and magic, and some of his stranger instruments. It would have been hard for himself even to say what he did or did not believe of such things. In certain moods, especially when under the influence of some fact he had just discovered without being able to account for it, he was ready to believe everything; in others, especially when he had just succeeded, right or wrong, in explaining anything to his own satisfaction, he doubted them all considerably. His imagination leaned lovingly towards them; his intellect required proofs which he had not yet found.

Hither then he had retired, to work out the sequences of the horoscopes he had that night constructed. He was far less doubtful of astrology than of magic. It would have been difficult, I suspect, to find at that time a man who did not more or less believe in the former, and the influence of his mechanical pursuits upon Lord Herbert's mind had not in any way interfered with his capacity for such belief. In the present case, however, he trusted for success rather to his knowledge of human nature than to his questioning of the stars.

Before this, the second day, was over, it was everywhere whispered that he was occupied in discovering the hidden way by which entrance and exit had been found through the defences of the castle; and the next day it was known by everybody that he had been successful, as who could doubt he must, with such powers at his command?

For a time curiosity got the better of fear, and there was not a soul in the place, except one bedridden old woman, who did not that day accept Lord Herbert's general invitation, and pass over the Gothic bridge to see the opening from the opposite side of the moat. To seal the conviction that the discovery had indeed been made, permission was given to any one who chose to apply to it the test of his own person, but of this only Shafto the groom availed himself. It was enough, however: he disappeared, and while the group which saw him enter the opening was yet anxiously waiting his return by the way he had gone, having re-entered by the western gate he came upon them from behind, to the no small consternation of those of weaker nerves, and so settled the matter for ever.

As soon as curiosity was satisfied, Lord Herbert gave orders which, in the course of a few days, rendered the drain as impassable to manor dog as the walls of the keep itself.

In the middle of the previous night, Marquis had returned, and announced himself by scratching and whining for admittance at the door of Dorothy's room. She let him in, but not until the morning discovered that he had a handkerchief tied round his neck, and in it a letter addressed to herself. Curious, perhaps something more than curious, to open it, she yet carried it straight to Lord Herbert.

'Canst not break the seal, Dorothy, that thou bringest it to me? I will not read it first, lest thou repent,' said his lordship.

'Will you open it then, madam?' she said, turning to Lady Margaret.

'What my Lord will not, why should I?' rejoined her mistress.

Dorothy opened the letter without more ado, crimsoned, read it to the end, and handed it again to Lord Herbert.

'Pray read, my lord,' she said.

He took it, and read. It ran thus—

'Mistress Dorothy, I think, and yet I know not, but I think thou wilt be pleased to learn that my Wound hath not proved mortal, though it hath brought me low, yea, very nigh to Death's Door. Think not I feared to enter. But it grieveth me to the Heart to ride another than my own Mare to the Wars, and it will pleasure thee to know that without my Lady I shall be but Half the Man I was. But do thou the Like again when thou mayest, for thou but didst thy Duty according to thy Lights; and according to what else should anyone do? Mistaken as thou art, I love thee as mine own Soul. As to the Ring I left for thee, with a safe Messenger, concerning whom I say Nothing, for thou wilt con her no Thanks for the doing of aught to pleasure me, I restored it not because it was thine, for thy mother gave it me, but because, if for Lack of my Mare I should fall in some Battle of those that are to follow, then would the Ring pass to a Hand whose Heart knew nought of her who gave it me. I am what thou knowest not, yet thine old Play-fellow Richard. When thou hearest of me in the Wars, as perchance thou mayest, then curse me not, but sigh an thou wilt, and say, he also would in his Blindness do the Thing that lay at his Door. God be with thee, mistress Dorothy. Beat not thy Dog for bringing thee this.

'RICHARD HEYWOOD.'

Lord Herbert gave the letter to his wife, and paced up and down the room while she read. Dorothy stood silent, with glowing face and downcast eyes. When Lady Margaret had finished it she handed it to her, and turned to her husband with the words—

'What sayest thou, Ned? Is it not a brave epistle?'

'There is matter for thought therein,' he answered. 'Wilt show me the ring whereof he writes, cousin?'

'I never had it, my lord.'

'Whom thinkest thou then he calleth his safe messenger? Not thy dog, plainly, for the ring had been sent thee before.'

'My lord, I cannot even conjecture,' answered Dorothy.

'There is matter herein that asketh attention. My lady, and cousin Dorothy, not a word of all this until I shall have considered what it may import! Beat not thy dog, Dorothy: that were other than he deserveth at thy hand. But he is a dangerous go-between, so prithee let him be at once chained up.'

'I will not beat him, my lord, and I will chain him up,' answered Dorothy, laughing.

Having then announced the discovery of the hidden passage, and given orders concerning it, Lord Herbert retired yet again to his secret chamber, and that night was once more seen of many consulting the stars from the top of the library tower.

The following morning another rumour was abroad—to the effect that his lordship was now occupied in questioning the stars as to who in the castle had aided the young roundhead in making his escape.

In the evening, soon after supper, there came a gentle tap to the door of Lady Margaret's parlour. At that time she was understood to be disengaged, and willing to see any of the household. Harry happened to be with her, and she sent him to the door to see who it was.

'It is Tom Fool,' he said, returning. 'He begs speech of you, madam—with a face as long as the baker's shovel, and a mouth as wide as an oven-door.'

With their Irish stepmother the children took far greater freedoms than would have been permitted them by the jealous care of their own mother over their manners.

Lady Margaret smiled: this was probably the first fruit of her husband's astrological investigations.

'Tell him he may enter, and do thou leave him alone with me, Harry,' she said.

Allowing for exaggeration, Harry had truly reported Tom's appearance. He was trembling from head to foot, and very white.

'What aileth thee, Tom, that thou lookest as thou had seen a hobgoblin?' said Lady Margaret.

'Please you, my lady,' answered Tom, 'I am in mortal terror of my Lord Herbert.'

'Then hast thou been doing amiss, Tom? for no well-doer ever yet was afeard of my lord. Comest thou because thou wouldst confess the truth?'

'Ah, my lady,' faltered Tom.

'Come, then; I will lead thee to my lord.'

'No, no, an't please you, my lady!' cried Tom, trembling yet more. 'I will confess to you, my lady, and then do you confess to my lord, so that he may forgive me.'

'Well, I will venture so far for thee, Tom,' returned her ladyship; 'that is, if thou be honest, and tell me all.'

Thus encouraged, Tom cleansed his stuffed bosom, telling all the part he had borne in Richard's escape, even to the disclosure of the watchword to his mother.

Is there not this peculiarity about the fear of the supernatural, even let it be of the lowest and most slavish kind, that under it men speak the truth, believing that alone can shelter them?

Lady Margaret dismissed him with hopes of forgiveness, and going straight to her husband in his secret chamber, amused him largely with her vivid representation, amounting indeed to no sparing mimicry of Tom's looks and words as he made his confession.

Here was much gained, but Tom had cast no ray of light upon the matter of Dorothy's imprisonment. The next day Lord Herbert sent for him to his workshop, where he was then alone. He appeared in a state of abject terror.

'Now, Tom,' said his lordship, 'hast thou made a clean breast of it?'

'Yes, my lord,' answered Tom; 'there is but one thing more.'

'What is that? Out with it.'

'As I went back to my chamber, at the top of the stair leading down from my lord's dining parlour to the hall, commonly called my lord's stair,' said Tom, who delighted in the pseudo-circumstantial, 'I stopped to recover my breath, of the which I was sorely bereft, and kneeling on the seat of the little window that commands the archway to the keep, I saw the prisoner—'

'How knewest thou the prisoner ere it was yet daybreak, and that in the darkest corner of all the court?'

'I knew him by the way my bones shook at the white sleeves of his shirt, my lord,' said Tom, who was too far gone in fear to make the joke of pretending courage.

'Hardly evidence, Tom. But go on.'

'And with him I saw mistress Dorothy—'

'Hold there, Tom!' cried Lord Herbert. 'Wherefore didst not impart this last night to my lady?'

'Because my lady loveth mistress Dorothy, and I dreaded she would therefore refuse to believe me.'

'What a heap of cunning goes to the making of a downright fool!' said Lord Herbert to himself, but so as Tom could not fail to hear him. 'And what saw'st thou pass between them?' he asked.

'Only a whispering with their heads together,' answered Tom.

'And what heard'st thou?'

'Nothing, my lord.'

'And what followed?'

'The roundhead left her, and went through the archway. She stood a moment and then followed him. But I, fearful of her coming up the stair and finding me, gat me quickly to my own place.'

'Oh, Tom, Tom! I am ashamed of thee. What! Afraid of a woman? Verily, thy heart is of wax.'

'That can hardly be, my lord, for I find it still on the wane.'

'An' thy wit were no better than thy courage, thou hadst never had enough to play the fool with.'

'No, my lord; I should have had to turn philosopher.'

'A fair hit, Tom! But tell me, why wast thou afeard of mistress Dorothy?'

'It might have come to a quarrel in some sort, my lord; and there is one thing I have remarked in my wanderings through this valley of Baca,' said Tom, speaking through his nose, and lengthening his face beyond even its own nature, 'namely, that he who quarrels with a woman goes ever to the wall.'

'One thing perplexes me, Tom: if thou sawest mistress Dorothy in the court with the roundhead, how came she thereafter, thinkest thou, locked up in his chamber?'

'It behoves that she went into it again, my lord.'

'How knowest thou she had been there before?'

'Nay, I know not, my lord. I know nothing of the matter.'

'Why say'st it then? Take heed to thy words, Tom. Who then, thinkest thou, did lock the door upon her?'

'I know not, my lord, and dare hardly say what I think. But let your lordship's wisdom determine whether it might not be one of those demons whereof the house hath been full ever since that night when I saw them rise from the water of the moat, that even now surrounds us, my lord! and rush into the fountain court.'

'Meddle thou not, even in thy thoughts, with things that are beyond thee,' said Lord Herbert. 'By what signs knewest thou mistress Dorothy in the dark as she stood talking to the roundhead?'

'There was light enough to know woman from man, my lord.'

'And were there then that night no women in the castle but mistress Dorothy?'

'Why, who else could it have been, my lord?'

'Why not thine own mother, Tom, rode thither on her broomstick to deliver her darling?'

Tom gaped with fresh terror at the awful suggestion.

'Now, hear me, Thomas Rees,' his lordship went on.

'Yes, my lord,' answered Tom.

'An' ever it come to my knowledge that thou say thou then saw mistress Dorothy, when all thou sawest was, as thou knowest, a woman who might have been thine own mother talking to the roundhead, as thou callest a man who might indeed have been Caspar Kaltoff in his shirt sleeves, I will set every devil at my command upon thy back and thy belly, thy sides and thy soles. Be warned, and not only speak the truth, as thou hast for a whole half-hour been trying hard to do, but learn to distinguish between thy fancies and God's facts; for verily thou art a greater fool than I took thee for, and that was no small one. Get thee gone, and send me hither mistress Watson.'

Tom crawled away, and presently mistress Watson appeared, looking offended, possibly at being called to the workshop, and a little frightened.

'I cannot but think thee somewhat remiss in thy ministrations to a sick man, mistress Watson,' he said, 'to leave him so long to himself. Had he been a king's officer now, wouldst thou not have shown him more favour?'

'That indeed may be, my lord,' returned mistress Watson with dignity. 'But an' the young fellow had been very sick, he had not made his escape.'

'And left the blame thereof with thee. Besides, that he did for his escape he may have done in the strength of the fever that followeth on such a wound.'

'My lord, I gave him a potion, wherefrom he should have slept until I sought him again.'

'Was he or thou to blame that he did not feel the obligation? When a man instead of sleeping runneth away, the potion was ill mingled, I doubt, mistress Watson, drove him crazy perchance.'

'She who waked him when he ought to have slept hath to bear the blame, not I, my lord.'

'Thou shouldst, I say, have kept better watch. But tell me whom meanest thou by that same SHE?'

'She who was found in his chamber, my lord,' said mistress Watson, compressing her lips, as if, come what might, she would stand on the foundation of the truth.

'Ah? By the way, I would gladly understand how it came to be known throughout the castle that thou didst find her there? I have the assurance of my lady, my Lord Marquis , and my Lord Charles, that never did one of them utter word so to slander an orphan as thou hast now done in my hearing. Who then can it be but her who is at the head of the meinie of this house, who hath misdemeaned herself thus to the spreading amongst those under her of evil reports and surmises affecting her lord's cousin, mistress Dorothy Vaughan?'

'You wrong me grievously, my lord,' cried mistress Watson, red with the wrath of injury and undeserved reproof.

'Thou hast thyself to thank for it then, for thou hast this night said in mine own ears that mistress Dorothy waked thy prisoner, importing that she thereafter set him free, when thou knowest that she denies the same, and is therein believed by my Lord Marquis and all his house.'

'Therein I believe her not, my lord; but I swear by all the saints and angels, that to none but your lordship have I ever said the word; neither have I ever opened my lips against her, lest I should take from her the chance of betterment.'

'I will be more just to thee than thou hast been to my cousin, mistress Watson, for I will believe thee that thou didst only harbour evil in thy heart, not send it from the doors of thy lips to enter into other bosoms. Was it thou then that did lock the door upon her?'

'God forbid, my lord!'

'Thinkest thou it was the roundhead?'

'No, surely, my lord, for where would be the need?'

'Lest she should issue and give the alarm.'

Mistress Watson smiled an acid smile.

'Then the doer of that evil deed,' pursued Lord Herbert, 'must be now in the castle, and from this moment every power I possess in earth, air, or sea, shall be taxed to the uttermost for the discovery of that evil person. Let this vow of mine be known, mistress Watson, as a thing thou hast heard me say, not commission thee to report. Prithee take heed to what I desire of thee, for I am not altogether powerless to enforce that I would.'

Mistress Watson left the workshop in humbled mood. To her spiritual benefit Lord Herbert had succeeded in punishing her for her cruelty to Dorothy; and she was not the less willing to mind his injunction as to the mode of mentioning his intent, that it would serve to the quenching of any suspicion that she had come under his disapproval.

And now Lord Herbert, depending more upon his wits than his learning, found himself a good deal in the dark. Confident that neither Richard, Tom Fool, nor mistress Watson had locked the door of the turret chamber after Dorothy's entrance, he gave one moment to the examination of the lock, and was satisfied that an enemy had done it. He then started his thoughts on another track, tending towards the same point: how was it that the roundhead, who had been carried insensible to the turret-chamber, had been able, ere yet more than a film of grey thinned the darkness, without alarming a single sleeper, to find his way from a part of the house where there were no stairs near, and many rooms, all occupied? Clearly by the help of her, whoever she was, whom Tom Fool had seen with him by the hall door. She had guided him down my lord's stair, and thus avoided the risk of crossing the paved court to the hall door within sight of the warders of the main entrance. To her indubitably the young roundhead had committed the ring for Dorothy. Here then was one secret agent in the affair: was it likely there had been two? If not, this woman was one and the same with the person who turned the key upon Dorothy. She probably had been approaching the snare while the traitress talked with the prisoner. What did her presence so soon again in the vicinity of the turret-chamber indicate? Possibly that her own chamber was near it. The next step then was to learn from the housekeeper who slept in the neighbourhood of the turret-chamber, and then to narrow the ground of search by inquiring which, if any of them, slept alone.

He found there were two who occupied each a chamber by herself; one of them was Amanda, the other mistress Watson.

Now therefore he knew distinctly in what direction first he must point his tentatives. Before he went farther, however, he drew from Dorothy an accurate description of the ring to which Richard's letter alluded, and immediately set about making one after it, from stage to stage of its progress bringing it to her for examination and criticism, until, before the day was over, he had completed a model sufficiently like to pass for the same.

The greater portion of the next day he spent in getting into perfect condition a certain mechanical toy which he had constructed many years before, and familiarising himself with its working. This done, he found himself ready for his final venture, to give greater solemnity to which he ordered the alarum-bell to be rung, and the herald of the castle to call aloud, first from the bell-tower in the grass-court, next from the roof of the hall-porch in the stone-court, communicating with the minstrels' gallery, that on the following day, after dinner, so soon as they should hear the sound of the alarum-bell, every soul in the castle, to the infant in arms, all of whatever condition, save old mother Prescot, who was bed-ridden, should appear in the great hall, that Lord Herbert might perceive which amongst them had insulted the Lord and the rule of the house by the locking of one of its doors to the imprisonment and wrong of his lordship's cousin, mistress Dorothy Vaughan. Three strokes of the great bell opened and closed the announcement, and a great hush of expectancy, not unmingled with fear, fell upon the place.

There was one in the household, however, who at first objected to the whole proceeding. That was sir Toby Mathews, the catholic chaplain. He went to the Marquis and represented that, if there was to be any exercise whatever of unlawful power, the obligations of the sacred office with which he was invested would not permit him to be present or connive thereat. The Marquis merrily insisted that it was a case of exorcism; that the devil was in the castle, and out he must go; that if Satan assisted in the detection of the guilty and the purging of the innocent, then was he divided against himself, and what could be better for the church or the world? But for his own part he had no hand in it, and if sir Toby had anything to say against it, he must go to his son. This he did at once; but Lord Herbert speedily satisfied him, pledging himself that there should be nothing done by aid from beneath, and making solemn assertion that if ever he had employed any of the evil powers to work out his designs, it had been as their master and not their accomplice.

CHAPTER XXXVIII

THE EXORCISM

It was the custom in Raglan to close the gates at eleven o'clock every morning, and then begin to lay the tables for dinner; nor were they opened again until the meal was over, and all had dispersed to their various duties. Upon this occasion directions were given that the gates should remain closed until the issue of further orders.

There was little talk in the hall during dinner that day, and not much in the Marquis 's dining-room.

In the midst of the meal at the housekeeper's table, mistress Amanda was taken suddenly ill, and nearly fell from her chair. A spoonful of one of mistress Watson's strong waters revived her, but she was compelled to leave the room.

When the remains of the dinner had been cleared away, the tables lifted from the trestles, and all removed, solemn preparations began to be made in the hall. The dais was covered with crimson cloth, and chairs were arranged on each side against the wall for the lords and ladies of the family, while in the wide space between was set the Marquis 's chair of state. Immediately below the dais, chairs were placed by the walls for the ladies and officers of the household. The minstrels' gallery was hung with crimson; long ladders were brought, and the windows, the great bay window and all save the painted one, were hung with thick cloth of the same colour, so that a dull red light filled the huge place. The floor was then strewn with fresh rushes, and candles were placed and lighted in sconces on the walls, and in two large candlesticks, one on each side of the Marquis 's chair. So numerous were the hands employed in these preparations, that about one o'clock the alarum-bell gave three great tolls, and then silence fell.

Almost noiselessly, and with faces more than grave, the people of the castle in their Sunday clothes began at once to come trooping in, amongst the rest Tom Fool, the very picture of dismay. Mrs. Prescot had refused to be left behind, partly from terror, partly from curiosity, and supine on a hand-barrow was borne in, and laid upon two of the table-trestles. Order and what arrangement was needful were enforced amongst them by Mr. Cook, one of the ushers. In came the garrison also, with clank and clang, and took their places with countenances expressive neither of hardihood nor merriment, but a grave expectancy.

Mostly by the other door came the ladies and officers, amongst them Dorothy, and seated themselves below the dais. When it seemed at length that all were present, the two doors were closed, and silence reigned.

A few minutes more and the ladies and gentlemen of the family, in full dress, entered by the door at the back of the dais, and were shown to their places by Mr. Moyle, the first usher. Next came the Marquis , leaning on Lord Charles, and walking worse than usual. He too was, wonderful to tell, in full dress, and, notwithstanding his corpulency and lameness, looked every inch a Marquis and the head of the house. He placed himself in the great chair, and sat upright, looking serenely around on the multitude of pale expectant faces, while Lord Charles took his station erect at his left hand. A moment yet, and by the same door, last of all, entered Lord Herbert, alone, in his garb of astrologer. He came before his father, bowed to him profoundly, and taking his place by his right hand, a little in front of the chair, cast a keen eye around the assembly. His look was grave, even troubled, and indeed somewhat anxious.

'Are all present?' he asked, and was answered only by silence. He then waved his right hand three times towards heaven, each time throwing open his palm outwards and upwards. At the close of the third wafture, a roar as of thunder broke and rolled about the place, making the huge hall tremble, and the windows rattle and shake fearfully. Some thought it was thunder, others thought it more like the consecutive discharge of great guns. It grew darker, and through the dim stained window many saw a dense black smoke rising from the stone-court, at sight of which they trembled yet more, for what could it be but the chariot upon which Modo, or Mahu, or whatever the demon might be called, rode up from the infernal lake? Again Lord Herbert waved his arm three times, and again the thunder broke and rolled vibrating about the place. A third time he gave the sign, and once more, but now close over their heads, the thunder broke, and in the midst of its echoes, high in the oak roof appeared a little cloud of smoke. It seemed to catch the eye of Lord Herbert. He made one step forward, and held out his hand towards it, with the gesture of a falconer presenting his wrist to a bird.

'Ha! art thou here?' he said.

And to the eyes of all, a creature like a bat was plainly visible, perched upon his forefinger, and waving up and down its filmy wings. He looked at it for a moment, bent his head to it, seemed to whisper, and then addressed it aloud.

'Go,' he said, 'alight upon the head of him or of her who hath wrought the evil thou knowest in this house. For it was of thine own kind, and would have smirched a fair brow.'

As he spoke he cast the creature aloft. A smothered cry came from some of the women, and Tom Fool gave a great sob and held his breath tight. Once round the wide space the bat flew, midway between floor and roof, and returning perched again upon Lord Herbert's hand.

'Ha!' said his lordship, stooping his head over it, 'what meanest thou? Is not the evil-doer in presence? What? Nay, but it cannot be? Not within the walls? Ha! "Not in the HALL" thou sayest!'

He lifted his head, turned to his father, and said,

'Your lordship's commands have been disregarded. One of your people is absent.'

The Marquis turned to Lord Charles.

'Call me the ushers of the hall, my lord,' he said.

In a moment the two officers were before him.

'Search and see, and bring me word who is absent,' said the Marquis .

The two gentlemen went down into the crowd, one from each side of the dais.

A minute or two passed, and then Mr. Cook came back and said—

'My lord, I cannot find Caspar Kaltoff.'

'Caspar! Art not there, Caspar?' cried Lord Herbert.

'Here I am, my lord,' answered the voice of Caspar from somewhere in the hall.

'I beg your lordship's pardon,' said Mr. Cook. 'I failed to find him.'

'It matters not, master usher. Look again,' said Lord Herbert.

At the moment, Caspar, the sole attendant spirit, that day at least, upon his lord's commands, stood in one of the deep windows behind the crimson cloth, more than twenty feet above the heads of the assembly. The windows were connected by a narrow gallery in the thickness of the wall, communicating also with the minstrels' gallery, by means of which, and a ladder against the porch, Caspar could come and go unseen.

As Lord Herbert spoke, Mr. Moyle came up on the dais, and brought his report that mistress Amanda Fuller was not with the rest of the ladies.

Lord Herbert turned to his wife.

'My lady,' he said, 'mistress Amanda is of your people: knowest thou wherefore she cometh not?'

'I know not, my lord, but I will send and see,' replied Lady Margaret. 'My Lady Broughton, wilt thou go and inquire wherefore the damsel disregardeth my Lord of Worcester's commands?'

She had chosen the gentlest-hearted of her women to go on the message.

Lady Broughton came back pale and trembling, indeed there was much pallor and trembling that day in Raglan, with the report that she could not find her. A shudder ran through the whole body of the hall. Plainly the impression was that she had been FETCHED. The thunder and the smoke had not been for nothing: the devil had claimed and carried off his own! On the dais the impression was somewhat different; but all were one in this, that every eye was fixed on Lord Herbert, every thought hanging on his pleasure.

For a whole minute he stood, apparently lost in meditation. The bat still rested on his hand, but his wings were still.

He had intended causing it to settle on Amanda's head, but now he must alter his plan. Nor was he sorry to do so, for it had involved no small risk of failure, the toy requiring most delicate adjustment, and its management a circumspection and nicety that occasioned him no little anxiety. It had indeed been arranged that Amanda should sit right under the window next the dais, so that he might have the assistance of Caspar from above; but if by any chance the mechanical bat should alight upon the head of another, mistress Doughty or Lady Broughton instead of Amanda, what then? He was not sorry to find himself rescued from this jeopardy, and scarcely more than a minute had elapsed ere he had devised a plan by which to turn the check to the advantage of all, even that of Amanda herself, towards whom, while he felt bound to bring her to shame should she prove guilty, he was yet willing to remember mercy; while, should she be innocent, no harm would now result from his mistaken suspicion. He turned and whispered to his father.

'I will back thee, lad. Do as thou wilt,' returned the Marquis , gravely nodding his head.

'Ushers of the hall,' cried Lord Herbert, 'close and lock both its doors. Lock also the door to the minstrels' gallery, and, with my lord's leave, that to my lord's stair. My Lord Charles, go thou prithee, and with chalk draw me a pentacle upon the threshold of each of the four; and do thou, sir Toby Mathews, make the holy sign thereabove upon the lintel and the doorposts. For the door to the pitched court, however, leave that until I am gone forth and it is closed behind me, and then do thereunto the same as to the others, after which let all sit in silence. Move not, neither speak, for any sound of fear or smell of horror. For the gift that is in him from his mother, Thomas Rees shall accompany me. Go to the door, and wait until I come.'

Having thus spoken he raised the bat towards his face, and, approaching his lips, seemed once more to be talking to it in whispers. The menials and the garrison had no doubt but he talked to his familiar spirit. Of their superiors, mistress Watson at least was of the same conviction. Then he bent his ear towards it as if he were listening, and it began to flutter its wings, at which sir Toby's faith in him began to waver. A moment more and he cast the creature from him. It flew aloft, traversed the whole length of the roof, and vanished.

It had in fact, as its master willed, alighted in the farthest corner of the roof, a little dark recess. Then, bowing low to his father, the magician stepped down from the dais, and walked through a lane of awe-struck domestics and soldiery to the door, where Tom stood waiting his approach. The fool was in a strange flutter of feelings, a conflict of pride and terror, the latter of which would, but for the former, have unnerved him quite; for not only was he doubtful of the magician's intent with regard to himself, but the hall seemed now the only place of security, and all outside it given over to goblins or worse.

The moment they crossed the threshold, the door was closed behind them, the holy sign was signed over the one, and the pentacle drawn upon the other.

All eyes were turned upon the Marquis . He sat motionless. Motionless, too, as if they had been carved in stone like the leopard and wyvern over their heads, sat all the lords and ladies, embodying in themselves the words of the motto there graven, Mulaxe Vel Timere Sperno. Motionless sat the ladies beneath the dais, but their faces were troubled and pale, for Amanda was one of them, and their imaginations were busy with what might now be befalling her. Dorothy sat in much distress, for although she could lay no evil intent to her own charge, she was yet the cause of the whole fearful business. As for Scudamore, though he too was white of blee, he said to himself, and honestly, that the devil might fly away with her and welcome for what he cared. One woman in the crowd fainted and fell, but uttered never a moan. The very children were hushed by the dread that pervaded the air, and the smell of sulphur, which from a suspicion grew to a plain presence, increased not a little the high-wrought awe.

After about half an hour, during which expectation of something frightful had been growing with every moment, three great knocks came to the porch door. Mr. Moyle opened it, and in walked Lord Herbert as he had issued, with Tom Fool, in whom the importance had now at length banished almost every sign of dread, at his heels. He reascended the dais, bowed once more to his father, spoke a few words to him in a tone too low to be overheard, and then turning to the assembly, said with solemn voice and stern countenance:

'The air is clear. The sin of Raglan is purged. Every one to his place.'

Had not Tom Fool, who had remained by the door, led the way from the hall, it might have been doubtful when any one would venture to stir; but, with many a deep-drawn breath and sigh of relief, they trooped slowly out after him, until the body of the hall was empty. In their hearts keen curiosity and vague terror contended like fire and water.

From that hour, while Raglan stood, the face of Amanda Serafina was no more seen within its walls. At midnight shrieks and loud wailings were heard, but if they came from Amanda, they were her last signs.

I shall not, however, hide the proceedings of Lord Herbert without the hall any more than he did himself when he reached the oak parlour with the members of his own family, in which Dorothy seemed now included. He had taken Tom Fool both because he knew the castle so well, and might therefore be useful in searching for Amanda, and because he believed he might depend, if not on his discretion, yet on his dread, for secrecy. They had scarcely left the hall before they were joined by Caspar, who, while his master and the fool went in one direction, set off in another, and after a long search in vain, at length found her in an empty stall in the subterranean stable, as if, in the agony of her terror at the awful noises and the impending discovery, she had sought refuge in the companionship of the innocent animals. She was crouching, the very image of fear, under the manger, gave no cry when he entered, but seemed to gather a little courage when she found that the approaching steps were those of a human being.

'Mistress Amanda Fuller,' said his lordship with awful severity, 'thou hast in thy possession a jewel which is not thine own.'

'A jewel, my lord?' faltered Amanda, betaking herself by the force of inborn propensity and habit, even when hopeless of success in concealment, to the falsehood she carried with her like an atmosphere; 'I know not what your lordship means. Of what sort is the jewel?'

'One very like this,' returned Lord Herbert, producing the false ring.

'Why, there you have it, my lord!'

'Traitress to thy king and thy lord, out of thine own mouth have I convicted thee. This is not the ring. See!'

As he spoke he squeezed it betwixt his finger and thumb to a shapeless mass, and threw it from him, then continued:

'Thou art she who did show the rebel his way from the prison into which her Lord had cast him.'

'He took me by the throat, my lord,' gasped Amanda, 'and put me in mortal terror.'

'Thou slanderest him,' returned Lord Herbert. 'The roundhead is a gentleman, and would not, to save his life, have harmed thee, even had he known what a worthless thing thou art. I will grant that he put thee in fear. But wherefore gavest thou no alarm when he was gone?'

'He made me swear that I would not betray him.'

'Let it be so. Why didst thou not reveal the way he took?'

'I knew it not.'

'Yet thou wentest after him when he left thee. And wherefore didst thou not deliver the ring he gave thee for mistress Dorothy?'

'I feared she would betray me, that I had held talk with the prisoner.'

'Let that too pass as less wicked than cowardly. But wherefore didst thou lock the door upon her when thou sawest her go into the roundhead's prison? Thou knewest that therefrom she must bear the blame of having set him free, with other blame, and worse for a maiden to endure?'

'It was a sudden temptation, my lord, which I knew not how to resist, and was carried away thereby. Have pity upon me, dear my lord,' moaned Amanda.

'I will believe thee there also, for I fear me thou hast had so little practice in the art of resisting temptation, that thou mightst well yield to one that urged thee towards such mere essential evil. But how was it that, after thou hadst had leisure to reflect, thou didst spread abroad·the report that she was found there, and that to the hurt not only of her loyal fame, but of her maidenly honour, understanding well that no one was there but herself, and that he alone who could bear testimony to her innocence and thy guilt was parted from her by everything that could divide them except hatred? Was the temptation to that also too sudden for thy resistance?'

At length Amanda was speechless. She hung her head, for the first time in her life ashamed of herself.

'Go before to thy chamber. I follow thee.'

She rose to obey, but she could scarcely walk, and he ordered the men to assist her. Arrived in her room she delivered up the ring, and at Lord Herbert's command proceeded to gather together her few possessions. That done, they led her away to the rude chamber in the watch tower, where stood the arblast, and there, seated on her chest, they left her with the assurance that if she cried out or gave any alarm, it would be to the publishing of her own shame.

At the dead of night Caspar and Tom, with four picked men from the guard, came to lead her away. Worn out by that time, and with nothing to sustain her from within, she fancied they were going to kill her, and giving way utterly, cried and shrieked aloud. Obdurate however, as gentle, they gave no ear to her petitions, but bore her through the western gate, and so to the brick gate in the rampart, placed her in a carriage behind six horses, and set out with her for Caerleon, where her mother lived in obscurity. At her door they set her down, and leaving the carriage at Usk, returned to Raglan one by one in the night, mounted on the horses. By the warders who admitted them they were supposed to be returned from distinct missions on the king's business.

Many were the speculations in the castle as to the fate of mistress Amanda Serafina Fuller, but the common belief continued to be that she had been carried off by Satan, body and soul.

VOLUME III

CHAPTER XXXIX

NEWBURY

Early the next morning, after Richard had left the cottage for Raglan castle, mistress Rees was awaked by the sound of a heavy blow against her door. When with difficulty she had opened it, Richard or his dead body, she knew not which, fell across her threshold. Like poor Marquis , he had come to her for help and healing.

When he got out of the quarry, he made for the highroad, but missing the way the dog had brought him, had some hard work in reaching it; and long before he arrived, at the cottage, what with his wound, his loss of blood, his double wetting, his sleeplessness after mistress Watson's potion, want of food, disappointment and fatigue, he was in a high fever. The last mile or two he had walked in delirium, but happily with the one dominant idea of getting help from mother Rees. The poor woman was greatly shocked to find that the teeth of the trap had closed upon her favourite and mangled him so terribly. A drop or two of one of her restoratives, however, soon brought him round so far that he was able to crawl to the chair on which he had sat the night before, now ages agone as it seemed, where he now sat shivering and glowing alternately, until with trembling hands the good woman had prepared her own bed for him.

'Thou hast left thy doublet behind thee,' she said, 'and I warrant me the cake I gave thee in the pouch thereof! Hadst thou eaten of that, thou hadst not come to this pass.'

But Richard scarcely heard her voice. His one mental consciousness was the longing desire to lay his aching head on the pillow, and end all effort.

Finding his wound appeared very tolerably dressed, Mrs. Rees would not disturb the bandages. She gave him a cooling draught, and watched by him till he fell asleep. Then she tidied her house, dressed herself, and got everything in order for nursing him. She would have sent at once to Redware to let his father know where and in what condition he was, but not a single person came near the cottage the whole day, and she dared not leave him before the fever had subsided. He raved a good deal, generally in the delusion that he was talking to Dorothy, who sought to kill him, and to whom he kept giving directions, at one time how to guide the knife to reach his heart, at another how to mingle her poison so that it should act with speed and certainty.

At length one fine evening in early autumn, when the red sun shone level through the window of the little room where he lay, and made a red glory on the wall, he came to himself a little.

'Is it blood?' he murmured. 'Did Dorothy do it? How foolish I am! It is but a blot the sun has left behind him! Ah! I see! I am dead and lying on the top of my tomb. I am only marble. This is Redware church. Oh, mother Rees, is it you! I am very glad! Cover me over a little. The pall there.'

His eyes closed, and for a few hours he lay in a deep sleep, from which he awoke very weak, but clear-headed. He remembered nothing, however, since leaving the quarry, except what appeared a confused dream of wandering through an interminable night of darkness, weariness, and pain. His first words were—

'I must get up, mother Rees: my father will be anxious about me. Besides, I promised to set out for Gloucester to-day.'

She sought to quiet him, but in vain, and was at last compelled to inform him that his father, finding he did not return, had armed himself, mounted Oliver, and himself led his little company to join the earl of Essex, who was now on his way, at the head of an army consisting chiefly of the trained bands of London, to raise the siege of Gloucester.

Richard started up, and would have leaped from the bed, but fell back helpless and unconscious. When at length his nurse had succeeded in restoring him, she had much ado to convince him that the best thing in all respects was to lie still and submit to be nursed, so to get well as soon as possible, and join his father.

'Alas, mother, I have no horse,' said Richard, and hid his face on the pillow.

'The Lord will provide what thee wants, my son,' said the old woman with emotion, neither asking nor caring whether the Lord was on the side of the king or of the parliament, but as little doubting that he must be on the side of Richard.

He soon began to eat hopefully, and after a day or two she found pretty nearly employment enough in cooking for him.

At last, weak as he still was, he would be restrained no longer. To Gloucester he must go, and relieve his father. Expostulation was unavailing: go he must, he said, or his soul would tear itself out of his body, and go without it.

'Besides, mother, I shall be getting better all the way,' he continued. '—I must go home at once and see whether there is anything left to go upon.'

He rose the same instant, and, regardless of the good woman's entreaties, crawled out to go to Redware. She followed him at a little distance, and, before he had walked a quarter of a mile, he was ready to accept her offered arm to help him back. But his recovery was now very rapid, and after a few days he felt able for the journey.

At home he found a note from his father, telling him where to find money, and informing him that he was ready to yield him Oliver the moment he should appear to claim him. Richard put on his armour, and went to the stable. The weather had been fine, and the harvest was wearing gradually to a close; but the few horses that were left were overworked, for the necessities of the war had been severe, and that part of the country had responded liberally on both sides. Besides, Mr. Heywood had scarce left an animal judged at all fit to carry a man and keep up with the troop.

When Richard reached the stable, there were in it but three, two of which, having brought loads to the barn, were now having their mid-day meal and rest. The first one was ancient in bones, with pits profound above his eyes, and grey hairs all about a face which had once been black.

'Thou art but fit for old Father Time to lay his scythe across when he is aweary,' said Richard, and turned to the next.

She was a huge-bodied, short-legged punch, as fat as butter, with lop ears and sleepy eyes. Having finished her corn, she was churning away at a mangerful of grass.

'Thou wouldst burst thy belly at the first charge,' said Richard, and was approaching the third, one he did not recognise, when a vicious, straight-out kick informed him that here was temper at least, probably then spirit. But when he came near enough to see into the stall, there stood the ugliest brute he thought that ever ate barley. He was very long-bodied and rather short-legged, with great tufts at his fetlocks, and the general look of a huge rat, in part doubtless from having no hair on his long undocked tail. He was biting vigorously at his manger, and Richard could see the white of one eye glaring at him askance in the gloom.

'Dunnot go nigh him, sir,' cried Jacob Fortune, who had come up behind. 'Thou knows not his tricks. His name be his nature, and we call him Beelzebub when master Stopchase be not by. I be right glad to see your honour up again.'

Jacob was too old to go to the wars, and too indifferent to regret it; but he was faithful, and had authority over the few men left.

'I thank you, Jacob,' said Richard. 'What brute is this? I know him not.'

'We all knows him too well, master Richard, though verily Stopchase bought him but the day before he rode, thinking belike he might carry an ear or two of wheat. If he be not very good he was not parlous dear; he paid for him but an old song. He was warranted to have work in him if a man but knew how to get it out.'

'He is ugly.'

'He is the ugliest horse, cart-horse, nag, or courser, on this creation-side,' said the old man, '—ugly enough to fright to death where he doth fail in his endeavour to kill. The men are all mortal feared on him, for he do kick and he do bite like the living Satan. He wonnot go in no cart, but there he do stand eating on his head off as fast as he can. An' the brute were mine, I would slay him; I would, in good sooth.'

'An' I had but time to cure him of his evil kicking! I fear I must ever ride the last in the troop,' said Richard.

'Why for sure, master, thee never will ride such a devil-pig as he to the wars! Will Farrier say he do believe he take his strain from the swine the devils go into in the miracle. All the children would make a mock of thee as thou did ride through the villages. Look at his legs: they do be like stile-posts; and do but look at his tail!'

'Lead him out, Jacob, and let me see his head.'

'I dare not go nigh him, sir. I be not nimble enough to get out of the way of his hoof. 'I be too old, master.'

Richard pulled on his thick buff glove and went straight into his stall. The brute made a grab at him with his teeth, met by a smart blow from Richard's fist, which he did not like, and, rearing, would have struck at him with his near fore-foot; but Richard caught it by the pastern, and with his left hand again struck him on the side of the mouth. The brute then submitted to be led out by the halter. And verily he was ugly to behold. His neck stuck straight out, and so did his tail, but the latter went off in a point, and the former in a hideous knob.

'Here is Jack!' cried the old man. 'He lets Jack ride him to the water. Here, Jack! Get thee upon the hog-back of Beelzebub, and mind the bristles do not flay thee, and let master Richard see what paces he hath.'

The animal tried to take the lad down with his hind foot as he mounted, but scarcely was he seated when he set off at a swinging trot, in which he plied his posts in manner astonishing. Spirit indeed he must have had, and plenty, to wield such clubs in such a fashion. His joints were so loose that the bones seemed to fly about, yet they always came down right.

'He is guilty of "hypocrisy against the devil,"' said Richard: 'he is better than he looks. Anyhow, if he but carry me thither, he will as well "fill a pit" as a handsomer horse. I'll take him. Have you got a saddle for him?'

'An' he had not brought a saddle with him, thou would not find one in Gwent to fit him,' said the old man.

Yet another day Richard found himself compelled to tarry, which he spent in caparisoning Beelzebub to the best of his ability, with the result of making him, if possible, appear still uglier than before.

The eve of the day of his departure, Marquis   paid mistress Rees a second visit. He wanted no healing or help this time, seeming to have come only to offer his respects. But the knowledge that here was a messenger, dumb and discreet, ready to go between and make no sign, set Richard longing to use him: what message he did send by him I have already recorded. Although, however, the dog left them that night, he did not reach Raglan till the second morning after, and must have been roaming the country or paying other visits all that night and the next day as well, with the letter about him, which he had allowed no one to touch.

At last Richard was on his way to Gloucester, mounted on Beelzebub, and much stared at by the inhabitants of every village he passed through. Apparently, however, there was something about the centaur-compound which prevented their rudeness from going farther. Beelzebub bore him well, and, though not a comfortable horse to ride, threw the road behind him at a wonderful rate, as often and as long as Richard was able to bear it. But he found himself stronger after every rest, and by the time he began to draw nigh to Gloucester, he was nearly as well as ever, and in excellent spirits; one painful thought only haunting him, the fear that he might, mounted on Beelzebub, have to encounter someone on his beloved mare. He was consoled, however, to think that the brute was less dangerous to one before than one behind him, heels being worse than teeth.

He soon became aware that something decisive had taken place: either Gloucester had fallen, or Essex had raised the siege, for army there was none, though the signs of a lately upbroken encampment were visible on all sides. Presently, inquiring at the gate, he learned that, on the near approach of Essex, the besieging army had retired, and that, after a few days' rest, the general had turned again in the direction of London. Richard, therefore, having fed Beelzebub and eaten his own dinner, which in his present condition was more necessary than usual to his being of service, mounted his hideous charger once more, and pushed on to get up with the army.

Essex had not taken the direct road to London, but kept to the southward. That same day he followed him as far as Swindon, and found he was coming up with him rapidly. Having rested a short night, he reached Hungerford the next morning, which he found in great commotion because of the intelligence that at Newbury, some seven miles distant only, Essex had found his way stopped by the king, and that a battle had been raging ever since the early morning.

Having given his horse a good feed of oats and a draught of ale, Richard mounted again and rode hard for Newbury. Nor had he rode long before he heard the straggling reports of carbines, looked to the priming of his pistols, and loosened his sword in its sheath. When he got under the wall of Craven park, the sounds of conflict grew suddenly plainer. He could distinguish the noise of horses' hoofs, and now and then the confused cries and shouts of hand-to-hand conflict. At Spain he was all but in it, for there he met wounded men, retiring slowly or carried by their comrades. These were of his own part, but he did not stop to ask any questions. Beelzebub snuffed at the fumes of the gunpowder, and seemed therefrom to derive fresh vigour.

The lanes and hedges between Spein and Newbury had been the scenes of many a sanguinary tussle that morning, for nowhere had either army found room to deploy. Some of them had been fought over more than once or twice. But just before Richard came up, the tide had ebbed from that part of the way, for Essex's men had had some advantage, and had driven the king's men through the town and over the bridge, so that he found the road clear, save of wounded men and a few horses. As he reached Spinhamland, and turned sharp to the right into the main street of Newbury, a bullet from the pistol of a royalist officer who lay wounded struck Beelzebub on the crest, what of a crest he had, and without injuring made him so furious that his rider had much ado to keep him from mischief. For, at the very moment, they were met by a rush of parliament pikemen, retreating, as he could see, over their heads, from a few of the kings cavalry, who came at a sharp trot down the main street. The pikemen had got into disorder pursuing some of the enemy who had divided and gone to the right and left up the two diverging streets, and when the cavalry appeared at the top of the main street, both parts, seeing themselves in danger of being surrounded, had retreated. They were now putting the Kennet with its narrow bridge between them and the long-feathered cavaliers, in the hope of gaining time and fit ground for forming and presenting a bristled front. In the midst of this confused mass of friends Richard found himself, the maddened Beelzebub every moment lashing out behind him when not rearing or biting.

Before him the bridge rose steep to its crown, contracting as it rose. At its foot, where it widened to the street, stood a single horseman, shouting impatiently to the last of the pikemen, and spurring his horse while holding him. As the last man cleared the bridge, he gave him rein, and with a bound and a scramble reached the apex, and stood, within half a neck of the foremost of the cavalier troop. A fierce combat instantly began between them. The bridge was wide enough for two to have fought side by side, but the roundhead contrived so to work his antagonist, who was a younger but less capable and less powerful man, that no comrade could get up beside him for the to-and-fro shifting of his horse.

Meantime Richard had been making his slow way through the swarm of hurrying pikemen, doing what he could to keep them off Beelzebub. The moment he was clear, he made a great bolt for the bridge, and the same moment perceived who the brave man was.

'Hold on, sir,' he shouted. 'Hold your own, father! Here I am! Here is Richard!'

And as he shouted he sent Beelzebub, like low-flying bolt from cross-bow, up the steep crown of the bridge, and wedged him in between Oliver and the parapet, just as a second cavalier made a dart for the place. At his horse Beelzebub sprang like a fury, rearing, biting, and striking out with his fore-feet in such manner as quite to make up to his rider for the disadvantage of his low stature. The cavalier's horse recoiled in terror, rearing also, but snorting and backing and wavering, so that, in his endeavours to avoid the fury of Beelzebub, which was frightful to see, for with ears laid back and gleaming teeth he looked more like a beast of prey, he would but for the crowd behind him have fallen backward down the slope. A bullet from one of Richard's pistols sent his rider over his tail, the horse fell sideways against that of Mr. Heywood's antagonist, and the path was for a moment barricaded.

'Well done, good Beelzebub!' cried Richard, as he reined him back on to the crest of the bridge.

'Boy!' said his father sternly, at the same instant dealing his encumbered opponent a blow on the head-piece which tumbled him also from his horse, 'is the sacred hour of victory a time to sully with profane and foolish jests? I little thought to hear such words at my side, not to say from the mouth of my own son!'

'Pardon me, father; I praised my horse,' said Richard. 'I think not he ever had praise before, but it cannot corrupt him, for he is such an ill-conditioned brute that they that named him did name him Beelzebub: Now that he hath once done well, who knoweth but it may cease to fit him!'

'I am glad thy foolish words were so harmless,' returned Mr. Heywood, smiling. 'In my ears they sounded so evil that I could ill accept their testimony. Verily the animal is marvellous ill-favoured, but, as thou sayest, he hath done well, and the first return we make him shall be to give him another name. The less man or horse hath to do with Satan the better, for what is he but the arch-foe of the truth?'

While they spoke, they kept a keen watch on the enemy, who could not get near to attack them, save with a few pistol-bullets, mostly wide-shot, for both horses were down, and their riders helpless if not slain.

'What shall we call him then, father?' asked Richard.

'He is amazing like a huge rat!' said his father. 'Let us henceforth call him Bishop.'

'Wherefore Bishop and not Beelzebub, sir?' inquired Richard.

Mr. Heywood laughed, but ere he could reply, a large troop of horsemen appeared at the top of the street. Glancing then behind in some anxiety, they saw to their relief that the pikemen had now formed themselves into a hollow square at the foot of the bridge, prepared to receive cavalry. They turned therefore, and, passing through them, rode to find their regiment.

From that day Bishop, notwithstanding his faults many and grievous, was regarded with respect by both father and son, Richard vowing never to mount another, let laugh who would, so long as the brute lived and he had not recovered Lady.

But they had to give him room for two on the march, and the place behind him was always left vacant, which they said gave no more space than he wanted, seeing he kicked out his leg to twice its walking length. Before long, however, they had got so used to his ways that they almost ceased to regard them as faults, and he began to grow a favourite in the regiment.

CHAPTER XL

DOROTHY AND ROWLAND

Such was the force of law and custom in Raglan that as soon as any commotion ceased things settled at once. It was so now. The minds of the Marquis and Lord Charles being at rest both as regarded the gap in the defences of the castle and the character of its inmates, the very next day all was order again. The fate of Amanda was allowed gradually to ooze out, but the greater portion both of domestics and garrison continued firm in the belief that she had been carried off by Satan. Young Delaware, indeed, who had been revelling late, I mean in the chapel with the organ, and who was always the more inclined to believe a thing the stranger it was, asserted that he SAW devil fly away with her, a testimony which gained as much in one way as it lost in another by the fact that he could not see at all.

To Scudamore her absence, however caused, was only a relief. She had ceased to interest him, while Dorothy had become to him like an enchanted castle, the spell of which he flattered himself he was the knight born to break. All his endeavours, however, to attract from her a single look such as indicated intelligence, not to say response, were disappointed. She seemed absolutely unsuspicious of what he sought, neither, having so long pretermitted what claim he might once have established to cousinly relations with her, could he now initiate any intimacy on that ground. Had she become an inmate of Raglan immediately after he first made her acquaintance, that might have ripened to something more hopeful; but when she came she was in sorrow, nor felt that there was any comfort in him, while he was beginning to yield to the tightening bonds mistress Amanda had flung around him. Nor since had he afforded her any ground for altering her first impressions, or favourably modifying a feature of the portrait Lady Margaret had presented of him.

Strange to say, however, poorly grounded as was the original interest he had taken in her, and little as he was capable of understanding her, he soon began, even while yet confident in his proved advantages of person and mind and power persuasive, to be vaguely wrought upon by the superiority of her nature. With this the establishment of her innocence in the eyes of the household had little to do; indeed, that threatened at first to destroy something of her attraction; a passionate, yielding, even erring nature, had of necessity for such as he far more enchantment than a nature that ruled its own emotions, and would judge such as might be unveiled to it. Neither was it that her cold courtesy and kind indifference roused him to call to the front any of the more valuable endowments of his being; something far better had commenced: unconsciously to himself, the dim element of truth that flitted vaporous about in him had begun to respond to the great pervading and enrounding orb of her verity. He began to respect her, began to feel drawn as if by another spiritual sense than that of which Amanda had laid hold. He found in her an element of authority. The conscious influences to whose triumph he had been so perniciously accustomed, had proved powerless upon her, while those that in her resided unconscious were subduing him. Her star was dominant over his.

At length he began to be aware that this was no light preference, no passing fancy, but something more serious than he had hitherto known, that in fact he was really, though uncomfortably and unsatisfactorily, in love with her. He felt she was not like any other girl he had made his shabby love to, and would have tried to make better to her, but she kept him at a distance, and that he began to find tormenting. One day, for example, meeting her in the court as she was crossing towards the keep—

'I would thou didst take apprentices, cousin,' he said, 'so I might be one, and learn of thee the mysteries of thy trade.'

'Wherefore, cousin?'

'That I might spare thee something of thy labour.'

'That were no kindness. I am not like thee; I find labour a thing to be courted rather than spared; I am not overwrought.'

Scudamore gazed into her grey eyes, but found there nothing to contradict, nothing to supplement the indifference of her words. There was no lurking sparkle of humour, no acknowledgment of kindness. There was a something, but he could not understand it, for his poor shapeless soul might not read the cosmic mystery embodied in their depths. He stammered, who had never known himself stammer before, broke the joints of an ill-fitted answer, swept the tiles with the long feather in his hat, and found himself parted from her, with the feeling that he had not of himself left her, but had been borne away by some subtle force emanating from her.

Lord Herbert had again left the castle. More soldiers and more must still be raised for the king. Now he would be paying his majesty a visit at Oxford, and inspecting the life-guards he had provided him, now back in South Wales, enlisting men, and straining every power in him to keep the district of which his father was governor in good affection and loyal behaviour.

Winter drew nigh, and stayed somewhat the rush of events, clogged the wheels of life as they ran towards death, brought a little sleep to the world and coolness to men's hearts, led in another Christmas, and looked on for a while.

Nor did the many troubles heaped on England, the drained purses, the swollen hearts, the anxious minds, the bereaved houses, the ruptures, the sorrows, and the hatreds, yet reach to dull in any large measure the merriment of the season at Raglan. Customs are like carpets, forever wearing out whether we mark it or no, but Lord Worcester's patriarchal prejudices, cleaving to the old and looking askance on the new, caused them to last longer in Raglan than almost anywhere else: the old were the things of his fathers which he had loved from his childhood; the new were the things of his children which he had not proven.

What a fire that was that blazed on the hall-hearth under the great chimney, which, dividing in two, embraced a fine window, then again becoming one, sent the hot blast rushing out far into the waste of wintry air! No one could go within yards of it for the fierce heat of the blazing logs, now and then augmented by huge lumps of coal. And when, on the evenings of special merry-making, the candles were lit, the musicians were playing, and a country dance was filling the length of the great floor, in which the whole household, from the Marquis himself, if his gout permitted, to the grooms and kitchen-maids, would take part, a finer outburst of homely splendour, in which was more colour than gilding, more richness than shine, was not to be seen in all the island.

On such an occasion Rowland had more than once attempted nearer approach to Dorothy, but had gained nothing. She neither repelled nor encouraged him, but smiled at his better jokes, looked grave at his silly ones, and altogether treated him like a boy, young, or old, enough to be troublesome if encouraged. He grew desperate, and so one night summoned up courage as they stood together waiting for the next dance.

'Why will you never talk to me, cousin Dorothy?' he said.

'Is it so, Mr. Scudamore? I was not aware. If thou spoke and I answered not, I am sorry.'

'No, I mean not that,' returned Scudamore. 'But when I venture to speak, you always make me feel as if I ought not to have spoken. When I call you COUSIN DOROTHY, you reply with MR. SCUDAMORE.'

'The relation is hardly near enough to justify a less measure of observance.'

'Our mothers loved each other.'

'They found each other worthy.'

'And you do not find me such?' sighed Scudamore, with a smile meant to be both humble and bewitching.

'N-n-o. Thou hast not made me desire to hold with thee much converse.'

'Tell me why, cousin, that I may reform that which offends thee.'

'If a man see not his faults with his own eyes, how shall he see them with the eyes of another?'

'Wilt thou never love me, Dorothy? Not even a little?'

'Wherefore should I love thee, Rowland?'

'We are commanded to love even our enemies.'

'Art thou then mine enemy, cousin?'

'No, forsooth! I am the most loving friend thou hast.'

'Then am I sorely to be pitied.'

'For having my love?'

'Nay; for having none better than thine. But thank God, it is not so.'

'Must I then be thine enemy indeed before thou wilt love me?'

'No, cousin: cease to be thine own enemy and I will call thee my friend.'

'Marry! wherein then am I mine own enemy? I lead a sober life enough, as thou seest, ever under the eye of my lord.'

'But what wouldst thou an' thou wert from under the eye of thy lord? I know thee better than thou thinkest, cousin. I have read thy title-page, if not thy whole book.'

'Tell me then how runneth my title-page, cousin.'

'The art of being wilfully blind, or The way to see no farther than one would.'

'Fair preacher,' began Rowland, but Dorothy interrupted him.

'Nay then, an' thou betake thee to thy jibes, I have done,' she said.

'Be not angry with me; it is but my nature, which for thy sake I will control. If thou canst not love me, wilt thou not then pity me a little?'

'That I may pity thee, answer me what good thing is there in thee wherefore I should love thee.'

'Wouldst thou have a man trumpet his own praises?'

'I fear not that of thee who hast but the trumpet, I will tell thee this much: I have never seen in thee that thou didst love save for the pastime thereof. I doubt if thou lovest thy master for more than thy place.'

'Oh cousin!'

'Be honest with thyself, Rowland. If thou would have me for thy cousin, it must be on the ground of truth.'

Rowland possessed at least good nature: few young men would have borne to be so severely handled. But then, while one's good opinion of himself remains untroubled, confesses no touch, gives out no hollow sound, shrinks not self-hurt with the doubt of its own reality, hostile criticism will not go very deep, will not reach to the quick. The thing that hurts is that which sets trembling the ground of self-worship, lays bare the shrunk cracks and wormholes under the golden plates of the idol, shows the ants running about in it, and renders the foolish smile of the thing hateful. But he who will then turn away from his imagined self, and refer his life to the hidden ideal self, the angel that ever beholds the face of the Father, shall therein be made whole and sound, alive and free.

The dance called them, and their talk ceased. When it was over, Dorothy left the hall and sought her chamber. But in the fountain court her cousin overtook her, and had the temerity to resume the conversation. The moth would still at any risk circle the candle. It was a still night, and therefore not very cold, although icicles hung from the mouth of the horse, and here and there from the eaves. They stood by the marble basin, and the dim lights and scarce dimmer shadows from many an upper window passed athwart them as they stood. The chapel was faintly lighted, but the lantern-window on the top of the hall shone like a yellow diamond in the air.

'Thou dost me scant justice, cousin,' said Rowland, 'maintaining that I love but myself or for mine own ends. I know that love thee better than so.'

'For thine own sake, I would, might I but believe it, be glad of the assurance. But—'

Amanda's behaviour to her having at last roused counter observation and speculation on Dorothy's part, she had become suddenly aware that there was an understanding between her and Rowland. It was gradually, however, that the question rose in her mind: could these two have been the nightly intruders on the forbidden ground of the workshop, and afterwards the victims of the water-shoot? But the suspicion grew to all but a conviction. Latterly she had observed that their behaviour to each other was changed, also that Amanda's aversion to herself seemed to have gathered force. And one thing she had found remarkable, that Rowland revealed no concern for Amanda's misfortunes, or anxiety about her fate. With all these things potentially present in her mind, she came all at once to the resolution of attempting a bold stroke.

'—But,' Dorothy went on, 'when I think how thou didst bear thee with mistress Amanda—'

'My precious Dorothy!' exclaimed Scudamore, filled with a sudden gush of hope, 'thou wilt never be so unjust to thyself as to be jealous of her! She is to me as nothing—as if she had never been; nor care I forsooth if the devil hath indeed flown away with her bodily, as they will have it in the hall and the guard-room.'

'Thou didst seem to hold friendly enough converse with her while she was yet one of us.'

'Ye-e-s. But she had no heart like thee, Dorothy, as I soon discovered. She had indeed a pretty wit of her own, but that was all. And then she was spiteful. She hated thee, Dorothy.'

He spoke of her as one dead.

'How knewest thou that? Wast thou then so far in her confidence, and art now able to talk of her thus? Where is thine own heart, Mr. Scudamore?'

'In thy bosom, lovely Dorothy.'

'Thou mistakest. But mayhap thou dost imagine I picked it up that night thou didst lay it at mistress Amanda's feet in my lord's workshop in the keep?'

Dorothy's hatred of humbug, which was not the less in existence then that they had not the ugly word to express the uglier thing, enabled her to fix her eyes on him as she spoke, and keep them fixed when she had ended. He turned pale, visibly pale through the shadowy night, nor attempted to conceal his confusion. It is strange how self-conviction will wait upon foreign judgment, as if often only the general conscience were powerful enough to wake the individual one.

'Or perhaps,' she continued, 'it was torn from thee by the waters that swept thee from the bridge, as thou didst venture with her yet again upon the forbidden ground.'

He hung his head, and stood before her like a chidden child.

'Think'st thou,' she went on, 'that my Lord would easily pardon such things?'

'Thou knewest it, and didst not betray me! Oh Dorothy!' murmured Scudamore. 'Thou art a very angel of light, Dorothy.'

He seized her hand, and but for the possible eyes upon them, he would have flung himself at her feet.

Dorothy, however, would not yet lay aside the part she had assumed as moral physician, surgeon rather.

'But notwithstanding all this, cousin Rowland, when trouble came upon the young lady, what comfort was there for her in thee? Never hadst thou loved her, although I doubt not thou didst vow and swear thereto an hundred times.'

Rowland was silent. He began to fear her.

'Or what love thou hadst was of such sort that thou didst encourage in her that which was evil, and then let her go like a haggard hawk. Thou marvellest, forsooth, that I should be so careless of thy merits! Tell me, cousin, what is there in thee that I should love? Can there be love for that which is nowise lovely? Thou wilt doubtless say in thy heart, "She is but a girl, and how then should she judge concerning men and their ways?" But I appeal to thine own conscience, Rowland, when I ask thee, is this well? And if a maiden truly loved thee, it were all one. Thou wouldst but carry thyself the same to her, if not to-day, then to-morrow, or a year hence.'

'Not if she were good, Dorothy, like thee,' he murmured.

'Not if thou wert good, Rowland, like Him that made thee.'

'Wilt thou not teach me then to be good like thee, Dorothy?'

'Thou must teach thyself to be good like the Rowland thou knowest in thy better heart, when it is soft and lowly.'

'Wouldst thou then love me a little, Dorothy, if I vowed to be thy scholar, and study to be good? Give me some hope to help me in the hard task.'

'He that is good is good for goodness' sake, Rowland. Yet who can fail to love that which is good in king or knave?'

'Ah! but do not mock me, Dorothy: such is not the love I would have of thee.'

'It is all thou ever canst have of me, and methinks it is not like thou wilt ever have it, for verily thou art of nature so light that any wind may blow thee into the Dead Sea.'

From a saint it was enough to anger any sinner.

'I see!' cried Scudamore. 'For all thy fine reproof, thou too canst spurn a heart at thy feet. I will lay my life thou lovest the roundhead, and art but a traitress for all thy goodness.'

'I am indeed traitress enough to love any roundhead gentleman better than a royalist knave,' said Dorothy; and turning from him she sought the grand staircase.

CHAPTER XLI

GLAMORGAN

The winter passed, with much running to and fro, in foul weather and fair; and still the sounds of war came no nearer to Raglan, which lay like a great lion in a desert that the hunter dared not arouse. The whole of Wales, except a castle or two, remained subject to the king; and this he owed in great measure to the influence and devotion of the Somersets, his obligation to whom he seemed more and more bent on acknowledging.

One day in early summer Lady Margaret was sitting in her parlour, busy with her embroidery, and Dorothy was by her side assisting her, when Lord Herbert, who had been absent for many days, walked in.

'How does my Lady Glamorgan?' he said gaily.

'What mean you, my Herbert?' returned his wife, looking in his eyes somewhat eagerly.

'Thy Herbert am I no more; neither plume I myself any more in the spare feathers of my father. Thou art, my dove, as thou deservest to be, countess of Glamorgan, in the right of thine own husband, first earl of the same; for such being the will of his majesty, I doubt not thou wilt give thy consent thereto, and play the countess graciously. Come, Dorothy, art not proud to be cousin to an earl?'

'I am proud that you should call me cousin, my lord,' answered Dorothy; 'but truly to me it is all one whether you be called Herbert or Glamorgan. So thou remain thou, cousin, and my friend, the king may call thee what he will, and if thou art pleased, so am I.'

It was the first time she had ever thou'd him, and she turned pale at her own daring.

'St. George! but thou hast well spoken, cousin!' cried the earl. 'Hath she not, wife?'

'So well that if she often saith as well, I shall have much ado not to hate her,' replied Lady Glamorgan. 'When didst thou ever cry "well spoken" to thy mad Irishwoman, Ned?'

'All thou dost is well, my lady. Thou hast all the titles to my praises already in thy pocket. Besides, cousin Dorothy is young and meek, and requireth a little encouragement.'

'Whereas thy wife is old and bold, and cares no more for thy good word, my new Lord of Glamorgan?'

Dorothy looked so grave that they both fell a-laughing.

'I would thou couldst teach her a merry jest or two, Margaret,' said the earl. 'We are decent people enough in Raglan, but she is much too sober for us. Cheer up, Dorothy! Good times are at hand: that thou mayest not doubt it, listen, but this is only for thy ear, not for thy tongue: the king hath made thy cousin, that is me, Edward Somerset, the husband of this fair lady, generalissimo of his three armies, and admiral of a fleet, and truly I know not what all, for I have yet but run my eye over the patent. And, wife, I verily do believe the king but bides his time to make my father duke of Somerset, and then one day thou wilt be a duchess, Margaret. Think on that!'

Lady Glamorgan burst into tears.

'I would I might have a kiss of my Molly!' she cried.

She had never before in Dorothy's hearing uttered the name of her child since her death. New dignity, strange as it may seem to some, awoke suddenly the thought of the darling to whom titles were but words, and the ice was broken. A pause followed.

'Yes, Margaret, thou art right,' said Glamorgan at length; 'it is all but folly; yet as the marks of a king's favour, such honours are precious.'

As to what a king's favour itself might be worth, that my Lord of Glamorgan lived to learn.

'It is I who pay for them,' said his wife.

'How so, my dove?'

'Do they not cost me thee, Herbert, and cost me very dear? Art not ever from my sight? Wish I not often as I lay awake in the dark, that we were all in heaven and well over with the foolery of it? The angels keep Molly in mind of us!'

'Yes, my Peggy, it is hard on thee, and hard on me too,' said the earl tenderly, 'yet not so hard as upon our liege lord, the king, who selleth his plate and jewels.'

'Pooh! what of that then, Herbert? An' he would leave me thee, he might have all mine, and welcome; for thou knowest, Ned, I but hold them for thee to sell when thou wilt.'

'I know; and the time may come, though, thank God, it is not yet. What wouldst thou say, countess, if with all thy honours thou did yet come to poverty? Canst be poor and merry, think'st thou?'

'So thou wert with me, Herbert, Glamorgan, I would say, but my lips frame not themselves to the word. I like not the title greatly, but when it means thee to me, then shall I love it.'

'Art thou poor, yet hast thou golden slumbers?
O sweet content!'

—sang the earl in a mellow tenor voice.

'My lord, an' I have leave to speak,' said Dorothy, 'did you not say the diamond in that ring Richard Heywood sent me was of some worth?'

'I did, cousin. It is a stone of the finest water, and of good weight, though truly I weighed it not.'

'Then would I cast it in the king's treasury, an' if your lordship would condescend to be the bearer of such a small offering.'

'No, child; the king robs not orphans.'

'Did the King of Kings rob the poor widow that cast in her two mites, then?'

'No; but perhaps the priests did. Still, as I say, the hour may come when all our mites may be wanted, and thine be accepted with the rest, but my father and I have yet much to give, and shall have given it before that hour come. Besides, as to thee, Dorothy, what would that handsome roundhead of thine say, if instead of keeping well the ring he gave thee, thou had turned it to the use he liked the least?'

'He will never ask me concerning it,' said Dorothy, with a faint smile.

'Be not over-sure of it, child. My lady asks me many things I never thought to tell her before the priest made us one. Dorothy, I have no right and no wish to spy into thy future, and fright thee with what, if it come at all, will come peacefully as June weather. I have not constructed thy horoscope to cast thy nativity, and therefore I speak as one of the ignorant; but let me tell thee, for I do say it confidently, that if these wars were once over, and the king had his own again, there will be few men in his three kingdoms so worthy of the hand and heart of Dorothy Vaughan as that same roundhead fellow, Richard Heywood. I would to God he were as good a catholic as he is a mistaken puritan! And now, my lady, may I not send thy maiden from us, for I would talk with thee alone of certain matters, not from distrust of Dorothy, but that they are not my own to impart, therefore I pray her absence.'

The parliament having secured the assistance of the Scots, and their forces having, early in the year, entered England, the king on his side was now meditating an attempt to secure the assistance of the Irish catholics, to which the devotion of certain of the old catholic houses at home encouraged him. But it was a game of terrible danger, for if he lost it, he lost everything; and that it should transpire before maturity would be to lose it absolutely; for the Irish catholics had, truly or falsely, been charged with such enormities during the rebellion, that they had become absolutely hateful in the eyes of all English protestants, and any alliance with them must cost him far more in protestants than he could gain by it in catholics. It was necessary therefore that he should go about it with the utmost caution; and indeed in his whole management of it, the wariness far exceeded the dignity, and was practised at the expense of his best friends. But the poor king was such a believer in his father's pet doctrine of the divine right of his inheritance, that not only would he himself sacrifice everything to the dim shadow of royalty which usurped the throne of his conscience, but would, without great difficulty or compunction, though not always without remorse, accept any sacrifice which a subject might have devotion enough to bring to the altar before which Charles Stuart acted as flamen.

In this my story of hearts rather than fortunes, it is not necessary to follow the river of public events through many of its windings, although every now and then my track will bring me to a ferry, where the boat bearing my personages will be seized by the force of the current, and carried down the stream while crossing to the other bank.

It must have been, I think, in view of his slowly-maturing intention to employ Lord Herbert in a secret mission to Ireland with the object above mentioned, that the king had sought to bind him yet more closely to himself by conferring on him the title of Glamorgan. It was not, however, until the following year, when his affairs seemed on the point of becoming desperate, that he proceeded, possibly with some protestant compunctions, certainly with considerable protestant apprehension, to carry out his design. Towards this had pointed the relaxation of his measures against the catholic rebels for some time previous, and may to some have indicated hopes entertained of them. It must be remembered that while these catholics united to defend the religion of their country, they, like the Scots who had joined the parliament, professed a sincere attachment to their monarch, and in the persons of their own enemies had certainly taken up arms against many of his.

Meantime the Scots had invaded England, and the parliament had largely increased their forces in the hope of a decisive engagement; but the king refused battle and gained time. In the north prince Rupert made some progress, and brought on the battle of Marston Moor, where the victory was gained by Cromwell, after all had been regarded as lost by the other parliamentary generals. On the other hand, the king gained an important advantage in the west country over Essex and his army.

The trial and execution of Laud, who died in the beginning of the following year, obeying the king rather than his rebellious lords, was a terrible sign to the house of Raglan of what the presbyterian party was capable of. But to Dorothy it would have given a yet keener pain, had she not begun to learn that neither must the excesses of individuals be attributed to their party, nor those of his party taken as embodying the mind of everyone who belongs to it. At the same time the old insuperable difficulty returned; how could Richard belong to such a party?

CHAPTER XLII

A NEW SOLDIER

Moments had scarcely passed after Dorothy left him at the fountain, ere Scudamore grievously repented of having spoken to her in such a manner, and would gladly have offered apology and what amends he might.

But Dorothy, neither easily moved to wrath, nor yet given to the nourishing of active resentment, was not therefore at all the readier to forget the results of moral difference, or to permit any nearer approach on the part of one such as her cousin had shown himself. As long as he continued so self-serene and unashamed, what satisfaction to her or what good to him could there be in it, even were he to content himself with the cousinly friendship which, as soon as he was capable of it, she was willing to afford him? As it was now, she granted him only distant recognition in company, neither seeking nor avoiding him; and as to all opportunity of private speech, entirely shunning him. For some time, in the vanity of his experience, he never doubted that these were only feminine arts, or that when she judged him sufficiently punished, she would relax the severity of her behaviour and begin to make him amends. But this demeanour of hers endured so long, and continued so uniform, that at length he began to doubt the universality of his experience, and to dread lest the maiden should actually prove what he had never found maiden before, inexorable. He did not reflect that he had given her no ground whatever for altering her judgment or feeling with regard to him. But in truth her thoughts rarely turned to him at all, and while his were haunting her as one who was taking pleasure in the idea that she was making him feel her resentment, she was simply forgetting him, busy perhaps with some self-offered question that demanded an answer, or perhaps brooding a little over the past, in which the form of Richard now came and went at its will.

So long as Rowland imagined the existence of a quarrel, he imagined therein a bond between them; when he became convinced that no quarrel, only indifference, or perhaps despisal, separated them, he began again to despair, and felt himself urged once more to speak. Seizing therefore an opportunity in such manner that she could not escape him without attracting very undesirable attention, he began a talk upon the old basis.

'Wilt thou then forgive me nevermore, Dorothy?', he said humbly.

'For what, Mr. Scudamore?'

'I mean for offending thee with rude words.'

'Truly I have forgotten them.'

'Then shall we be friends?'

'Nay, that follows not.'

'What quarrel then hast thou with me?'

'I have no quarrel with thee; yet is there one thing I cannot forgive thee.'

'And what is that, cousin? Believe me I know not. I need but to know, and I will humble myself.'

'That would serve nothing, for how should I forgive thee for being unworthy? For such thing there is no forgiveness. Cease thou to be unworthy, and then is there nothing to forgive. I were an unfriendly friend, Rowland, did I befriend the man who befriendeth not himself.'

'I understand thee not, cousin.'

'And I understand not thy not understanding. Therefore can there be no communion between us.'

So saying Dorothy left him to what consolation he could find in such china-pastoral abuse as the gallants of the day would, with the aid of poetic penny-trumpet, cast upon offending damsels, Daphnes and Chloes, and, in the mood, heathen shepherdesses in general. But, fortunately for himself, how great soever had been the freedom with which he had lost and changed many a foolish liking, he found, let his hopelessness or his offence be what it might, he had not the power to shake himself free from the first worthy passion ever roused in him. It had struck root below the sandy upper stratum of his mind into a clay soil beneath, where at least it was able to hold, and whence it could draw a little slow reluctant nourishment.

During his poetic anger, he wrote no small amount of fair verse, tried by the standard of Cowley, Carew, and Suckling, so like theirs indeed that the best of it might have passed for some of their worst, although there was not in it all a single phrase to remind one of their best. But when the poetic spring began to run dry, he fell once more into a sort of wilful despair, and disrelished everything, except indeed his food and drink, so much so that his master perceiving his altered cheer, one day addressed him to know the cause.

'What aileth thee, Rowland?' he said kindly. 'For this se'en-night past, thou lookest like one that oweth the hangman his best suit.'

'I rust, my lord,' said Rowland, with a tragic air of discontent.

The notion had arisen in his foolish head that the way to soften the heart of Dorothy would be to ride to the wars, and get himself slain, or, rather severely but not mortally wounded. Then he would be brought back to Raglan, and, thinking he was going to die, Dorothy would nurse him, and then she would be sure to fall in love with him. Yes, he would ride forth on the fellow Heywood's mare, seek him in the field of battle, and slay him, but be himself thus grievously wounded.

'I rust, my lord,' he said briefly.

'Ha! Thou wouldst to the wars! I like thee for that, boy. Truly the king wanteth soldiers, and that more than ever. Thou art a good cupbearer, but I will do my best to savour my claret without thee. Thou shalt to the king, and what poor thing my word may do for thee shall not be wanting.'

Scudamore had expected opposition, and was a little nonplussed. He had judged himself essential to his master's comfort, and had even hoped he might set Dorothy to use her influence towards reconciling him to remain at home. But although self-indulgent and lazy, Scudamore was constitutionally no coward, and had never had any experience to give him pause: he did not know what an ugly thing a battle is after it is over, and the mind has leisure to attend to the smarting of the wounds.

'I thank your lordship with all my heart,' he said, putting on an air of greater satisfaction than he felt, 'and with your lordship's leave would prefer a further request.'

'Say on, Rowland. I owe thee something for long and faithful service. An' I can, I will.'

'Give me the roundhead's mare that I may the better find her master.'

For Lady was still within the walls. The Marquis could not restore her, but neither could he bring himself to use her, cherishing the hope of being one day free to give her back to a reconciled subject. But alas! there were very few horses now in Raglan stalls.

'No, Rowland,' he said, 'thou art the last who ought to get any good of her. It were neither law nor justice to hand the stolen goods to the thief.'

He sat silent, and Rowland, not very eager, stood before him in silence also, meaning it to be read as indicating that to the wars except on that mare's back he would not ride. But the thought of the Marquis had now taken another turn.

'Thou shalt have her, my boy. Thou shalt not rust at home for the sake of a gouty old man and his claret. But ere thou go, I will write out certain maxims for thy following both in the field and in quarters. Ere thou ride, look well to thy girths, and as thou ridest say thy prayers, for it pleaseth not God that every man on the right side should live, and thou mayst find the presence in which thou standest change suddenly from that of mortal man to that of living God. I say nothing of orthodoxy, for truly I am not one to think that because a man hath been born a heretic, which lay not in his choice, and hath not been of his parents taught in the truth, that therefore he must howl for ever. Not while blessed Mary is queen of heaven, will all the priests in Christendom persuade me thereof. Only be thou fully persuaded in thine own mind, Rowland; for if thou cared not, that were an evil thing indeed. And of all things, my lad, remember this, that a weak blow were ever better unstruck. Go now to the armourer, and to him deliver my will that he fit thee out as a cuirassier for his majesty's service. I can give thee no rank, for I have no regiment in the making at present, but it may please his majesty to take care of thee, and give thee a place in my Lord Glamorgan's regiment of body-guards.'

The prospect thus suddenly opened to Scudamore of a wider life and greater liberty, might have dazzled many a nobler nature than his. Lord Worcester saw the light in his eyes, and as he left the room gazed after him with pitiful countenance.

'Poor lad! poor lad!' he said to himself; 'I hope I see not the last of thee! God forbid! But here thou didst but rust, and it were a vile thing in an old man to infect a youth with the disease of age.'

Rowland soon found the master of the armoury, and with him crossed to the keep, where it lay, above the workshop. At the foot of the stair he talked loud, in the hope that Dorothy might be with the fire-engine, which he thought he heard at work, and would hear him. Having chosen such pieces as pleased his fancy, and needed but a little of the armourer's art to render them suitable, he filled his arms with them, and following the master down, contrived to fall a little behind, so that he should leave the tower before him, when he dropped them all with a huge clatter at the foot of the stair. The noise was sufficient, for it brought out Dorothy. She gazed for a moment as, pretending not to have seen her, he was picking them up with his back towards her.

'Do I see thee arming at length, cousin?' she said. 'I congratulate thee.'

She held out her hand to him. He took it and stared. The reception of his noisy news was different from what he had been vain enough to hope. So little had Dorothy's behaviour in the capture of Rowland enlightened him as to her character!

'Thou wouldst have me slain then to be rid of me, Dorothy?' he gasped.

'I would have any man slain where men fight,' returned Dorothy, 'rather than idling within stone walls!'

'Thou art hard-hearted, Dorothy, and knowest not what love is, else wouldst thou pity me a little.'

'What! art afraid, cousin?'

'Afraid! I fear nothing under heaven but thy cruelty, Dorothy.'

'Then what wouldst thou have me pity thee for?'

'I would, an' I had dared, have said—Because I must leave thee. But thou wouldst mock at that, and therefore I say instead—Because I shall never return; for I see well that thou never hast loved me even a little.'

Dorothy smiled.

'An' I had loved thee, cousin,' she rejoined, 'I had never let thee rest, or left soliciting thee, until thou hadst donned thy buff coat and buckled on thy spurs, and departed to be a man among men, and no more a boy among women.'

So saying she returned to her engine, which all the time had been pumping and forcing with fiery inspiration.

Scudamore mounted and rode, followed by one of the grooms. He found the king at Wallingford, presented the Marquis 's letter, proffered his services, and was at once placed in attendance on his majesty's person.

In the eyes of most of his comrades the mare he rode seemed too light for cavalry work, but she made up in spirit and quality of muscle for lack of size, and there was not another about the king to match in beauty the little black Lady. Sweet-tempered and gentle although nervous and quick, and endowed with a rare docility and a faith which supplied courage, it was clear, while nothing was known of her pedigree, both from her form and her nature, that she was of Arab descent. No feeling of unreality in his possession of her intruding to disturb his satisfaction in her, Scudamore became very fond of her. Having joined the army, however, only after the second battle of Newbury, he had no chance till the following summer of learning how she bore herself in the field.

CHAPTER XLIII

LADY AND BISHOP

In the meantime a succession of events had contributed to enhance the influence of Cromwell in the parliament, and his position and power in the army. He was now, therefore, more able to put in places of trust such men as came nearest his own way of thinking, and amongst the rest Roger Heywood, whom, once brought into the active service for which modesty had made him doubt his own fitness, he would not allow to leave it again, but made colonel of one of his favourite regiments of horse, with his son as major.

Richard continued to ride Bishop, which became at length famous for courage, as he had become at once for ugliness. Fortunately they found that he had developed friendly feelings towards one of the mares of the troop, never lashing out when she happened to be behind him; so they gave her that place, and were freed from much anxiety. Still the rider on each side of him had to keep his eyes open, for every now and then a sudden fury of biting would seize him, and bring chaos in the regiment for a moment or two. When his master was made an officer, the brute's temptations probably remained the same, but his opportunities of yielding to them became considerably fewer.

It was strange company in which Richard rode. Nearly all were of the independent party in religious polity, all holding, or imagining they held, the same or nearly the same tenets. The opinions of most of them, however, were merely the opinions of the man to whose influences they had been first and principally subjected: to say what their belief was, would be to say what they were, which is deeper judgment than a man can reach. In Roger Heywood and his son dwelt a pure love of liberty; the ardent attachment to liberty which most of the troopers professed, would have prevented few of them indeed from putting a quaker in the stocks, or perhaps whipping him, had such an obnoxious heretic as a quaker been at that time in existence. In some was the devoutest sense of personal obligation, and the strongest religious feeling; in others was nothing but talk, less injurious than some sorts of pseudo-religious talk, in that it was a jargon admitting of much freedom of utterance and reception, mysterious symbols being used in commonest interchange. That they all believed earnestly enough to fight for their convictions, will not go very far in proof of their sincerity even, for to most of them fighting came by nature, and was no doubt a great relief to the much oppressed old Adam not yet by any means dead in them.

At length the king led out his men for another campaign, and was followed by Fairfax and Cromwell into the shires of Leicester and Northampton. Then came the battle at the village of Naseby.

Prince Rupert, whose folly so often lost what his courage had gained, having defeated Ireton and his horse, followed them from the field, while Cromwell with his superior numbers turned Sir Marmaduke Langdale's flank, and thereby turned the scale of victory.

But Sir Marmaduke and his men fought desperately, and while the contest was yet undecided, the king saw that Rupert, returned from the pursuit, was attacking the enemy's artillery, and dispatched Rowland in hot haste to bring him to the aid of Sir Marmaduke.

The straightest line to reach him lay across a large field to the rear of Sir Marmaduke's men. As he went from behind them, Richard caught sight of him and his object together, struck spurs into Bishop's flanks, bored him through a bull-fence, was in the same field with Rowland, and tore at full speed to head him off from the prince.

Rowland rode for some distance without perceiving that he was followed; if Richard could but get within pistol-shot of him, for alas, he seemed to be mounted on the fleeter animal! Heavens! Could it be? Yes it was! it was his own lost Lady the cavalier rode! For a moment his heart beat so fast that he felt as if he should fall from his horse.

Rowland became aware that he was pursued, but at the first glimpse of the long, low, rat-like animal on which the roundhead came floundering after him, burst into a laugh of derision, and jumping a young hedge found himself in a clayish fallow, which his mare found heavy. Soon Richard jumped the hedge also, and immediately Bishop had the advantage. But now, beyond the tall hedge they were approaching, they heard the sounds of the conflict near: there was no time to lose. Richard breathed deep, and uttered a long, wild, peculiar cry. Lady started, half-stopped, raised her head high, and turned round her ears. Richard cried again. She wheeled, and despite spur, and rein, though the powerful bit with which Rowland rode her seemed to threaten breaking her jaw, bore him, at short deer-like bounds, back towards his pursuer.

Not until the mare refused obedience did Rowland begin to suspect who had followed him. Then a vague recollection of something Richard had said the night he carried him home to Raglan, crossed his mind, and he grew furious. But in vain he struggled with the mare, and all the time Richard kept ploughing on towards him. At length he saw Rowland take a pistol from his holster. Instinctively Richard did the same, and when he saw him raise the butt-end to strike her on the head, firmed, and missed, but saved Lady the blow, and ere Rowland recovered from the start it gave him to hear the bullet whistle past his ear, uttered another equally peculiar but different cry. Lady reared, plunged, threw her heels in the air, emptied her saddle, and came flying to Richard.

But now arose a fresh anxiety:-what if Bishop should, as was most likely, attack the mare? At her master's word, however, she stood, a few yards off, and with arched neck and forward-pricked ears, waited, while Bishop, moved possibly with admiration of the manner in which she had unseated her rider, scanned her with no malign aspect.

By this time Rowland had got upon his feet, and mindful of his duty, hopeful also that Richard would be content with his prize, set off as hard as he could run for a gap he spied in the hedge. But in a moment Bishop, followed by Lady, had headed him.

'Thou wert better cry quarter,' said Richard.

The reply was a bullet, that struck Bishop below the ear. He stood straight up, gave one yell, and tumbled over. Scudamore ran towards the mare, hoping to catch her and be off ere the roundhead could recover himself. But, although Bishop had fallen on his leg, Richard was unhurt. He lay still and watched. Lady seemed bewildered, and Rowland coming softly up, seized her bridle, and sprung into the saddle. The same moment Richard gave his cry a second time, and again up went Rowland in the air, and Lady came trotting daintily to her master, scared, but obedient. Rowland fell on his back, and before he came to himself, Richard had drawn his leg from under his slain charger, and his sword from its sheath. And now first he perceived who his antagonist was, and a pang went to his heart at the remembrance of his father's words.

'Mr. Scudamore,' he cried, 'I would thou hadst not stolen my mare, so that I might fight with thee in a Christian fashion.'

'Roundhead scoundrel!' gasped Scudamore, wild with wrath. 'Thy unmannerly varlet tricks shall cost thee dear. Thou a soldier? A juggler with a mountebank jade, a vile hackney which thou hast taught to caper! A soldier indeed!'

'A soldier and seatless!' returned Richard. 'A soldier and rail! A soldier and steal my mare, then shoot my horse! Bah! an' the rest were like thee, we might take the field with dog-whips.'

Scudamore drew a pistol from his belt, and glanced towards the mare.

'An' thou lift thine arm, I will kill thee,' cried Richard. 'What! shall a man not teach his horse lest the thief should find him not broke to his taste? Besides, did I not give thee warning while yet I judged thee an honest man, and a thief but in jest? Go thy ways. I shall do my country better service by following braver men than by taking thee. Get thee back to thy master. An' I killed thee, I should do him less hurt than I would. See yonder how thy master's horse do knot and scatter!'

He approached Lady to mount and ride away.

But Rowland, who had now with the help of his anger recovered from the effects of his fall, rushed at Richard with drawn sword. The contest was brief. With one heavy blow that beat down his guard and wounded him severely in the shoulder, dividing his collarbone, for he was but lightly armed, Richard stretched his antagonist on the ground; then seeing prince Rupert's men returning, and sir Marmaduke's in flight and some of them coming his way, he feared being surrounded, and leaping into the saddle, flew as if the wind were under him back to his regiment, reaching it just as in the first heat of pursuit. Cromwell called them back, and turned them upon the rear of the royalist infantry.

This decided the battle. Ere Rupert returned, the affair was so hopeless that not even the entreaties of the king could induce his cavalry to form again and charge.

His majesty retreated to Leicester and Hereford.

CHAPTER XLIV

THE KING

Some months before the battle of Naseby, which was fought in June early, that is, in the year 1645, the plans of the king having now ripened, he gave a secret commission for Ireland to the earl of Glamorgan, with immense powers, among the rest that of coining money, in order that he might be in a position to make proposals towards certain arrangements with the Irish catholics, which, in view of the prejudices of the king's protestant council, it was of vital importance to keep secret. Glamorgan therefore took a long leave of his wife and family, and in the month of March set out for Dublin. At Caernarvon, they got on board a small barque, laden with corn, but, in rough weather that followed, were cast ashore on the coast of Lancashire. A second attempt failed also, for, pursued by a parliament vessel, they were again compelled to land on the same coast. It was the middle of summer before they reached Dublin.

During this period there was of course great anxiety in Raglan, the chief part of which was lady Glamorgan's. At times she felt that but for the sympathy of Dorothy, often silent but always ministrant, she would have broken down quite under the burden of ignorance and its attendant anxiety.

In the prolonged absence of her husband, and the irregularity of tidings, for they came at uncertain as well as wide intervals, her yearnings after her vanished Molly, which had become more patient, returned with all their early vehemence, and she began to brood on the meeting beyond the grave of which her religion waked her hope. Nor was this all: her religion itself grew more real; for although there is nothing essentially religious in thinking of the future, although there is more of the heart of religion in the taking of strength from the love of God to do the commonest duty, than in all the longing for a blessed hereafter of which the soul is capable, yet the love of a little child is very close to the love of the great Father; and the loss that sets any affection aching and longing, heaves, as on a wave from the very heart of the human ocean, the labouring spirit up towards the source of life and restoration. In like manner, from their common love to the child, and their common sense of loss in her death, the hearts of the two women drew closer to each other, and protestant mistress Dorothy was able to speak words of comfort to catholic Lady Glamorgan, which the hearer found would lie on the shelf of her creed none the less quietly that the giver had lifted them from the shelf of hers.

One evening, while yet Lady Glamorgan had had no news of her husband's arrival in Ireland, and the bright June weather continued clouded with uncertainty and fear, Lady Broughton came panting into her parlour with the tidings that a courier had just arrived at the main entrance, himself pale with fatigue, and his horse white with foam.

'Alas! alas!' cried Lady Glamorgan, and fell back in her chair, faint with apprehension, for what might not be the message he bore? Ere Dorothy had succeeded in calming her, the Marquis himself came hobbling in, with the news that the king was coming.

'Is that all?' said the countess, heaving a deep sigh, while the tears ran down her cheeks.

'Is that all?' repeated her father-in-law. 'How, my lady! Is there then nobody in all the world but Glamorgan? Verily I believe thou wouldst turn thy back on the angel Gabriel, if he dared appear before thee without thy Ned under his arm. Bless the Irish heart! I never gave thee MY Ned that thou shouldst fall down and worship the fellow.'

'Bear with me, sir,' she answered faintly. 'It is but the pain here. Thou knowest I cannot tell but he lieth at the bottom of the Irish Sea.'

'If he do lie there, then lieth he in Abraham's bosom, daughter, where I trust there is room for thee and me also. Thou rememberest how thy Molly said once to thee, 'Madam, thy bosom is not so big as my Lord Abraham's. What a big bosom my Lord Abraham must have!'

Lady Glamorgan laughed.

'Come then—"to our work alive!" which is now to receive his majesty,' said the Marquis . 'My wild Irishwoman—'

'Alas, my lord! tame enough now,' sighed the countess.

'Not too tame to understand that she must represent her husband before the king's majesty,' said Lord Worcester.

Lady Glamorgan rose, kissed her father-in-law, wiped her eyes, and said—

'Where, my lord, do you purpose lodging his majesty?'

'In the great north room, over the buttery, and next the picture-gallery, which will serve his majesty to walk in, and the windows there have the finest prospect of all. I did think of the great tower, but—Well—the chamber there is indeed statelier, but it is gloomy as a dull twilight, while the one I intend him to lie in is bright as a summer morning. The tower chamber makes me think of all the lords and ladies that have died therein; the north room, of all the babies that have been born there.'

'Spoken like a man!' murmured Lady Glamorgan. 'Have you given directions, my lord?'

'I have sent for sir Ralph. Come with me, Margaret: you and Mary must keep your old father from blundering. Run, Dorothy, and tell Mr. Delaware and Mr. Andrews that I desire their presence in my closet. I miss the rogue Scudamore. They tell me he hath done well, and is sorely wounded. He must feel the better for the one already, and I hope he will soon be nothing the worse for the other.'

As he thus talked, they left the room and took their way to the study, where they found the steward waiting them.

The whole castle was presently alive with preparations for the king's visit. That he had been so sorely foiled of late, only roused in all the greater desire to receive him with every possible honour. Hope revived in Lady Glamorgan's bosom: she would take the coming of the king as a good omen for the return of her husband.

Dorothy ran to do the Marquis 's pleasure. As she ran, it seemed as if some new spring of life had burst forth in her heart. The king! the king actually coming! The God-chosen monarch of England! The head of the church! The type of omnipotence! The wronged, the saintly, the wise! He who fought with bleeding heart for the rights, that he might fulfil the duties to which he was born! She would see him! she would breathe the same air with him! gaze on his gracious countenance unseen until she had imprinted every feature of his divine face upon her heart and memory! The thought was too entrancing. She wept as she ran to find the master of the horse and the master of the fish-ponds.

At length, on the evening of the third of July, a pursuivant, accompanied by an advanced guard of horsemen, announced the king, and presently on the north road appeared the dust of his approach. Nearer they came, all on horseback, a court of officers. Travel-stained and weary, with foam-flecked horses, but flowing plumes, flashing armour, and ringing chains, they arrived at the brick gate, where Lord Charles himself threw the two leaves open to admit them, and bent the knee before his king. As they entered the marble gate, they saw the Marquis descending the great white stair to meet them, leaning for his lameness on the arm of his brother sir Thomas of Troy, and followed by all the ladies and gentlemen and officers in the castle, who stood on the stair while he approached the king's horse, bent his knee, kissed the royal hand, and, rising with difficulty, for the gout had aged him beyond his years, said:

'Domine, non sum dignus.'

I would I had not to give this brief dialogue; but it stands on record, and may suggest something worth thinking to him who can read it aright.

The king replied:

'My lord, I may very well answer you again: I have not found so great faith in Israel; for no man would trust me with so much money as you have done.'

'I hope your majesty will prove a defender of the faith,' returned the Marquis .

The king then dismounted, ascended the marble steps with his host, nearly as stiff as he from his long ride, crossed the moat on the undulating drawbridge, passed the echoing gateway, and entered the stone court.

The Marquis turned to the king, and presented the keys of the castle. The king took them and returned them.

'I pray your majesty keep them in so good a hand. I fear that ere it be long I shall be forced to deliver them into the hands of who will spoil the compliment', said the Marquis .

'Nay,' rejoined his majesty, 'but keep them till the King of kings demand the account of your stewardship, my lord.'

'I trust your majesty's name will then be seen where it stands therein,' said the Marquis , 'for so it will fare the better with the steward.'

In the court, the garrison, horse and foot, a goodly show, was drawn up to receive him, with an open lane through, leading to the north-western angle, where was the stair to the king's apartment. At the draw-well, which lay right in the way, and around which the men stood off in a circle, the king stopped, laid his hand on the wheel, and said gaily:

'My lord, is this your lordship's purse?'

'For your majesty's sake, I would it were,' returned the Marquis .

At the foot of the stair, on plea of his gout, he delivered his majesty to the care of Lord Charles, sir Ralph Blackstone, and Mr. Delaware, who conducted him to his chamber.

The king supped alone, but after supper, Lady Glamorgan and the other ladies of the family, having requested permission to wait upon him, were ushered into his presence. Each of them took with her one of her ladies in attendance, and Dorothy, being the one chosen by her mistress for that honour, not without the rousing of a strong feeling of injustice in the bosoms of the elder ladies, entered trembling behind her mistress, as if the room were a temple wherein no simulacrum but the divinity himself dwelt in visible presence.

His majesty received them courteously, said kind things to several of them, but spoke and behaved at first with a certain long-faced reserve rather than dignity, which, while it jarred a little with Dorothy's ideal of the graciousness that should be mingled with majesty in the perfect monarch, yet operated only to throw her spirit back into that stage of devotion wherein, to use a figure of the king's own, the awe overlays the love.

A little later the Marquis entered, walking slowly, leaning on the arm of Lord Charles, but carrying in his own hands a present of apricots from his brother to the king.

Meantime Dorothy's love had begun to rise again from beneath her awe; but when the Marquis came in, old and stately, reverend and slow, with a silver dish in each hand and a basket on his arm, and she saw him bow three times ere he presented his offering, himself serving whom all served, himself humble whom all revered, then again did awe nearly overcome her. When the king, however, having graciously received the present, chose for each of the ladies one of the apricots, and coming to Dorothy last, picked out and offered the one he said was likest the bloom of her own fair cheek, gratitude again restored the sway of love, and in the greatness of the honour she almost let slip the compliment. She could not reply, but she looked her thanks, and the king doubtless missed nothing.

The next day his majesty rested, but on following days rode to Monmouth, Chepstow, Usk, and other towns in the neighbourhood, whose loyalty, thanks to the Marquis, had as yet stood out. After dinner he generally paid the Marquis a visit in the oak parlour, then perhaps had a walk in the grounds, or a game on the bowling-green.

But although the Marquis was devoted to the king's cause, he was not therefore either blinded or indifferent to the king's faults, and as an old man who had long been trying to grow better, he made up his mind to risk a respectful word in the matter of kingly obligation.

One day, therefore, when his majesty entered the oak parlour, he found his host sitting by the table with his Gower lying open before him, as if he had been reading, which doubtless was the case.

'What book have you there, my lord?' asked the king—while some of his courtiers stood near the door, and others gazed from the window on the moat and the swelling, towering mass of the keep. 'I like to know what books my friends read.'

'Sir, it is old master John Gower's book of verses, entitled Confessio Amantis,' answered his lordship.

'It is a book I have never seen before,' said the king, glancing at its pages.

'Oh!' returned the Marquis, 'it is a book of books, which if your majesty had been well versed in, it would have made you a king of kings.'

'Why so, my lord?' asked the king.

'Why,' said the Marquis, 'here is set down how Aristotle brought up and instructed Alexander the Great in all his rudiments, and the principles belonging to a prince. Allow me, sir, to read you such a passage as will show your majesty the truth of what I say.'

He opened the book and read:

'Among the vertues one is chefe,
And that is trouthe, which is lefe (dear)
To God and eke to man also.
And for it hath ben ever so,
Taught Aristotle, as he well couth, (knew)
To Alisaundre, how in his youth
He shulde of trouthe thilke grace (that same)

With all his hole herte embrace,
So that his word be trewe and pleine
Toward the world, and so certeine,
That in him be no double speche.
For if men shulde trouthe seche,
And found it nought within a king,
It were an unfittende thing
The worde is token of that within;
There shall a worthy king begin
To kepe his tunge and to be trewe,
So shall his price ben ever newe.'

'And here, sir, is what he saith as to the significance of the kingly crown, if your majesty will allow me
to read it.'

'Read on, my lord; all is good and true,' said the king.

'The gold betokneth excellence,
That men shuld done him reverence,
As to her lege soveraine. (their liege)
The stones, as the bokes saine,
Commended ben in treble wise.
First, they ben hard, and thilke assise (that attribute)
Betokeneth in a king constaunce,
So that there shall be no variaunce
Be found in his condicion.
And also by description
The vertue, whiche is in the stones,
A verray signe is for the nones
Of that a king shall ben honest,
And holde trewely his behest (promise)
Of thing, which longeth to kinghede.' (belongeth)

'And so on, for I were loath to weary your majesty, of the colour of the stones, and the circular form
of the crown.'

'Read on, my lord,' said the king.

Several passages, therefore, did the Marquis pick out and read, amongst which probably were
certain concerning flatterers, taking care still to speak of Alexander and Aristotle, and by no means
of king and Marquis, until at length he had 'read the king such a lesson,' as Dr. Bayly informs us,
'that the bystanders were amazed at his boldness.'

'My lord, have you got your lesson by heart, or speak you out of the book?' asked the king, taking
the volume.

'Sir,' the Marquis replied, 'if you could read my heart, it may be you might find it there; or if your
majesty please to get it by heart, I will lend you my book.'

'I would willingly borrow it,' said the king.

'Nay,' said the Marquis , 'I will lend it to you upon these conditions: first, that you read it; and, second, that you make use of it.'

Here, glancing round, well knowing the nature of the soil upon which his words fell, he saw 'some of the new-made lords displeased, fretting and biting their thumbs,' and thus therefore resumed:—

'But, sir, I assure you that no man was so much for the absolute power of the king as Aristotle. If your majesty will allow me the book again, I will show you one remarkable passage to that purpose.'

Having searched the volume for a moment, and found it, he read as follows:—

'Harpaghes first his tale tolde,
And said, how that the strength of kinges
Is mightiest of alle thinges.
For king hath power over man,
And man is he, which reson can,
As he, which is of his nature
The most noble creature
Of alle tho that God hath wrought.
And by that skill it seemeth nought, (for that reason)
He saith that any erthly thing
May be so mighty as a king.
A king may spille, a king may save,
A king may make of lorde a knave,
And of a knave a Lord also;
The power of a king stant so
That he the lawes overpasseth.
What he will make lasse, he lasseth;
What he will make more, he moreth;
And as a gentil faucon soreth,
He fleeth, that no man him reclaimeth.
But he alone all other tameth,
And slant him self of lawe fre.'

'There, my liege! So much for Aristotle and the kinghood! But think not he taketh me with him all the way. By our Lady, I go not so far.'

Lifting his head again, he saw, to his wish, that 'divers new-made lords' had 'slunk out of the room.'

'My lord,' said the king, 'at this rate you will drive away all my nobility.'

'I protest unto your majesty,' the Marquis replied, 'I am as new a made Lord as any of them all, but I was never called knave or rogue so much in all my life as I have been since I received this last honour: and why should they not bear their shares?'

In high good-humour with his success, he told the story the same evening to Lady Glamorgan in Dorothy's presence. It gave her ground for thought: she wondered that the Marquis should think the king required such lessoning. She had never dreamed that a man and his office are not only metaphysically distinct, but may be morally separate things; she had hitherto taken the office as the pledge for the man, the show as the pledge for the reality; and now therefore her notion of the king received a rude shock from his best friend.

The arrival of his majesty had added to her labours, for now again horse must spout every day, with no Molly to see it and rejoice. Every fountain rushed heavenwards, 'and all the air' was 'filled with pleasant noise of waters.' This required the fire-engine to be kept pretty constantly at work, and Dorothy had to run up and down the stair of the great tower several times a-day. But she lingered on the top as often and as long as she might.

One glorious July afternoon, gazing from the top of the keep, she saw his majesty, the Marquis , some of the courtiers, and a Mr. Prichard of the neighbourhood, on the bowling-green, having a game together. It was like looking at a toy-representation of one, for, so far below, everything was wondrously dwarfed and fore-shortened. But certainly it was a pretty sight-the gay garments, the moving figures, the bowls rolling like marbles over the green carpet, while the sun, and the blue sky, and just an air of wind, enough to turn every leaf into a languidly waved fan, enclosed it in loveliness and filled it with life. It was like a picture from a CAMERA OBSCURA dropped right at the foot of the keep, for the surrounding walk, moat, and sunk walk beyond, were, seen from that height, but enough to keep the bowling-green, which came to the edge of the sunk walk, twelve feet below it, from appearing to cling to the foundations of the tower. The circle of arches filled with shell-work and statues of Roman emperors, which formed the face of the escarpment of the sunk walk, looked like a curiously-cut fringe to the carpet.

While Dorothy aloft was thus looking down and watching the game—

'What a lovely prospect it is!' said his majesty below, addressing Mr. Prichard, while the Marquis bowled.

Making answer, Mr. Prichard pointed out where his own house lay, half hidden by a grove, and said, 'May it please your majesty, I have advised my Lord to cut down those trees, so that when he wants a good player at bowls, he may have but to beckon.'

'Nay,' returned the king, 'he should plant more trees, that so he might not see thy house at all.'

The Marquis , who had bowled, and was coming towards them, heard what the king said, and fancying he aimed at the fault of the greedy buying-up of land—

'If your majesty hath had enough of the game,' he said, 'and will climb with me to the top of the tower, I will show you what may do your mind some ease.'

'I should be sorry to set your Lordship such an arduous task,' replied the king. 'But I am very desirous of seeing your great tower, and if you will permit me, I will climb the stair without your attendance.'

'Sir, it will pleasure me to think that the last time ever I ascended those stairs, I conducted your majesty. For indeed it shall be the last time. I grow old.'

As the Marquis spoke, he led towards the twin-arched bridge over the castle-moat, then through the western gate, and along the side of the court to the Gothic bridge, on their way despatching one of his gentlemen to fetch the keys of the tower.

'My lord,' said the king when the messenger had gone, 'there are some men so unreasonable as to make me believe that your lordship hath good store of gold yet left within the tower; but I, knowing how I have exhausted you, could never have believed it, until now I see you will not trust the keys with any but yourself.'

'Sir,' answered the Marquis , 'I was so far from giving your majesty any such occasion of thought by this tender of my duty, that I protest unto you that I was once resolved that your majesty should have lain there, but that I was loath to commit your majesty to the Tower.'

'You are more considerate, my lord, than some of my subjects would be if they had me as much in their keeping,' answered the king sadly. 'But what are those pipes let into the wall up there?' he asked, stopping in the middle of the bridge and looking up at the keep.

'Nay, sire, my son Edward must tell you that. He taketh strange liberties with the mighty old hulk. But I will not injure his good grace with your majesty by talking of that I understand not. I trust that one day, when you shall no more require his absence, you will yet again condescend to be my guest, when my son, by your majesty's favour now my Lord Glamorgan, will have things to show you that will delight your eyes to behold.'

'I have ere now seen something of his performance,' answered the king; 'but these naughty times give room for nothing in that kind but guns and swords.'

Leaving the workshop unvisited, his lordship took the king up the stair, and unlocking the entrance to the first floor, ushered him into a lofty vaulted chamber, old in the midst of antiquity, dark, vast, and stately.

'This is where I did think to lodge your majesty,' he said, 'but—but—your majesty sees it is gloomy, for the windows are narrow, and the walls are ten feet through.'

'It maketh me very cold,' said the king, shuddering. 'Good sooth, but I were loath to be a prisoner!'

He turned and left the room hastily. The Marquis rejoined him on the stair, and led him, two stories higher, to the armoury, now empty compared to its former condition, but still capable of affording some supply. The next space above was filled with stores, and the highest was now kept clear for defence, for the reservoir so fully occupied the top that there was no room for engines of any sort; and indeed it took up so much of the storey below with its depth that it left only such room as between the decks of a man of war, rendering it hardly fit for any other use.

Reaching the summit at length, the king gazed with silent wonder at the little tarn which lay there as on the crest of a mountain. But the Marquis conducted him to the western side, and, pointing with his finger, said—

'Sir, you see that line of trees, stretching across a neck of arable field, where to the right the brook catches the sun?'

'I see it, my lord,' answered the king.

'And behind it a house and garden, small but dainty?'

'Yes, my lord.'

'Then I trust your majesty will release me from suspicion of being of those to whom the prophet Isaias saith, "Vae qui conjungitis domum ad domum, et agrum agro copulatis usque ad terminum loci: numquid habitabitis vos soli in medio terrae?" May it please your majesty, I planted those trees to hoodwink mine eyes from such temptations, hiding from them the vineyard of Naboth, lest they should act the Jezebel and tempt me to play the Ahab thereto. If I did thus when those trees and I were young, shall I do worse now that I stand with one foot in the grave, and purgatory itself in the other?'

The king seemed to listen politely, but only listened half and did not perceive his drift. He was looking at Dorothy where she stood at the opposite side of the reservoir, unable, because of the temporary obstruction occasioned by certain alterations and repairs about the cocks now going on, to reach the stair without passing the king and the Marquis . The king asked who she was; and the Marquis , telling him a little about her, called her. She came, courtesied low to his majesty, and stood with beating heart.

'I desire,' said the Marquis , 'thou shouldst explain to his majesty that trick of thy cousin Glamorgan, the water-shoot, and let him see it work.'

'My lord,' answered Dorothy, trembling betwixt devotion and doubtful duty, 'it was the great desire of my Lord Glamorgan that none in the castle should know the trick, as it pleases your lordship to call it.'

'What, cousin! cannot his majesty keep a secret? And doth not all that Glamorgan hath belong to the king?'

'God forbid I should doubt either, my lord,' answered Dorothy, turning very pale, and ready to sink, 'but it cannot well be done in the broad day without someone seeing. At night, indeed—'

'Tut, tut! it is but a whim of Glamorgan's. Thou wilt not do a jot of ill to show the game before his majesty in the sunlight.'

'My lord, I promised.'

'Here standeth who will absolve thee, child! His majesty is paramount to Glamorgan.'

'My lord! my lord!' said Dorothy almost weeping, 'I am bewildered, and cannot well understand. But I am sure that if it be wrong, no one can give me leave to do it, or absolve me beforehand. God himself can but pardon after the thing is done, not give permission to do it. Forgive me, sir, but so master Matthew Herbert hath taught me.'

'And very good doctrine, too,' said the Marquis emphatically, 'let who will propound it. Think you not so, sir?'

But the king stood with dull imperturbable gaze fixed on the distant horizon, and made no reply. An awkward silence followed. The king requested his host to conduct him to his apartment.

'I marvel, my lord,' said his majesty as they went down the stair, seeing how lame his host was, 'that, as they tell me, your lordship drinks claret. All physicians say it is naught for the gout.'

'Sir,' returned the Marquis , 'it shall never be said that I forsook my friend to pleasure my enemy.'

The king's face grew dark, for ever since the lecture for which he had made Gower the textbook, he had been ready to see a double meaning of rebuke in all the Marquis said. He made no answer, avoided his attendants who waited for him in the fountain court, expecting him to go by the bell-tower, and, passing through the hall and the stone court, ascended to his room alone, and went into the picture-gallery, where he paced up and down till supper-time.

The Marquis rejoined the little company of his own friends who had left the bowling-green after him, and were now in the oak parlour. A little troubled at the king's carriage towards him, he entered with a merrier bearing than usual.

'Well, gentlemen, how goes the bias?' he said gayly.

'We were but now presuming to say, my lord,' answered Mr. Prichard, 'that there are who would largely warrant that if you would you might be duke of Somerset.'

'When I was earl of Worcester,' returned the Marquis , 'I was well to do; since I was Marquis , I am worse by a hundred thousand pounds; and if I should be a duke, I should be an arrant beggar. Wherefore I had rather go back to my earldom, than at this rate keep on my pace to the dukedom of Somerset.'

CHAPTER XLV

THE SECRET INTERVIEW

Between the third of July, when he first came, and the fifteenth of September, when he last departed, the king went and came several times. During his last visit a remarkable interview took place between him and his host, the particulars of which are circumstantially given by Dr. Bayly in the little book he calls Certamen Religiosum: to me it falls to recount after him some of the said particulars, because, although Dorothy was brought but one little step within the sphere of the interview, certain results were which bore a large influence upon her history.

'Though money came from him,' that is, the Marquis , 'like drops of blood,' says Dr. Bayly, 'yet was he contented that every drop within his body should be let out,' if only he might be the instrument of bringing his majesty back to the bosom of the catholic church, a bosom which no doubt the Marquis found as soft as it was capacious, but which the king regarded as a good deal resembling that of a careless nurse rather than mother, frized with pins, and here and there a cruel needle. Therefore, expecting every hour that the king would apply to him for more money, the Marquis had resolved that, at such time as he should do so, he would make an attempt to lead the stray sheep within the fold, for the Marquis was not one of those who regarded a protestant as necessarily a goat.

But the king shrank from making the request in person, and having learned that the Marquis had been at one point in his history under the deepest obligation to Dr. Bayly, who having then preserved both his lordship's life and a large sum of money he carried with him, by 'concealing both for the space that the moon useth to be twice in riding of her circuit,' had thereafter become a member of his family and a sharer in his deepest confidence, greatly desired that the doctor should take the office of mediator between him and the Marquis .

The king's will having been already conveyed to the doctor, in the king's presence colonel Lingen came up to him and said,

'Dr. Bayly, the king, much wishing your aid in this matter, saith he delights not to be a beggar, and yet is constrained thereunto.'

'I am at his majesty's disposal,' returned the doctor, 'although I confess myself somewhat loath to be the beetle-head that must drive this wedge.'

'Nay,' said the colonel, 'they tell me that no man can make a divorce between the Babylonish garment and the wedge of gold sooner than thyself, good doctor.'

The end was that he undertook the business, though with reluctance, unwilling to be 'made an instrument to let the same horse bleed whom the king himself had found so free', and sought the Marquis in his study.

'My lord,' he said, 'the thing that I feared is now fallen upon me. I am made the unwelcome messenger of bad news: the king wants money.'

'Hold, sir! that's no news,' interrupted the Marquis . 'Go on with your business.'

'My lord,' said the doctor, 'there is one comfort yet, that, as the king is brought low, so are his demands, and, like his army, are come down from thousands to hundreds, and from paying the soldiers of his army to buying bread for himself and his followers. My lord, it is the king's own expression, and his desire is but three hundred pound.'

Lord Worcester remained a long time silent, and Dr. Bayly waited, 'knowing by experience that in such cases it was best leaving him to himself, and to let that nature that was so good work itself into an act of the highest charity, like the diamond which is only polished with its own dust.'

'Come hither, come nearer, my good doctor,' said his lordship at length: 'hath the king himself spoken unto thee concerning any such business?'

'The king himself hath not, my lord, but others did, in the king's hearing.'

'Might I but speak unto him—,' said the Marquis . 'But I was never thought worthy to be consulted with, though in matters merely concerning the affairs of my own country! I would supply his wants, were they never so great, or whatsoever they were.'

'If the king knew as much, my lord, you might quickly speak with him,' remarked the doctor.

'The way to have him know so much is to have somebody to tell him of it,' said the Marquis testily.

'Will your lordship give me leave to be the informer?' asked the doctor.

'Truly I spake it to the purpose,' answered the Marquis .

Away ran the little doctor, ambling through the picture-gallery, 'half going and half running,' like some short-winged bird, his heart trembling lest the Marquis should change his mind and call him back, and so his pride in his successful mediation be mortified, to the king's chamber, where he told his majesty with diplomatic reserve, and something of diplomatic cunning, enhancing the difficulties, that he had perceived his lordship desired some conference with him, and that he believed, if the king granted such conference, he would find a more generous response to his necessities than perhaps he expected. The king readily consenting, the doctor went on to say that his lordship much wished the interview that very night. The king asked how it could be managed, and the doctor told him the Marquis had contrived it before his majesty came to the castle, having for that reason appointed the place where they were for his bed-chamber, and not that in the great tower, which the Marquis himself liked the best in the castle.

'I know my lord's drift well enough,' said the king, smiling: 'either he means to chide me, or else to convert me to his religion.'

'I doubt not, sire,' returned the doctor, 'but your majesty is temptation-proof as well as correction-free, and will return the same man you go, having made a profitable exchange of gold and silver for words and sleep.'

Upon Dr. Bayly's report of his success, the Marquis sent him back to tell the king that at eleven o'clock he would be waiting his majesty in a certain room to which the doctor would conduct him.

This was the room the Marquis's father had occupied and in which he died, called therefore 'my Lord Privy-seal's chamber.' Since then the Marquis had never allowed any one to sleep in it, hardly any one to go into it; whence it came that although all the rest of the castle was crowded, this one room remained empty and fit for their purpose.

To understand the precautions taken to keep their interview a secret, we must remember that, although he had not a better friend in all England, such reason had the king to fear losing his protestant friends from their jealousy of catholic influence, that he had never invited the Marquis of Worcester to sit with him in council; and that the Marquis on his part was afraid both of injuring the cause of the king, and of being himself impeached for treason. Should any of the king's attendant lords discover that they were closeted together, he dreaded the suspicion and accusation of another Gowry conspiracy even. His lordship therefore instructed Dr. Bayly to go, as the time drew nigh, to the drawing-room, which was next the Marquis's chamber, and the dining parlour, through both of which he must pass to reach the appointed place, and clear them of the company which might be in them. The chaplain desiring to know how he was to manage it, so that it should not look strange and arouse suspicion, and what he should do if any were unwilling to go —

'I will tell you what you shall do,' said the Marquis hastily, 'so that you shall not need to fear any such thing. Go unto the yeoman of the wine-cellar, and bid him leave the keys of the wine-cellar with you, and all that you find in your way, invite them down into the cellar, and show them the keys, and I warrant you, you shall sweep the room of them, if there were a hundred. And when you have done, leave them there.'

But having thus arranged, the Marquis grew anxious again. He remembered that it was not unusual to pass to the hall from the northern side of the fountain court, where were most of the rooms of the ladies' gentlewomen, through the picture-gallery, entering it by a passage and stair which connected the bell-tower with one of its deep window recesses, and leaving it by a door in the middle of the opposite side, admitting to a stair in the thickness of the wall, which led downwards, opening to the minstrels' gallery on the left hand, and a little further below, to the organ loft in the chapel on the right hand. It was not the least likely that any of the ladies or their attendants would be passing that way so late at night, but there was a possibility, and that was enough, the Marquis being anxious and nervous, to render him more so.

There was, however, another and more threatening possibility of encounter. He remembered that Mr. Delaware, the master of his horse, had lately removed to that part of the house: and the fear came upon him lest his blind son, who frequently turned night into day in his love for the organ, and was uncertain in his movements between chapel and chamber, the direct way being that just described, should by evil chance appear at the very moment of the king's passing, and alarm him, for through the gallery Dr. Bayly must lead his majesty to reach my Lord Privy-seal's chamber. The Marquis , therefore, although reluctant to introduce another even to the externals of the plot, felt that the assistance of a second confidant was more than desirable, and turning the matter over, could think of no one whom he could trust so well, and who at the same time would, if seen, be so little liable to the sort of suspicion he dreaded, as Dorothy. He therefore sent for her, told her as much as he thought proper, gave her the key of his private passage to the gallery, leading across the top of the hall-door, the only direct communication from the southern side of the castle, and generally kept closed, and directed her to be in the gallery ten minutes before eleven, to lock the door at the top of the stair leading down into the hall, and take her stand in the window at the foot of the stair from the bell-tower, where the door was without a lock, and see that no one entered by order of the Marquis for the king's repose, enjoining upon her that, whatever she saw or heard from any other quarter, she must keep perfectly still, nor let anyone discover that she was there. With these instructions, his lordship, considerably relieved, dismissed her, and went to lie down upon his bed, and have a nap if he could. He had already given the chaplain the key of his chamber, the door of which he always locked, that he might enter and wake him when the appointed hour was at hand.

As soon as he began to feel that eleven o'clock was drawing near, Dr. Bayly proceeded to reconnoitre. The Marquis 's plan, although he could think of none better, was not altogether satisfactory, and it was to his relief that he found nobody in the dining-room. When he entered the drawing-room, however, there, to his equal annoyance, he saw in the light of one expiring candle the dim figure of a lady; he could not offer HER the keys of the wine-cellar! What was he to do? What could she be there for? He drew nearer, and, with a positive pang of relief, discovered that it was Dorothy. A word was enough between them. But the good doctor was just a little annoyed that a second should share in the secret of the great ones.

The next room was the antechamber to the Marquis 's bedroom: timorously on tiptoe he stepped through it, fearful of waking the two young gentlemen, for Scudamore's place had been easily supplied, who waited upon his lordship. Opening the inner door as softly as he could, he crept in, and found the Marquis fast asleep. So slowly, so gently did he wake him, that his lordship insisted he had not slept at all; but when he told him that the time was come—

'What time?' he asked.

'For meeting the king,' replied the doctor.

'What king?' rejoined the Marquis , in a kind of bewildered horror.

The more he came to himself, the more distressed he seemed, and the more unwilling to keep the appointment he had been so eager to make, so that at length even Dr. Bayly was tempted to doubt something evil in the 'design that carried with it such a conflict within the bosom of the actor.' It soon became evident, however, that it was but the dread of such possible consequences as I have already indicated that thus moved him.

'Fie, fie!' he said; 'I would to God I had let it alone.'

'My lord,' said the doctor, 'you know your own heart best. If there be nothing in your intentions but what is good and justifiable, you need not fear; if otherwise, it is never too late to repent.'

'Ah, doctor!' returned the Marquis with troubled look, 'I thought I had been sure of one friend, and that you would never have harboured the least suspicion of me. God knows my heart: I have no other intention towards his majesty than to make him a glorious man here, and a glorified saint hereafter.'

'Then, my lord,' said Dr. Bayly, 'shake off these fears together with the drowsiness that begat them. Honi soit qui mal y pense.'

'Oh, but I am not of that order!' said the Marquis ; 'but I thank God I wear that motto about my heart, to as much purpose as they who wear it about their arms.'

'He then,' reports the doctor, 'began to be a little pleasant, and took a pipe of tobacco, and a little glass full of aqua mirabilis, and said, "Come now, let us go in the name of God," crossing himself.'

My love for the Marquis has led me to recount this curious story with greater minuteness than is necessary to the understanding of Dorothy's part in what follows, but the worthy doctor's account is so graphic that even for its own sake, had it been fitting, I would gladly have copied it word for word from the Certamen Religiosum.

It is indeed a strange story, king and Marquis , attended by a doctor of divinity, of the faith of the one, but the trusted friend of the other, meeting, at midnight, although in the house of the Marquis , to discuss points of theology, both king and Marquis in mortal terror of discovery.

Meantime Dorothy had done as she had been ordered, had felt her way through the darkness to the picture-gallery, had locked the door at the top of the one stair, and taken her stand in the recess at the foot of the other, in pitch darkness, close to the king's bedchamber, for the gallery was but thirteen feet in width, keeping watch over him! The darkness felt like awe around her.

The door of the chamber opened: it gave no sound, but the glimmer of the night-light shone out. By that she saw a figure enter the gallery. The door closed softly and slowly, and all was darkness again. No sound of movement across the floor followed: but she heard a deep sigh, as from a sorely burdened heart. Then, in an agonised whisper, as if wrung by torture from the depths of the spirit, came the words: 'Oh Stafford, thou art avenged! I left thee to thy fate, and God hath left me to mine. Thou didst go for me to the scaffold, but thou wilt not out of my chamber. O God, deliver me from blood-guiltiness.'

Dorothy stood in dismay, a mere vessel containing a tumult of emotions. The king re-entered his chamber, and closed the door. The same instant a light appeared at the further end of the gallery, a long way off, and Dr. Bayly came, like a Will o' the wisp, gliding from afar; till, softly walking up, he stopped within a yard or two of the king's door, and there stood, with his candle in his hand. His round face was pale that should have been red, and his small keen eyes shone in the candle light with mingled importance and anxiety. He saw Dorothy, but the only notice he took of her presence was to turn from her with his face towards the king's door, so that his shadow might shroud the recess where she stood.

A minute or so passed, and the king's door re-opened. He came out, said a few words in a whisper to his guide, and walked with him down the gallery, whispering as he went.

Dorothy hastened to her chamber, threw herself on the bed, and wept. The king was cast from the throne of her conscience, but taken into the hospital of her heart.

What followed between the king and the Marquis belongs not to my tale. When, after a long talk, the chaplain had conducted the king to his chamber and returned to Lord Worcester, he found him in the dark upon his knees.

CHAPTER XLVI

GIFTS OF HEALING

Soon after the king's departure, the Marquis received from him a letter containing another addressed 'To our Attorney or Solicitor-General for the time being,' in which he commanded the preparation of a bill for his majesty's signature, creating the Marquis of Worcester duke of Somerset. The enclosing letter required, however, that it should—'be kept private, until I shall esteem the time convenient.' In the next year we have causes enough for the fact that the king's pleasure never reached any attorney or solicitor-general for the time being.

About a month after the battle of Naseby, and while yet the king was going and coming as regards Raglan, the wounded Rowland, long before he was fit to be moved from the farm-house where his servant had found him shelter, was brought home to the castle. Shafto, faithful as hare-brained, had come upon him almost accidentally, after long search, and just in time to save his life. Mistress Watson received him with tears, and had him carried to the same turret-chamber whence Richard had escaped, in order that she might be nigh him. The poor fellow was but a shadow of his former self, and looked more likely to vanish than to die in the ordinary way. Hence he required constant attention, which was so far from lacking that the danger, both physical and spiritual, seemed rather to lie in over-service. Hitherto, of the family, it had been the Marquis chiefly that spoiled him; but now that he was so sorely wounded for the king, and lay at death's door, all the ladies of the castle were admiring, pitiful, tender, ministrant, paying him such attentions as nobody could be trusted to bear uninjured except a doll or a baby. One might have been tempted to say that they sought his physical welfare at the risk of his moral ruin. But there is that in sickness which leads men back to a kind of babyhood, and while it lasts there is comparatively little danger. It is with returning health that the peril comes. Then self and self-fancied worth awake, and find themselves again, and the risk is then great indeed that all the ministrations of love be taken for homage at the altar of importance. How often has not a mistress found that after nursing a servant through an illness, perhaps an old servant even, she has had to part with her for unendurable arrogance and insubordination? But present sickness is a wonderful antidote to vanity, and nourisher of the gentle primeval simplicities of human nature. So long as a man feels himself a poor creature, not only physically unable, but without the spirit to desire to act, kindness will move gratitude, and not vanity. In Rowland's case happily it lasted until something better was able to get up its head a little. But no one can predict what the first result of suffering will be, not knowing what seeds lie nearest the surface. Rowland's self-satisfaction had been a hard pan beneath which lay thousands of germinal possibilities invaluable; and now the result of its tearing up remained to be seen. If in such case Truth's never-ceasing pull at the heart begins to be felt, allowed, considered; if conscience begin, like a thing weary with very sleep, to rouse itself in motions of pain from the stiffness of its repose, then is there hope of the best.

He had lost much blood, having lain a long time, as I say, in the fallow-field before Shafto found him. Oft-recurring fever, extreme depression, and intermittent and doubtful progress life-wards followed. Through all the commotion of the king's visits, the coming and going, the clang of hoofs and clanking of armour, the heaving of hearts and clamour of tongues, he lay lapped in ignorance and ministration, hidden from the world and deaf to the gnarring of its wheels, prisoned in a twilight dungeon, to which Richard's sword had been the key. The world went grinding on and on, much the same, without him whom it had forgotten; but the over-world remembered him, and now and then looked in at a window: all dungeons have one window which no gaoler and no tyrant can build up.

The Marquis went often to see him, full of pity for the gay youth thus brought low; but he would lie pale and listless, now and then turning his eyes, worn large with the wasting of his face, upon him, but looking as if he only half heard him. His master grew sad about him. The next time his majesty came, he asked him if he remembered the youth, telling him how he had lain wounded ever since the battle at Naseby. The king remembered him well enough, but had never missed him. The Marquis then told him how anxious he was about him, for that nothing woke him from the weary heartlessness into which he had fallen.

'I will pay him a visit,' said the king.

'Sir, it is what I would have requested, had I not feared to pain your majesty,' returned the Marquis .

'I will go at once,' said the king.

When Rowland saw him his face flushed, the tears rose in his eyes, he kissed the hand the king held out to him, and said feebly:—

'Pardon, sire: if I had rode better, the battle might have been yours. I reached not the prince.'

'It is the will of God,' said the king, remembering for the first time that he had sent him to Rupert. 'Thou didst thy best, and man can do no more.'

'Nay, sire, but an' I had ridden honestly,' returned Rowland; '—I mean had my mare been honestly come by, then had I done your majesty's message.'

'How is that?' asked the king.

'Ha!' said the Marquis ; 'then it was Heywood met thee, and would have his own again? Told I not thee so? Ah, that mare, Rowland! that mare!'

But Rowland had to summon all his strength to keep from fainting, for the blood had fled again to his heart, and could not reply.

'Thou didst thy duty like a brave knight and true, I doubt not,' said the king, kindly wishful to comfort him; 'and that my word may be a true one,' he added, drawing his sword and laying it across the youth's chest, 'although I cannot tell thee to rise and walk, I tell thee, when thou dost arise, to rise up sir Rowland Scudamore.'

The blood rushed to sir Rowland's face, but fled again as fast.

'I deserve no such honour, sire,' he murmured.

But the Marquis struck his hands together with pleasure, and cried,

'There, my boy! There is a king to serve! Sir Rowland Scudamore! There is for thee! And thy wife will be MY LADY! Think on that!'

Rowland did think on it, but bitterly. He summoned strength to thank his majesty, but failed to find anything courtier-like to add to the bare thanks. When his visitors left him, he sighed sorely and said to himself,

'Honour without desert! But for the roundhead's taunts, I might have run to Rupert and saved the day.'

The next morning the Marquis went again to see him.

'How fares sir Rowland?' he said.

'My lord,' returned Scudamore, in beseeching tone, 'break not my heart with honour unmerited.'

'How! Darest thou, boy, set thy judgment against the king's?' cried the Marquis . 'Sir Rowland thou art, and SIR ROWLAND will the archangel cry when he calls thee from thy last sleep.'

'To my endless disgrace,' added Scudamore.

'What! hast not done thy duty?'

'I tried, but I failed, my lord.'

'The best as often fail as the worst,' rejoined his lordship.

'I mean not merely that I failed of the end. That, alas! I did. But I mean that it was by my own fault that I failed,' said Rowland.

Then he told the Marquis all the story of his encounter with Richard, ending with the words,

'And now, my lord, I care no more for life.'

'Stuff and nonsense!' exclaimed the Marquis . 'Thinkest though the roundhead would have let thee run to Rupert? It was not to that end he spared thy life. Thy only chance was to fight him.'

'Does your lordship think so indeed?' asked Rowland, with a glimmer of eagerness.

'On my soul I do. Thou art weak-headed from thy sickness and weariness.'

'You comfort me, my lord—a little. But the stolen mare, my lord?'

'Ah! there indeed I can say nothing. That was not well done, and evil came thereof. But comfort thyself that the evil is come and gone; and think not that such chances are left to determine great events. Naseby fight had been lost, spite of a hundred messages to Rupert. Not care for life, boy! Leave that to old men like me. Thou must care for it, for thou hast many years before thee.'

'But nothing to fill them with, my lord.'

'What meanest thou there, Rowland? The king's cause will yet prosper, and—'

'Pardon me, my lord; I spoke not of the king's majesty or his affairs. Hardly do I care even for them. It is a nameless weight, or rather emptiness, that oppresseth me. Wherefore is there such a world? I ask, and why are men born thereinto? Why should I live on and labour on therein? Is it not all vanity and vexation of spirit? I would the roundhead had but struck a little deeper, and reached my heart.'

'I admire at thee, Rowland. Truly my gout causeth me so great grief that I have much ado to keep my unruly member within bounds, but I never yet was aweary of my life, and scarce know what I should say to thee.'

A pause followed. The Marquis did not think what a huge difference there is between having too much blood in the feet and too little in the brain.

'I pray, sir, can you tell me if mistress Dorothy knoweth it was before Heywood I fell?' said Rowland at length.

'I know not; but methinks had she known, I should sooner have heard the thing myself. Who indeed should tell her, for Shafto knew it not? And why should she conceal it?'

'I cannot tell, my lord: she is not like other ladies.'

'She is like all good ladies in this, that she speaketh the truth: why then not ask her?'

'I have had no opportunity, my lord. I have not seen her since I left to join the army.'

'Tut, tut!' said his lordship, and frowned a little. 'I thought not the damsel had been over nice. She might well have favoured a wounded knight with a visit.'

'She is not to blame. It is my own fault,' sighed Rowland.

The Marquis looked at him for a moment pitifully, but made no answer, and presently took his leave.

He went straight to Dorothy, and expostulated with her. She answered him no farther or otherwise than was simply duteous, but went at once to see Scudamore.

Mistress Watson was in the room when she entered, but left it immediately: she had never been in spirit reconciled to Dorothy: their relation had in it too much of latent rebuke for her. So Dorothy found herself alone with her cousin.

He was but the ghost of the gay, self-satisfied, good-natured, jolly Rowland. Pale and thin, with drawn face and great eyes, he held out a wasted hand to Dorothy, and looked at her, not pitifully, but despairingly. He was one of those from whom take health and animal spirits, and they feel to themselves as if they had nothing. Nor have they in themselves anything. With those he could have borne what are called hardships fairly well; those gone, his soul sat aghast in an empty house.

'My poor cousin!' said Dorothy, touched with profound compassion at sight of his lost look. But he only gazed at her, and said nothing. She took the hand he did not offer, and held it kindly in hers. He burst into tears, and she gently laid it again on the coverlid.

'I know you despise me, Dorothy,' he sobbed, 'and you are right: I despise myself.'

'You have been a good soldier to the king, Rowland,' said Dorothy, 'and he has acknowledged it fitly.'

'I care nothing for king or kingdom, Dorothy. Nothing is worth caring for. Do not mistake me. I am not going to talk presumptuously. I love not thee now, Dorothy. I never did love thee, and thou dost right to despise me, for I am unworthy. I would I were dead. Even the king's majesty hath been no whit the better for me, but rather the worse; for another man, one, I mean, who was not mounted on a stolen mare, would have performed his hest unhindered of foregone fault.'

'Thou didst not think thou wast doing wrong when thou stolest the mare,' said Dorothy, seeking to comfort him.

'How know'st thou that, Dorothy? There was a spot in my heart that felt ashamed all the time.'

'He that is sorry is already pardoned, I think, cousin. Then what thou hast done evil is gone and forgotten.'

'Nay, Dorothy. But if it were forgotten, yet would it BE. If I forgot it myself, yet would I not cease to be the man who had done it. And thou knowest, Dorothy, in how many things I have been false, so false that I counted myself honourable all the time. Tell me wherefore should I not kill myself, and rid the world of me; what withholdeth?'

'That thou art of consequence to him that made thee.'

'How can that be, when I know myself worthless? Will he be mistaken in me?'

'No, truly. But he may have regard to that thou shalt yet be. For surely he sent thee here to do some fitting work for him.'

More talk followed, but Dorothy did not seem to herself to find the right thing to say, and retired to the top of the Tower with a sense of failure, and oppressed with helpless compassion for the poor youth.

The doctors of divinity and of medicine differed concerning the cause of his sad condition. The doctor of medicine said it arose entirely from a check in the circulation of the animal spirits; the doctor of divinity thought, but did not say, only hinted, that it came of a troubled conscience, and that he would have been well long ago but for certain sins, known only to himself, that bore heavy upon his life. This gave the Marquis a good ground of argument for confession, the weight of which argument was by the divine felt and acknowledged. But both doctors were right, and both were wrong. Could his health have been at once restored, a great reaction would have ensued, his interest in life would have reawaked, and most probably he would have become indifferent to that which now oppressed him; but on the slightest weariness or disappointment, the same overpowering sense of desolation would have returned, and indeed at times amidst the warmest glow of health and keenest consciousness of pleasure. On the other hand, if by any argument addressed to his moral or religious nature his mind could have been a little eased, his physical nature would most likely have at once responded in improvement; but he had no individual actions of such heavy guilt as the divine presumed to repent of, nor could any amount or degree of sorrow for the past have sufficed to restore him to peace and health. It was a poet of the time who wrote,

'The soul's dark cottage, battered and decayed,
Lets in new light, through chinks that time has made:'

sickness had done the same thing as time with Rowland, and he saw the misery of his hovel. The cure was a deeper and harder matter than Dr. Bayly yet understood, or than probably Rowland himself would for years attain to, while yet the least glimmer of its approach would be enough to initiate physical recovery.

CHAPTER XLVII

THE POET-PHYSICIAN

Time passed, but with little change in the condition of the patient. Winter began to draw on, and both doctors feared a more rapid decline.

Early in the month of November, Dorothy received a letter from Mr. Herbert, informing her that her cousin, Henry Vaughan, one of his late twin pupils, would, on his way from Oxford, be passing near Raglan, and that he had desired him to call upon her. Willing enough to see her relative, she thought little more of the matter, until at length the day was at hand, when she found herself looking for his arrival with some curiosity as to what sort of person he might prove of whom she had heard so often from his master.

When at length he was ushered into Lady Glamorgan's parlour, where her mistress had desired her to receive him, both her ladyship and Dorothy were at once prejudiced in his favour. They saw a rather tall young man of five or six and twenty, with a small head, a clear grey eye, and a sober yet changeful countenance. His carriage was dignified yet graceful, self-restraint and no other was evident therein; a certain sadness brooded like a thin mist above his eyes, but his smile now and then broke out like the sun through a grey cloud. Dorothy did not know that he was just getting over the end of a love-story, or that he had a book of verses just printed, and had already begun to repent it.

After the usual greetings, and when Dorothy had heard the last news of Mr. Herbert, for Mr. Vaughan had made several journeys of late between Brecknock and Oxford, taking Llangattock Rectory in his way, and could tell her much she did not know concerning her friend, Lady Glamorgan, who was not sorry to see her interested in a young man whose royalist predilections were plain and strong, proposed that Dorothy should take him over the castle.

She led him first to the top of the tower to show him the reservoir and the prospect; but there they fell into such a talk as revealed to Dorothy that here was a man who was her master in everything towards which, especially since her mother's death and her following troubles, she had most aspired, and a great hope arose in her heart for her cousin Scudamore. For in this talk it had come out that Mr. Vaughan had studied medicine, and was now on his way to settle for practice at Brecknock. As soon as Dorothy learned this, she entreated her cousin Vaughan to go and visit her cousin Scudamore. He consented, and Dorothy, scarcely allowing him to pause even under the admirable roof of the great hall as they passed through, led him straight to the turret-chamber, where the sick man was.

They found him sitting by the fire, folded in blankets, listless and sad.

When Dorothy had told him whom she had brought to see him, she would have left them, but Rowland turned on her such beseeching eyes, that she remained, by no means unwillingly, and seated herself to hear what this wonderful young physician would say.

'It is very irksome to be thus prisoned in your chamber, sir Rowland,' he said.

'No,' answered Scudamore, 'or yes: I care not.'

'Have you no books about you?' asked Mr. Vaughan, glancing round the room.

'Books!' repeated Scudamore, with a wan contemptuous smile.

'You do not then love books?'

'Wherefore should I love books? What can books do for me? I love nothing. I long only to die.'

'And go—?' suggested, rather than asked, Mr. Vaughan.

'I care not whither, anywhere away from here, if indeed I go anywhere. But I care not.'

'That is hardly what you mean, sir Rowland, I think. Will you allow me to interpret you? Have you not the notion that if you were hence you would leave behind you a certain troublesome attendant who is scarce worth his wages?'

Scudamore looked at him but did not reply; and Mr. Vaughan went on.

'I know well what aileth you, for I am myself but now recovering from a similar sickness, brought upon me by the haunting of the same evil one who torments you.'

'You think, then, that I am possessed?' said Rowland, with a faint smile and a glance at Dorothy.

'That verily thou art, and grievously tormented. Shall I tell thee who hath possessed thee? for the demon hath a name that is known amongst men, though it frighteneth few, and draweth many, alas! His name is Self, and he is the shadow of thy own self. First he made thee love him, which was evil, and now he hath made thee hate him, which is evil also. But if he be cast out and never more enter into thy heart, but remain as a servant in thy hall, then wilt thou recover from this sickness, and be whole and sound, and shall find the varlet serviceable.'

'Art thou not an exorciser, then, Mr. Vaughan, as well as a discerner of spirits? I would thou couldst drive the said demon out of me, for truly I love him not.'

'Through all thy hate thou lovest him more than thou knowest. Thou seest him vile, but instead of casting him out, thou mournest over him with foolish tears. And yet thou dreamest that by dying thou wouldst be rid of him. No, it is back to thy childhood thou must go to be free.'

'That were a strange way to go, sir. I know it not. There seems to be a purpose in what you say, Mr. Vaughan, but you take me not with you. How can I rid me of myself, so long as I am Rowland Scudamore?'

'There is a way, sir Rowland, and but one way. Human words at least, however it may be with some high heavenly language, can never say the best things but by a kind of stumbling, wherein one contradiction keepeth another from falling. No man, as thou sayest, truly, can rid him of himself and live, for that involveth an impossibility. But he can rid himself of that haunting shadow of his own self, which he hath pampered and fed upon shadowy lies, until it is bloated and black with pride and folly. When that demon king of shades is once cast out, and the man's house is possessed of God instead, then first he findeth his true substantial self, which is the servant, nay, the child of God. To rid thee of thyself thou must offer it again to him that made it. Be thou empty that he may fill thee. I never understood this until these latter days. Let me impart to thee certain verses I found but yesterday, for they will tell thee better what I mean. Thou knowest the sacred volume of the blessed George Herbert?'

'I never heard of him or it,' said Scudamore.

'It is no matter as now: these verses are not of his. Prithee, hearken:

'I carry with, me, Lord, a foolish fool,
That still his cap upon my head would place.
I dare not slay him, he will not to school,
And still he shakes his bauble in my face.

'I seize him, Lord, and bring him to thy door;
Bound on thine altar-threshold him I lay.
He weepeth; did I heed, he would implore;
And still he cries ALACK and WELL-A-DAY!

'If thou wouldst take him in and make him wise,
 I think he might be taught to serve thee well;
If not, slay him, nor heed his foolish cries,
He's but a fool that mocks and rings a bell.'

Something in the lines appeared to strike Scudamore.

'I thank you, sir,' he said. 'Might I put you to the trouble, I would request that you would write out the verses for me, that I may study their meaning at my leisure.'

Mr. Vaughan promised, and, after a little more conversation, took his leave.

Now, whether it was from anything he had said in particular, or that Scudamore had felt the general influence of the man, Dorothy could not tell, but from that visit she believed Rowland began to think more and to brood less. By and by he began to start questions of right and wrong, suppose cases, and ask Dorothy what she would do in such and such circumstances. With many cloudy relapses there was a suspicion of dawn, although a rainy one most likely, on his far horizon.

'Dost thou really believe, Dorothy,' he asked one day, 'that a man ever did love his enemy? Didst thou ever know one who did?'

'I cannot say I ever did,' returned Dorothy. 'I have however seen few that were enemies. But I am sure that had it not been possible, we should never have been commanded thereto.'

'The last time Dr. Bayly came to see me he read those words, and I thought within myself all the time of the only enemy I had, and tried to forgive him, but could not.'

'Had he then wronged thee so deeply?'

'I know not, indeed, what women call wronged, least of all what thou, who art not like other women, wouldst judge; but this thing seems to me strange, that when I look on thee, Dorothy, one moment it seems as if for thy sake I could forgive him anything, except that he slew me not outright, and the next that never can I forgive him even that wherein he never did me any wrong.'

'What! hatest thou then him that struck thee down in fair fight? Sure thou art of meaner soul than I judged thee. What man in battle-field hates his enemy, or thinks it less than enough to do his endeavour to slay him?'

'Know'st thou whom thou wouldst have me forgive? He who struck me down was thy friend, Richard Heywood.'

'Then he hath his mare again?' cried Dorothy, eagerly.

Rowland's face fell, and she knew that she had spoken heartlessly, knew also that, for all his protestations, Rowland yet cherished the love she had so plainly refused. But the same moment she knew something more.

For, by the side of Rowland, in her mind's eye, stood Henry Vaughan, as wise as Rowland was foolish, as accomplished and learned as Rowland was narrow and ignorant; but between them stood Richard, and she knew a something in her which was neither tenderness nor reverence, and yet included both. She rose in some confusion, and left the chamber.

This good came of it, that from that moment Scudamore was satisfied she loved Heywood, and, with much mortification, tried to accept his position. Slowly his health began to return, and slowly the deeper life that was at length to become his began to inform him.

Heartless and poverty-stricken as he had hitherto shown himself, the good in him was not so deeply buried under refuse as in many a better-seeming man. Sickness had awakened in him a sense of requirement, of need also, and loneliness, and dissatisfaction. He grew ashamed of himself and conscious of defilement. Something new began to rise above and condemn the old. There are who would say that the change was merely the mental condition resulting from and corresponding to physical weakness; that repentance, and the vision of the better which maketh shame, is but a mood, sickly as are the brain and nerves which generate it; but he who undergoes the experience believes he knows better, and denies neither the wild beasts nor the stars, because they roar and shine through the dark.

Mr. Vaughan came to see him again and again, and with the concurrence of Dr. Spott, prescribed for him. As the spring approached he grew able to leave his room. The ladies of the family had him to their parlours to pet and feed, but he was not now so easily to be injured by kindness as when he believed in his own merits.

CHAPTER XLVIII

HONOURABLE DISGRACE

January of 1646, according to the division of the year, arrived, and with it the heaviest cloud that had yet overshadowed Raglan.

One day, about the middle of the month, Dorothy, entering Lady Glamorgan's parlour, found it deserted. A moan came to her ears from the adjoining chamber, and there she found her mistress on her face on the bed.

'Madam,' said Dorothy in terror, 'what is it? Let me be with you. May I not know it?'

'My Lord is in prison,' gasped Lady Glamorgan, and bursting into fresh tears, she sobbed and moaned.

'Has my Lord been taken in the field, madam, or by cunning of his enemies?'

'Would to God it were either,' sighed Lady Glamorgan. 'Then were it a small thing to bear.'

'What can it be, madam? You terrify me,' said Dorothy.

No words of reply, only a fresh outburst of agonised, could it also be angry? Weeping followed.

'Since you will tell me nothing, madam, I must take comfort that of myself I know one thing.'

'Prithee, what knowest thou?' asked the countess, but as if careless of being answered, so listless was her tone, so nearly inarticulate her words.

'That is but what bringeth him fresh honour, my lady,' answered Dorothy.

The countess started up, threw her arms about her, drew her down on the bed, kissed her, and held her fast, sobbing worse than ever.

'Madam! madam!' murmured Dorothy from her bosom.

'I thank thee, Dorothy,' she sighed out at length: 'for thy words and thy thoughts have ever been of a piece.'

'Sure, my lady, no one did ever yet dare think otherwise of my lord,' returned Dorothy, amazed.

'But many will now, Dorothy. My God! they will have it that he is a traitor. Wouldst thou believe it, child, he is a prisoner in the castle of Dublin!'

'But is not Dublin in the hands of the king, my lady?'

'Ay! there lies the sting of it! What treacherous friends are these heretics! But how should they be anything else? Having denied their Saviour they may well malign their better brother! My Lord Marquis of Ormond says frightful things of him.'

'One thing more I know, my lady,' said Dorothy, '—that as long as his wife believes him the true man he is, he will laugh to scorn all that false lips may utter against him.'

'Thou art a good girl, Dorothy, but thou knowest little of an evil world. It is one thing to know thyself innocent, and another to carry thy head high.'

'But, madam, even the guilty do that; wherefore not the innocent then?'

'Because, my child, they ARE innocent, and innocence so hateth the very shadow of guilt that it cannot brook the wearing it. My Lord is grievously abused, Dorothy, I say not by whom.'

'By whom should it be but his enemies, madam?'

'Not certainly by those who are to him friends, but yet, alas! by those to whom he is the truest of friends.'

'Is my Lord of Ormond then false? Is he jealous of my Lord Glamorgan? Hath he falsely accused him? I would I understood all, madam.'

'I would I understood all myself, child. Certain papers have been found bearing upon my lord's business in Ireland, all ears are filled with rumours of forgery and treason, coupled with the name of my lord, and he is a prisoner in Dublin castle.'

She forced the sentence from her, as if repeating a hated lesson, then gave a cry, almost a scream of agony.

'Weep not, madam,' said Dorothy, in the very foolishness of sympathetic expostulation.

'What better cause could I have out of hell!' returned the countess, angrily.

'That it were no lie, madam.'

'It is true, I tell thee.'

'That my Lord is a traitor, madam?'

Lady Glamorgan dashed her from her, and glared at her like a tigress. An evil word was on her lips, but her better angel spoke, and ere Dorothy could recover herself, she had listened and understood.

'God forbid!' she said, struggling to be calm. 'But it is true that he is in prison.'

'Then give God thanks, madam, who hath forbidden the one and allowed the other, said Dorothy; and finding her own composure on the point of yielding, she courtesied and left the room. It was a breach of etiquette without leave asked and given, but the face of the countess was again on her pillow, and she did not heed.

For some time things went on as in an evil dream. The Marquis was in angry mood, with no gout to lay it upon. The gloom spread over the castle, and awoke all manner of conjecture and report. Soon, after a fashion, the facts were known to everybody, and the gloom deepened. No further enlightenment reached Dorothy. At length one evening, her mistress having sent for her, she found her much excited, with a letter in her hand.

'Come here, Dorothy: see what I have!' she cried, holding out the letter with a gesture of triumph, and weeping and laughing alternately.

'Madam, it must be something precious indeed,' said Dorothy, 'for I have not heard your ladyship laugh for a weary while. May I not rejoice with you, madam?'

'You shall, my good girl: hearken: I will read: 'My dear Heart,' Who is it from, think'st thou, Dorothy? Canst guess? 'My dear Heart, I hope these will prevent any news shall come unto you of me since my commitment to the Castle of Dublin, to which I assure thee I went as cheerfully and as willingly as they could wish, whosoever they were by whose means it was procured; and should as unwillingly go forth, were the gates both of the Castle and Town open unto me, until I were cleared: as they are willing to make me unserviceable to the king, and lay me aside, who have procured for me this restraint; when I consider thee a Woman, as I think I know you are, I fear lest you should be apprehensive. But when I reflect that you are of the House of Thomond, and that you were once pleased to say these words unto me, That I should never, in tenderness of you, desist from doing what in honour I was obliged to do, I grow confident, that in this you will now show your magnanimity, and by it the greatest testimony of affection that you can possibly afford me; and am also confident, that you know me so well, that I need not tell you how clear I am, and void of fear, the only effect of a good conscience; and that I am guilty of nothing that may testify one thought of disloyalty to his Majesty, or of what may stain the honour of the family I come of, or set a brand upon my future posterity.'

The countess paused, and looked a general illumination at Dorothy.

'I told you so, madam,' returned Dorothy, rather stupidly perhaps.

'Little fool!' rejoined the countess, half-angered: 'dost suppose the wife of a man like my Ned needs to be told such things by a green goose like thee? Thou wouldst have had me content that the man was honest, me, who had forgotten the word in his tenfold more than honesty! Bah, child! thou knowest not the love of a woman. I could weep salt tears over a hair pulled from his noble head. And thou to talk of TELLING ME SO, hussy! Marry, forsooth!'

And taking Dorothy to her bosom, she wept like a relenting storm.

One sentence more she read ere she hurried with the letter to her father-in-law. The sentence was this:

'So I pray let not any of my friends that's there, believe anything, until ye have the perfect relation of it from myself.'

The pleasure of receiving news from his son did but little, however, to disperse the cloud that hung about the Marquis . I do not know whether, or how far, he had been advised of the provision made for the king's clearness by the anticipated self-sacrifice of Glamorgan, but I doubt if a full knowledge thereof gives any ground for disagreement with the judgment of the Marquis , which seems, pretty plainly, to have been, that the king's behaviour in the matter was neither that of a Christian nor a gentleman. As in the case of Strafford, he had accepted the offered sacrifice, and, in view of possible chances, had in Glamorgan's commission pretermitted the usual authoritative formalities, thus keeping it in his power, with Glamorgan's connivance, it must be confessed, but at Glamorgan's expense, to repudiate his agency. This he had now done in a message to the parliament, and this the Marquis knew.

His majesty had also written to Lord Ormond as follows: 'And albeit I have too just cause, for the clearing of my honour, to prosecute Glamorgan in a legal way, yet I will have you suspend the execution,' &c. At the same time his secretary wrote thus to Ormond and the council: 'And since the warrant is not' 'sealed with the signet,' &c., &c., 'your lordships cannot but judge it to be at least surreptitiously gotten, if not worse; for his majesty saith he remembers it not;' and thus again privately to Ormond: 'The king hath commanded me to advertise your lordship that the patent for making the said Lord Herbert of Raglan earl of Glamorgan is not passed the great seal here, so as he is no peer of this kingdom; notwithstanding he styles himself, and hath treated with the rebels in Ireland, by the name of earl of Glamorgan, which is as vainly taken upon him as his pretended warrant (if any such be) was surreptitiously gotten.' The title had, meanwhile, been used by the king himself in many communications with the earl.

These letters never came, I presume, to the Marquis 's knowledge, but they go far to show that his feeling, even were it a little embittered by the memory of their midnight conference and his hopes therefrom, went no farther than the conduct of his majesty justified. It was no wonder that the straight-forward old man, walking erect to ruin for his king, should fret and fume, yea, yield to downright wrath and enforced contempt.

Of the king's behaviour in the matter, Dorothy, however, knew nothing yet.

One day towards the end of February, a messenger from the king arrived at Raglan, on his way to Ireland to Lord Ormond. He had found the roads so beset, for things were by this time, whether from the successes of the parliament only, or from the negligence of disappointment on the part of Lord Worcester as well, much altered in Wales and on its borders, that he had been compelled to leave his despatches in hiding, and had reached the castle only with great difficulty and after many adventures. His chief object in making his way thither was to beg of Lord Charles a convoy to secure his despatches and protect him on his farther journey. But Lord Charles received him by no means cordially, for the whole heart of Raglan was sore. He brought him, however, to his father, who, although indisposed and confined to his chamber, consented to see him. When Mr. Boteler was admitted, Lady Glamorgan was in the chamber, and there remained.

Probably the respect to the king's messenger which had influenced the Marquis to receive him, would have gone further and modified the expression of his feelings a little when he saw him, but that, like many more men, his lordship, although fairly master of his temper-horses when in health, was apt to let them run away with him upon occasion of even slighter illness than would serve for an excuse.

'Hast thou in thy despatches any letters from his majesty to my son Glamorgan, master Boteler?' he inquired, frowning unconsciously.

'Not that I know of, my lord,' answered Mr. Boteler, 'but there may be such with the Lord Marquis of Ormond's.'

He then proceeded to give a friendly message from the king concerning the earl. But at this the 'smouldering fire out-brake' from the bosom of the injured father and subject.

'It is the grief of my heart,' cried his lordship, wrath predominating over the regret which was yet plainly enough to be seen in his face and heard in his tone, 'It is the grief of my heart that I am enforced to say that the king is wavering and fickle. To be the more his friend, it too plainly appeareth, is but to be the more handled as his enemy.'

'Say not so, my lord,' returned Mr. Boteler. 'His gracious majesty looketh not for such unfriendly judgment from your lips. Have I not brought your lordship a most gracious and comfortable message from him concerning my Lord Glamorgan, with his royal thanks for your former loyal expressions?'

'Mr. Boteler, thou knowest nought of the matter. That thou has brought me a budget of fine words, I go not to deny. But words may be but schismatics; deeds alone are certainly of the true faith. Verily the king's majesty setteth his words in the forefront of the battle, but his deeds lag in the rear, and let his words be taken prisoners. When his majesty was last here, I lent him a book to read in his chamber, the beginning of which I know he read, but if he had ended, it would have showed him what it was to be a fickle prince.'

'My lord! my lord! surely your lordship knoweth better of his majesty.'

'To know better may be to know worse, master Boteler. Was it not enough to suffer my Lord Glamorgan to be unjustly imprisoned by my Lord Marquis of Ormond for what he had His majesty's authority for, but that he must in print protest against his proceedings and his own allowance, and not yet recall it? But I will pray for him, and that he may be more constant to his friends, and as soon as my other employments will give leave, you shall have a convoy to fetch securely your despatches.'

Herewith Mr. Boteler was dismissed, Lord Charles accompanying him from the room.

'False as ice!' muttered the Marquis to himself, left as he supposed alone. 'My boy, thou hast built on a quicksand, and thy house goeth down to the deep. I am wroth with myself that ever I dreamed of moving such a bag of chaff to return to the bosom of his honourable mother.'

'My lord,' said Lady Glamorgan from behind the bed-curtains, 'have you forgotten that I and my long ears are here?'

'Ha! art thou indeed there, my mad Irishwoman! I had verily forgotten thee. But is not this king of ours as the Minotaur, dwelling in the labyrinths of deceit, and devouring the noblest in the land? There was his own Strafford, next his foolish Laud, and now comes my son, worth a host of such!'

'In his letter, my Lord of Glamorgan complaineth not of his majesty's usage,' said the countess.

'My Lord of Glamorgan is patient as Grisel. He would pass through the pains of purgatory with never a grumble. But purgatory is for none such as he. In good sooth I am made of different stuff. My soul doth loath deceit, and worse in a king than a clown. What king is he that will lie for a kingdom!'

Day after day passed, and nothing was done to speed the messenger, who grew more and more anxious to procure his despatches and be gone; but Lord Worcester, through the king's behaviour to his honourable and self-forgetting son, with whom he had never had a difference except on the point of his blind devotion to his majesty's affairs, had so lost faith in the king himself that he had no heart for his business. It seems also that for his son's sake he wished to delay Mr. Boteler, in order that a messenger of his own might reach Glamorgan before Ormond should receive the king's despatches. For a whole fortnight therefore no further steps were taken, and Boteler, wearied out, bethought him of applying to the countess to see whether she would not use her influence in his behalf. I am thus particular about Boteler's affair, because through it Dorothy came to know what the king's behaviour had been, and what the Marquis thought of it; she was in the room when Mr. Boteler waited on her mistress.

'May it please your ladyship,' he said, 'I have sought speech of you that I might beg your aid for the king's business, remembering you of the hearty affection my master the king beareth towards your Lord and all his house.'

'Indeed you do well to remember me of that, master Boteler, for it goeth so hard with my memory in these troubled times that I had nigh forgotten it,' said the countess dryly.

'I most certainly know, my lady, that his majesty hath gracious intentions towards your lord.'

'Intention is but an addled egg,' said the countess. 'Give me deeds, if I may choose.'

'Alas! the king hath but little in his power, and the less that his business is thus kept waiting.'

'Your haste is more than your matter, master Boteler. Believe me, whatsoever you consider of it, your going so hurriedly is of no great account, for to my knowledge there are others gone already with duplicates of the business.'

'Madam, you astonish me.'

'I speak not without book. My own cousin, William Winter, is one, and he is my husband's friend, and hath no relation to my Lord Marquis of Ormond,' said Lady Glamorgan significantly.

'My lord, madam, is your lord's very good friend, and I am very much his servant; but if his majesty's business be done, I care not by whose hand it is. But I thank your honour, for now I know wherefore I am stayed here.'

With these words Boteler withdrew, and withdraws from my story, for his further proceedings are in respect of it of no consequence.

When he was gone, Lady Glamorgan, turning a flushed face, and encountering Dorothy's pale one, gave a hard laugh, and said:

'Why, child! thou lookest like a ghost! Was afeard of the man in my presence?'

'No, madam; but it seemed to me marvellous that his majesty's messenger should receive such words from my mistress, and in my Lord of Worcester's house.'

'I' faith, marvellous it is, Dorothy, that there should be such good cause so to use him!' returned Lady Glamorgan, tears of vexation rising as she spoke. 'But an' thou think I used the man roughly, thou shouldst have heard my father speak to him his mind of the king his master.'

'Hath the king then shown himself unkingly, madam?' said Dorothy aghast.

Whereupon Lady Glamorgan told her all she knew, and all she could remember of what she had heard the Marquis say to Boteler.

'Trust me, child,' she added, 'my Lord Worcester, no less than I am, is cut to the heart by this behaviour of the king's. That my husband, silly angel, should say nothing, is but like him. He would bear and bear till all was borne.'

'But,' said Dorothy, 'the king is still the king.'

'Let him be the king then,' returned her mistress. 'Let him look to his kingdom. Why should I give him my husband to do it for him and be disowned therein? I thank heaven I can do without a king, but I can't do without my Ned, and there he lies in prison for him who cons him no thanks! Not that I would overmuch heed the prison if the king would but share the blame with him; but for the king to deny him, to say that he did all of his own motion and without authority! why, child, I saw the commission with my own eyes, nor count myself under any farther obligation to hold my peace concerning it! I know my husband will bear all things, even disgrace itself, undeserved, for the king's sake: he is the loveliest of martyrs; but that is no reason why I should bear it. The king hath no heart and no conscience. No, I will not say that; but I will say that he hath little heart and less conscience. My good husband's fair name is gone, blasted by the king, who raiseth the mist of Glamorgan's dishonour that he may hide himself safe behind it. I tell thee, Dorothy Vaughan, I should not have grudged his majesty my lord's life, an' he had been but a right kingly king. I should have wept enough and complained too much, in womanish fashion, doubtless; but I tell thee earl Thomond's daughter would not have grudged it. But my lord's truth and honour are dear to him, and the good report of them is dear to me. I swear I can ill brook carrying the title he hath given me. It is my husband's and not mine, else would I fling it in his face who thus wrongs my Herbert.'

This explosion from the heart of the wild Irishwoman sounded dreadful in the ears of the king-worshipper. But he whom she thus accused the king of wronging, had been scarcely less revered of her, even while the idol with the feet of clay yet stood, and had certainly been loved greatly more, than the king himself. Hence, notwithstanding her struggle to keep her heart to its allegiance, such a rapid change took place in her feelings, that ere long she began to confess to herself that if the puritans could have known what the king was, their conduct would not have been so unintelligible, not that she thought they had an atom of right on their side, or in the least feared she might ever be brought to think in the matter as they did; she confessed only that she could then have understood them.

The whole aspect and atmosphere of Raglan continued changed. The Marquis was still very gloomy; Lord Charles often frowned and bit his lip; and the flush that so frequently overspread the face of Lady Glamorgan as she sat silent at her embroidery, showed that she was thinking in anger of the wrong done to her husband. In this feeling all in the castle shared, for the matter had now come to be a little understood, and as they loved the earl more than the king, they took the earl's part.

Meantime he for whose sake the fortress was troubled, having been released on large bail, was away, with free heart, to Kilkenny, busy as ever on behalf of the king, full of projects, and eager in action. Not a trace of resentment did he manifest, only regret that his majesty's treatment of him, in destroying his credit with the catholics as the king's commissioner, had put it out of his power to be so useful as he might otherwise have been. His brain was ever contriving how to remedy things, but parties were complicated, and none quite trusted him now that he was disowned of his master.

CHAPTER XLIX

SIEGE

Things began to look threatening. Raglan's brooding disappointment and apprehension was like the electric overcharge of the earth, awaiting and drawing to it the hovering cloud: the lightning and thunder of the war began at length to stoop upon the Yellow Tower of Gwent. When the month of May arrived once more with its moonlight and apple-blossoms, the cloud came with it. The doings of the earl of Glamorgan in Ireland had probably hastened the vengeance of the parliament.

There was no longer any royal army. Most of the king's friends had accepted the terms offered them; and only a few of his garrisons, amongst the rest that of Raglan, held out, no longer, however, in such trim for defence as at first. The walls, it is true, were rather stronger than before, the quantity of provisions was large, and the garrison was sufficient; but their horses were now comparatively few, and, which was worse, the fodder in store was, in prospect of a long siege, scanty. But the worst of all, indeed the only weak and therefore miserable fact, was, that the spirit, I do not mean the courage, of the castle was gone; its enthusiasm had grown sere; its inhabitants no longer loved the king as they had loved him, and even stern-faced general Duty cannot bring up his men to a hand-to-hand conflict with the same elans as queen love.

The rumour of approaching troops kept gathering, and at every fresh report Scudamore's eyes shone.

'Sir Rowland,' said the governor one day, 'hast not had enough of fighting yet for all thy lame shoulder?'

''Tis but my left shoulder, my lord,' answered Scudamore.

'Thou lookest for the siege as an' it were but a tussle and over, a flash and a roar. An' thou had to answer for the place like me, well!'

'Nay, my lord, I would fain show the roundheads what an honest house can do to hold out rogues.'

'Ay, but there's the rub!' returned Lord Charles: 'will the house hold out the rogues? Bethink thee, Rowland, there is never a spot in it fit for defence except the keep and the kitchen.'

'We can make sallies, my lord.'

'To be driven in again by ten times our number, and kept in while they knock our walls about our ears! However, we will hold out while we can. Who knows what turn affairs may take?'

It was towards the end of April when the news reached Raglan that the king, desperate at length, had made his escape from beleaguered Oxford, and in the disguise of a serving man, betaken himself to the headquarters of the Scots army, to find himself no king, no guest even, but a prisoner. He sought shelter and found captivity. The Marquis dropped his chin on his chest and murmured, 'All is over.'

But the pang that shot to his heart awoke wounded loyalty: he had been angry with his monarch, and justly, but he would fight for him still.

'See to the gates, Charles,' he cried, almost springing, spite of his unwieldiness, from his chair. 'Tell Caspar to keep the powder-mill going night and day. Would to God my boy Ned were here! His majesty hath wronged me, but throned or prisoned he is my king still, the church must come down, Charles. The dead are for the living, and will not cry out.' For in St. Cadocus' church lay the tombs of his ancestors.

On deliberation it was resolved, however, that only the tower, which commanded some portions of the castle, should fall. To Dorothy it was like taking down the standard of the Lord. She went with some of the ladies to look a last look at the ancient structure, and saw mass after mass fall silent from the top to clash hideous at the foot amidst the broken tomb-stones. It was sad enough! but the destruction of the cottages around it, that the enemy might not have shelter there, was sadder still. The women wept and wailed; the men growled, and said what was Raglan to them that their houses should be pulled from over their heads. The Marquis offered compensation and shelter. All took the money, but few accepted the shelter, for the prospect of a siege was not attractive to any but such as were fond of fighting, of whom some would rather attack than defend.

The next day they heard that sir Trevor Williams was at Usk with a strong body of men. They knew colonel Birch was besieging Gutbridge castle. Two days passed, and then colonel Kirk appeared to the north, and approached within two miles. The ladies began to look pale as often as they saw two persons talking together: there might be fresh news. His father and his wife were not the only persons in the castle who kept sighing for Glamorgan. Every soul in it felt as if, not to say fancied that, his presence would have made it impregnable.

But a strange excitement seized upon Dorothy, which arose from a sense of trust and delegation, outwardly unauthorised. She had not the presumption to give it form in words, even to Caspar, but she felt as if they two were the special servants of the absent power. Ceaselessly therefore she kept open eyes, and saw and spoke and reminded and remedied where she could, so noiselessly, so unobtrusively, that none were offended, and all took heed of the things she brought before them. Indeed what she said came at length to be listened to almost as if it had been a message from Glamorgan. But her chief business was still the fire-engine, whose machinery she anxiously watched, for if anything should happen to Caspar and then to the engine, what would become of them when driven into the tower?

Discipline, which of late had got very drowsy, was stirred up to fresh life. Watch grew strict. The garrison was drilled more regularly and carefully, and the guard and sentinels relieved to the minute. The armoury was entirely overhauled, and every smith set to work to get the poor remainder of its contents into good condition.

One evening Lord Charles came to his father with the news that some score of fresh horses had arrived.

'Have they brought provender with them, my lord?' asked the Marquis .

'Alas, no, my lord, only teeth,' answered the governor.

'How stands the hay?'

'At low ebb, my lord. There is plenty of oats, however.'

'We hear to-day nothing of the roundheads: what say you to turning them out and letting them have a last bellyful of sweet grass under the walls?'

'I say 'tis so good a plan, my lord, that I think we had better extend it, and let a few of the rest have a parting nibble.'

The Marquis approved.

There was a postern in the outermost wall of the castle on the western side, seldom used, commanded by the guns of the tower, and opening upon a large field of grass, with nothing between but a ditch. It was just wide enough to let one horse through at a time, and by this the governor resolved to turn them out, and as soon as it was nearly dark, ordered a few thick oak planks to be laid across the ditch, one above another, for a bridge. The field was sufficiently fenced to keep them from straying, and with the first signs of dawn they would take them in again.

Dorothy, leaving the tower for the night, had reached the archway, when to her surprise she saw the figure of a huge horse move across the mouth of it, followed by another and another. Except Richard's mare on that eventful night she had never seen horse-kind there before. One after another, till she had counted some five-and-twenty, she saw pass, then heard them cross the fountain court with heavy foot upon the tiles. At length, dark as it was, she recognised her own little Dick moving athwart the opening. She sprang forward, seized him by the halter, and drew him in beside her. On and on they came, till she had counted eighty, and then the procession ceased.

Presently she heard the voice of Lord Charles, as he crossed the hall and came out into the court, saying,

'How many didst thou count, Shafto?'

'Seventy-nine, my lord,' answered the groom, coming from the direction of the gate.

'I counted eighty at the hall-door as they went in.'

'I am certain no more than seventy-nine went through the gate, my lord.'

'What can have become of the eightieth? He must have gone into the chapel, or up the archway, or he may be still in the hall. Art sure he is not grazing on the turf?'

'Certain sure, my lord,' answered Shafto.

'I am the thief, my lord,' said Dorothy, coming from the archway behind him, leading her little horse. '—Good, my lord, let me keep Dick. He is as useful as another, more useful than some.'

'How, cousin!' cried Lord Charles, 'didst imagine I was sending off thy genet to save the hay? No, no! An' thou hadst looked well at the other horses, thou wouldst have seen they are such as we want for work, such as may indeed save the hay, but after another fashion. I but mean to do thy Dick a kindness, and give him a bite of grass with the rest.'

'Then you are turning them out into the fields, my lord?'

'Yes, at the little postern.'

'Is it safe, my lord, with the enemy so near?'

'It is my father's idea. I do not think there is any danger. There will be no moon to-night.'

'May not the scouts ride the closer for that,' my lord?'

'Yes, but they will not see the better.'

'I hope, my lord, you will not think me presumptuous, but, please let me keep my Dick inside the walls.'

'Do what thou wilt with thine own, cousin. I think thou art over-fearful; but do as thou wilt, I say.'

Dorothy led Dick back to his stable, a little distressed that Lord Charles seemed to dislike her caution.

But she had a strong feeling of the risk of the thing, and after she went to bed was so haunted by it that she could not sleep. After a while, however, her thoughts took another direction: Might not Richard come to the siege? What if they should meet? That his party had triumphed, no whit altered the rights of the matter, and she was sure it had not altered her feelings; yet her feelings were altered: she was no longer so fiercely indignant against the puritans as heretofore! Was she turning traitor? or losing the government of herself? or was the right triumphing in her against her will? Was it St. Michael for the truth conquering St. George for the old way of England? Had the king been a tyrant indeed? and had the powers of heaven declared against him, and were they now putting on their instruments to cut down the harvest of wrong? Had not Richard been very sure of being in the right? But what was that shaking, not of the walls, but the foundations? What was that noise as of distant thunder? She sprang from her bed, caught up her night-light, for now she never slept in the dark as heretofore, and hurried to the watch-tower. From its top she saw, by the faint light of the stars, vague forms careering over the fields. There was no cry except an occasional neigh, and the thunder was from the feet of many horses on the turf. The enemy was lifting the castle horses!

She flew to the chamber beneath, where, since the earl's departure, in the stead of the cross-bow, a small minion gun had been placed by Lord Charles, with its muzzle in the round where the lines of the loop-hole crossed. A piece of match lay beside it. She caught it up, lighted it at her candle, and fired the gun. The tower shook with its roar and recoil. She had fired the first gun of the siege: might it be a good omen!

In an instant the castle was alive. Warders came running from the western gate. Dorothy had gone, and they could not tell who had fired the gun, but there were no occasion to ask why it had been fired, for where were the horses? They could hear, but no longer see them. There was mounting in hot haste, and a hurried sally. Lord Charles flung himself on little Dick's bare back, and flew to reconnoitre. Fifty of the garrison were ready armed and mounted by the time he came back, having discovered the route they were taking, and off they went at full speed in pursuit. But, encumbered as they were at first with the driven horses, the twenty men who had carried them off had such a start of their pursuers that they reached the high road where they could not stray, and drove them right before them to sir Trevor Williams at Usk.

'The fodder will last the longer,' said the Marquis , with a sigh sent after his eighty horses.

'Mistress Dorothy,' said Lord Charles the next day, 'methinks thou art as Cassandra in Troy. I shall tremble after this to do aught against thy judgment.'

'My lord,' returned Dorothy, 'I have to ask your pardon for my presumption, but it was borne in upon me, as Tom Fool says, that there was danger in the thing. It was scarcely judgment on my part, rather a womanish dread.'

'Go thou on to speak thy mind like Cassandra, cousin Dorothy, and let us men despise it at our peril. I am humbled before thee,' said Lord Charles, with the generosity of his family.

'Truly, child,' said Lady Glamorgan, 'the mantle of my husband hath fallen upon thee!'

The next day sir Trevor Williams and his men sat down before the castle with a small battery, and the siege was fairly begun. Dorothy, on the top of the keep, watching them, but not understanding what they were about in particulars, heard the sudden bellow of one of their cannon. Two of the battlements beside her flew into one, and the stones of the parapet between them stormed into the cistern. Had her presence been the attraction to that thunderbolt? Often after this, while she watched the engine below in the workshop, she would hear the dull thud of an iron ball against the body of the tower; but although it knocked the parapet into showers of stones, their artillery could not make the slightest impression upon that.

The same night a sally was prepared. Rowland ran to Lord Charles, begging leave to go. But his lordship would not hear of it, telling him to get well, and he should have enough of sallying before the siege was over. The enemy were surprised, and lost a few men, but soon recovered themselves and drove the royalists home, following them to the very gates, whence the guns of the castle sent them back in their turn.

Many such sallies and skirmishes followed. Once and again there was but time for the guard to open the gate, admit their own, and close it, ere the enemy came thundering up, to be received with a volley and gallop off. At first there was great excitement within the walls when a party was out. Eager and anxious eyes followed them from every point of vision. But at length they got used to it, as to all the ordinary occurrences of siege.

By and by colonel Morgan appeared with additional forces, and made his head-quarters to the south, at Llandenny. In two days more the castle was surrounded, and they began to erect a larger battery on the east of it, also to dig trenches and prepare for mining. The chief point of attack was that side of the stone court which lay between the towers of the kitchen and the library. Here then came the hottest of the siege, and very soon that range of building gave show of affording an easy passage by the time the outer works should be taken.

After the first ball, whose execution Dorothy had witnessed, there came no more for some time. Sir Trevor waited until the second battery should be begun and captain Hooper arrive, who was to be at the head of the mining operations. Hence most of the inmates of the castle began to imagine that a siege was not such an unpleasant thing after all. They lacked nothing; the apple trees bloomed; the moon shone; the white horse fed the fountain; the pigeons flew about the courts, and the peacock strutted on the grass. But when they began digging their approaches and mounting their guns on the east side, sir Trevor opened his battery on the west, and the guns of the tower replied. The guns also from the kitchen tower, and another between it and the library tower, played upon the trenches, and the noise was tremendous. At first the inhabitants were nearly deafened, and frequently failed to hear what was said; but at length they grew hardened, so much so that they were often unaware of the firing altogether, and began again to think a siege no great matter. But when the guns of the eastern battery opened fire, and at the first discharge a round shot, bringing with it a barrowful of stones, came down the kitchen chimney, knocking the lid through the bottom of the cook's stewpan, and scattering all the fire about the place; when the roof of one of the turrets went clashing over the stones of the paved court; when a spent shot struck the bars of the Great Mogul's cage, and sent him furious, making them think what might happen, and wishing they were sure of the politics of the wild beasts; when the stones and slates flew about like sudden showers of hail; when every now and then a great rumble told of a falling wall, and that side of the court was rapidly turning to a heap of ruins; then were cries and screams, many more however of terror than of injury, to be heard in the castle, and they began to understand that it was not starvation, but something more peremptory still, to which they were doomed to succumb. At times there would fall a lull, perhaps for a few hours, perhaps but for a few moments, to end in a sudden fury of firing on both sides, mingled with shouts, the rattling of bullets, and the falling of stones, when the women would rush to and fro screaming, and all would imagine the storm was in the breach.

But the gloom of the Marquis seemed to have vanished with the breaking of the storm, as the outburst of the lightning takes the weight off head and heart that has for days been gathering. True, when his house began to fall, he would look for a moment grave at each successive rumble, but the next he would smile and nod his head, as if all was just as he had expected and would have it. One day when sir Toby Mathews and Dr. Bayly happened both to be with him in his study, an ancient stack of chimneys tumbled with tremendous uproar into the stone court. The two clergymen started visibly, and then looked at each other with pallid faces. But the Marquis smiled, kept the silence for an instant, and then, in slow solemn voice, said:

'Scimus enim quoniam si terrestris domus nomus nostra hujus habitationis dissolvatur, quod aedificationem ex Deo habemus, domum non manufactam, aeternam in coelis.'

The clergymen grasped each other by the hand, then turning bowed together to the Marquis , but the conversation was not resumed.

One evening in the drawing-room, after supper, the Marquis , in good spirits, and for him in good health, was talking more merrily than usual. Lady Glamorgan stood near him in the window. The captain of the garrison was giving a spirited description of a sally they had made the night before upon colonel Morgan in his quarters at Llandenny, and sir Rowland was vowing that come of it what might, leave or no leave, he would ride the next time, when crash went something in the room, the Marquis put his hand to his head, and the countess fled in terror, crying, 'O Lord! O Lord!' A bullet had come through the window, knocked a little marble pillar belonging to it in fragments on the floor, and glancing from it, struck the Marquis on the side of the head. The countess, finding herself unhurt, ran no farther than the door.

'I ask your pardon, my lord, for my rudeness,' she said, with trembling voice, as she came slowly back. 'But indeed, ladies,' she added, 'I thought the house was coming down. You gentlemen, who know not what fear is, I pray you to forgive me, for I was mortally frightened.'

'Daughter, you had reason to run away, when your father was knocked on the head,' said the Marquis .

He put his finger on the flattened bullet where it had fallen on the table, and turning it round and round, was silent for a moment evidently framing aright something he wanted to say. Then with the pretence that the bullet had been flattened upon his head,

'Gentlemen,' he remarked, 'those who had a mind to flatter me were wont to tell me that I had a good head in my younger days, but if I don't flatter myself, I think I have a good head-piece in my old age, or else it would not have been musket-proof.'

But although he took the thing thus quietly and indeed merrily, it revealed to him that their usual apartments were no longer fit for the ladies, and he gave orders therefore that the great rooms in the tower should be prepared for them and the children.

Dorothy's capacity for work was not easily satisfied, but now for a time she had plenty to do. In the midst of the roar from the batteries, and the answering roar from towers and walls, the ladies betook themselves to their stronger quarters: a thousand necessaries had to be carried with them, and she, as a matter of course, it seemed, had to superintend the removal. With many hands to make light work she soon finished, however, and the family was lodged where no hostile shot could reach them, although the frequent fall of portions of its battlemented summit rendered even a peep beyond its impenetrable shell hazardous. Dorothy would lie awake at night, where she slept in her mistress's room, and listen, now to the baffled bullet as it fell from the scarce indented wall, now to the roar of the artillery, sounding dull and far away through the ten-foot thickness; and ever and again the words of the ancient psalm would return upon her memory: 'Thou hast been a shelter for me, and a strong tower from the enemy.'

She tended the fire-engine if possible yet more carefully than ever, kept the cistern full, and the water lipping the edge of the moat, but let no fountain flow except that from the mouth of the white horse. Her great fear was lest a shot should fall into the reservoir and injure its bottom, but its contriver had taken care that, even without the protection of its watery armour, it should be indestructible.

The Marquis would not leave his own rooms and the supervision they gave him. The domestics were mostly lodged within the kitchen tower, which, although in full exposure to the enemy's fire, had as yet proved able to resist it. But all between that and the library tower was rapidly becoming a chaos of stones and timber. Lord Glamorgan's secret chamber was shot through and through; but Caspar, as soon as the direction and force of the battery were known, had carried off his books and instruments.

CHAPTER L

A SALLY

Meantime Mr. Heywood had returned home to look after his affairs, and brought Richard with him. In the hope that peace was come they had laid down their commissions. Hardly had they reached Redware when they heard the news of the active operations at Raglan, and Richard rode off to see how things were going, not a little anxious concerning Dorothy, and full of eagerness to protect her, but entirely without hope of favour either at her hand or her heart. He had no inclination to take part in the siege, and had had enough of fighting for any satisfaction it had brought him. It might be the right thing to do, and so far the only path towards the sunrise, but had he ground for hope that the day of freedom had in himself advanced beyond the dawn? His confidence in Milton and Cromwell, with his father's, continued unshaken, but what could man do to satisfy the hunger for freedom which grew and gnawed within him? Neither political nor religious liberty could content him. He might himself be a slave in a universe of freedom. Still ready, even for the sake of mere outward freedom of action and liberty of worship, to draw the sword, he yet had begun to think he had fought enough.

As he approached Raglan he missed something from the landscape, but only upon reflection discovered that it was the church tower. Entering the village, he found it all but deserted, for the inhabitants had mostly gone, and it was too near the gates and too much exposed to the sudden sallies of the besieged for the occupation of the enemy. That day, however, a large reinforcement, sent from Oxford by Fairfax to strengthen colonel Morgan, having arrived at Llandenny, some of its officers, riding over to inspect captain Hooper's operations, had halted at the White Horse, where they were having a glass of ale when Richard rode up. He found them old acquaintances, and sat down with them. Almost evening when he arrived, it was quite dusk when they rose and called for their horses.

They had placed a man to keep watch towards Raglan, while the rest of their attendants, who were but few, leaving their horses in the yard, were drinking their ale in the kitchen; but seeing no signs of peril, and growing weary of his own position and envious of that of his neighbours, the fellow had ventured, discipline being neither active nor severe, to rejoin his companions.

The host, being a tenant of the Marquis, had decided royalist predilections, but whether what followed was of his contriving I cannot tell; news reached the castle somehow that a few parliamentary officers with their men were drinking at the White Horse.

Rowland was in the chapel, listening to the organ, having in his illness grown fond of hearing Delaware play. The brisker the cannonade, the blind youth always praised the louder, and had the main stops now in full blast; but through it all, Scudamore heard the sound of horses' feet on the stones, and running along the minstrels' gallery and out on the top of the porch, saw over fifty horsemen in the court, all but ready to start. He flew to his chamber, caught up his sword and pistols, and without waiting to put on any armour, hurried to the stables, laid hold of the first horse he came to, which was fortunately saddled and bridled, and was in time to follow the last man out of the court before the gate was closed behind the issuing troop.

The parliamentary officers were just mounting, when their sentinel, who had run again into the road to listen, for it was now too dark to see further than a few yards, came running back with the alarm that he heard the feet of a considerable body of horse in the direction of the castle. Richard, whose mare stood unfastened at the door, was on her back in a moment. Being unarmed, save a brace of pistols in his holsters, he thought he could best serve them by galloping to captain Hooper and bringing help, for the castle party would doubtless outnumber them. Scarcely was he gone, however, and half the troopers were not yet in their saddles, when the place was surrounded by three times their number. Those who were already mounted, escaped and rode after Heywood, a few got into a field, where they hid themselves in the tall corn, and the rest barricaded the inn door and manned the windows. There they held out for some time, frequent pistol-shots being interchanged without much injury to either side. At length, however, the Marquis 's men had all but succeeded in forcing the door, when they were attacked in the rear by Richard with some thirty horse from the trenches, and the runaways of colonel Morgan's men, who had met them and turned with them. A smart combat ensued, lasting half an hour, in which the parliament men had the advantage. Those who had lost their horses recovered them, and a royalist was taken prisoner. From him Richard took his sword, and rode after the retreating cavaliers.

One of their number, a little in the rear, supposing Richard to be one of themselves, allowed him to get ahead of him, and, facing about, cut him off from his companions. It was the second time he had headed Scudamore, and again he did not know him, this time because it was dark. Rowland, however, recognised his voice as he called him to surrender, and rushed fiercely at him. But scarcely had they met, when the cavalier, whose little strength had ere this all but given way to the unwonted fatigue, was suddenly overcome with faintness, and dropped from his horse. Richard got down, lifted him, laid him across Lady's shoulders, mounted, raised him into a better position, and, leading the other horse, brought him back to the inn. There first he discovered that he was his prisoner whom he feared he had killed at Naseby.

When Rowland came to himself,

'Are you able to ride a few miles, Mr Scudamore?' asked Richard.

At first Rowland was too much chagrined, finding in whose power he was, to answer.

'I am your prisoner,' he said at length. 'You are my evil genius, I think. I have no choice. Thy star is in the ascendant, and mine has been going down ever since first I met thee, Richard Heywood.'

Richard attempted no reply, but got Rowland's horse, and assisted him to mount.

'I want to do you a good turn, Mr Scudamore,' he said, after they had ridden a mile in silence.

'I look for nothing good at thy hand,' said Scudamore.

'When thou findest what it is, I trust thou wilt change thy thought of me, Mr Scudamore.'

'SIR ROWLAND, an' it please you,' said the prisoner, his boyish vanity roused by misfortune, and passing itself upon him for dignity.

'Mere ignorance must be pardoned, sir Rowland,' returned Richard: 'I was unaware of your dignity. But think you, sir Rowland, you do well to ride on such rough errands, while yet not recovered, as is but too plain to see, from former wounds?'

'It seems not, Mr. Heywood, for I had not else been your prize, I trust. The wound I caught at Naseby has cost the king a soldier, I fear.'

'I hope it will cost no more than is already paid. Men must fight, it seems, but I for one would gladly repair, an' I might, what injuries I had been compelled to cause.'

'I cannot say the like on my part,' returned sir Rowland. 'I would I had slain thee!'

'So would not I concerning thee, in proof whereof do I now lead thee to the best leech I know, one who brought me back from death's door, when through thee, if not by thy hand, I was sore wounded. With her, as my prisoner, I shall leave thee. Seek not to make thy escape, lest, being a witch, as they saw of her, she chain thee up in alabaster. When thou art restored, go thy way whither thou pleasest. It is no longer as it was with the cause of liberty: a soldier of hers may now afford to release an enemy for whom he has a friendship.'

'A friendship!' exclaimed sir Rowland. 'And wherefore, prithee, Mr Heywood? On what ground?'

But they had reached the cottage, and Richard made no reply. Having helped his prisoner to dismount, led him through the garden, and knocked at the door,

'Here, mother!' he said as mistress Rees opened it, 'I have brought thee a king's-man to cure this time.'

'Praise God!' returned mistress Rees, not that a king's-man was wounded, but that she had him to cure: she was an enthusiast in her art. Just as she had devoted herself to the puritan, she now gave all her care and ministration to the royalist. She got her bed ready for him, asked him a few questions, looked at his shoulder, not even yet quite healed, said it had not been well managed, and prepared a poultice, which smelt so vilely that Rowland turned from it with disgust. But the old woman had a singular power of persuasion, and at length he yielded, and in a few moments was fast asleep.

Calling the next morning, Richard found him very weak, partly from the unwonted fatigue of the previous day, and partly from the old woman's remedies, which were causing the wound to threaten suppuration. But somehow he had become well satisfied that she knew what she was about, and showed no inclination to rebel.

For a week or so he did not seem to improve. Richard came often, sat by his bedside, and talked with him; but the moment he grew angry, called him names, or abused his party, would rise without a word, mount his mare, and ride home, to return the next morning as if nothing unpleasant had occurred.

After about a week, the patient began to feel the benefit of the wise woman's treatment. The suppuration carried so much of an old ever-haunting pain with it, that he was now easier than he had ever been since his return to Raglan. But his behaviour to Richard grew very strange, and the roundhead failed to understand it. At one time it was so friendly as to be almost affectionate; at another he seemed bent on doing and saying everything he could to provoke a duel. For another whole week, aware of the benefit he was deriving from the witch, as he never scrupled to call her, nor in the least offended her thereby, apparently also at times fascinated in some sort by the visits of his enemy, as he persisted in calling Richard, he showed no anxiety to be gone.

'Heywood,' he said one morning suddenly, with quite a new familiarity, 'dost thou consider I owe thee an apology for carrying off thy mare? Tell me what look the thing beareth to thee.'

'Put thy case, Scudamore,' returned Richard.

And sir Rowland did put his case, starting from the rebel state of the owner, advancing to the natural outlawry that resulted, going on to the necessity of the king, &c., and ending thus:

'Now I know thou regardest neither king nor right, therefore I ask thee only to tell me how it seemeth to thee I ought on these grounds to judge myself, since for thy judgment in thy own person and on thy own grounds, or rather no grounds, I care not at all.'

'Come, then, let it be but a question of casuistry. Yet I fear me it will be difficult to argue without breaking bounds. Would my Lord Marquis now walk forth of his castle at the king's command as certainly as he will at the voice of the nation, that is, the cannons of the parliament?'

'The cannons of the cursed parliament are not the voice of the nation? Our side is the nation, not yours.'

'How provest thou that?'

'We are the better born, to begin with.'

'Ye have the more titles, I grant ye, but we have the older families. Let it be, however, that I was or am a rebel, then I can only say that in stealing, no, I will not say STEALING, for thou didst it with a different mind, all I will say is this, sir Rowland, that I should have scorned so to carry off thine or any man's horse.'

'Ah, but thou wouldst have no right, being but a rebel!'

'Bethink thee, thou must judge on my grounds when thou judgest me.'

'True; then am I driven to say thou wast made of the better earth, curse thee! I am ashamed of having taken thy mare, only because it was in a half-friendly passage with thee I learned her worth. But, hang thee! it was not through thee I learned to know my cousin, Dorothy Vaughan.'

The recoiling blood stung Richard's heart like the blow of a whip, but he manned himself to answer with coolness.

'What then of her?' he said. 'Hast thou been wooing her favour, sir Rowland? Thou owest me nothing there, I admit, even had she not sent me from her. Besides, I am scarce one to be content with a mistress whose favour depended on the not coming between of some certain other, known or unknown. This I say not in pride, but because in such case I were not the right man for her, neither she the woman for me.'

'Then thou bearest me no grudge in that I have sought the prize of my cousin's heart?'

'None,' answered Richard, but could not bring himself to ask how he had sped.

'Then will I own to thee that I have gained as little. I will madden myself telling thee whom I hate, and to thy comfort, that she despises me like any Virginia slave.'

'Nay, that I am sure she doth not. She can despise nothing that is honourable.'

'Dost thou then count me honourable, Heywood?' said Scudamore, in a voice of surprise, putting forth a thin white hand, and placing it on Richard's where it lay huge and brown on the coverlid: 'Then honourable I will be.'

'And, in that resolve, art, sir Rowland.'

'I will be honourable,' repeated Scudamore, angrily, with flushing cheek, and hard yet flashing eye, 'because thou thinkest me such, although my hate would, an' it might, damn thee to lowest hell.'

'Nay, but thou wilt be honourable for honour's sake,' said Richard. 'Bethink thee, when first we met, we were but boys: now are we men, and must put away boyish things.'

'Dost call it a boyish thing to be madly in love with the fairest and noblest and bravest mistress that ever trod the earth, though she be half a puritan, alack?'

'She half a puritan!' exclaimed Heywood. 'She hates the very wind of the word.'

'She may hate the word, but she is the thing. She hath read me such lessons as none but a puritan could.'

'Were they not then good lessons, that thou joinest with them a name hateful to thee?'

'Ay, truly, much too good for mortal like me, or thee either, Heywood. They are but hypocrites that pretend otherwise.'

'Callest thou thy cousin a hypocrite?'

'No, by heaven! she is not. She is a woman, and it is easy for women to say prayers.'

'I never rode into a fight but I said my prayer,' returned Richard.

'None the less art thou a hypocrite. I should scorn to be forever begging favours as thou. Dost think God heareth such prayers as thine?'

'Not if He be such as thou, sir Rowland, and not if he who prays be such as thou thinkest him. Prithee, what sort of prayer thinkest thou I pray ere I ride into the battle?'

'How should I know? My Lord Marquis would have had me say my prayers at such a time, but, good sooth! I always forgot. And if I had done it, where would have been the benefit thereof, so long as thou, who wast better used to the work, wast praying against me? I say it is a cowardly thing to go praying into the battle, and not take thy fair chance as other men do.'

'Then will I tell thee to what purpose I pray. But, first of all, I must confess to thee that I have had my doubts, not whether my side were more in the right than thine, but whether it were worth while to raise the sword even in such cause. Now, still when that doubt cometh, ever it taketh from my arm the strength, and going down into the very legs of my mare causeth that she goeth dull, although willing, into the battle. Moreover, I am no saint, and therefore cannot pray like a saint, but only like Richard Heywood, who hath got to do his duty, and is something puzzled. Therefore pray I thus, or to this effect:

'"O God of battles! who, thyself dwelling in peace, beholdest the strife, and workest thy will thereby, what that good and perfect will of thine is I know not clearly, but thou hast sent us to be doing, and thou hatest cowardice. Thou knowest I have sought to choose the best, so far as goeth my poor ken, and to this battle I am pledged. Give me grace to fight like a soldier of thine, without wrath and without fear. Give me to do my duty, but give the victory where thou pleasest. Let me live if so thou wilt; let me die if so thou wilt, only let me die in honour with thee. Let the truth be victorious, if not now, yet when it shall please thee; and oh! I pray, let no deed of mine delay its coming. Let my work fail, if it be unto evil, but save my soul in truth."

'And in truth, sir Rowland, it seemeth to me then as if the God of truth heard me. Then say I to my mare, "Come, Lady, all is well now. Let us go. And good will come of it to thee also, for how should the Father think of his sparrows and forget his mares? Doubtless there are of thy kind in heaven, else how should the apostle have seen them there? And if any, surely thou, my Lady!" So ride we to the battle, merry and strong, and calm, as if we were but riding to the rampart of the celestial city.'

Rowland lay gazing at Richard for a few moments, then said:

'By heaven, but it were a pity you should not come together! Surely the same spirit dwelleth in you both! For me, I should show but as the shadow cast from her brightness. But I tell thee, roundhead, I love her better than ever roundhead could.'

'I know not, Scudamore. Nor do I mean to judge thee when I say that no man who loves not the truth can love a woman in the grand way a woman ought to be loved.'

'Tell me not I do not love her, or I will rise and kill thee. I love her even to doing what my soul hateth for her sake. Damned roundhead, she loves THEE.'

The last words came from him almost in a shriek, and he fell back panting.

Richard sat silent for a few moments, his heart surging and sinking. Then he said quietly:

'It may be so, sir Rowland. We were boy and girl together, fed rabbits, flew kites, planted weeds to make flowers of them, played at marbles; she may love me a little, roundhead as I am.'

'By heaven, I will try her once more! Who knows the heart of a woman?' said Rowland through his teeth.

'If thou should gain her, Scudamore, and afterward she should find thee unworthy?'

'She would love me still.'

'And break her heart for thee, and leave thee young to marry another, while I—'

He laughed a low, strangely musical laugh, and ceased, then resumed:—

'But what if, instead of dying, she should learn to despise thee, finding thou hadst not only deceived her, but deceived thy better self, and should turn from thee with loathing, while thou didst love her still, as well as thy nature could? what then, sir Rowland?'

'Then I should kill her.'

'And thou lovest her better than any roundhead could! I will find thee man after man from amongst Ireton's or Cromwell's horse, I know not the foot so well: fanatic enough they are, God knows! and many of them fools enough to boot! but I will find thee man after man who is fanatic or fool enough, which thou wilt, to love better than thou, thou poor atom of solitary selfishness!'

Rowland half flung himself from the bed, seized Richard by the throat, and with all the strength he could summon did his best to strangle him. For a time Richard allowed him to spend his rage, then removed his grasp as gently as he could, and holding both his wrists in his left hand, rose and stood over him.

'Sir Rowland,' he said, 'I am not angry with thee that thou art weak and passionate. But bethink thee, thou liest in God's hands a thousandfold more helpless than now thou liest in mine, and like Saul of Tarsus thou wilt find it hard to kick against the pricks. For the maiden, do as thou wilt, for thou canst not do other than the will of God. But I thank thee for what thou hast told me, though I doubt it meaneth little better for me than for thee. Thou hast a kind heart. I almost love thee, and will when I can.'

He let go his hands, and walked from the room.

'Canting hypocrite!' cried sir Rowland in the wrath of impotence, but knew while he said the words that they were false.

And with the words the bitterness of life seized his heart, and his despair shrouded the world in the blackness of darkness. There was nothing more to live for, and he turned his face to the wall.

CHAPTER LI

UNDER THE MOAT

It was some time ere they discovered that Scudamore was missing from the castle, but there was the hope that he had been taken prisoner; and things were growing so bad within the walls, that there was little leisure for lamentation over individual misfortunes. Unless some change as entire as unexpected, for there seemed no chance of any except the king should win over the Scots to take his part, should occur, it was evident that the enemy must speedily make the assault, nor could there be a doubt of their carrying the place, an anticipation which, as the inevitable drew nearer, became nothing less than terrible to both household and garrison. True, their conquerors would be of their own people, but battle and bloodshed and victory, and, worst of all, party-spirit, the Marquis knew, destroy not nationality merely, but humanity as well, rousing into full possession the feline beast which has his lair in every man, in many, it is true, dwindled to the household cat, but in many others a full-sized, only sleepy tiger. To what was he about to expose his men, not to speak of his ladies and their children!

On the other hand, ever since the balls had been flying about his house, and the stones of it leaving their places to keep them company, the loyalty of the Marquis had been rising, and he had thought of his prisoner-king ever with growing tenderness, of his faults with more indulgence, and of the wrongs he had done his family with more magnanimity and forgiveness, so that, for his own part, he would have held out to the very last.

'And truly were it not better to be well buried under the ruins,' he would say to himself, looking down with a sigh at his great bulk, which added so much to the dismalness of the prospect of being, in his seventieth year, a prisoner or a wanderer, the latter a worse fate even than the former. To be no longer the master of his own great house, of many willing servants, of all ready appliances for liberty and comfort, while the weight of his clumsy person must still hang about him, and his unfitness to carry the same go on increasing with the bulk to be carried, such a prospect required something more than loyalty to meet it with equanimity. To the young and strong, adventure ought always to be more attractive than ease, but none save those who are themselves within sight of old age can truly imagine what an utter horror the breach of old habits and loss of old comforts is to the aged.

But to the good Marquis it was consolation enough to repeat to himself the text from his precious Vulgate: SCIMUS ENIM; FOR WE KNOW THAT IF OUR EARTHLY HOUSE OF THIS TABERNACLE WERE DISSOLVED, WE HAVE A BUILDING OF GOD, AN HOUSE NOT MADE WITH HANDS, ETERNAL IN THE HEAVENS.

For the ladies, so long as their father-chief was with them, they were at least not too anxious. Whatever was done must be the right thing, and in the midst of tumult and threat they were content. If only their Edward had been with them too!

But surrender, even when the iron shot was driving his stately house into showers of dirt, the Marquis found it hard indeed to contemplate. The eastern side of the stone court was now little better than a heap of rubbish, and the hour of assault could not be far off, although as yet there had been no second summons; but he could not forget that, though the castle was his, it was not for himself but for his king he held it garrisoned, and how could he yield it without the approval of his sovereign? The governor shared in the same chivalry with his father, and was equally anxious for a word from the king. But that king was a prisoner in the hands of a hostile nation, and how was he to receive message or return answer? Nay, how were they to send message or receive answer, not even knowing with certainty where his majesty was, and but presuming that he was still at Newcastle? And not to mention difficulties at every step of the way, their house itself was so beset that no one could issue from its gates without risk of being stopped, searched, detained until it should have fallen. For the besiegers knew well enough that Lord Glamorgan was still in Ireland, straining his utmost on behalf of the king; and what more likely than that he should, with the men he was still raising in Ireland, make some desperate attempt to turn the scales of war, striking first, it might well be, for the relief of his father's castle?

These things were all pretty freely spoken of in the family, and Dorothy understood the position of affairs as well as anyone. And now at length it seemed to her that the hour had arrived for attempting some return for Raglan's hospitality. No service she had hitherto stumbled upon had any magnitude in her eyes, but now, to be the bearer of dispatches to the king! It would suffice at least, even if it turned out a failure, to prove her not ungrateful. But she too had her confidant, and in the absence of Lord Glamorgan would consult with Caspar.

Meantime the Marquis had made matters worse by sending a request to Colonel Morgan that he would grant safe passage for a messenger to the king, without whose command he was not at liberty to surrender the place. The answer was to the effect that they acknowledged no jurisdiction of the king in the business, and that the Marquis might keep his mind easy as far as his supposed duty to his majesty was concerned, for they would so compel a surrender that there could be no reflection upon him for making it.

Caspar, fearful of the dangers she would have to encounter, sought to dissuade Dorothy from her meditated proposal, but feebly, for everyone who had anything noble in his nature, and Caspar had more than his share, was influenced by the magnanimity that ruled the place. Indeed he told her one thing which served to clench her resolution, that there was a secret way out of the castle, provided by his master Glamorgan for communication during siege: more he was not at liberty to disclose. Dorothy went straight to the Marquis and laid her plan before him, which was that she should make her escape to Wyfern, and thence, attended by an old servant, set out to seek the king.

'There is no longer time, alas!' returned the Marquis . 'I look for the final summons every hour.'

'Could you not raise the report, my lord, that you have undermined the castle, and laid a huge quantity of gunpowder, with the determination of blowing it up the moment they enter? That would make them fall back upon blockade, and leave us a little time. Our provisions are not nearly exhausted, and when fodder fails, we can eat the horses first.'

'Thou art a brave lady, cousin Dorothy,' said the Marquis . 'But if they caught and searched thee, and found papers upon thee, it would go worse with us than before.'

'Please your lordship, my Lord Glamorgan once showed me such a comb as a lady might carry in her pocket, but so contrived that the head thereof was hollow and could contain despatches. Methinks Caspar could lay his hand on the comb. If I were but at Wyfern! and thither my little horse would carry me in less than hour, giving all needful time for caution too, my lord.'

'By George, thou speakest well, cousin!' said the Marquis . 'But who should attend thee?'

'Let me have Tom Fool, my lord, for now have I thought of a betterment of my plan: he will guide me to his mother's house by by-ways, and thence can I cross the fields to my own, as easily as the great hall, my lord.'

'Tom Fool is a mighty coward,' objected the Marquis .

'So much the better, my lord. He will not get me into trouble through displaying his manhood before me. He hath besides a face long enough for three roundheads, and a tongue that can utter glibly enough what soundeth very like their jargon. Tom is the right fool to attend me, my lord.'

'He can't ride; he never backed a horse in his life, I believe. No, no, Dorothy. Shafto is the man.'

'Shafto is much too ready, my lord. He would ride over my hounds. I want Tom no farther than his mother's, and there will be no need for him to ride.'

'Well, it is a brave offer, my child, and I will think thereupon,' said his lordship.

All the rest of the day the Marquis and Lord Charles, with two or three of the principal officers of house and garrison, were in conference, and letters were written both to his majesty and Lord Glamorgan. Before they were finally written out in cipher, Kaltoff was sent for, the comb found, its contents gauged, and the paper cut to suit.

About an hour after midnight, Dorothy, Lord Charles, and Caspar stood together in the workshop, waiting for Tom Fool, who had gone to fetch Dick from the stables. Dorothy had the comb in her pocket. She looked pale, but her grey eyes shone with courage and determination. She carried nothing but a whip. A keen little lamp borne by Caspar was all their light.

Presently they heard the sound of Dick's hoofs on the bridge. A moment more and Tom led him in, both man and horse looking somewhat scared at the strangeness of the midnight proceeding. But Tom was, notwithstanding, glad of the office, and ready to risk a good deal in order to get out of the castle, where he expected nothing milder at last than a general massacre.

Lord Charles himself lifted foot after foot of the little horse to be satisfied that his shoes were sound, then made a sign to Caspar, and gave his hand to Dorothy. Caspar took Dick by the bridle, and led him up to the wall near the door. Lord Charles and Dorothy followed. But Tom, observing that they placed themselves within a chalk-drawn circle, hung back in terror; he fancied Caspar was going to raise the devil. Yet he knew that within the circle was the only safety; a word from Dorothy turned the scale, and he stood trembling by her side. Nor was he greatly consoled to find that, as he now thought, instead of the devil coming to them, they were going to him, as, with the circle upon which they stood, they began to sink, through a stone-faced shaft, slowly into the foundations of the keep. Dick also was frightened, but happily his faith was stronger than his imagination, and a word now and then from his mistress, and an occasional pat from her well-known hand, sufficed to keep him quiet.

At the depth of about thirty feet they stopped, and found themselves facing a ponderous door, studded and barred with iron. Caspar took from his pocket a key about the size of a goose quill, felt about for a moment, and then with a slight movement of finger and thumb threw back a dozen ponderous bolts with a great echoing clang; the door slowly opened, and they entered a narrow vaulted passage of stone. Lord Charles took the lamp from Caspar, and led the way with Dorothy; Tom Fool came next, and Caspar followed with Dick. The lamp showed but a few feet of the walls and roof, and revealed nothing in front until they had gone about a furlong, when it shone upon what seemed the live rock ending their way. But again Caspar applied the little key somewhere, and immediately a great mass of rock slowly turned on a pivot, and permitted them to pass.

When they were all on the other side of it, Lord Charles turned and held up the light. Dorothy turned also and looked: there was nothing to indicate whence they had come. Before her was the rough rock, seemingly solid, certainly slimy and green, and over its face was flowing a tiny rivulet.

'See there,' said Lord Charles, pointing up; 'that little stream comes the way thy dog Marquis and the roundhead Heywood came and went. But I challenge anything larger than a rat to go now.'

Dorothy made no answer, and they went on again for some distance in a passage like the former, but soon arrived at the open quarry, whence Tom knew the way across the fields to the high road as well, he said, as the line of life on his own palm. Lord Charles lifted Dorothy to the saddle, said good-luck and good-bye, and stood with Caspar watching as she rode up the steep ascent, until for an instant her form stood out dark against the sky, then vanished, when they turned and re-entered the castle.

CHAPTER LII

THE UNTOOTHSOME PLUM

It was a starry night, with a threatening of moonrise, and Dorothy was anxious to reach the cottage before it grew lighter. But they must not get into the high road at any nearer point than the last practicable, for then they would be more likely to meet soldiers, and Dick's feet to betray their approach. Over field after field, therefore, they kept on, as fast as Tom, now and then stopping to peer anxiously over the next fence or into a boundary ditch, could lead the way. At last they reached the place by the side of a bridge, where Marquis led Richard off the road, and there they scrambled up.

'O Lord!' cried Tom, and waked a sentry dozing on the low parapet.

'Who goes there?' he cried, starting up, and catching at his carbine, which leaned against the wall.

'Oh, master!' began Tom, in a voice of terrified appeal; but Dorothy interrupted him.

'I am an honest woman of the neighbourhood,' she said. 'An' thou wilt come home with me, I will afford thee a better bed than thou hast there, and also a better breakfast, I warrant thee, than thou had a supper.'

'That is, an' thou be one of the godly,' supplemented Tom.

'I thank thee, mistress,' returned the sentinel, 'but not for the indulgence of carnal appetite will I forsake my post. Who is he goeth with thee?'

'A fellow whose wit is greater than his courage, and yet he goeth with many for a born fool. A parlous coward he is, else might he now be fighting the Amalekites with the sword of the Lord and of Gideon. Yet in good sooth he serveth me well for the nonce.'

The sentry glanced at Tom, but could see little of him except a long white oval, and Tom was now collected enough to put in exercise his best wisdom, which consisted in holding his tongue.

'Answer me then, mistress, how, being a godly woman, as I doubt not from thy speech thou art, thee rides thus late with none but a fool to keep thee company? Knowest thou not that the country is full of soldiers, whereof some, though that they be all true-hearted and right-minded men, would not mayhap carry themselves so civil to a woman as corporal Bearbanner? And now, I bethink me, thou comest from the direction of Raglan!'

Here he drew himself up, summoned a voice from his chest a storey or two deeper, and asked in magisterial tone:

'Whence comest thou, woman? and on what business gaddest thou so late?'

'I am come from visiting at a friend's house, and am now almost on my own farm,' answered Dorothy.

The man turned to Tom, and Dorothy began to regret she had brought him: he was trembling visibly, and his mouth was wide open with terror.

'See,' she said, 'how thy gruff voice terrifieth the innocent! If now he should fall in a fit thou wert to blame.'

As she spoke she put her hand in her pocket, and taking from it her untoothsome plum, popped it into Tom's mouth. Instantly he began to make such strange uncouth noises that the sentinel thought he had indeed terrified him into a fit.

'I must get him straightway home. Good-night, friend,' said Dorothy, and giving Dick the rein, she was off like the wind, heedless of the shouts of the sentinel or the feeble cries of pursuing Tom, who, if he could not fight, could run. Following his mistress at great speed, he was instantly lost in the darkness, and the sentinel, who had picketed his horse in a neighbouring field, sat down again on the parapet of the bridge, and began to examine all that Dorothy had said with a wondrous inclination to discover the strong points in it.

Having galloped a little way, Dorothy drew bridle and halted for Tom. As soon as he came up, she released him, and telling him to lay hold of Dick's mane and run alongside, kept him at a fast trot all the way to his mother's house.

The moon had risen before they reached it, and Dorothy was therefore glad, when she dismounted at the gate, to think she need ride no further. But while Tom went in to rouse his mother, she let Dick have a few bites of the grass before taking him into the kitchen, lest the roundheads should find him. The next moment, however, out came Tom in terror, saying there was a man in his mother's closet, and he feared the roundheads were in possession.

'Then take care of thyself, Tom,' said Dorothy; and mounting instantly, she made Dick scramble up into the fields that lay between the cottage and her own house, and set off at full speed across the grass in the moonlight, an ethereal pleasure which not even an anxious secret could blast.

Through a gap in the hedge she had just popped into the second field, when she heard the click of a flint-lock, and a voice she thought she knew ordering her to stand: within a few yards of her was again a roundhead soldier. If she rode away, he would fire at her; that mode of escape therefore she would keep for a last chance. The moon by this time was throwing an unclouded light from more than half a disc upon the field.

Keeping a sharp eye upon the man's movements, she allowed him to come within a pace or two, but the moment he would have taken Dick by the bridle she was three or four yards away.

'Fright not my horse, friend,' she said. 'But how!' she added, suddenly remembering him, 'is it possible? Master Upstill! Gently, gently, little Dick! Master Upstill is an old friend. What! hast thou too turned soldier? Left thy last and lapstone and turned soldier, master Upstill?'

'I have left all and followed him, mistress,' answered Cast-down.

'Art sure he called thee, master Upstill?'

'I heard him with my own ears.'

'Called thee to be a shedder of blood, master Upstill?'

'Called me to be a fisher of men, and thee I catch, mistress, thus,' returned the man, stepping quickly forward and making another grasp at Dick's bridle.

It was all Dorothy could do to keep herself from giving him a smart blow across the face with her whip, and riding off. But she gave Dick the cut instead, and sent him yards away.

'Poor Dick! poor Dick!' she said, patting his neck; 'be quiet; master Upstill will do thee no wrong. Be quiet, little man.'

As she thus talked to her genet, Upstill again drew near, now more surly than at first.

'Say what manner of woman art thou?' he demanded with pompous anger. 'Whence comes thou, and whither does thee go?'

'Home,' answered Dorothy.

'What place calls thee home?'

'Why! dost not know me, master Upstill? When I was a little one, thou didst make my shoes for me.'

'I trust it will be forgiven me, mistress. Truly I had ne'er made shoe for thee an' I had foreseen what thee would come to! For I make no farther doubt thou art a consorter with malignants, harlots, and papists.'

Again he clutched at her bridle, and this time, whether it was Dorothy or Dick's fault, with success. Dorothy dropped the bridle, put her hand in her pocket, struck Dick smartly with her whip, and as he reared in consequence, drew it across Upstill's eyes, and so found the chance of administering her bolus.

It was thoroughly effective. The fellow left his hold of the bridle, and began a series of efforts to remove it, which rapidly grew wilder and wilder, until at last his gestures were those of a maniac.

'There!' she cried, as she bounded from him, 'take thy first lesson in good manners. No one can rid thee of that mouthful, which is as thy evil words returned to choke thee! Thou hadst better keep me in sight,' she added, as she gave Dick his head, 'for no one else can free thee.'

Upstill ceased his futile efforts, caught up his carbine, and fired, not without risk to Dorothy, for he was far too wrathful to take the aim that would have ensured her safety. But she rode on unhurt, meditating how to secure Upstill when she got him to Wyfern, whither she doubted not he would follow her. Her difficulties were not yet past, however, for just as she reached her own ground, she was once again met by the order to stand.

This time it came in a voice which, notwithstanding the anxiety it brought with it, was almost as welcome as well known, and yet made her tremble for the first time that night: it was the voice of Richard Heywood. Dick also seemed to know it, for he stood without a hint from his mistress, while, through the last hedge that parted her from the little yet remaining of the property of her fathers, came the man she loved, an enemy between her and her own.

The Marquis 's request to be allowed to communicate with the king had been an unfortunate one. It increased suspicion of all kinds, rendered the various reports of the landing of the Irish army under

Lord Glamorgan more credible, roused the resolution to render all communication impossible, and led to the drawing of a cordon around the place that not a soul should pass unquestioned. The measure would indeed have been unavailing had the garrison been as able as formerly to make sallies; but ever since colonel Morgan received his reinforcement, the issuing troopers had been invariably met at but a few yards from home, and immediately driven in again by largely superior numbers. Still the cordon required a good many more men than the besieging party could well spare without too much weakening their positions, and they had therefore sought the aid of all the gentlemen of puritian politics in the vicinity, and of course that of Mr. Heywood. With the men his father sent, Richard himself offered his services, in the hope that, at the coming fall of the stronghold, he might have a chance of being useful to Dorothy. They had given the cordon a wide extension, in order that an issuing messenger might not perceive his danger until he was too far from the castle to regain it, and then by capturing him might acquire information. Hence it came that posts could be assigned to Richard and his men within such a distance of Redware as admitted of their being with their own people when off duty.

CHAPTER LIII

FAITHFUL FOES

Hearing Upstill's shot, and then Dick's hoofs on the sward, Richard fortunately judged well and took the right direction. What was his astonishment and delight when, passing hurriedly through the hedge in the expectation of encountering a cavalier, he saw Dorothy mounted on Dick! What form but hers had been filling soul and brain when he was startled by the shot! And there she was before him! He felt like one who knows the moon is weaving a dream in his brain.

'Dorothy,' he murmured tremblingly, and his voice sounded to him like that of someone speaking far away. He drew nearer, as one might approach a beloved ghost, anxious not to scare her. He laid his hand on Dick's neck, half fearful of finding him but a shadow.

'Richard!' said Dorothy, looking down on him benignant as Diana upon Endymion.

Then suddenly, at her voice and the assurance of her bodily presence, a great wave from the ocean of duty broke thunderous on the shore of his consciousness.

'Dorothy, I am bound to question thee,' he said: 'whence comest thou? and whither art thou bound?'

'If I should refuse to answer thee, Richard?' returned Dorothy with a smile.

'Then must I take thee to headquarters. And bethink thee, Dorothy, how that would cut me to the heart.'

The moon shone full upon his face, and Dorothy saw the end of a great scar that came from under his hat down on to his forehead.

'Then will I answer thee, Richard,' she said, with a strange trembling in her voice. '—I come from Raglan.'

'And whither art going, Dorothy?'

'To Wyfern.'

'On what business?'

'Were it then so wonderful, Richard, if I should desire to be at home, seeing Wyfern is now safer than Raglan? It was for safety I went thither, thou knowest.'

'It might not be wonderful in another, Dorothy, but in thee it were truly wonderful; for now are they of Raglan thy friends, and thou art a brave woman, and lovest thy friends. I would not believe it of thee even from the mouth of thy mother. Confess, thou bearest about thee that thou wouldst not willingly show me.'

Dorothy, as if in embarrassment, drew from her pocket her handkerchief, and with it a comb, which fell on the ground.

'Prithee, Richard, pick me up my comb,' she said; then, answering his question, continued, '—No, I have nothing about me I would not show thee, Richard: wilt thou take my word for it?'

When she had spoken, she held out her hand, and receiving from him the comb, replaced it in her pocket. But a keen pang of remorse went through her heart.

'I am a man under authority,' said Richard, 'and my orders will not allow me. Besides thou knowest, Dorothy, although it involves such questions in casuistry as I cannot meet, men say thou art not bound to tell the truth to thine enemy.'

'An' thou be mine enemy, Richard, then must thou satisfy thyself,' said Dorothy, trying to speak in a tone of offence. But while she sat there looking at him, it seemed as if her heart were floating on the top of a great wave out somewhere in the moonlight. Yet the conscience-dog was awake in his kennel.

Richard stood for a moment in silent perplexity.

'Wilt thou swear to me, Dorothy,' he said at length, 'that thou hast no papers about thee, neither art the bearer of news or request or sign to any of the king's party?'

'Richard,' returned Dorothy, 'thou hast thyself taken from my words the credit: I say to thee again, satisfy thyself.'

'Dorothy, what AM I to do?' he cried.

'Thy duty, Richard,' she answered.

'My duty is to search thee,' he said.

Dorothy was silent. Her heart was beating terribly, but she would see the end of the path she had taken ere she would think of turning. And she WOULD trust Richard. Would she then have him fail of his duty? Would she have the straight-going Richard swerve? Even in the face of her maidenly fears, she would encounter anything rather than Richard should for her sake be false. But Richard would not turn aside. Neither would he shame her. He would find some way.

'Do then thy duty, Richard,' she said, and sliding from her saddle, she stood before him, one hand grasping Dick's mane.

There was no defiance in her tone. She was but submitting, assured of deliverance.

What was Richard to do? Never man was more perplexed. He dared not let her pass. He dared no more touch her than if she had been Luna herself standing there. He would not had he dared, and yet he must. She was silent, seemed to herself cruel, and began bitterly to accuse herself. She saw his hazel eyes slowly darken, then began to glitter, was it with gathering tears? The glitter grew and overflowed. The man was weeping! The tenderness of their common childhood rushed back upon her in a great wave out of the past, ran into the rising billow of present passion, and swelled it up till it towered and broke; she threw her arm round his neck and kissed him. He stood in a dumb ecstasy. Then terror lest he should think she was tempting him to brave his conscience overpowered her.

'Richard, do thy duty. Regard not me,' she cried in anguish.

Richard gave a strange laugh as he answered,

'There was a time when I had doubted the sun in heaven as soon as thy word, Dorothy. This is surely an evil time. Tell me, yea or nay, hast thou missives to the king or any of his people? Palter not with me.'

But such an appeal was what Dorothy would least willingly encounter. The necessity yet difficulty of escaping it stimulated the wits that had been overclouded by feeling. A light appeared. She broke into a real merry laugh.

'What a pair of fools we are, Richard!' she said. 'Is there never an honest woman of thy persuasion near, one who would show me no favour? Let such an one search me, and tell thee the truth.'

'Doubtless,' answered Richard, laughing very differently now at his stupidity, yet immediately committing a blunder: 'there is mother Rees!'

'What a baby thou art, Richard!' rejoined Dorothy. 'She is as good a friend of mine as of thine, and would doubtless favour the wiles of a woman.'

'True, true! Thou wast always the keener of wit, Dorothy, as becometh a woman. What say'st thou then to dame Upstill? She is even now at the farm there, whence she watches over her husband while he watches over Raglan. Will she answer thy turn?'

'She will,' replied Dorothy. 'And that she may show me no favour, here comes her husband, who shall bear a witness against me shall rouse in her all the malice of vengeance for her injured spouse, whom for his evil language, as thou shalt see, I have so silenced as neither thou nor any man can restore him to speech.'

While she spoke, Upstill, who had followed his enemy as the sole hope of deliverance, drew near, in such plight as the dignity of narrative refuses to describe.

'Upstill,' said Richard, 'what meaneth this? Wherefore hast thou left thy post? And above all, wherefore hast thou permitted this lady to pass unquestioned?'

Sounds of gurgle and strangulation, with other cognate noises, was all Upstill's response.

'Indeed, Mr. Heywood,' said Dorothy, 'he was so far from neglecting his duty and allowing me to pass unquestioned, that he insulted me grievously, averring that I consorted with malignant rogues and papists, and worse, the which drove me to punish him as thou seest.'

'Cast-down Upstill, thou hast shamed thy regiment, carrying thyself thus to a gentlewoman,' said Richard.

'Then he fired his carbine after me,' said Dorothy.

'That may have been but his duty,' returned Richard.

'And worst of all,' continued Dorothy, 'he said that had he known what I should grow to, he would never have made shoes for me when I was an infant. Think on that, master Heywood!'

'Ask the lady to pardon thee, Upstill. I can do nothing for thee,' said Richard.

Upstill would have knelt, in lack of other mode of petition strong enough to express the fervour of his desires for release, but Dorothy was content to see him punished, and would not see him degraded.

'Nay, master Upstill,' she said, 'I desire not that thou shouldst take the measure of my foot to-night. Prithee, master Heywood, wilt thou venture thy fingers in the godly man's mouth for me? Here is the key of the toy, a sucket which will pass neither teeth nor throat. I warrant thee it were no evil thing for many a married woman to possess. I will give it thee when thou marriest, master Heywood, though, good sooth, it were hardly fair to my kind!'

So saying she took a ring from her finger, raised from it a key, and directed Richard how to find its hole in the plum.

'There! Follow us now to the farm, and find thy wife, for we need her aid,' said Richard as he drew by the key the little steel instrument from Upstill's mouth, and restored him to the general body of the articulate.

Thereupon he took Dick by the bridle, and Dorothy and he walked side by side, as if they had been still boy and girl as of old, for of old it already seemed.

As they went, Richard washed both plum and ring in the dewy grass, and restored them, putting the ring upon her finger.

'With better light I will one day show thee how the thing worketh,' she said, thanking him. 'Holding it thus by the ends, thou seest, it will bear to be pressed; but remove thy finger and thumb, and straight upon a touch it shooteth its stings in all directions. And yet another day, when these troubles are over, and honest folk need no longer fight each other, I will give it thee, Richard.'

'Would that day were here, Dorothy! But what can honest people do, while St. George and St. Michael are themselves at odds?'

'Mayhap it but seemeth so, and they but dispute across the Yule-log,' said Dorothy; 'and men down here, like the dogs about the fire, take it up, and fall a-worrying each other. But the end will crown all.'

'Discrown some, I fear,' said Richard to himself.

As they reached the farm-house, it was growing light. Upstill fetched his dame from her bed in the hayloft, and Richard told her, in formal and authoritative manner, what he required of her.

'I will search her!' answered the dame from between her closed teeth.

'Mistress Vaughan,' said Richard, 'if she offer thee evil words, give her the same lesson thou gavest her husband. If all tales be true, she is not beyond the need of it. Search her well, mistress Upstill, but show her no rudeness, for she hath the power to avenge it in a parlous manner, having gone to school to my Lord Herbert of Raglan. Not the less must thou search her well, else will I look upon thee as no better than one of the malignants.'

The woman cast a glance of something very like hate, but mingled with fear, upon Dorothy.

'I like not the business, captain Heywood,' she said.

'Yet the business must be done, mistress Upstill. And hark'ee, for every paper thou findest upon her, I will give thee its weight in gold. I care not what it is. Bring it hither, and the dame's butter-scales withal.'

'I warrant thee, captain!' she returned. '—Come with me, mistress, and show what thou hast about thee. But, good sooth, I would the sun were up!'

She led the way to the rick-yard, and round towards the sunrise. It was the month of August, and several new ricks already stood facing the east, yellow, and beginning to glow like a second dawn. Between the two, mistress Upstill began her search, which she made more thorough than agreeable. Dorothy submitted without complaint.

At last, as she was giving up the quest in despair, her eyes or her fingers discovered a little opening inside the prisoner's bodice, and there sure enough was a pocket, and in the pocket a slip of paper! She drew it out in triumph.

'That is nothing,' said Dorothy: 'give it me.' And with flushed face she made a snatch at it.

'Holy Mary!' cried dame Upstill, whose protestantism was of doubtful date, and thrust the paper into her own bosom.

'That paper hath nothing to do with state affairs, I protest,' expostulated Dorothy. 'I will give thee ten times its weight in gold for it.'

But mistress Upstill had other passions besides avarice, and was not greatly tempted by the offer. She took Dorothy by the arm, and said,

'An' thou come not quickly, I will cry that all the parish shall hear me.'

'I tell thee, mistress Upstill, on the oath of a Christian woman, it is but a private letter of mine own, and beareth nothing upon affairs. Prithee read a word or two, and satisfy thyself.'

'Nay, mistress, truly I will pry into no secrets that belong not to me,' said the searcher, who could read no word of writing or print either. 'This paper is no longer thine, and mine it never was. It belongeth to the high court of parliament, and goeth straight to captain Heywood, whom I will inform concerning the bribe wherewith thou didst seek to corrupt the conscience of a godly woman.'

Dorothy saw there was no help, and yielded to the grasp of the dame, who led her like a culprit, with burning cheek, back to her judge.

When Richard saw them his heart sank within him.

'What hast thou found?' he asked gruffly.

'I have found that which young mistress here would have had me cover with a bribe of ten times that your honour promised me for it,' answered the woman. 'She had it in her bosom, hid in a pocket little bigger than a crown-piece, inside her bodice.'

'Ha, mistress Dorothy! is this true?' asked Richard, turning on her a face of distress.

'It is true,' answered Dorothy, with downcast eyes, far more ashamed however, of that which had not been discovered, and which might have justified Richard's look, than of that which he now held in his hand. 'Prithee,' she added, 'do not read it till I am gone.'

'That may hardly be,' returned Richard, almost sullenly. 'Upon this paper it may depend whether thou go at all.'

'Believe me, Richard, it hath no importance,' she said, and her blushes deepened. 'I would thou wouldst believe me.'

But as she said it, her conscience smote her.

Richard returned no answer, neither did he open the paper, but stood with his eyes fixed on the ground.

Dorothy meantime strove to quiet her conscience, saying to herself: 'It matters not; I must marry him one day, an' he will now have me. Hath not the woman told him where the silly paper was hid? And when I am married to him, then will I tell him all, and doubtless he will forgive me. Nay, nay, I must tell him first, for he might not then wish to have me. Lord! Lord! what a time of lying it is! Sure for myself I am no better than one of the wicked!'

But now Richard, slowly, reluctantly, with eyes averted, opened the paper, stood for an instant motionless, then suddenly raised it, and looked at it. His face changed at once from midnight to morning, and the sunrise was red. He put the paper to his lips, and thrust it inside his doublet. It was his own letter to her by Marquis ! She had not thought to remove it from the place where she had carried it ever since receiving it.

'And now, master Heywood, I may go where I will?' said Dorothy, venturing a half-roguish, but wholly shamefaced glance at him.

But Dame Upstill was looking on, and Richard therefore brought as much of the midnight as would obey orders, back over his countenance as he answered:

'Nay, mistress. An' we had found aught upon thee of greater consequence it might have made a question. But this hardly accounts for thy mission. Doubtless thou bearest thy message in thy mind.'

'What! thou wilt not let me go to Wyfern, to my own house, master Heywood?' said Dorothy in a tone of disappointment, for her heart now at length began to fail her.

'Not until Raglan is ours,' answered Richard. 'Then shalt thou go where thou wilt. And go where thou wilt, there will I follow thee, Dorothy.'

From the last clause of this speech he diverted mistress Upstill's attention by throwing her a gold noble, an indignity which the woman rightly resented but stooped for the money!

'Go tell thy husband that I wait him here,' he said.

'Thou shalt follow me nowhither,' said Dorothy, angrily. 'Wherefore should not I go to Wyfern and there abide? Thou canst there watch her whom thou trustest not.'

'Who can tell what manner of person might not creep to Wyfern, to whom there might messages be given, or whom thou mightest send, credenced by secret word or sign?'

'Whither, then, am I to go?' asked Dorothy, with dignity.

'Alas, Dorothy!' answered Richard, 'there is no help: I must take thee to Raglan. But comfort thyself, soon shalt thou go where thou wilt.'

Dorothy marvelled at her own resignation the while she rode with Richard back to the castle. Her scheme was a failure, but through no fault, and she could bear anything with composure except blame.

A word from Richard to colonel Morgan was sufficient. A messenger with a flag of truce was sent instantly to the castle, and the firing on both sides ceased. The messenger returned, the gate was opened, and Dorothy re-entered, defeated, but bringing her secrets back with her.

'Tit for tat,' said the Marquis when she had recounted her adventures. 'Thou and the roundhead are well matched. There is no avoiding of it, cousin! It is your fate, as clear as if your two horoscopes had run into one. Mind thee, hearts are older than crowns, and love outlives all but leasing.'

'All but leasing!' repeated Dorothy to herself, and the BUT was bitter.

CHAPTER LIV

DOMUS DISSOLVITUR

Scudamore was now much better, partly from the influence of reviving hopes with regard to Dorothy, for his disposition was such that he deceived himself in the direction of what he counted advantage; not like Heywood, who was ever ready to believe what in matters personal told against him. Tom Fool had just been boasting of his exploit in escaping from Raglan, and expressing his conviction that Dorothy, whom he had valiantly protected, was safe at Wyfern, and Rowland was in consequence dressing as fast as he could to pay her a visit, when Tom caught sight of Richard riding towards the cottage, and jumping up, ran into the chimney corner beyond his mother, who was busy with Scudamore's breakfast. She looked from the window, and spied the cause of his terror.

'Silly Tom!' she said, for she still treated him like a child, notwithstanding her boastful belief in his high position and merits, 'he will not harm thee. There never was hurt in a Heywood.'

'Treason, flat treason, witch!' cried the voice of Scudamore from the closet.

'Thee of all men, sir Rowland, has no cause to say so,' returned mistress Rees. 'But come and break thy fast while he talks to thee, and save the precious time which runneth so fast away.'

'I might as well be in my grave for any value it hath to me!' said Rowland, who was for the moment in a bad mood. His hope and his faith were ever ready to fall out, and a twinge in his shoulder was enough to set them jarring.

'Here comes master Heywood, anyhow,' said the old woman, as Richard, leaving Lady at the gate, came striding up the walk in his great brown boots; 'and I pray you, sir Rowland, to let by-gones be by-gones, for my sake if not for your own, lest thou bring the vengeance of general Fairfax upon my poor house.'

'Fairfax!' cried Scudamore; 'is that villain come hither?'

'Sir Thomas Fairfax arrived two days agone, answered mistress Rees. 'Alas, it is but too sure a sign that for Raglan the end is near!'

'Good morrow, mother Rees,' said Richard, looking in at the door, radiant as an Apollo. The same moment out came Scudamore from the closet, pale as a dying moon.

'I want my horse, Heywood!' he cried, deigning no preliminaries.

'Thy horse is at Redware, Scudamore; I carry him not in my pocket. I saw him yesterday; his flesh hath swallowed a good many of his bones since I looked on him last. What wouldst thou with him?'

'What is that to thee? Let me have him.'

'Softly, sir Rowland! It is true I promised thee thy liberty, but liberty doth not necessarily include a horse.'

'Thou wast never better than a shifting fanatic!' cried sir Rowland.

'An' I served thee as befitted, thou shouldst never see thy horse again,' returned Richard. 'Yet I promise thee that so soon as Raglan hath fallen, he shall again be thine. Nay, I care not. Tell me whither thou goest, and—Ha! art thou there?' he cried, interrupting himself as he caught sight of Tom in the chimney corner; and pausing, he stood silent for a moment. '—Wouldst like to hear, thou rascal,' he resumed presently, 'that mistress Dorothy Vaughan got safe to Wyfern this morning?'

'God be praised!' said Tom Fool.

'But thou shalt not hear it. I will tell thee better if less welcome news, that I come from conducting her back to Raglan in safety, and have seen its gates close upon her. Thou shalt have thy horse, sir Rowland, an' thou can wait for him an hour; but for thy ride to Wyfern, that, thou seest, would not avail thee. Thy cousin rode by here this morning, it is true, but, as I say, she is now within Raglan walls, whence she will not issue again until the soldiers of the parliament enter. It is no treason to tell thee that general Fairfax is about to send his final summons ere he storm the rampart.'

'Then mayst thou keep the horse, for I will back to Raglan on foot,' said Scudamore.

'Nay, that wilt thou not, for nought greatly larger than a mouse can any more pass through the lines. Dost think because I sent back thy cousin Dorothy, lest she should work mischief outside the walls, I will therefore send thee back to work mischief within them?'

'And thou art the man who professeth to love mistress Dorothy!' cried Scudamore with contempt.

'Hark thee, sir Rowland, and for thy good I will tell thee more. It is but just that as I told thee my doubts, whence thou didst draw hope, I should now tell thee my hopes, whence thou mayst do well to draw a little doubt.'

'Thou art a mean and treacherous villain!' cried Scudamore.

'Thou art to blame in speaking that thou dost not believe, sir Rowland. But wilt thou have thy horse or no?'

'No; I will remain where I am until I hear the worst.'

'Or come home with me, where thou wilt hear it yet sooner. Thou shalt taste a roundhead's hospitality.'

'I scorn thee and thy false friendship,' cried Rowland, and turning again into the closet, he bolted the door.

That same morning a great iron ball struck the marble horse on his proud head, and flung it in fragments over the court. From his neck the water bubbled up bright and clear, like the life-blood of the wounded whiteness.

'Poor Molly!' said the Marquis , when he looked from his study-window, then smiled at his pity.

Lord Charles entered: a messenger had come from general Fairfax, demanding a surrender in the name of the parliament.

'If they had but gone on a little longer, Charles, they might have saved us the trouble,' said his lordship, 'for there would have been nothing left to surrender. But I will consider the proposal,' he added. 'Pray tell sir Thomas that whatever I do, I look first to have it approved of the king.'

But there was no longer the shadow of a question as to submission. All that was left was but the arrangement of conditions. The Marquis was aware that captain Hooper's trenches were rapidly approaching the rampart; that six great mortars for throwing shells had been got into position; and that resistance would be the merest folly.

Various meetings, therefore, of commissioners appointed on both sides for the settling of the terms of submission took place; and at last, on the fifteenth of August, they were finally arranged, and the surrender fixed for the seventeenth.

The interval was a sad time. All day long tears were flowing, the ladies doing their best to conceal, the servants to display them. Everyone was busy gathering together what personal effects might be carried away. It was especially a sad time for Lord Glamorgan's children, for they were old enough not merely to love the place, but to know that they loved it; and the thought that the sacred things of their home were about to pass into other hands, roused in them wrath and indignation as well as grief; for the sense of property is, in the minds of children who have been born and brought up in the midst of family possessions, perhaps stronger than in the minds of their elders.

As the sun was going down on the evening of the sixteenth, Dorothy, who had been helping now one and now another of the ladies all day long, having, indeed, little of her own to demand her attention, Dick and Marquis being almost her sole valuables, came from the keep, and was crossing the fountain court to her old room on its western side. Everyone was busy indoors, and the place appeared deserted. There was a stillness in the air that SOUNDED awful. For so many weeks it had been shattered with roar upon roar, and now the guns had ceased to bellow, leaving a sense of vacancy and doubt, an oppression of silence. The hum that came from the lines outside seemed but to enhance the stillness within. But the sunlight lived on sweet and calm, as if all was well. It seemed to promise that wrath and ruin would pass, and leave no lasting desolation behind them. Yet she could not help heaving a great sigh, and the tears came streaming down her cheeks.

'Tut, tut, cousin! Wipe thine eyes. The dreary old house is not worth such bright tears.'

Dorothy turned, and saw the Marquis seated on the edge of the marble basin, under the headless horse, whose blood seemed still to well from his truncated form. She saw also that, although his words were cheerful, his lip quivered. It was some little time before she could compose herself sufficiently to speak.

'I marvel your lordship is so calm,' she said.

'Come hither, Dorothy,' he returned kindly, 'and sit thee down by my side. Thou wast right good to my little Molly. Thou hast been a ministering angel to Raglan and its people. I did thee wrong, and thou forgavest me with a whole heart. Thou hast returned me good for evil tenfold, and for all this I love thee; and therefore will I now tell thee what maketh me quiet at heart, for I am as thou seest me, and my heart is as my countenance. I have lived my life, and have now but to die my death. I am thankful to have lived, and I hope to live hereafter. Goodness and mercy went before my birth, and goodness and mercy will follow my death. For the ills of this life, if there was no silence there would be no music. Ignorance is a spur to knowledge. Darkness is a pavilion for the Almighty, a foil to the painter to make his shadows. So are afflictions good for our instruction, and adversities for our amendment. As for the article of death, shall I shun to meet what she who lay in my bosom hath passed through? And look you, fair damsel, thou whose body is sweet, and comely to behold, wherefore should I not rejoice to depart? When I see my house lying in ruins about me, I look down upon this ugly overgrown body of mine, the very foundations whereof crumble from beneath me, and I thank God it is but a tent, and no enduring house even like this house of Raglan, which yet will ere long be a dwelling of owls and foxes. Very soon will Death pull out the tent-pins and let me fly, and therefore am I glad; for, fair damsel Dorothy, although it may be hard for thee, beholding me as I am, to comprehend it, I like to be old and ugly as little as wouldst thou, and my heart, I verily think, is little, older than thine own. One day, please God, I shall yet be clothed upon with a house that is from heaven, nor shall I hobble with gouty feet over the golden pavement, if so be that my sins overpass not mercy. Pray for me, Dorothy, my daughter, for my end is nigh, that I find at length the bosom of father Abraham.'

As he ended, a slow flower of music bloomed out upon the silence from under the fingers of the blind youth hid in the stony shell of the chapel; and, doubtful at first, its fragrance filled at length the whole sunset air. It was the music of a Nunc dimittis of Palestrina. Dorothy knelt and kissed the old man's hand, then rose and went weeping to her chamber, leaving him still seated by the broken yet flowing fountain.

Of all who prepared to depart, Caspar Kaltoff was the busiest. What best things of his master's he could carry with him, he took, but a multitude he left to a more convenient opportunity, in the hope of which, alone and unaided, he sunk his precious cabinet, and a chest besides, filled with curious inventions and favourite tools, in the secret shaft. But the most valued of all, the fire-engine, he could not take and would not leave. He stopped the fountain of the white horse, once more set the water-commanding slave to work, and filled the cistern until he heard it roar in the waste-pipe. Then he extinguished the fire and let the furnace cool, and when Dorothy entered the workshop for the last time to take her mournful leave of the place, there lay the bones of the mighty creature scattered over the floor, here a pipe, there a valve, here a piston and there a cock. Nothing stood but the furnace and the great pipes that ran up the grooves in the wall outside, between which there was scarce a hint of connection to be perceived.

'Mistress Dorothy,' he said, 'my master is the greatest man in Christendom, but the world is stupid, and will forget him because it never knew him.'

Amongst her treasures, chief of them all, even before the gifts of her husband, Lady Glamorgan carried with her the last garments, from sleeve-ribbons to dainty little shoes and rosettes, worn by her Molly.

Dr. Bayly carried a bag of papers and sermons, with his doctor's gown and hood, and his best suit of clothes.

The Marquis with his own hand put up his Vulgate, and left his Gower behind. Ever since the painful proofs of its failure with the king, he had felt if not a dislike yet a painful repugnance to the volume, and had never opened it.

It was a troubled night, the last they spent in the castle. Not many slept. But the Lord of it had long understood that what could cease to be his never had been his, and slept like a child. Dr. Bayly, who in his loving anxiety had managed to get hold of his key, crept in at midnight, and found him fast asleep; and again in the morning, and found him not yet waked.

When breakfast was over, proclamation was made that at nine o'clock there would be prayers in the chapel for the last time, and that the Marquis desired all to be present. When the hour arrived, he entered leaning on the arm of Dr. Bayly. Dorothy followed with the ladies of the family. Young Delaware was in his place, and 'with organ voice and voice of psalms,' praise and prayer arose for the last time from the house of Raglan. All were in tears save the Marquis . A smile played about his lips, and he looked like a child giving away his toy. Sir Toby Mathews tried hard to speak to his flock, but broke down, and had to yield the attempt. When the services were over, the Marquis rose and said,

'Master Delaware, once more play thy Nunc dimittis, and so meet me every one in the hall.'

Thither the Marquis himself walked first, and on the dais seated himself in his chair of state, with his family and friends around him, and the officers of his household waiting. On one side of him stood sir Ralph Blackstone, with a bag of gold, and on the other Mr. George Wharton, the clerk of the accounts, with a larger bag of silver. Then each of the servants, in turn according to position, was called before him by name, and with his own hand the Marquis , dipping now into one bag, now into the other, gave to each a small present in view of coming necessities: they had the day before received their wages. To each he wished a kind farewell, to some adding a word of advice or comfort. He then handed the bags to the governor, and told him to distribute their contents according to his judgment amongst the garrison. Last, he ordered everyone to be ready to follow him from the gates the moment the clock struck the hour of noon, and went to his study.

When Lord Charles came to tell him that all were marshalled, and everything ready for departure, he found him kneeling, but he rose with more of agility than he had for a long time been able to show, and followed his son.

With slow pace he crossed, the courts and the hall, which were silent as the grave, bending his steps to the main entrance. The portcullises were up, the gates wide open, the drawbridge down, all silent and deserted. The white stair was also vacant, and in solemn silence the Marquis descended, leaning on Lord Charles. But beneath was a gallant show, yet, for all its colour and shine, mournful enough. At the foot of the stair stood four carriages, each with six horses in glittering harness, and behind them all the officers of the household and all the guests on horseback. Next came the garrison-music of drums and trumpets, then the men-servants on foot, and the women, some on foot and some in waggons with the children. After them came the waggons loaded with such things as they were permitted to carry with them. These were followed by the principal officers of the garrison, colonels and captains, accompanied by their troops, consisting mostly of squires and gentlemen, to the number of about two hundred, on horseback. Last came the foot-soldiers of the garrison and those who had lost their horses, in all some five hundred, stretching far away, round towards the citadel, beyond the sight. Colours were flying and weapons glittering, and though all was silence except for the pawing of a horse here and there, and the ringing of chain-bridles, everything looked like an ordered march of triumph rather than a surrender and evacuation. Still there was a something in the silence that seemed to tell the true tale.

In the front carriage were Lady Glamorgan and the ladies Elizabeth, Anne, and Mary. In the carriages behind came their gentlewomen and their lady visitors, with their immediate attendants. Dorothy, mounted on Dick, with Marquis 's chain fastened to the pommel of her saddle, followed the last carriage. Beside her rode young Delaware, and his father, the master of the horse.

'Open the white gate,' said the Marquis from the stair as he descended.

The great clock of the castle struck, and with the last stroke of the twelve came the blast of a trumpet from below.

'Answer, trumpets,' cried the Marquis .

The governor repeated the order, and a tremendous blare followed, in which the drums unbidden joined.

This was the signal to the warders at the brick gate, and they flung its two leaves wide apart.

Another blast from below, and in marched on horseback general Fairfax with his staff, followed by three hundred foot. The latter drew up on each side of the brick gate, while the general and his staff went on to the marble gate.

As soon as they appeared within it, the Marquis , who had halted in the midst of his descent, came down to meet them. He bowed to the general, and said:—

'I would it were as a guest I received you, sir Thomas, for then might I honestly bid you welcome. But that I cannot do when you so shake my poor nest that you shake the birds out of it. But though I cannot bid you welcome, I will notwithstanding heartily bid you farewell, sir Thomas, and I thank you for your courtesy to me and mine. This nut of Raglan was, I believe, the last you had to crack. Amen. God's will be done.'

The general returned civil answer, and the Marquis , again bowing graciously, advanced to the foremost carriage, the door of which was held for him by sir Ralph, the steward, while Lord Charles stood by to assist his father. The moment he had entered, the two gentlemen mounted the horses held for them one on each side of the carriage, Lord Charles gave the word, the trumpets once more uttered a loud cry, the Marquis 's moved, the rest followed, and in slow procession Lord Worcester and his people, passing through the gates, left for ever the house of Raglan, and in his heart Henry Somerset bade the world good-bye.

General Fairfax and his company ascended the great white stair, crossed the moat on the drawbridge, passed under the double portcullis and through the gates, and so entered the deserted court. All was frightfully still; the windows stared like dead eyes, the very houses seemed dead; nothing alive was visible except one scared cat: the cannonade had driven away all the pigeons, and a tile had killed the patriarch of the peacocks. They entered the great hall and admired its goodly proportions, while not a few expressions of regret at the destruction of such a magnificent house escaped them; then as soldiers they proceeded to examine the ruins, and distinguish the results wrought by the different batteries.

'Gentlemen,' said sir Thomas, 'had the walls been as strong as the towers, we should have been still sitting in yonder field.'

In the meantime the army commissioner, Thomas Herbert by name, was busy securing with the help of his men the papers and valuables, and making an inventory of such goods as he considered worth removing for sale in London.

Having satisfied his curiosity with a survey of the place, and left a guard to receive orders from Mr. Herbert, the general mounted again and rode to Chepstow, where there was a grand entertainment that evening to celebrate the fall of Raglan, the last of the strongholds of the king.

CHAPTER LV

R. I. P.

As the sad, shining company of the Marquis went from the gates, running at full speed to overtake the rear ere it should have passed through, came Caspar, and mounting a horse led for him, rode near Dorothy.

As they left the brick gate, a horseman joined the procession from outside. Pale and worn, with bent head and sad face, sir Rowland Scudamore fell into the ranks amongst his friends of the garrison, and with them rode in silence.

Many a look did Dorothy cast around her as she rode, but only once, on the crest of a grassy hill that rose abrupt from the highway a few miles from Raglan, did she catch sight of Richard mounted on Lady. All her life after, as often as trouble came, that figure rose against the sky of her inner world, and was to her a type of the sleepless watch of the universe.

Soon, from flank and rear, in this direction and that, each to some haven or home, servants and soldiers began to drop away. Before they reached the forest of Dean, the cortege had greatly dwindled, for many belonged to villages, small towns, and farms on the way, and their orders had been to go home and wait better times. When he reached London, except the chief officers of his household, one of his own pages, and some of his daughters' gentlewomen and menials, the Marquis had few attendants left beyond Caspar and Shafto.

It was a long and weary journey for him, occupying a whole week. One evening he was so tired and unwell that they were forced to put up with what quarters they could find in a very poor little town. Early in the morning, however, they were up and away. When they had gone some ten miles, Lord Charles was riding beside the coach and chatting with his sisters, a remark was made not complimentary to their accommodation of the previous night.

'True,' said Lord Charles; 'it was a very scurvy inn, but we must not forget that the reckoning was cheap.'

While he spoke, one of the household had approached the Marquis , who sat on the other side of the carriage, and said something in a low voice.

'Say'st thou so!' returned his lordship. '—Hear'st thou, my Lord Charles? Thou talkest of a cheap reckoning! I never paid so dear for a lodging in my life. Here is master Wharton hath just told me that they have left a thousand pound under a bench in the chamber we broke our fast in. Truly they are overpaid for what we had!'

'We have sent back after it, my lord,' said Mr. Wharton.

'You will never see the money again,' said Lord Charles.

'Oh, peace!' said the Marquis . 'If they will not be known of the money, you shall see it in a brave inn in a short time.'

Nothing more was said on the matter, and the Marquis seemed to have forgotten it. Late at night, at their next halting-place, the messenger rejoined them, having met a drawer, mounted on a sorry horse, riding after them with the bag, but little prospect of overtaking them before they reached London.

'I thought our hostess seemed an honest woman!' said Lady Anne.

'It is a poor town, indeed, Lord Charles, but you see it is an honest one nevertheless!' said Dr. Bayly.

'It may be the town never saw so much money before,' said the Marquis , 'and knew not what to make of it.'

'Your lordship is severe,' said the doctor.

'Only with my tongue, good doctor, only with my tongue,' said the Marquis , laughing.

When they reached London, Lord Worcester found himself, to his surprise, in custody of the Black Rod, who, as now for some three years Worcester House in the Strand had been used for a state-paper office, conducted him to a house in Covent Garden, where he lodged him in tolerable comfort and mild imprisonment. Parliament was still jealous of Glamorgan and his Irish doings, as indeed well they might be.

But his confinement was by no means so great a trial to him as his indignant friends supposed; for, long willing to depart, he had at length grown a little tired of life, feeling more and more the oppression of growing years, of gout varied with asthma, and, worst of all to the once active man, of his still increasing corpulence, which last indeed, by his own confession, he found it hard to endure with patience. The journey had been too much for him, and he began to lead the life of an invalid.

There being no sufficient accommodation in the house for his family, they were forced to content themselves with lodging as near him as they could, and in these circumstances Dorothy, notwithstanding Lady Glamorgan's entreaties, would have returned home. But the Marquis was very unwilling she should leave him, and for his sake she concluded to remain.

'I am not long for this world, Dorothy,' he said. 'Stay with me and see the last of the old man. The wind of death has got inside my tent, and will soon blow it out of sight.'

Lady Glamorgan's intention from the first had been to go to Ireland to her husband as soon as she could get leave. This however she did not obtain until the first of October, five weeks after her arrival in London. She would gladly have carried Dorothy with her, but she would not leave the Marquis, who was now failing visibly. As her ladyship's pass included thirty of her servants, Dorothy felt at ease about her personal comforts, and her husband would soon supply all else.

The ladies Elizabeth and Mary were in the same house with their father; Lady Anne and Lord Charles were in the house of a relative at no great distance, and visited him every day. Sir Toby Mathews also, and Dr. Bayly, had found shelter in the neighbourhood, so that his lordship never lacked company. But he was going to have other company soon.

Gently he sank towards the grave, and as he sank his soul seemed to retire farther within, vanishing on the way to the deeper life. They thought he lost interest in life: it was but that the brightness drew him from the glimmer. Every now and then, however, he would come forth from his inner chamber, and standing in his open door look out upon his friends, and tell them what he had seen.

The winter drew on. But first November came, with its 'saint Martin's summer, halcyon days' and the old man revived a little. He stood one morning and looked from his window on the garden behind the house, all glittering with molten hoar-frost. A few leaves, golden with death, hung here and there on a naked bough. A kind of sigh was in the air. The very light had in it as much of resignation as hope. He had forgotten that Dorothy was in the room.

There was Celtic blood in the Marquis, and at times his thoughts took shapes that hardly belonged to the Teuton.

'Cometh my youth hither again?' he murmured. 'As a stranger he cometh whom yet I know so well! Or is it but the face of my old age lighted with a parting smile? Either way, change cometh, and change will be good. Domine, in manus tuas.'

He turned and saw Dorothy.

'Child!' he exclaimed, 'good sooth, I had forgotten thee. Yet I spake no treason. Dorothy, I hold not with them who say that from dust we came and to dust we return. Neither my blessed countess, whom thou knewest not, nor my darling Molly, whom thou knewest so well, were born of the dust. From some better where they came, for, say, can dust beget love? Whither they have gone I follow, in the hope that their prayers have smoothed for me the way. Lord, lay not my sins to my charge. Mary, mother, hear my wife who prayeth for me. Hear my little Molly: she was ever dainty and good.'

Again he had forgotten Dorothy, and was with his dead.

But St. Martin's summer is only the lightening of the year that comes before its death; and November, although it brought not then such evil fogs as it now afflicts London withal, yet brought with it November weather, one of God's hounds, with which he hunts us out of the hollows of our own moods, and teaches us to sit on the arch of the cellar. But though the Marquis fought hard and kept it out of his mind, it got into his troubled body. The gout left his feet; he coughed distressingly, breathed with difficulty, and at length betook himself to bed.

For some time his interest in politics, save in so much as affected the king's person, had been gradually ceasing.

'I trust I have done my part,' he said once to the two clergymen, as they sat by his bedside. 'Yet I know not. I fear me I clove too fast to my money. Yet would I have parted with all, even to my shirt, to make my Lord the king a good catholic. But it may be, sir Toby, we make more of such matters down here than they do in the high countries; and in that case, good doctor, ye are to blame who broke away from your mother, even were she not perfect.'

He crossed himself and murmured a prayer, in fear lest he had been guilty of laxity of judgment. But neither clergyman said a word.

'But tell me, gentlemen, ye who understand sacred things,' he resumed, 'can a man be far out of the way so long as, with full heart and no withholding, he saith, Fiat voluntas tua, and that after no private interpretation, but Sicut in caelo?'

'That, my lord, I also strive to say with all my heart,' said Dr. Bayly.

'Mayhap, doctor,' returned the Marquis , 'when thou art as old as I, and hast learned to see how good it is, how all-good, thou wilt be able to say it without any striving. There was a time in my life when I too had to strive, for the thought that he was a hard master would come, and come again. But now that I have learned a little more of what he meaneth with me, what he would have of me and do for me, how he would make me pure of sin, clean from the very bottom of my heart to the crest of my soul, from spur to plume a stainless knight, verily I am no more content to SUBMIT to his will: I cry in the night time, "Thy will be done: Lord, let it be done, I entreat thee;" and in the daytime I cry, "Thy kingdom come: Lord, let it come, I pray thee."'

He lay silent. The clergymen left the room, and Lord Charles came in, and sat down by his bedside. The Marquis looked at him, and said kindly,

'Ah, son Charles! art thou there?'

'I came to tell you, my lord, the rumour goeth that the king hath consented to establish the presbyterian heresy in the land,' said Lord Charles.

'Believe it not, my lord. A man ought not to believe ill of another so long as there is space enough for a doubt to perch. Yet, alas! what shall be hoped of him who will yield nothing to prayers, and everything to compulsion? Had his majesty been a true prince, he had ere now set his foot on the neck of his enemies, or else ascended to heaven a blessed martyr. "Protestant," say'st thou? In good sooth, I force not. What is he now but a football for the sectaries to kick to and fro! But I shall pray for him whither I go, if indeed the prayers of such as I may be heard in that country. God be with his majesty. I can do no more. There are other realms than England, and I go to another king. Yet will I pray for England, for she is dear to my heart. God grant the evil time may pass, and Englishmen yet again grow humble and obedient!'

He closed his eyes, and his face grew so still that, notwithstanding the labour of his breathing, he would have seemed asleep, but that his lips moved a little now and then, giving a flutter of shape to the eternal prayer within him.

Again he opened his eyes, and saw sir Toby, who had re-entered silent as a ghost, and said, feebly holding out his hand, 'I am dying, sir Toby: where will this swollen hulk of mine be hid?'

'That, my lord,' returned sir Toby, 'hath been already spoken of in parliament, and it hath been wrung from them, heretics and fanatics as they are, that your lordship's mortal remains shall lie in Windsor castle, by the side of earl William, the first of the earls of Worcester.'

'God bless us all!' cried the Marquis , almost merrily, for he was pleased, and with the pleasure the old humour came back for a moment: 'they will give me a better castle when I am dead than they took from me when I was alive!'

'Yet is it a small matter to him who inherits such a house as awaiteth my lord, domum non manufactam, in caelis aeternam,' said sir Toby.

'I thank thee, sir Toby, for recalling me. Truly for a moment I was uplifted somewhat. That I should still play the fool, and the old fool, in the very face of Death! But, thank God, at thy word the world hath again dwindled, and my heavenly house drawn the nearer. Domine, nunc dimittis. Let me, so soon as you judge fit, sir Toby, have the consolations of the dying.'

When the last rites, wherein the church yields all hold save that of prayer, had been administered, and his daughters with Dorothy and Lord Charles stood around his bed.

'Now have I taken my staff to be gone,' he said cheerfully, 'like a peasant who hath visited his friends, and will now return, and they will see him as far upon the road as they may. I tremble a little, but I bethink me of him that made me and died for me, and now calleth me, and my heart revives within me.'

Then he seemed to fall half asleep, and his soul went wandering in dreams that were not all of sleep, just as it had been with little Molly when her end drew near.

'How sweet is the grass for me to lie in, and for thee to eat! Eat, eat, old Ploughman.'

It was a favourite horse of which he dreamed, one which in old days he had named after Piers Ploughman, the Vision concerning whom, notwithstanding its severity on catholic abuses, he had at one time read much.

After a pause he went on—

'Alack, they have shot off his head! What shall I do without my Ploughman, my body groweth so large and heavy! Hark, I hear Molly! "Spout, horse," she crieth. See, it is his life-blood he spouteth! O Lord, what shall I do, for I am heavy, and my body keepeth down my soul. Hark! Who calleth me? It is Molly! No, no! it is the Master. Lord, I cannot rise and come to thee. Here have I lain for ages, and my spirit groaneth. Reach forth thy hand, Lord, and raise me. Thanks, Lord, thanks!'

And with the word he was neither old man nor Marquis any more.

The parliament, with wondrous liberality, voted five hundred pounds for his funeral, and Dr. Bayly tells us that he laid him in his grave with his own hands. But let us trust rather that Anne and Molly received him into their arms, and soon made him forget all about castles and chapels and dukedoms and ungrateful princes, in the everlasting youth of the heavenly kingdom, whose life is the presence of the Father, whose air to breathe is love, and whose corn and wine are truth and graciousness.

There surely, and nowhere else as surely, can the prayer be for a man fulfilled: Requiescat in Pace.

CHAPTER LVI

RICHARD AND CASPAR

I have now to recount a small adventure, to which it would scarcely be worth while to afford a place, were it not for the important fact that it opened to Richard a great window not only in Dorothy's history while she lived at the castle, but, which was of far more importance, into the character moulding that history, for character has far more to do with determining history than history has to do with determining character. Without the interview whose circumstances I am about to narrate, Richard could not so soon at least have done justice to a character which had been, if not keeping parallel pace with his own, yet advancing rapidly in the same direction.

The decree of the parliament had gone forth that Raglan should be destroyed. The same hour in which the sad news reached Caspar, he set out to secure, if possible, the treasures he had concealed. He had little fear of their being discovered, but great fear of their being rendered inaccessible from the workshop.

Having reached the neighbourhood, he hired a horse and cart from a small farmer whom he knew, and, taking the precaution to put on the dress of a countryman, got on it and drove to the castle. The huge oaken leaves of the brick gate, bound and riveted with iron, lay torn from their hinges, and he entered unquestioned. But instead of the solitude of desertion, for which he had hoped, he found the whole place swarming with country people, men and women, most of them with baskets and sacks, while the space between the outer defences and the moat of the castle itself was filled with country vehicles of every description, from a wheelbarrow to a great waggon.

When the most valuable of the effects found in the place had been carried to London, a sale for the large remainder had been held on the spot, at which not a few of the neighbouring families had been purchasers. After all, however, a great many things were left unhid for, which were not, from a money point of view, the sole one taken, worth removing; and now the peasantry were, like jackals, admitted to pick the bones of the huge carcase, ere the skeleton itself should be torn asunder. Nor could the invading populace have been disappointed of their expectations: they found numberless things of immense value in their eyes, and great use in their meagre economy. For years, I might say centuries after, pieces of furniture and panels of carved oak, bits of tapestry, antique sconces and candlesticks of brass, ancient horse-furniture, and a thousand things besides of endless interest, were to be found scattered in farm-houses and cottages all over Monmouth and neighbouring shires. I should not wonder if, even now in the third century, and after the rage for the collection of such things has so long prevailed, there were some of them still to be discovered in places where no one has thought of looking.

When Caspar saw what was going on, he judged it prudent to turn and drive his cart into the quarry, and having there secured it, went back and entered the castle. There was a great divided torrent of humanity rushing and lingering through the various lines of rooms, here meeting in whirlpools, there parted into mere rivulets, man and woman searching for whatever might look valuable in his or her eyes. Things that nowadays would fetch their weight in silver, some of them even in gold, were passed by as worthless, or popped into a bag to be carried home for the amusement of cottage children. The noises of hobnailed shoes on the oak floors, and of unrestrained clownish and churlish voices everywhere, were tremendous. Here a fat cottager might be seen standing on a lovely quilt of patchwork brocade, pulling down, rough in her cupidity, curtains on which the new-born and dying eyes of generations of nobles had rested, henceforth to adorn a miserable cottage, while her husband was taking down the bed, larger perhaps, than the room itself in which they would in vain try to set it up, or cruelly forcing a lid, which, having a spring lock, had closed again after the carved chest had been already rifled by the commissioner or his men. The kitchen was full of squabbling women, and the whole place in the agonies of dissolution. But there was a small group of persons, fortuitously met, but linked together by an old painful memory of the place itself, strongly revived by their present meeting, to whom a fanatical hatred of everything catholic, coupled with a profound sense of personal injury, had prevailed over avarice, causing them to leave the part of acquisition to their wives, and aspire to that of pure destruction. It was the same company, almost to a man, whose misadventures in their search of Raglan for arms, under the misguidance of Tom Fool, I have related in an early chapter. In their hearts they nursed a half-persuasion that Raglan had fallen because of their wrongs within its walls, and the shame that there had been heaped upon the godly.

These men, happening to meet, as I say, in the midst of the surrounding tumult, had fallen into a conversation chiefly occupied with reminiscences of that awful experience, whose terrors now looked like an evil dream, and, in a place thus crowded with men and women, buzzing with voices, and resounding with feet, as little likely to return as a vanished thundercloud. In the course of their conversation, therefore, they grew valiant; grew conscious next of a high calling, and resolved therewith to take to themselves the honour of giving the first sweep of the besom of destruction to Raglan Castle. Satisfying themselves first therefore that their wives were doing their duty for their household, mistress Upstill was as good as two men at least at appropriation, they set out, Cast-down taking the lead, master Sycamore, John Croning, and the rest following, armed with crowbars, for the top of the great tower, ambitious to commence the overthrow by attacking the very summit, the high places of wickedness, the crown of pride; and after some devious wandering, at length found the way to the stair.

When Caspar Kaltoff entered the castle, he made straight for the keep, and to his delight found no one in the lower part. To make certain however that he was alone in the place, ere he secured himself from intrusion, he ran up the stair, gave a glance at the doors as he ran, and reached the top just as Upstill in fierce discrowning pride was heaving the first capstone from between two battlements. Caspar was close by the cocks; instantly he turned one, and as the dislodged stone struck the water of the moat, a sudden hollow roaring invaded their ears, and while they stood aghast at the well-remembered sound, and ere yet the marrow had time to freeze in their stupid bones, the very moat itself into which they had cast the insulted stone, storming and spouting, seemed to come rushing up to avenge it upon them were they stood. The moment he turned the cock, Caspar shot half-way down the stair, but as quietly as he could, and into a little chamber in the wall, where stood two great vessels through which the pipes of the fire-engine inside had communicated with the pipes in the wall outside. There he waited until the steps which, long before he reached his refuge, he heard come thundering down the stairs after him, had passed in headlong haste, when he sprang up again to save the water for another end, and to attach the drawbridge to the sluice, so that it would raise it to its full height. Then he hurried down to the water trap under the bridge and set it, after which he could hardly help wasting a little of his precious time, lurking in a convenient corner to watch the result.

He had not to wait long. The shrieks of the yokels as they ran, and their looks of horror when they appeared, quickly gathered around them a gaping crowd to hear their tale, the more foolhardy in which, partly doubting their word, for the fountains no longer played, and partly ambitious of showing their superior courage, rushed to the Gothic bridge. Down came the drawbridge with a clang, and with it in sheer descent a torrent of water fit to sweep a regiment away, which shot along the stone bridge and dashed them from it bruised and bleeding, and half drowned with the water which in their terror and surprise found easy way into their bodies. Caspar withdrew satisfied, for he now felt sure of all the time he required to get some other things he had thought of saving down into the shaft with the cabinet and chest.

Having effected this, and with much labour and difficulty, aided by rollers, got all into the quarry and then into the cart, he did not resist the temptation to go again amongst the crowd, and enjoy listening to the various remarks and conjectures and terrors to which doubtless his trick had given rise. He therefore got a great armful of trampled corn from the field above, and laid it before his patient horse, then ran round and re-entered the castle by the main gate.

He had not been in the crowd many minutes, however, when he saw indications of suspicion ripening to conviction. What had given ground for it he could not tell, but at some point he must have been seen on the other side of the tower-moat. All this time Upstill and his party had been recounting with various embellishment their adventures both former and latter, and when Kaltoff was recognised, or at least suspected in the crowd, the rumour presently arose and spread that he was either the devil himself, or an accredited agent of that potentate.

'Be it then the old Satan himself?' Caspar heard a man say anxiously to his neighbour, as he tried to get a look at his feet, which was not easy in such a press. Caspar, highly amused, and thinking such evil reputation would rather protect than injure him, showed some anxiety about his feet, and made as if he would fain keep them out of the field of observation. But thereupon he saw the faces and gestures of the younger men begin to grow threatening; evidently anger was succeeding to fear, and some of them, fired with the ambition possibly of thrashing the devil, ventured to give him a rough shove or two from behind. Neither outbreak of sulphurous flashes nor even kick of cloven hoof following, they proceeded with the game, and rapidly advanced to such extremities, expostulation in Caspar's broken English, for such in excitement it always became, seeming only to act as fresh incitement and justification, that at length he was compelled in self-defence to draw a dagger. This checked them a little, and ere audacity had had time to recover itself, a young man came shoving through the crowd, pushing them all right and left until he reached Caspar, and stood by his side. Now there was that about Richard Heywood to give him influence with a crowd: he was a strong man and a gentleman, and they drew back.

'De fools dink I was de tuyfel!' said Caspar.

Richard turned upon them with indignation.

'You Englishmen!' he cried, 'and treat a foreigner thus!'

But there was nothing about him to show that he was a roundhead, and from behind rose the cry: 'A malignant! A royalist!' and the fellows near began again to advance threateningly.

'Mr. Heywood,' said Caspar hurriedly, for he recognised his helper from the time he had seen him a prisoner, 'let us make for the hall. I know the place and can bring us both off safe.'

It was one of Richard's greatest virtues that he could place much confidence. He gave one glance at his companion, and said, 'I will do as thou sayest.'

'Follow me then, sir,' said Caspar, and turning with brandished dagger, he forced his way to the hall-door, Richard following with fists, his sole weapons, defending their rear.

There were but few in the hall, and although their enemies came raging after them, they were impeded by the crowd, so that there was time as they crossed it for Caspar to say:

'Follow me over the bridge, but, for God's sake, put your feet exactly where I put mine as we cross. You will see why in a moment after.'

'I will,' said Richard, and, delayed a little by needful care, gained the other side just as the foremost of their pursuers rushed on the bridge, and with a clang and a roar were swept from it by the descending torrent.

They lost no time in explanations. Caspar hurried Richard to the workshop, down the shaft, through the passage, and into the quarry, whence, taking no notice of his cart, he went with him to the White Horse, where Lady was waiting him.

And Richard was well rewarded for the kindness he had shown, for ere they said good bye, the German, whose heart was full of Dorothy, and understood, as indeed everyone in the castle did, something of her relation to Richard, had told him all he knew about her life in the castle, and how she had been both before and during the siege a guardian angel, as the Marquis himself had said, to Raglan. Nor was the story of her attempted visit to her old playfellow in the turret chamber, or the sufferings she had to endure in consequence, forgotten; and when Caspar and he parted, Richard rode home with fresh strength and light and love in his heart, and Lady shared in them all somehow, for she constantly reflected, or imaged rather, the moods of her master. As much as ever he believed Dorothy mistaken, and yet could have kneeled in reverence before her. He had himself tried to do the truth, and no one but he who tries to do the truth can perceive the grandeur of another who does the same. Alive to his own shortcomings, such a one the better understands the success of his brother or sister: there the truth takes to him shape, and he worships at her shrine. He saw more clearly than before what he had been learning ever since she had renounced him, that it is not correctness of opinion, could he be SURE that his own opinions were correct? that constitutes rightness, but that condition of soul which, as a matter of course, causes it to move along the lines of truth and duty, the LIFE going forth in motion according to the law of light: this alone places a nature in harmony with the central Truth. It was in the doing of the will of his Father that Jesus was the son of God, yea the eternal son of the eternal Father.

Nor was this to make little of the truth intellectually considered, of the FACT of things. The greatest fact of all is that we are bound to obey the truth, and that to the full extent of our knowledge thereof, however LITTLE that may be. This obligation acknowledged and OBEYED, the road is open to all truth, and the ONLY road. The way to know is to do the known.

Then why, thought Richard with himself, should he and Dorothy be parted? Why should Dorothy imagine they should? All depended on their common magnanimity, not the magnanimity that pardons faults, but the magnanimity that recognises virtues. He who gladly kneels with one who thinks largely wide from himself, in so doing draws nearer to the Father of both than he who pours forth his soul in sympathetic torrent only in the company of those who think like himself. If a man be of the truth, then and only then is he of those who gather with the Lord.

In forms natural to the age and his individual thought, if not altogether in such as I have here put down, Richard thus fashioned his insights as he sauntered home upon Lady, his head above the clouds, and his heart higher than his head, as it ought to be once or twice a day at least. Poor indeed is any worldly success compared to a moment's breathing in divine air, above the region where the miserable word SUCCESS yet carries a meaning.

CHAPTER LVII

THE SKELETON

The death of the Marquis took place in December, long before which time the second Marquis of Worcester, ever busy in the king's affairs, and unable to show himself with safety in England, or there be useful, had gone from Ireland to Paris.

As the country was now a good deal quieter, and there was nothing to detain her in London, and much to draw her to Wyfern, Dorothy resolved to go home, and there, if possible, remain. Indeed, there was now nothing else she could well do, except visit Mr. Herbert at Llangattock. But much as she revered and loved the old man, and would have enjoyed his company, she felt now such a longing for activity, that she must go and look after her affairs. What with the words of the good Marquis and her own late experiences and conflicts, Dorothy had gained much enlightenment. She had learned that well-being is a condition of inward calm, resting upon yet deeper harmonies of being, and resulting in serene activity, the prevention of which natural result reacts in perturbation and confusion of thought and feeling. But for many sakes the thought of home was in itself precious and enticing to her. It was full of clear memories of her mother, and vague memories of her father, not to mention memories of the childhood Richard and she had spent together, from which the late mists had begun to rise, and reveal them sparkling with dew and sunshine. As soon, therefore, as Marquis Henry had gone to countess Anne, Dorothy took her leave, with many kind words between, of the ladies Elizabeth, Anne, and Mary, and set out, attended by her old bailiff and some of the men of her small tenantry, who having fought the king's battle in vain, had gone home again to fight their own.

At Wyfern she found everything in rigid order, almost cataleptic repose. How was it ever to be home again? What new thing could restore the homefulness where the revered over-life had vanished? And how shall the world be warmed and brightened to him who knows no greater or better man than himself therein, no more skilful workman, no diviner thinker, no more godlike doer than himself? And what can the universe have in it of home, of country, nay even of world, to him who cannot believe in a soul of souls, a heart of hearts? I should fall out with the very beating of the heart within my bosom, did I not believe it the pulse of the infinite heart, for how else should it be heart of MINE? I made it not, and any moment it may SEEM to fail me, yet never, if it be what I think it, can it betray me. It is no wonder then, that, with only memories of what had been to render it lovely in her eyes, Dorothy should have soon begun to feel the place lonely.

The very next morning after her rather late arrival, she sent to saddle Dick once more, called Marquis , and with no other attendant, set out to see what they had done to dear old Raglan. Marquis had been chained up almost all the time they were in London, and freedom is blessed even to a dog: Dick was ever joyful under his mistress, and now was merry with the keen invigorating air of a frosty December morning, and frolicsome amidst the early snow, which lay unusually thick on the ground, notwithstanding his hundred and twenty miles' ride, for they had taken nearly a week to do it; so that between them they soon raised Dorothy's spirits also, and she turned to her hopes, and grew cheerful.

This mood made her the less prepared to encounter the change that awaited her. What a change it was! While she approached, what with the trees left, and the towers, the rampart, and the outer shell of the courts, little injured to the distant eye, she had not an idea of the devastation within. But when she rode through one entrance after another with the gates torn from their hinges, crossed the moat by a mound of earth instead of the drawbridge, and rode through the open gateway, where the portcullises were wedged up in their grooves and their chains gone, into the paved court, she beheld a desolation, at sight of which her heart seemed to stand still in her bosom. The rugged horror of the heaps of ruins was indeed softly covered with snow, but what this took from the desolation in harshness, it added in coldness and desertion and hopelessness. She felt like one who looks for the corpse of his friend, and finds but his skeleton.

The broken bones of the house projected gaunt and ragged. Its eyes returned no shine, they did not even stare, for not a pane of glass was left in a window: they were but eye-holes, black and blank with shadow and no-ness. The roofs were gone, all but that of the great hall, which they had not dared to touch. She climbed the grand staircase, open to the wind and slippery with ice, and reached her own room. Snow lay on the floor, which had swollen and burst upwards with November rains. Through room after room she wandered with a sense of loneliness and desolation and desertion such as never before had she known, even in her worst dreams. Yet was there to her, in the midst of her sorrow and loss, a strange fascination in the scene. Such a hive of burning human life now cold and silent! Even Marquis appeared aware of the change, for with tucked-in tail he went about sadly sniffing, and gazing up and down. Once indeed, and only once, he turned his face to the heavens, and gave a strange protesting howl, which made Dorothy weep, and a little relieved her oppressed heart.

She would go and see the workshop. On the way, she would first visit the turret chamber. But so strangely had destruction altered the look of what it had spared, that it was with difficulty she recognised the doors and ways of the house she had once known so well. Here was a great hole to the shining snow where once had been a dark corner; there a heap of stones where once had been a carpeted corridor. All the human look of indwelling had past away. Where she had been used to go about as if by instinct, she had now to fall back upon memory, and call up again, with an effort sometimes painful in its difficulty, that which had vanished altogether except from the minds of its scattered household.

She found the door of the turret chamber, but that was all she found: the chamber was gone. Nothing was there but the blank gap in the wall, and beyond it, far down, the nearly empty moat of the tower. She turned, frightened and sick at heart, and made her way to the bridge. That still stood, but the drawbridge above was gone.

She crossed the moat and entered the workshop. A single glance took in all that was left of the keep. Not a floor was between her and the sky! The reservoir, great as a little mountain-tarn, had vanished utterly! All was cleared out; and the white wintry clouds were sailing over her head. Nearly a third part of the walls had been brought within a few feet of the ground. The furnace was gone, all but its mason-work. It was like the change of centuries rather than months. The castle had half-melted away. Its idea was blotted out, save from the human spirit. She turned from the workshop, in positive pain of body at the sight, and wandered she hardly knew whither, till she found herself in Lady Glamorgan's parlour. There was left a single broken chair: she sat down on it, closed her eyes, and laid back her head.

She opened them with a slight start: there stood Richard a yard or two away.

He had heard of her return, and gone at once to Wyfern. There learning whither she had betaken herself, he had followed, and tracking what of her footsteps he could discover, had at length found her.

CHAPTER LVIII

LOVE AND NO LEASING

Their eyes met in the flashes of a double sunrise. Their hands met, but the hand of each grasped the heart of the other. Two honester purer souls never looked out of their windows with meeting gaze. Had there been no bodies to divide them, they would have mingled in a rapture of faith and high content.

The desolation was gone; the desert bloomed and blossomed as the rose. To Dorothy it was for a moment as if Raglan were rebuilt; the ruin and the winter had vanished before the creative, therefore prophetic, throb of the heart of love; then her eyes fell, not defeated by those of the youth, for Dorothy's faith gave her a boldness that was lovely even against the foil of maidenly reserve, but beaten down by conscience: the words of the Marquis shot like an arrow into her memory: 'Love outlives all but leasing,' and her eyes fell before Richard's.

But Richard imagined that something in his look had displeased her, and was ashamed, for he had ever been, and ever would be, sensitive as a child to rebuke. Even when it was mistaken or unjust he would always find within him some ground whereon it MIGHT have alighted.

'Forgive me, Dorothy,' he said, supposing she had found his look presumptuous.

'Nay, Richard,' returned Dorothy, with her eyes fast on the ground, whence it seemed rosy mists came rising through her, 'I know no cause wherefore thou shouldst ask me to forgive thee, but I do know, although thou knowest not, good cause wherefore I should ask thee to forgive me. Richard, I will tell thee the truth, and thou wilt tell me again how I might have shunned doing amiss, and how far my lie was an evil thing.'

'Lie, Dorothy! Thou hast never lied!'

'Hear me, Richard, first, and then judge. Thou rememberest I did tell thee that night as we talked in the field, that I had about me no missives: the word was true, but its purport was false. When I said that, thou didst hold in thy hand my comb, wherein were concealed certain papers in cipher.'

'Oh thou cunning one!' cried Richard, half reproachfully, half humorously, but the amusement overtopped the seriousness.

'My heart did reproach me; but Richard, what WAS I to do?'

'Wherefore did thy heart reproach thee, Dorothy?'

'That I told a falsehood, that I told THEE a falsehood, Richard.'

'Then had it been Upstill, thou wouldst not have minded?'

'Upstill! I would never have told Upstill a falsehood. I would have beaten him first.'

'Then thou didst think it better to tell a falsehood to me than to Upstill?'

'I would rather sin against thee, an' it were a sin, Richard. Were it wrong to think I would rather be in thy hands, sin or none, or sin and all, than in those of a mean-spirited knave whom I despised? Besides I might one day, somehow or other, make it up to thee, but I could not to him. But was it sin, Richard? tell me that. I have thought and thought over the matter until my mind is maze. Thou seest it was my Lord Marquis 's business, not mine, and thou hadst no right in the matter.'

'Prithee, Dorothy, ask not me to judge.'

'Art thou then so angry with me that thou will not help me to judge myself aright?'

'Not so, Dorothy, but there is one command in the New Testament for the which I am often more thankful than for any other.'

'What is that, Richard.'

'JUDGE NOT. Prythee, between whom lieth the quarrel, Dorothy? Bethink thee.'

'Between thee and me, Richard.'

'No, verily, Dorothy. I accuse thee not.'

Dorothy was silent for a moment, thinking.

'I see, Richard,' she said. 'It lieth between me and my own conscience.'

'Then who am I, Dorothy, that I should dare step betwixt thee and thy conscience? God forbid. That were a presumption deserving indeed the pains of hell.'

'But if my conscience and I seek a daysman betwixt us?'

'Mortal man can never be that daysman, Dorothy. Nay, an' thou need an umpire, thou must seek to him who brought thee and thy conscience together and told thee to agree. Let God, over all and in all, tell thee whether or no thou wert wrong. For me, I dare not. Believe me, Dorothy, it is sheer presumption for one man to intermeddle with the things that belong to the spirit of another man.'

'But these are only the things of a woman,' said Dorothy, in pure childish humility born of love.

'Sure, Dorothy, thou wouldst not jest in such sober matters.'

'God forbid, Richard! I but spoke that which was in me. I see now it was foolishness.'

'All a man can do in this matter of judgment,' said Richard, 'is to lead his fellow man, if so be he can, up to the judgment of God. He must never dare judge him for himself. An' thou cannot tell whether thou did well or ill in what thou didst, thou shouldst not vex thy soul. God is thy refuge, even from the wrongs of thine own judgment. Pray to him to let thee know the truth, that if needful thou mayst repent. Be patient and not sorrowful until he show thee. Nor fear that he will judge thee harshly because he must judge thee truly. That were to wrong God. Trust in him even when thou fearest wrong in thyself, for he will deliver thee therefrom.'

'Ah! how good and kind art thou, Richard.'

'How should I be other to thee, beloved Dorothy?'

'Thou art not then angry with me that I did deceive thee?'

'If thou didst right, wherefore should I be angry? If thou didst wrong, I am well content to know that thou wilt be sorry therefor as soon as thou seest it, and before that thou canst not, thou must not, be sorry. I am sure that what thou knowest to be right that thou will do, and it seemeth as if God himself were content with that for the time. What the very right thing is, concerning which we may now differ, we must come to see together one day, the same, and not another, to both, and this doing of what we see, is to each of us the path thither. Let God judge us, Dorothy, for his judgment is light in the inward parts, showing the truth and enabling us to judge ourselves. For me to judge thee and thee me, Dorothy, would with it bear no light. Why, Dorothy, knowest thou not, yet how shouldst thou know? that this is the very matter for the which we, my father and his party, contend, that each man, namely, in matters of conscience, shall be left to his God, and remain unjudged of his brother? And if I fight for this on mine own part, unto whom should I accord it if not to thee, Dorothy, who art the highest in soul and purest in mind and bravest in heart of all women I have known? Therefore I love thee with all the power of a heart that loves that which is true before that which is beautiful, and that which is honest before that which is of good report.'

What followed I leave to the imagination of such of my readers as are capable of understanding that the truer the nature the deeper must be the passion, and of hoping that the human soul will yet burst into grander blossoms of love than ever poet has dreamed, not to say sung. I leave it also to the hearts of those who understand that love is greater than knowledge. For those who have neither heart nor imagination, only brains, to them I presume to leave nothing, knowing what self-satisfying resources they possess of their own.

The pair wandered all over the ruins together, and Dorothy had a hundred places to take Richard to, and tell him what they had been and how they had looked in their wholeness and use, amongst the rest her own chamber, whither Marquis had brought her the letter which mistress Upstill had found so badly concealed.

Then Richard's turn came, and he gave Dorothy a sadly vivid account of what he had seen of the destruction of the place; how, as if with whole republics of ants, it had swarmed all over with men paid to destroy it; how in every direction the walls were falling at once; how they dug and drained at fish-ponds and moat in the wild hope of finding hidden treasure, and had found in the former nothing but mud and a bunch of huge old keys, the last of some lost story of ancient days, and in the latter nothing but a pair of silver-gilt spurs, which he had himself bought of the fellow who found them. He told her what a terrible shell the Tower of towers had been to break, how after throwing its battlemented crown into the moat, they had in vain attacked the walls, might almost as well have sought with pickaxes and crowbars to tear asunder the living rock, and at last, but this was hearsay, he had not seen it, had undermined the wall, propped it up with timber, set the timber on fire, and so succeeded in bringing down a portion of the hard, tough massy defence.

'What became of the wild beasts in the base of the kitchen-tower, dost know, Richard?'

'I saw their cages,' answered Richard, 'but they were empty. I asked what they were, and what had become of the animals, of which all the country had heard, but no one could tell me. I asked them questions until they began to puzzle themselves to answer them, and now I believe all Gwent is divided between two opinions as to their fate, one, that they are roaming the country, the other that Lord Herbert, as they still call him, has by his magic conveyed them away to Ireland to assist him in a general massacre of the Protestants.'

Mighty in mutual faith, neither politics, nor morals, nor even theology was any more able to part those whose plain truth had begotten absolute confidence. Strive they might, sin they could not, against each other. They talked, wandering about, a long time, forgetting, I am sorry to say, even their poor shivering horses, which, after trying to console themselves with the renewal of a friendship which a broad white line across Lady's face had for a moment, on Dick's part, somewhat impeded, had become very restless. At length an expostulatory whinny from Lady called Richard to his duty, and with compunctions of heart the pair hurried to mount. They rode home together in a bliss that would have been too deep almost for conscious delight but that their animals were eager after motion, and as now the surface of the fields had grown soft, they turned into them, and a tremendous gallop soon brought their gladness to the surface in great fountain throbs of joy.

CHAPTER LIX

AVE! VALE! SALVE!

And now must I bury my dead out of my sight, bid farewell to the old resplendent, stately, scarred, defiant Raglan, itself the grave of many an old story, and the cradle of the new, and alas! in contrast with the old, not merely the mechanical, but the unpoetic and commonplace, yes vulgar era of our island's history. Little did Lord Herbert dream of the age he was initiating, of the irreverence and pride and destruction that were about to follow in his footsteps, wasting, defiling, scarring, obliterating, turning beauty into ashes, and worse! That divine mechanics should thus, through selfishness and avarice, be leagued with filth and squalor and ugliness! When one looks upon Raglan, indignation rises, not at the storm of iron which battered its walls to powder, hardly even at the decree to level them with the dust, but at the later destroyer who could desecrate the beauty yet left by wrath and fear, who with the stones of my lady's chamber would build a kennel, or with the carved stones of chapel or hall a barn or cowhouse! What would the inventor of the water-commanding engine have said to the pollution of our waters, the destruction of the very landmarks of our history, the desecration of ruins that ought to be venerated for their loveliness as well as their story! Would he not have broken it to pieces, that the ruin it must occasion might not be laid to his charge? May all such men as for the sake of money constitute themselves the creators of ugliness, not to speak of far worse evils in the land, live, or die, I care not which, to know in their own selves what a lovely human Psyche lies hid even in the chrysalis of a railway-director, and to loathe their past selves as an abomination, incredible but that it had been. He who calls such a wish a curse, must undergo it ere his being can be other than a blot.

But this era too will pass, and truth come forth in forms new and more lovely still.

The living Raglan has gone from me, and before me rise the broken, mouldering walls which are the monument of their own past. My heart swells as I think of them, lonely in the deepening twilight, when the ivy which has flung itself like a garment about the bareness of their looped and windowed raggedness is but as darker streaks of the all prevailing dusk, and the moon is gathering in the east. Fain would the soul forsake the fettersome body for a season, to go flitting hither and thither, alighting and flitting, like a bat or a bird, now drawing itself slow along a moulding to taste its curve and flow, now creeping into a cranny, and brooding and thinking back till the fancy feels the tremble of an ancient kiss yet softly rippling the air, or descries the dim stain which no tempest can wash away. Ah, here is a stair! True there are but three steps, a broken one and a fragment. What said I? See how the phantom-steps continue it, winding up and up to the door of my lady's chamber! See its polished floor, black as night, its walls rich with tapestry, lovelily old, and harmoniously withered, for the ancient time had its ancient times, and its things that had come down from solemn antiquity, see the silver sconces, the tall mirrors, the part-open window, long, low, carved latticed, and filled with lozenge panes of the softest yellow green, in a multitude of shades! There stands my lady herself, leaning from it, looking down into the court! Ah, lovely lady! is not thy heart as the heart of my mother, my wife, my daughters? Thou hast had thy troubles. I trust they are over now, and that thou art satisfied with God for making thee!

The vision fades, and the old walls rise like a broken cenotaph. But the same sky, with its clouds never the same, hangs over them; the same moon will fold them all night in a doubtful radiance, befitting the things that dwell alone, and are all of other times, for she too is but a ghost, a thing of the past, and her light is but the light of memory; into the empty crannies blow the same winds that once refreshed the souls of maiden and man-at-arms, only the yellow flower that grew in its gardens now grows upon its walls. And however the mind, or even the spirit of man may change, the heart remains the same, and an effort to read the hearts of our forefathers will help us to know the heart of our neighbour.

Whoever cares to distinguish the bones of fact from the drapery of invention in the foregone tale, will find them all in the late Mr. Dirck's 'Life of the Marquis of Worcester,' and the 'Certamen Religiosum' and 'Golden Apophthegms' of Dr. Bayly.

George MacDonald – A Short Biography

George MacDonald was born on December 10th 1824 at Huntly, Aberdeenshire, Scotland.

The MacDonald family had proud and long historical roots. His father, was a farmer, was a direct descendant of one of the families that suffered in the infamous massacre of 1692 when the Campbells set upon the MacDonalds.

George grew up with the Congregational Church, with its atmosphere of Calvinism to which George never really attached himself. A story often told is that the young George on hearing that life was already mapped out and pre-destined burst into tears and was only comforted by the re-assurance that he was one of the elect.

When he was only 8, his mother Helen died. His father re-married 7 years later in 1839. The next year George was successful in obtaining a bursary to study at King's College in Aberdeen and from which he also received his M.A.

In 1846 George was first published, anonymously, but his poem was there in print in the Scottish Congregational Magazine.

In 1848 he attended Highbury Theological College to study for the Congregational ministry. That same year he became engaged to Louisa Powell. An enduring relationship that would see them as life long companions coupled with a marriage of over fifty years.

By 1850 George was appointed as the pastor of Trinity Congregational Church in Arundel. His sermons were however sometimes at odds with the Church and their more segmented views.

It is also at this time that George's health becomes a major concern. In November he suffered what would be termed 'a severe haemorrhage'. However Louisa was by his side and her support and nursing ensured his recovery.

On March 8th 1851 George and Louisa married. As a Christmas gift to friends later that year he had printed his translation of Twelve of the Spiritual Songs of Novalis.

The year of 1852 started on a very bright note with the birth of his daughter on January 4th – Lilia.

Meanwhile George preached that with God's universal love and the possibility that none would, ultimately, fail to unite with God were deemed to be almost heretical by the Church elders and as a punishment his salary was cut in half in June of 1852.

In May 1853 George could no longer reconcile with the Church's demands and he resigned from the pulpit. Interestingly in his later novels, such as Robert Falconer and Lilith, there is common theme for distaste at the idea that God's electing love is limited to some and denied to others running through.

Happier news for 1853 was the birth of his daughter Mary Josephine born on July 23rd.

And with this the family decided to move to Manchester where he continued his ministerial work but his health again deteriorated. Another daughter, Caroline Grace was born on September 16th 1854. In 1855 his collection of poems 'Within and Without' was published.

On 20th January 1856 his son Greville was born. The year brought further good news when Lady Byron decided to become his patron. However his health once more deteriorated and the family moved to Algiers to recuperate over the winter.

The following spring he was back in London and teaching at the University of London.

On August 31st 1857 a fourth daughter, Irene, was born and the family decided to settle in Hastings.

1858 brought bitter sweet times. His brother and Father both died but another daughter, Winifrid Louisa was born and his classic work 'Phantastes' was published.

The following year, 1859, George returned again to London and became the Professor of English Literature at Bedford College.

The following few years brought several more children into the ever growing family and a growing literary reputation.

In 1869 George accepted the editorship of Good Words for the Young and embarked on a lecture tour of Scotland.

In 1871 'At the Back of the North Wind' was published followed by such other classics as Wilfrid Cumbermede, The Princess and the Goblin and in 1876, Exotics.

In 1877 came the beginning of a new chapter in his life with his first trip to Italy and the award of a Civil List pension.

Sadly in 1878 his daughter, Mary Josephine and the following year his son, Maurice both died.

From 1880 he and his family moved to Bordighera on the Riviera dei Fiori in Liguria, Italy, almost on the French border. Locally there also was an Anglican Church, which he attended. Deeply enamoured of the Riviera, he spent 20 years there, writing almost half of his literary canon and predominantly the fantasy works.

George founded a literary studio named Casa Coraggio (Bravery House), which soon became one of the most celebrated cultural centres of its age, well attended by British and Italian travellers, and locals. Representations were often held of classic plays, and readings were given of Dante and Shakespeare.

In 1882 The Princess and Curdie was published and his reputation to grow. But again tragedy was never far away; in 1884 Grace died followed 7 years later by Lilia. Despite these impossible blows George continued to work. Lilith was published in 1895 and two years later Salted with Fire, which was to be his last novel.

Ill health now fastened its hold on George and by 1898 a stroke had taken his voice.

In 1900 he moved into St George's Wood, Haslemere, a house designed and overseen by his two sons, Robert Falconer and Greville.

1901   George and Louisa were able to celebrate their Golden Wedding anniversary but so sadly Louisa was to pass away on January 13th, 1902 whilst at Bordighera.

On 18th September 1905 George MacDonald died at Sagamore, Ashtead in Surrey. He was cremated and his ashes buried at Bordighera, in the English cemetery, along with his wife Louisa and daughters Lilia and Grace.

He is writing is popular to this day and as he said "I write, not for children, but for the child-like, whether they be of five, or fifty, or seventy-five."

As a writer he was easily placed among a very distinguished group. Indeed there is a photograph of him amongst such Victorian and literary luminaries as Tennyson, Dickens, Wilkie Collins, Trollope, Ruskin, Lewes, and Thackeray. While in America he was a friend of the famed poets Longfellow and Walt Whitman.

His use of fantasy as a way of exploring the human condition influenced authors such as C. S. Lewis and J. R. R. Tolkien whilst his realistic Scottish novels, and as such MacDonald have seen him established as the founder of the "kailyard school" of Scottish writing.

George MacDonald – An Obituary.

The Manchester Guardian. Wednesday, 20th September, 1905

We regret to announce the death of George MacDonald, which took place on Monday at Sagamore, Ashtead, Surrey.

George MacDonald was a compound of Highland birth and Lowland education. He was descended from the ill-fated MacDonald's of Glencoe. Two of his ancestors fought on the losing side at Culloden. One of them who had been blinded in the battle but contrived to escape further punishment settled at Portsoy, on the shores of the Moray Firth, and there reared a family. Tradition records that the blind Highlander was noted in all the country as a famous piper. Later the family moved to Huntly, in Aberdeenshire, where George MacDonald's grandfather exercised the double trade of farmer and banker. The late novelist's father confined himself to farming, but it was at the bank, in the present Bogie-street, of Huntly that George MacDonald was born in 1824. His boyhood was spent on his father's farm.

Among the chief formative influences on his character he used to reckon the teaching and example of his father and his grandmother. The former was described by a contemporary as "a singularly handsome man, and noted for the sweetness and chivalry of his disposition", qualities which his son inherited to the full. The grandmother is known to a far wider circle than she ever moved in by the genius of the "laddie" whom she taught and chastened. The early chapters of his seventh novel reflect her severe virtues; "our grandmother will be known," MacDonald once said, "as long as 'Robert Falconer' is read." Old Mrs. MacDonald was the original of Robert Falconer's grandmother, "a woman," as an unsympathetic critic once said, "in whom the detestable creed of Calvinism had wrought its almost inevitable results." Like Macaulay, MacDonald might have said, "After the straitest sect of our religion was I brought up a Pharisee." Nominally his parents belonged to the sect of the Congregationalists, but practically they were rigid Calvinists of the type that MacDonald has drawn, with equal sympathy for their virtues and comprehension of their defects, in so many of his books. But in his father even the strictest Calvinism was unable to kill the Celtic mysticism and the human sympathy that he transmitted in fuller measure to his son. In a few simple lines MacDonald has indicated the nature of the teaching that had most effect on him -

Once more I paced the fields
With him whose love had made me long for God
So good a father that, needs must, I sought
A better still, Father of him and me.

Another passage from a still more directly autobiographical poem will serve to indicate the more worldly influences that formed his mind:

The boy knew little: but he read old tales
Of Scotland's warriors till his blood ran swift
As charging knights upon their death-career.
He chanted ancient tunes till the wild blood
Was charmed back into its fountain-well,
And tears arose instead. That poet's songs,
Whose music evermore recalls his name,
His name of waters babbling as they run,
And met the skylarks, raining from the clouds.
But only as the poet-birds he sang
From rooted impulse of essential song.
The earth was fair, he knew not it was fair;
His heart was glad, he knew not it was glad;
He walked as in a twilight of the sense.

From the farm at Huntly young MacDonald went to King's College, that stately fabric of the sixteenth century which has since been welded with its sister foundation into the University of Aberdeen, and:

Four years long his life swung to and fro,
Alternating the red gown and the blue coat,
The garret study and the wide-floored barn,
The wintry city and the sunny fields.

He helped to support himself, in the frugal Scottish way, by taking pupils while he was studying for his own degree, and did not disdain to help on the farm in the long summer vacation. A contemporary at Aberdeen describes him as "a very handsome lad, very punctilious about his dress, but not specially distinguished as a scholar." The physical delicacy which hampered but did not shorten his life was already conspicuous, and it was a flight from east winds as well as Scottish Calvinism that sent him, when his mind was assured that he had a call to the ministry, to Study at the Independent College at Highbury, never to return to his native land except as a visitor. After passing through the usual course, he was called to the pastorate of Trinity Congregational Church at Arundel in 1850. This enabled him to marry the lady to whom he had already engaged himself, a Miss Powell of Hampstead, with whom he lived very long and happily. His brief residence at Arundel was rather a failure, though his personal popularity and pastoral care of his flock were undoubted. One of his successors says: "The tall form, the blue and dreamy eyes, the full beard, the long hair, the appearance at once weird and winning, was a familiar sight in the streets, and the older inhabitants delight to recall how, to something of the knight errant he added true chivalry, tenderness for suffering, scorn of insincerity, and strong love of right." But his theological doctrines, which were rapidly passing away from the Congregational standpoint to that inherited mysticism which is easier to admire than to define, speedily failed to commend themselves to the plain Sussex folk, and in 1853 he was obliged to resign his charge at the request of his deacons. The next three years were passed in our own neighbourhood. MacDonald preached regularly in Manchester and Bolton, where his remarkable power in the pulpit gained him a larger circle of hearers than the vagueness of his creed could keep. Among the fragments that remain from this period one may quote his "Manchester Poem," which begins with a picture that most of us can recognise:

"Tis a poor, drizzly morning, dark and sad.
The cloud has fallen and filled with fold on fold
The chimneyed city; and the smoke is caught
And spreads diluted in the cloud, and sinks,

A black precipitate, on miry streets.
And faces grey glide through the darkened fog.

About this time MacDonald made three friends to whom he was wont in after years to ascribe great influence on his mental development, Lady Byron, whom Robertson, of Brighton, used to call "one of the noblest and purest women he had ever met"; A J Scott, the first principal of Owens College, to whom, with his

Intellect unrivalled in its sway,
Upheld and ordered by a regnant will.

MacDonald has expressed his obligations in more than one poem; and Frederick Denison Maurice. It is largely under their influence that George MacDonald ventured to commit himself to the troubled waters of literature and "commenced author" with the two books of verse that he brought out in 1856 and 1857. These neither attracted nor deserved much notice; but the remarkable "fairy romance" of "Phantastes," which was produced in the following year, revealed a new and original talent. By this time MacDonald had definitely abandoned any attempt to return to the Independent ministry, and had enrolled himself as a lay member of the Church of England where the teaching of men like Robertson and Maurice had much in common with his own views. From this time the history of his life is mainly that of his writings. He himself has, we understand, expressed the desire that no memoir of him should be written, and we shall nor endeavour to raise the veil over his private life in his later years. It is enough to say that following a lecturing tour to the United States in 1872-3, that he received a Civil List pension of £100 in 1877, that much of his later life was spent at Bordighera to avoid the English east winds, and that he made the remarkable, but very successful, experiment of giving dramatic representations of the "Pilgrims Progress," in which he himself enacted Greatheart, while the other parts were largely filled by members of his own family. It only remains to speak of the literary work of forty years, by which George MacDonald is best known to the world.

The late Sir William Geddes, who was a contemporary of MacDonald's at the university of which he afterwards became principal, maintained that MacDonald was "a poet by nature and the gift of God" who wasted his powers in writing second-rate novels to keep the pot boiling. Few readers will agree with Geddes that MacDonald was really "the most richly gifted of Victorian poets after Tennyson," though those who know his prose will admit that it possesses a uniform distinction and "fundamental brain-work" which are less fully marked in the work of many more popular writers. It is a little hard on MacDonald that his name should be universally associated with that rather insincere and mawkish set of verses beginning -

Where did you come from, baby dear?

Hardly any poetic reputation could survive that inane popularity; even Longfellow never really got over "Excelsior." But MacDonald was not a great poet, though few recent writers have touched the chord of mysticism with more success. As a novelist also one can hardly rank him higher than second-rate, though it is extremely unfair to slight his tales as mere pot-boilers, like those of the late Grant Allen. "The mainspring of the interest," as a critic said of one of the first of them, "lies in the development of the inner life and spiritual history of all the characters." It is no pot-boiler of which that can be said. In all his stories there are passages of singular beauty and revelations of thought "on man, on Nature and on human life" that entirely account for and justify a popularity which even the tendency to introduce unneccesary metaphysics and to subordinate the development of the story to religious conversations could not destroy. "Malcolm" and its sequel, "David Elginbrod," which first showed MacDonald his true field; "The Annals of a Quiet Neighbourhood," which was the most successful of all from the publishers point of view; "Sir Gibbie," "Alec Forbes of Howglen," with its inimitable pictures of boyish life in the Aberdeenshire villages; "Robert Falconer," with its grim sketches of the severest Calvinism in its bearing on "life and death and the deep heart of man," certainly entitle MacDonald to a place beside Trollope and Charles Reade and Mrs. Oliphant and the other Victorian novelists of the second rank, through no one will contend that they should place him higher. Yet one must add that he was the best interpreter of Scottish life and character who appeared between Miss Ferriman and Mr. Barrie. His books are rather the unstudied productions of a beautiful and well-stored mind than works of literary art. To our own taste, his most original and best work was that which he produced when he wrote for children, especially during the years in which he edited the short-lived "Good Words for the Young." It is not easy to find a parallel to "The Princess and the Goblins," "At the back of the North Wind," and "The Light Princess," with their delicacy of touch and vivacity of fancy informing a deep moral purpose. Moral purpose in fact was the secret of both the strength and the weakness of George MacDonald; but he seldom managed to surround the powder with jam as well as in these charming fairy-tales.

George MacDonald – A Concise Bibliography

Fantasy
Phantastes: A Fairie Romance for Men and Women (1858)
"Cross Purposes" (1862)
Adela Cathcart (1864)
The Portent: A Story of the Inner Vision of the Highlanders, Commonly Called "Second Sight" (1864)
Dealings with the Fairies (1867)
At the Back of the North Wind (1871)
Works of Fancy and Imagination (1871)
The Princess and the Goblin (1872)
The Wise Woman: A Parable (1875)
The Gifts of the Child Christ and Other Tales (1882)
The Day Boy and the Night Girl (1882)
The Princess and Curdie (1883)
The Flight of the Shadow (1891)
Lilith: A Romance (1895)

Realistic fiction
David Elginbrod (1863; republished as The Tutor's First Love), originally published in three volumes
Alec Forbes of Howglen (1865; republished as The Maiden's Bequest)
Annals of a Quiet Neighbourhood (1867)
Guild Court: A London Story (1868)
Robert Falconer (1868; republished as The Musician's Quest)
The Seaboard Parish (1869)
Ranald Bannerman's Boyhood (1871)
Wilfrid Cumbermede (1871–72)
The Vicar's Daughter (1871–72)
The History of Gutta Percha Willie, the Working Genius (1873)
Malcolm (1875)
St. George and St. Michael (1876)
Thomas Wingfold, Curate (1876; republished as The Curate's Awakening)
The Marquis of Lossie (1877; republished as The Marquis' Secret)
Paul Faber, Surgeon (1879; republished as The Lady's Confession)

Sir Gibbie (1879; republished as The Baronet's Song)
Mary Marston (1881; republished as A Daughter's Devotion)
Warlock o' Glenwarlock (1881; republished as Castle Warlock and The Laird's Inheritance)
Weighed and Wanting (1882; republished as A Gentlewoman's Choice)
Donal Grant (1883; republished as The Shepherd's Castle)
What's Mine's Mine (1886; republished as The Highlander's Last Song)
Home Again: A Tale (1887; republished as The Poet's Homecoming)
The Elect Lady (1888; republished as The Landlady's Master)
A Rough Shaking (1891)
There and Back (1891; republished as The Baron's Apprenticeship)
Heather and Snow (1893; republished as The Peasant Girl's Dream)
Salted with Fire (1896; republished as The Minister's Restoration)
Far Above Rubies (1898)

Poetry
Twelve of the Spiritual Songs of Novalis (1851), translation of the poetry of Novalis
Within and Without: A Dramatic Poem (1855)
Poems (1857)
"A Hidden Life" and Other Poems (1864)
"The Disciple" and Other Poems (1867)
Exotics: A Translation of the Spiritual Songs of Novalis, the Hymn-book of Luther, and Other Poems
from the German and Italian (1876)
Dramatic and Miscellaneous Poems (1876)
A Book of Strife, in the Form of the Diary of an Old Soul (1880)
The Threefold Cord: Poems by Three Friends (1883) with Greville Matheson and John Hill MacDonald
Poems (1887)
The Poetical Works of George MacDonald, 2 Volumes (1893)
Scotch Songs and Ballads (1893)
Rampolli: Growths from a Long-planted Root (1897)

Nonfiction
Unspoken Sermons (1867)
England's Antiphon (1868, 1874)
The Miracles of Our Lord (1870)
Cheerful Words from the Writing of George MacDonald (1880), compiled by E. E. Brown
Orts: Chiefly Papers on the Imagination, and on Shakespeare (1882)
"Preface" (1884) to Letters from Hell (1866) by Valdemar Adolph Thisted
The Tragedie of Hamlet, Prince of Denmarke: A Study With the Test of the Folio of 1623 (1885)
Unspoken Sermons, Second Series (1885)
Unspoken Sermons, Third Series (1889)
A Cabinet of Gems, Cut and Polished by Sir Philip Sidney; Now, for the More Radiance, Presented
Without Their Setting by George MacDonald (1891)
The Hope of the Gospel (1892)
A Dish of Orts (1893)
Beautiful Thoughts from George MacDonald (1894), compiled by Elizabeth Dougall

www.ingramcontent.com/pod-product-compliance
Lightning Source LLC
Chambersburg PA
CBHW071410090426
42737CB00011B/1419